*Allegro's Secret*

# *Allegro's Secret*

Ramon Harris

Writers Club Press
San Jose  New York  Lincoln  Shanghai

Allegro's Secret

All Rights Reserved © 2001 by Ramon Harris

No part of this book may be reproduced or transmitted in any form or by any means, graphic, electronic, or mechanical, including photocopying, recording, taping, or by any information storage retrieval system, without the permission in writing from the publisher.

Writers Club Press
an imprint of iUniverse.com, Inc.

For information address:
iUniverse.com, Inc.
5220 S 16th, Ste. 200
Lincoln, NE 68512
www.iuniverse.com

This is a work of fiction. Any resembleance to real people or events is purely coincidental and unintended.

ISBN: 0-595-19590-3

Printed in the United States of America

*To my often patient wife Diane.*

# Forward

The United States conducted illegal intelligence flights for 15 years before Francis Gary Powers U2 was shot down and made world headlines. In the early days, young Americans flew outmoded equipment and often died. For one, there would be a lifetime of consequences.

# Chapter 1

**South China Sea, December 29, 1949.**

He was tiring now; it would end soon. A voice came from somewhere and he concentrated fiercely to understand.

"Identify yourself: turn on the IFF, waggle your wings, or hold up a hand. Anything."

He turned left gently, but his shattered skull sent points of pain. He stopped. It was hopeless to the right, that eye didn't work. He thought a while and finally raised his right hand. The voice spoke to someone else.

"PEACHTREE 4 to OCTAVE. I found it. It's ours, but no markings except some nose-art: *EyeCatcher*. One of those old Army night-fighters I think. Some damage, flak damage it looks like. The pilot's hurt, he seems to be out of it. What do you want me to do?"

He waited now, hoping for the voice again. It came.

"What's your fuel situation, how much gas?"

He didn't know what the words meant. He sat very still.

"Gas! How much gas? Look at your fuel gauges. Hold up a finger for every hour of fuel you have left."

He leaned forward without conscious thought and studied the six gauges, then made a zero with thumb and index finger. The voice was alarmed now, he could tell.

"OK, OK. I'll get you down; we'll put you in the water. Something…someone will be there for you, don't worry. But listen pal, you have to wake up and fly the thing, I can't do it for you."

He didn't think he could survive a water landing.

# CHAPTER 2

## The Present

Leonard Lavendar was about to be handed the story of his life, but he didn't know it. He looked asleep but he was awake, worrying about ratings. He sat tilted back in his chair; big feet in Mephistos planted on the desktop, puzzling over the April ratings sweeps.

He had been recruited to a stellar position in this outfit: producer of a prime-time news magazine in a fresh new format. Now he wondered if he had done the right thing. Being a producer was more difficult than he had ever imagined, certainly harder than his reporting career had ever been. His World Weekly Summary was interesting, even great at times. Presentations were always polished and precise. But the ratings fell in a downward spiral in spite of his efforts.

One humiliating consequence of the ratings drop was a required meeting each Monday evening with the Audience Share Analysis Team: a group of four statisticians who spoke to him in tongues. They prattled about geographic regions, cultural regions, demographics and technology. They explained that Pennsylvania equaled Mississippi, except for the cultural islands of Pittsburgh and Philadelphia. They spoke of East Indians and American Indians, of teens, of GEN X'ers, of boomers and yuppies, and the burgeoning population of oldsters. They said there was almost no real news in a peacetime economy: the kind of news that made people sit up and listen. They wanted universal themes. Our country cried out for themes that would span the thousand inner-directed cells of America's balkanized New-Millennium culture.

Monday nights gave him a headache. The handful of truly bright people he had known in his life spoke simple English. The ASAT team did not.

And in the end it was all a guess, a crock of shit. He made the crucial choices pretty much by himself, and then he waited for the chorus of bitching from upstairs. It was a lonely life.

The cell phone beeped and he studied the caller ID display: an unfamiliar number. Still, it was his private line, used by only a select handful of associates.

"Len here."

"I have something unusual for you. Cost you ten."

He recognized the voice, a wormy GS8 in the DOD Office of Media Coordination.

"Hell it will; we won't pay that kind of money. If it's really good I can get you a couple grand—after we see the material."

"OK, fine: a major mistake. You'll love this on CNN or ABC or even FOX. It's huge—or it will be when you've done your research. I've never handed you a dud, have I?"

"Will you hold on for a day, let me see what I can do?"

The caller sounded irritated.

"Tomorrow at ten. Yes or no. All the money up front."

"You get nothing until we understand what you have, no negotiation on that point at all."

The receiver clicked in the middle of his sentence.

Lavendar took the matter to his boss: the final say on dubious expenditures.

"The guy's a creep, Ray, but he's never given me bad information and he's never been greedy—before."

Raymond Durand looked like he was being forced to smell a July afternoon doggie deposit.

"In addition to the ratings issue, Len, you're behind in programming. We only have seven months of programming, and you're through ten months of funding. The money boys upstairs think you ought to pay modest attention to your budget. So this would have to be something cosmic, something the viewers could get a grip on; like World War 3, a dog that can whistle Bach's Prelude, gas prices going to $20 per gallon."

Lavendar needed a blockbuster; he knew that.

"I want to call the guy's hand, Ray. I covered the Pentagon for 10 years. Once in a blue moon the bosses release very sensitive information without attribution. I've seen some snarky stuff that was never traced to anyone, but I knew from informants that the Service Chiefs were behind the material. They try to make it look like a slipup. We may be looking at something like that here and it could be sensational. It could be just what I need."

Durand didn't want to hear it.

"You're headed in the wrong direction. Pentagon dogfights aren't big these days. Commerce wags the dog, not Communism. Communism is the news industry's dead dog now; it's road-kill. Anyway, why would a responsible Service Chief knowingly release damaging information about the military? It seems like a losing proposition."

"Here's the way the game is played; they release hints about some gray laundry concerning a rival service program that's stealing funding from them. Then, when the material is out and developed by the press, they can put the knock on their rivals, maybe keep the bucks for their own programs. It happens, Ray. It all depends on how they see the competition and who they think their friends are."

"Jesus: it sounds like a locker room shoving match, juvenile bullshit."

Durand sighed, because he had always been a sucker for the next sensation.

"But if you want to take a flyer, go ahead."

Lavendar smiled. Durand continued.

"Listen to me now—it all comes right in here for review: names, dates, numbers, and facts. Then we decide together how much to pay this jerk. And keep this to yourself for the moment. Just you and me."

The Civil Service employee was back the next morning.

"So, are you going or not?"

"OK. The contingency is we have two weeks to evaluate the material. If it's good you get your price. If it's dogshit, you get nothing."

There was a long pause while the caller evaluated probabilities.

"It's good, don't worry about that. Request the service record of 1st Lieutenant L. A. Deforest, USAF. It's been mistakenly released from a 75-year diplomatic and security hold. Study the combat entries. You'll need to invoke the Freedom of Information Act, they won't release it voluntarily."

# Chapter 3

He was in his beloved workshop studying disassembled pieces of the ancient Jaguar transmission. He probed a hairline crack in the beautifully cast delicate aluminum transmission case. His dental pick twanged and went deep in several places. No question about it, the crack went clear through. Should he just drill the end of the crack, then epoxy the thing, strap it, and hope for the best?

No, that was a half-assed approach; he couldn't do it. He needed to perform an aluminum weld, a risky thing. If the weld was unsuccessful the case would be ruined and he would be S.O.L. There were no replacements for this rare piece. He could reduce the risk by sending the case out to his friend Ron Cord, known in the trade as "Sparthantuous", for his welding prowess. But then he would be ducking responsibility for the restoration. He wouldn't be much of a restorer, would he?

The speaker above the workbench interrupted his ruminations.

"Mr. Deforest? Front gate security here, Devon speaking. A gentleman is here for you, a Mr. Lavendar. Shall I send him in?"

Al didn't know the name.

"Must be a mistake Devon, I don't know any Mr. Lavendar. He's got the wrong man."

A second voice came from the speaker.

"Mr. Deforest? My name is Leonard Lavendar. I'm with World Weekly Summary, may I speak with you?"

Warning flags flew up.

"About what?"

"It would be better if we spoke privately I think."

Al closed his eyes: what had the goddamned fools done?

"Let him in Devon. Give him directions to the house."

Lavendar followed a tortured set of curving roads through the gated community, pausing frequently to consult a map marked with lime-colored highlighter. He turned in at a broad driveway designed in a long climbing sweep to enhance rich desert landscaping surrounding the Deforest home. The rambling prairie house was set low in an upland slope that broke sharply behind the home becoming a 1200 foot mountain strewn with huge granite boulders: a giant desert wave. It was a carefully chosen backdrop for the elegant structure.

Lavendar tried to remain unimpressed; he needed an edge for this interview. Still, it was clear that the Deforest's had done well in life, and this somehow irritated him. He punched a doorbell beside the massive etched-glass front door and waited several moments before a tall thin man came into the foyer to open the door. The broad lined face and white widows-peaked hair failed to give an age: a person who might be 55 or 75. The man smiled cautiously and spoke in a disarmingly young California-Surfer voice.

"Afternoon. You Lavendar?"

Len nodded, bothered by his nervousness.

"Yes I am. Thank you for seeing me with no notice."

Deforest led the way down a granite-floored hall, past a large living room containing several expensive paintings in an abstract southwest style. He continued to a small library-office where he gestured to the leather couch in front of a massive, battered teak desk.

"Please sit down. Something to drink?"

Len nodded gratefully: he was thirsty, unused to the heat.

"Just some spring-water please."

Al Deforest settled into a small leather chair beside the desk after preparing drinks. He studied Lavendar, forming an impression: thirty five or so, mid-height, brown straight hair done in the side-combed Washington Bureaucrat style, intelligent face, not handsome, looked vaguely familiar but Al couldn't place the source. Well built but going to fat: looked OK in a suit, but the garment was expertly cut to disguise a substantial paunch.

Al left the evaluation in neutral, deliberately not forming an opinion.

"I think you have me confused with someone else Mr. Lavendar."

Lavendar looked out the window a moment to formulate his approach, decided to go straight at it.

"It's possible Mr. Deforest, but I doubt it. We've obtained a copy of a military service record. The physical metrics appear similar to yours and the ID card photo, even in our poor copy, certainly looks like a younger version of you."

He paused again, not wanting to make a mistake with this man.

"Of course fingerprints would be definitive if you would allow a comparison."

Al suppressed irritation.

"I'm not in the fingerprint business."

"Of course you're not; you have nothing to prove. So I take it you're denying a connection with the service file in our possession?"

"I'm not confirming or denying, I'm listening."

"Yes. Well, the person in question served as an enlisted man in the Army Air Force from 1945 to 1947. He was accepted into the Pilot Training program in 1947, just as the Army Air Force was being converted into the United States Air Force."

Lavendar paused for dramatic effect, eyes locked to Al's.

"Here the record becomes unusual, highly unusual. There is no indication of graduation from his training class: Class 48N, I believe. There is no record of a commission, yet the file lists an Officer's serial number and a rank of First Lieutenant. According to the file, the man was qualified to fly the P-80, and later, the P-61. The P-61 was an obsolete airplane even back then, it had been retired from service at the end of the war, years before the qualification date in the service record. That entry is rather strange, don't you think?"

"Damned if I could tell you."

"But those things are incidental details, not a reason for me to be meeting with you. The power in this service file, the story, lies in the entries under flight experience: 23 combat missions, but no indication of where they took place. And there's more, three more entries about combat victories, all in 1949. By the end of the year, this guy is credited with 13 kills. Then, in the awards section, the Medal of Honor was awarded on November 21, 1950, for an action on October 22, 1949. There are no citation details in the file."

Lavendar met the old man's eyes, looking defiant.

"If this is a true record, not some gross mistake, the air history of the twentieth century needs a touch-up. L. A. Deforest became an ace during a time when the United States was not at war. You can imagine the media interest."

Al smiled gently. This was trouble, but he would have some fun anyway.

"Yow! That fellow sounds like one of those Beta males they're always telling you about."

"Excuse me? Oh, I think you mean the Alpha male, the one that leads the pack."

Al's green eyes twinkled, but his face remained somber.

"I guess that's it. Well, you have an interesting story there, Mr. Lavendar. But I'm not much concerned with heroics any more, all that Alpha and Beta stuff. I was a sensitive kid back then, probably a Beta. You know what I say to myself nowadays? I look around me and say, thank you Lord for getting me this far, and if it isn't too much trouble deal me another five while you're at it."

He put his hands behind his head, looking for words that would deflect this shark.

"Funerals. I was in the funeral business son, forty years in the funeral business. Owned 15 establishments at one time: still own three. So you can see you're at a dead end with me—no pun intended. You need to look elsewhere."

Al stood. The interview was over.

"Come on, I'll see you out. Do you have that map the guard gave you? It's real easy to get lost in here."

"One last thing if you will sir."

Al waved a hand impatiently. He wanted the man out of his house but was not quite willing to be rude.

Lavender's cold eyes sent a sniper's bullet: one he hoped would be the tiebreaker.

"Let me sketch the methods we use to develop a feature with this sort of appeal, I'll only need a moment. We always prefer a story from the principals, but if that's not possible, we hire investigators to go after every verifiable detail and do a circumstantial reconstruction. For instance, the man in question was injured while on duty. We already know he was treated aboard the aircraft carrier BON HOMME RICHARD and sent on to Osaka, Japan for emergency surgery. Then, three weeks later he was sent to Tripler Army Medical Center in Honolulu. Some time after that we believe he underwent extensive rehabilitation at the Veterans Administration Hospital in Long Beach-we'll have an answer on that in a few days."

Al interrupted.

"So what? Nothing to do with me."

"By next week, Mr. Deforest, we'll have lists of all the medical personnel assigned to those facilities in 1950 and 1951. We'll interview every surviving person to piece together just that one portion of the story if we have to. And we have initiatives underway in other areas. I'm sure we'll have something that will stand up in two months, with or without the cooperation of the principals, with or without the cooperation of the Department of Defense. I just hope you may reconsider your position."

The phrase "without the co-operation of the principals" sunk into Al's gut like a drop of hot solder: worrisome. He tried to look unimpressed.

"Power of the press, huh?"

"Something like that, yes."

"Like I said, use the map to get out of here."

Afterward, he went to the garage to sit in his BarcaLounger. The garage was a three-bay affair: his truck, Mandy's car, and an extra large third bay and workshop for his restoration projects. The floor was painted in 2-part epoxy and immaculate, the walls enclosed in drywall and finished in a soft neutral tone. There was strong overhead fluorescent lighting, and air conditioning. And then there was the BarcaLounger. Mandy hated the goddamned scruffy chair: cheap black covering gone mottled-gray with age and sweat, fabric ruptured, sitting there looking like a sore carbuncle in the middle of all that junk. But Al loved it; he sat in the lounger and closed his eyes when puzzled or uncertain about a restoration project. Often, sitting in the middle of all the pieces and parts, a solution would come to him as if by magic.

Mandy found him when she came home from her weekly bridge party two hours later, sound asleep in the chair. She picked her way through fenders and running boards to shake him gently awake. He told her of the visitor. He wanted her views on what they should do.

"It will all come out now, Mandy; some kind of a screw up, I guess. Your Federal Government in action. The media has a sniff and there's no way to stop it."

"Do you mean the official version, or what really happened?"

Al grinned slyly.

"The official version, of course. If anyone knew what really happened out there, I'd still be hoeing potatoes up at the Federal Farm."

# CHAPTER 4

The call came sooner than he thought. He had figured early afternoon, allowing time for all the Washington gears to engage before an organ of the government could come awake and speak. But it was just after seven a.m. when Mandy came through the granite tiled great-room toward him, waving the portable phone.

"Stop that, Al. A young man from Washington wants to speak with you."

Al was sitting at their fashionably distressed redwood breakfast table drinking a second double cup of Starbucks, binoculars to his eyes, peering through huge glazed sliding doors at the rear patio. He was looking upward to the magnificent boulder-strewn hill behind the house.

"Yeah, yeah: in a minute. But first take a look up there, in that rocky saddle above the first tee box. Unbelievable."

Mandy put down the phone and took the glasses. She could see nothing at first because Al always adjusted the binoculars for his bad eye, the right lens was far out of focus and she saw only a blur. She turned the adjustment until the view became clear, then swept up the hill and laughed in delight. A Javelina sow with four babies was getting breakfast: she had a huge prickly pear arm in her mouth, gently testing various grips with her teeth before she firmed her small cloven feet in the sandy soil, wiggling for purchase. With a muscular neck jerk, she wrenched the arm off the plant, scattering pear ears down the hillside.

The babies were quickly on them, chewing voraciously at their breakfast.

"How can they possibly eat those things, I get a million tiny thorns if I even look at a prickly pear."

"I don't know: it's amazing. What a great place to live. Who did you say was calling?"

Mandy widened her eyes in a look of mock amazement.

"Washington."

He knew the call would come, still he felt a surge of apprehension. A knot formed at the top of his stomach. He picked up the phone and cleared his throat.

"This is Al Deforest."

"Sir, this is Captain Ruben Greenlee, Assistant Adjutant in the office of the Chief of Staff, United States Air Force. That's in the Pentagon, sir."

Al's mouth quirked with humor at the words.

"I know it son: third floor, E ring, pretty good view of the Potomac; but not as good as the Navy guy upstairs from you. I got a medal there once."

Captain Greenlee continued without acknowledging Al's compelling observations.

"Yes sir. Well, the General is most anxious to meet with you at your earliest convenience on a private matter. You wouldn't need to travel here; we could send an airplane to get you. We were hoping you could be at the Business Terminal at Scottsdale Airport tomorrow afternoon at three. That would put you in here about ten in the evening; our guests usually stay at the Hay-Adams. The General has opened his schedule for all of Thursday. Actually, it wouldn't be the Chief: you would meet with Lieutenant General Goldkette, our Operations Deputy. May we prevail on you for this meeting, sir?"

Al looked at Mandy and pointed to the east, eyebrows raised. She smiled and nodded enthusiastically.

"Captain, I'm pleased to accept your invitation, but we need a couple of changes: have the airplane ready for us at seven tomorrow morning; my wife is coming with me and you are going to put us up at Hay-Adams for a week, then fly us home. We'll need a staff car to drive around town. Oh, one more thing; have an airport limo pick us up at home here at six am."

He cradled the telephone and strolled into the pantry to grab a handful of Raisin Bran from the box. He waggled his eyebrows at Mandy and walked silently to the heavy patio doors to let himself out, bracing against the morning heat: only May and already the days were over 100 degrees. He moved past the pool and through his horticultural specimen garden to the low adobe pony wall that separated landscaping from the natural desert acreage beyond. He stood waiting.

Presently a Northern Flicker woodpecker left his perch on a massive granite boulder eight hundred feet up the hillside and flew down toward the standing man, making the peculiar bobbing flight of the species: flap and up, pause, gravity and down, flap and up. The large handsome bird settled on a tall saguaro cactus, looked about for predator Harris hawks, and then turned to greet the familiar figure with a shrill "doop-doop-doop."

He did not smile but pleasure softened his granitelike features. He released his grip on the Raisin Bran, showering the ground with raisins and wheat flakes. He stood thinking about the call, remembering fifty years ago, getting mad again. He had never been able to purge the rage.

Then another thought tugged the corners of his mouth upward. In the long run the two of them had prevailed, even with no one to help them. They'd brought the ball game up to a tie, by God. They'd made a life.

And now, this might be the end of it. Bad timing. Well even if it was, they'd had a good run, hadn't they? A melody from youth popped into his head. A moment later the title came: Let's Face the Music and Dance.

Knowing the bird would not eat while he was nearby, he turned and went back to the house. Mandy looked up from nibbling her toast.

"The Birdman. I wish you wouldn't feed that thing, Al."

"Woodpeckers have rights. They deserve rewards now and again."

"Uh huh. And my reward is that he shits all over the wall back there."

"A noble bird. We must make sacrifices."

"I don't see you out there with a bucket of water and a scrub brush every weekend."

"I handle the feeding end."

She was reluctant to bring up the serious matter.

"They'll try to take it all away, won't they?"

"Maybe, if someone knows something. I doubt they do, it's been a long time."

Her jaw set stubbornly and she turned hot angry eyes to him. The look said she was prepared to go miles and miles with this. He grinned; she had always been a toughie.

* * *

They took the subway from the Hay-Adams to the Pentagon station and exited directly into an area known as The Mall. Al pushed through the considerable crowd to a security booth at the subterranean entrance to the building.

"Mr. and Mrs. Deforest to see General Goldkette."

The Marine Corporal looked down at his roster and nodded.

"Yes sir, I have your badges here. An escort will be down from the General's office in a minute."

Ten minutes later a female Major, striking in summer blue uniform, appeared and took them expertly in tow. Mandy was bewildered by the system of elevators, ramps and stairwells through which they passed. The building walls seemed all askew with each other, furthering her disorientation as they walked down dimly lit, brown-linoleum covered hallways. Al talked as they proceeded.

"This is the most confusing building in the world in addition to being the ugliest; five concentric rings and five levels and not a straight wall in the place. Not too many straight people either."

After what seemed like miles, they arrived at a crinkle-glass door marked ' LTG P.G.T. Goldkette, DCS OPS '. They were ushered into a small anterior office, well lit from a bank of external windows. Mandy was pleased by a view of the outside; it helped to dispel her sense of disorientation. The Major smiled encouragingly and gestured toward two government-issue leather and mahogany chairs, handsomely decorated by closely spaced antique brass buttons.

Al studied the chairs they sat in; he was sure he had seen the very same chairs here in the Pentagon in 1950. He wondered if the chairs had been around for the Civil War, or maybe even the Revolutionary War. The Major punched an intercom.

"The guests are here now Colonel."

In a moment a youngish, preppy Lt. Colonel in shirtsleeves appeared and sat on the desk opposite them, looking sheepish.

"Folks, we're delighted to welcome you but we seem to have a small problem. Mrs. Deforest has no security status: she has no clearances for the conversations we wish to have with you, sir."

Al had anticipated this move. He was ready.

"That's right. And neither do I, Colonel."

The man studied Al a moment, no expression on his face.

"I see. Well, please excuse me a moment."

Mandy thought the man looked irritated. When he was gone she turned to Al anxiously.

"Don't make a fuss, Al. I don't want to cause a problem."

Al made a face, talking loudly enough for the Major to hear.

"I know dear, don't worry. After all we've been through you deserve to know everything about this. And besides, they've already decided to clear you. There wouldn't have been two badges downstairs otherwise. This is just dumb stuff they try to do: limit access to sensitive information. If we went for that sucker play they'd have you out shopping with the girls and I'd be here alone, pining away."

The Major was studying papers on her desk. Frown lines appeared and her lips thinned.

Presently the Lt. Colonel reappeared carrying two crudely mimeographed sheets. In three-inch tall letters the title proclaimed, ' **Access Request** *Project Heat Lightning,* **requires TQ, LL**'. Two paragraphs of text followed, then a signature block. The Colonel recited a standard preamble in a bored voice, warned Mandy of the treason penalty, and required her signature. Al signed his form and looked at the Colonel a moment before speaking.

"Been a while since I've seen that name."

The man smiled.

"Yes sir. If you'll come with me the General will see you now."

P.G.T. Goldkette was a small compactly built man. His thick straight blond hair, gone grayish, was combed straight back in the European style. He had huge blue eyes behind glasses, a small potbelly, and stood in a slightly forward stance so his short arms actually hung a few inches in front of his belt buckle, like a New Age Jimmy Cagney.

Mandy thought he looked like a bewildered baby toddling about the large office.

Al squinted at the General a moment; then he suddenly stabbed an index finger.

"Cajun! The P.G.T. stands for Pierre Gustave Toutant."

Goldkette threw back his head and roared with laughter.

"I see you are a student of the Civil War, Mr. Deforest. I am guilty as charged."

He spoke in the pleasing patois of New Orleans: half Southern, half French, and half Brooklyn all stirred together. He smiled at Mandy.

"Let us tell you the secret, Mrs. Deforest: my Daddy named me after the famous Civil War General P.G.T. Beauregard. He would have it no other way."

They sat at a large mahogany conference table with a view across well-cut lawns to the muddy Potomac River. The Washington Monument obelisk and the Capitol Hill dome jutted in the background. The historic Custis-Lee mansion stood on a hillcrest to the south.

Goldkette sobered as he studied a thin folder before him.

"Mr. Deforest we are most distressed at the accidental release of your service record. Inquiries are being made: ears will be pinned back. But that is neither here nor there; the damage is done. We know that a certain media individual is aggressively pursuing the matter and our experience tells us he will have the story, at least in part, in a few weeks. My job is damage control. I have read thoroughly the archival summary of *Project Heat Lightning*."

Suddenly, he scooted his chair backwards and sailed away from the conference table across the room to his desk. Mandy could tell he enjoyed the maneuver, like a kid on a board flying down a snow bank. She decided she liked him. If Al got stubborn, she would lend a hand. Not with everything, but enough to deflect the momentum.

Goldkette picked another folder from his desk and returned, laboriously waddling the chair forward across the office.

"And I have taken the trouble to review all the combat de-briefs, including yours. But this is all history, mere paper and rather dry into the bargain. Just now I feel a great need for insight into the attitudes, the reasoning behind this…uh, remarkable activity. Will you help me? It seems there is no one else left."

Al was not listening. He had been looking at Goldkette's tunic, hanging over a chair near his desk: seven rows of medals below Command Pilot wings. So many medals that the uppermost were hidden under the jacket lapel. Al could read medals: a natural if somewhat useless gift. There were "been there" medals and "done that" medals: the former for having been in a certain place at a certain time, the latter for individual performance. Goldkette had lots of "done that" medals, high-level ones, including the Air Force Cross and the Silver Star.

Al was on the fence about cooperation. He was still bitter about his treatment, about the treatment they had all received. But it was clear Goldkette had stuck his neck in the noose a few times. Now, without conscious thought, he decided that the man was probably OK. He would tell him of that time.

"There's one other man, Douglas Trapnell, in North Carolina."

"I am sorry to tell you Mr. Trapnell suffered a stroke two weeks ago. He cannot speak now; the prognosis is unfavorable. You are our hope, sir."

Al was deeply stricken by this unwelcome news. Now suddenly, with nothing to soften the shock, he was the last old prune on the tree.

"I didn't know. He's my close friend. I used to see him every year. Then as we got older it was the telephone, we talked a couple of times a year. I'll miss those conversations."

Tears came to his eyes and he wiped angrily at them.

"I'll miss Doug."

Al sat thinking, going back to another time, remembering events that had begun mercifully to dim. The late spring sun lit his troubled face for a long while. Mandy and Goldkette understood, waited. Eventually he spoke, anger in his voice.

"I'll tell you what I know General, but you won't like it; won't like my version of the thing at all. We were just kids, dumb kids trained to do a job we didn't understand. And we were used by the politicians; badly used. And the Air Force did nothing to protect us, nothing meaningful. Twenty-two of us went out to that shithole and two came back: Doug had no legs and half my brains were blown out."

Al glared at Goldkette as if he were personally responsible, seeing the system rather than the man.

"I think I'm a reasonably strong man: no hero, but able to stay the course. I don't whine and I don't spend a lot of time blaming others. But your Air Force shit on me, mister: threw me out with a quarter-pay medical retirement. Then I had to fight to get VA rehabilitation over at the Naval Hospital: no help from you on that one either. Then, when I struggled back from my disability, you sons of bitches canceled my medical retirement. I was left in the street with no help, not even that paltry disability check. I couldn't eat the goddamned medals. Mandy took me in before we were married; I was a half-wit. We lived a year on her secretary's salary because no one would hire me: the speech therapy hadn't kicked in and I sounded like a drunk. Finally I got a job as an assistant embalmer, they were happy to have me because no one wanted to do that work. No sir, you're not going to like this story at all."

Goldkette looked at him calmly.

"Nevertheless, I need to hear it."

Now Al turned to Mandy. A tear had formed in the bad eye and slowly made its crooked way down the furrows of his cheek.

"And those kids that didn't come home, they were all good ones: Dave Rey was a Senator's son, he saved me that day. And all the others; no one knows where they fell in that jungle. Fifty years gone by and no one can go to mourn them, to say an Ave over them."

He paused now, chest heaving, embarrassed to lose control in front of this stranger. He had hoped for dignity.

"And your Air Force did nothing to find them. Not a fucking thing: goddamned cowardly politicians. What got broken over there, I could never put it back together."

He turned again to Mandy.

"A lot of times I wonder why I'm still around, and they're gone. They didn't get all these good years we've had. Fall is the worst for me you know, when the leaves turn. I never told you, I didn't know what to say."

Mandy looked at him and simply nodded. She could not speak. She looked down at her lap. There was extended silence before she turned to the man she had known for 60 years; the man she had always loved.

"I didn't think…Oh, but I knew Al, I always knew. I just couldn't do anything. I saw how powerful it was."

He made a helpless gesture.

"I guess I'm getting sentimental in my old age. Old guys get sentimental you know. No one knows why."

Goldkette's hands were arranged primly on the table before him. He knew enough of the ghastly affair not to contest Al's accusations: they were generally correct. But he couldn't let his service go entirely undefended. He softly spoke.

"We're fighting men, Mr. Deforest: we fight when we're ordered to. Not perfect, not even close. By mandate, we respond to civilian authority, to elected officials in the White House, modulated by certain individuals in the Congress. We don't always do the right thing, but in my experience we try: we try hard. And we have two sides, the fighters and the bureaucrats. We can't do our job without both sides, but it isn't always pretty. I'm sorry for what happened to you, and I suppose it will happen again to others, but I won't apologize for my service: we're not that bad."

He paused, looking to the handsome couple across the conference table, thinking he was ill prepared to argue this case.

"And I still need your help."

He turned mournfully to Mandy and saw the striking face, saddened now. The wrinkles were there, the delicate transparent skin of old age. But the facial structure: eyes, cheeks, mouth, had not changed from her youth. Gravity and the adipose deposits of age had not had their way with her. He thought she must have been a beauty—was a beauty.

"My wife Edith and I would be honored to have you in our home this evening, Mrs. Deforest. We'll eat Creole: She-Devil Prawns and Hoppin' Joe."

# Chapter 5

## June 1948

The briefer wore wool in the humid summer heat of Washington. The briefing was badly hampered by sweat rolling down his forehead, darkening his tight starched collar. Assistant Secretary Penrod Taylor, a recipient of the briefing and mid-senior executive in the newly created Department of Defense, wondered if the man's conclusions were as illogical as the wool suit he wore in this ancient tarpaper and stick building at the Naval Annex in Arlington, where the air conditioning system was a small rotating fan at the front of the room.

"I have a question for you Dr. Jackson, if you will allow an interruption."

Dr. Jackson was an old-fashioned briefer: he used a wooden pointer to strike the words on the silver screen before him, lending emphasis to his analysis. Now he put the pointer on the desk before him and began to roll it about, not looking up.

"Yes?"

The remaining audience of three turned to hear Taylor.

"Well. It just seems to me the construction site you're showing us here could be making roasted peanuts, or umbrellas, or atomic bombs. The choices are equally likely: there really isn't enough detail to be certain of anything. What do you say to that?"

Dr. Jackson of the CIA, another newly created entity, stared at Secretary Taylor through thick glasses, his eyes huge behind them.

"I will cover your conundrum in my conclusions, but as you ask the question now let me answer you directly: no, we cannot tell with certainty what product will issue from these works. I would guess two more years are required to be certain, at the rate the Chinese are now progressing. But my purpose here today is to point out what is possible, based on current intelligence information. I cannot tell you what the plant will produce: it's too early to know. The quality of the photography is not good, but it is the best we have."

He paused and looked over his shoulder toward the blackboard as if some interloper might have crept behind him.

"You all know the price we pay for these pictures. Our men are dying on almost every attempt."

He turned back and looked directly at each person in his small audience.

"So I tell you this: the Peoples Republic of China is pouring vast sums into this project and they are a strapped government, economically broken by the world war and now by their internecine civil war. We see no other activity like this across the nation. The technical indications do not rule out an atomic assembly facility, indeed they support such capability rather strongly. Therefore it is prudent to believe the Chinese will have an atomic capability in the early 1950's, and to take a defensive posture accordingly."

He stood there, flatfooted and heavy, breathing with difficulty in the awful heat, his huge eyes rolling about the room.

"The Administration does not care for this theory, they don't want to spend more money. They badger me with questions about how such a primitive society could come by atomic capability in so short a time.

Alas, I do not know, or even care. I care only for my inescapable conclusion: the Chinese are about to make a bomb. That is my position, and it is strongly supported by the Agency."

Taylor had to wait until eight that evening to get into the Defense Secretary's office. A carefully crafted system was in place across the government: Cabinet-level personnel did not attend the INDICATIONS AND WARNINGS briefings, ever. Lower levels attended these briefings, formed opinions, outlined plans, and then discreetly approached the bosses for approvals. That way, the seniors could deny knowledge if things turned bad and they were subpoenaed to testify before Congress. The lesser figures, men like Taylor, could invoke national security and escape public testimony.

Taylor was pumped up now, not the same man who had practiced wit upon Dr. Jackson that morning.

"Jackson is taking the position that it's the assembly plant, the final link. The other sites we know about are making components. The Agency will back him, sir."

Abner Day shook his head, hoping this wasn't true.

"Well, I don't know Pen; it's certainly not welcome news. You're very close to this issue, what do you think?"

"We just don't know. But if we ignore the thing and it turns out to be a bomb plant, we would never be forgiven: it would be a grave breach. We need to find a better way to get in there, to get better intelligence. We'd continue the photography for sure, but also get communications intercepts. We need to get into their new microwave telephone links. But we'll have to be right in the main microwave beam, just a few hundred feet above the ground to do that."

Taylor liked this new idea of telephone intercepts in the enemy's lair. He very much preferred to hear what the builders themselves had to say about their site, rather than look at incomplete construction photographs and make guesses as to the ultimate use.

Day looked to the third man in the room, sitting silently in a darkened corner chair.

"He's right, John, we're asking too much of your aircrews now and yet we need even better data. I guess we need to look under more technical rocks to do this job successfully."

Air Force Chief of Staff John Stenzell shook his head and shifted uncomfortably in his chair.

"I agree that we should stir the pot again Abner, but I can't give you much hope. Right now the B-29 is the only airplane we have with the range to get to your target and return safely. The neutrals won't cooperate, so we have nowhere to refuel for almost 3700 miles in and out. It takes a big airplane to carry the reconnaissance payloads and enough fuel to do the job. It's unfortunate, tragic that we're forced to make the entire trip at high altitude. Our loss rate is close to the worst we saw during the war: 1942 and 43 over Germany."

Day leaned back in his chair and closed his eyes, it had been a very long day and no end was in sight.

"What about that new thing; the jet, the B-47?"

"It's very fast, and that would help survivability some, but it just gulps the fuel down: the range is much shorter than the B-29. Even if we could solve that problem, there aren't enough of them yet to even deploy a bombing squadron. If the few we have on operations started to disappear, you can bet the Congress would be over here in short order, demanding answers. We're only able to do the missions now because the

B-29 is in such plentiful supply: the overseers don't notice when 20 or so are diverted to other uses."

Stenzell produced an unneeded lecture.

"What we're doing isn't exactly legal you know. We're in muddy waters, violating another nation's sovereign territory during peacetime. We get away with it because a handful of Senators and Congressmen have been briefed into the program to offer protection if things go sour."

He thought of the lethal B-29 missions. The courage and determination of his aircrews weighed on him like stone.

"Pen, I want you to go out to Wright Field tomorrow. Lay out the technical elements of the mission for our engineering staff: get creative, open the thing up, blue-sky it. You know, I was thinking of the P-38M just the other day: the last of the P-38 line. They gussied the old bird up with extra engine power and fuel tanks right near the end of the war, and used it for long-range reconnaissance. I think the range of a stripped down-version got up around 4500 miles: no armament of course. Throw that airplane on the table, and anything else anyone can think of."

He searched for more.

"And you might bring up the P-61. I'm not sure how many are left now, it's a long shot, but have them check on it."

Penrod Taylor looked to his boss for approval. Day nodded.

"Do it, Pen. We lost another B-29 this afternoon. The Chinese used the new high altitude YAK-9 fighter. They can't quite get up to the B-29's altitude, so they zoom up from below and shoot into the belly just before the fighter stalls. The crew almost got home; the plane went out of control just short of Formosa and crashed in the China Sea. The air-sea rescue boys are out now: no sign of survivors. God help us, that's ten aircraft we've lost: 100 men. I am growing almighty tired of lying to the families about mid-air collisions and weather accidents."

Taylor rose from his chair and started for the door.

"I'll call Wright Field now and ask the Chief Engineer to assemble a group first thing tomorrow, then I'll get on over to Andrews and catch the midnight shuttle out there."

Day stopped him on the way out.

"I need a story for the Hill; a different approach. We'll need new funding for this program. How much, what shall I tell them?"

Penrod Taylor thought a moment. He looked at Stenzell.

"I think we should use the P-38M for now. I know there are still quite a few around. I'm not so sure about the P-61. Emphasize the need for communications intercepts, the need to actually hear what Chinese Government officials are saying on the telephone. Tell them about the new Hallicrafter intercept payload and the need for extremely low altitude. We can never do that with the B-29. We need a new capability to go low in the target area: new capability equals new funds. They'll be worried about using old airplanes, tell them we'll do refurbishment at the Lockheed plant in Burbank. And we'll need to train a new group of pilots; thirty or forty I would guess. So I think we're looking at 30 plus million here. We might be able to reprogram 10 or so. We'd need about 20 million in new funding, that should be safe."

Taylor thought of final important advice.

"Keep the discussion general, we don't have the details. We'll need time to plan the details."

Day turned wearily to his intercom after the men left.

"I'll need the limo now. Capitol Hill."

There was one more chore before the long day ended, a private chat with four members of Congress, all very senior men with seats on the important Defense Committees: two Republicans and two Democrats.

The limousine pulled up to the side of the Capitol Building in the dark. Even at this hour the humid heat was wretched. A young staff member met them and escorted the Secretary through a basement door to a small room used for this sort of sensitive topic: a few comfortable chairs, reading lamps, coffee tables and service, a small bar, and the pleasant, timeless odor of furniture polish and tobacco smoke.

The elected officials preferred to be consulted in this comfortable, collegiate atmosphere: no harsh lights, no prepared speeches, and no observers. Day chatted for 20 minutes, occasionally referring to handwritten notes, often stopping to field questions: tough questions.

Senator Evan Meyer, R, Rhode Island, Chairman of the Select Committee on Intelligence, had a good one. Eyes closed, four ounces of excellent brandy in his stomach, nodding toward sleep, he interrupted Day's monologue.

"Tell me again why we're doing this, Abner. If we just ignored the whole thing, what's so bad about that? After all, the Chinese are certainly large in numbers but not very close to our borders, and hardly a sophisticated enemy. And where could they possibly get the funds for such a massive undertaking? Mao and Chiang Kai-Shek have been fighting tooth and nail since the end of the war while the United States vacillates and supports neither. We say we want a coalition government, but it will never happen with those two. What a joke it all is; weak and shortsighted."

Meyer held up his index finger without opening his eyes.

"Before you answer, let me tell you what's good about taking no action in this damnable affair: no requests for new funds, no battle on the floor, no press clacking about a bunch of hysterics seeing Communists under every bush. And so on."

Abner Day, a Democrat and Defense Secretary in the present Administration, thought a moment. He was in dangerous territory. He needed to reconcile the threat of an attack from the Oriental Pacific with the possibility that these men would read him as another grasping bureaucrat building an empire from imagined enemies. He chose a course of explanation and began, knowing the Congressmen were looking for their own defensible arguments as much as they were listening to his.

"Let me address the funding question first, Senator. We believe Mao recovered almost $500 million in U.S. lend-lease funding from the Nanking banks when he overran the city in 1947 while Chiang Kai-Shek sat on his mountaintop, pouting about our lack of support for his anti-communist policies. Mao stole our money."

The men around him were shaking their heads. He was afraid they were disagreeing with him. After a silent moment he understood the head shaking was disgust at the weak role the United States was playing in keeping China out of Communist hands.

Meyer had another question.

"We're already building the DEW radar line across Canada and Alaska to stop the Russian IL28 bomber. Won't that handle the Chinese, too?

"The DEW line handles attacks across the North Pole, Senator. The Chinese are getting IL28's now, too. They'll come in from the West, where we don't have a DEW line. We'll have a funding problem here; the Administration is already uneasy about military expenditures. They would much prefer to spend on schools and teachers and a better cross-country transportation program. But the Russian airplanes are real, being deployed now in large numbers; they're not some intelligence analysts dream. So we're spending, but reluctantly. Even at that, I think we can agree on the wisdom of the DEW line, we all lived through Pearl Harbor."

They wouldn't argue with him about DEW line expenditures. There would never be another undefended attack upon the United States, not while these men were in office.

"Now, if the Chinese add an atomic bomb to the IL28, we'll be forced to come over here with a request to extend the DEW line down the West Coast: it will be a request you can't deny and there will be a political firestorm"

He stopped a moment to be sure he had their attention, saw four pairs of eyes riveted on his face.

"Last September we took in a defector who worked constructing a huge facility in the Takli Makan Desert in far western China, out of range of our reconnaissance aircraft. We sent a special B-29 all the way in just before Christmas and recovered decent high altitude photography. It was a shock I can tell you: a facility under construction that sprawls over two square miles. We've authorized 30 missions since then. Today I learned of our tenth B-29 loss, and the loss rate has increased sharply over the past two months. The Chinese see them on radar at very long range and they have become adept at interception."

Day rubbed his face wearily, rose, and went to the small bar for another brandy before continuing.

"If it's the final assembly plant for an atomic bomb, we must anticipate an atomic attack from the China as early as 1950 or 51. We'll be coming over here to the Hill with a massive new funding request. We need the bedrock truth."

Congressman Levi Jones, D, Iowa, Chairman of the House Defense Appropriations Committee, interrupted.

"All well and good, Abner, but I don't see how a bunch of ancient WW2 airplanes will increase your chances. It sounds like a disaster to me, a waste of our young men, possibly worse than these damned B-29 missions. And what's the tab for this deal?"

Day nodded, happy to be moving to firmer ground.

"The P-38M is faster and longer range than the B-29. We plan to use some of that extra range to execute a low altitude final approach to the target; a luxury we do not have with the B-29. You're right, Congressmen, the airplanes are old. We'll send them to the Lockheed Burbank plant for a major overhaul; bring them back to new condition. In a few months we'll select a group of pilots and start training for this very difficult flight operation. There will be cameras of course, but we'll also install the new Hallicrafter voice intercept payload. The pilots will fly right down into the new microwave telephone beams, just a few hundred feet above the ground. They'll record actual conversations dealing with matters at the site. Gentlemen, the idea of actually eavesdropping on the enemy in his sanctuary is very exciting. We'll need about 20 million for the program."

Day knew his arguments were strong and simple. Senator Meyer looked around the room.

"Are we agreed Gentlemen, shall we authorize the Secretary to proceed?"

A new activity would be born. The tax-paying public would never know.

# Chapter 6

Corporal Lockwood Allegro Deforest, radio mechanic, sat in a chair in front of his boss, Lt. Col. Roy "Doc" Mendes, Commander of the 4712th Airways and Air Communications Squadron. Deforest was quite relaxed because Mendes was a fine leader, a motivator known for taking care of his men. Mendes was thick-shouldered, beer-bellied, and he sported a pencil-thin Ramon Navarro silent film mustache.

He wore half-glasses to study the yellow one-page Teletype sheet on the desk before him. Winter sunlight illuminated his lined face but did little to take the chill off the room. Ticks and muffled hisses from the overworked steam radiator were the only sound for several minutes as Mendes continued his reading. Eventually he peered above the half-glasses.

"Got two Buck Sergeant slots in this month, Al. Gonna give one to Lewis because he deserves it: he's smart and hard working. You should get the other one, but you won't: it's going to Hambone. You want to know why?"

Al grinned. He liked the Colonel and knew he would be taken care of eventually.

"Yes sir I would, especially since you claim it should go to me."

Mendes smiled benignly.

"It's going to Hambone because he's blood: he's my sisters' boy. The kid isn't right bright, he's a little lazy, and we have him driving a truck because he's a menace doing the technical work. Still, I'll make him a Sergeant because he's family."

His head moved as if shaking off a disturbing thought.

"I just thought you should know the truth of it, since you're the one getting screwed here. Shortsighted and unfair isn't it? Ugly. Well, consider it a lesson in life."

"Yes sir it is ugly, but I'm not going to worry about it. I like my job here and I like the outfit. I guess I'll be a Sergeant when the time is right. Is that all?"

He rose to leave, but Mendes held up a hand dramatically. He enjoyed drama.

"Hold it boy, that is not all. See this Teletype? It's from Headquarters USAF."

He pronounced USAF phonetically: you-saff, rolling the tones off his tongue and smiling wonderingly. He had been a pilot in the Army Air Service in WW1. He had been in the Army Air Corps, the Army Air Force, and now he was in the United States Air Force. He had lived through the entire development of modern aviation and he remained amazed at the technical progress he had witnessed. He continued to wave the yellow sheet as he spoke.

"This is your ticket to the big time boy; your brass ring. It says here our leaders are going to open up the Pilot, Navigator, and Bombardier training programs to exceptional enlisted men: men who can pass the OCS tests and are recommended by their CO's. They're waving the requirement for 2 years of college. You want to know why?"

Al had a sinking feeling; he knew where Doc was headed and he was less than sure he wanted to expose himself to the possibility of failing. He excelled at his job, but he was painfully shy and in this way not particularly suited to the military life. He felt safe and competent right here doing his job: a little frog in a little pond. He nodded vaguely and spoke without enthusiasm.

"I guess I do, sir."

Mendes failed to notice the spiritless reply. He dropped the yellow sheet and stood to pace the room, full of nervous energy, eager to get this opportunity across to the exceptional young man.

"Well, it's two things. First, the war kind of tired everyone out: young fella's all seem to want to be civilians now and it's been hard for us to attract the right kind. And second, it's our Captains bulge. See, when the war ended we tried to keep the best officers in the service: offered to give them Regular Commissions, to send them to college for graduate work, that sort of thing. But so many of them just wanted out, didn't want to be part of the military, that we fell a little short. Then, to compound the problem, the boys who did want to stay were too often just interested in flying their airplanes—they didn't want to manage things and they weren't particularly good leaders. So a lot of these fellas aren't progressing: they aren't able to make it over the hump to the field-grade ranks, Major and up. That means we have too many Captains, and not enough Majors. That's the Captain's bulge. It's awful."

Mendes paused to scratch a gray eyebrow. He looked at Al to see how his pitch was going.

"Then some smart person up at Headquarters had a wonderful idea, an idea I really believe in: use the talent pool in our enlisted ranks. Take a smart enlisted kid, give him an education and the right training, and make him part of our future, one of our leaders. The training will be very different from years past, though. This new Air Force will teach you to fly all right, but there will be a lot more emphasis on teaching our kids to be good managers, and gentlemen too. Sort of like a military version of Harvard, you could say."

He stopped pacing and returned to the desk, eyes boring into Al.

"You've got to do this, boy: it's a break for you. I've seen all kinds in the past thirty years and I know: you'll be a good officer, a good leader. So you think about it and come see me tomorrow. And don't disappoint me Al, you hear?"

Mendes had a last comment as Al left.

"Of course they'll want a seven year commitment from you, but that's peanuts."

Al spent a sleepless night full of doubt about leaving his secure nest and venturing into a more demanding world. He had joined the Army Air Force two years ago just as the war was ending. He joined not to fight, but to enjoy the benefits of the GI Bill, which would underwrite the college training his parents could not afford.

He was not at all sure he wanted to be a manager, or a gentleman. He wasn't even sure he wanted to be a pilot. Still, it was clearly a way for him to learn new things, expensive new things.

Al knew his Dad would approve of the training. Curtis Deforest lost his accounting business during the Depression and now he kept the books for a local machine shop, scraping by at a minimal standard of living. Al remembered endless meals of beans and rice. He remembered going hungry some nights when there weren't even beans. He remembered hunting rabbits along the railroad tracks for meat. His Dad would give him two .22 cartridges and their ancient single shot rifle every Friday night. If Al missed, there was no meat for a week. They had survived somehow, but these days Curtis Deforest believed above all else in training and a regular paycheck.

Birdie was harder to anticipate. Al's mother was a gifted musician who supplemented the family income with part time work playing the cello and viola in local quartets: weddings and garden parties and special events around Northwest Oregon. She occasionally substituted with the Portland Philharmonic. Birdie was fey and abstract and brilliant, and Al was the center of her life. The Army bothered her, but she understood about the GI Bill.

Then there was Mandy with her curly cap of red-gold hair and dark brown eyes that radiated fire when she was mad. Mandy had never learned feminine indirection: she said exactly what she thought, and she thought the Army was a terrible idea. In Mandy's opinion, Al could do much better than the Army.

The cloud dissolved at breakfast. He would just have to trust Doc, trust that he knew enough about Al to be doing the right thing. After all, Doc was both a pilot and a medical doctor who had practiced in the years between the wars.

He saw him that afternoon and said he would do his best. Mendes beamed; another good kid sent down the correct path.

"By God that's OK, Al, that's just fine. Now you scoot over to the Adjutant and get some travel orders, you're going down to Moody Field in Georgia to take those tests. And hurry up, they start on Monday, there's not a moment to lose."

# Chapter 7

Corporal Deforest joined several hundred young enlisted men at the small base in South Georgia late Sunday afternoon. He was assigned an upper bunk in a barracks controlled by the Air Training Command, sponsors of this new initiative, charged with administering a battery of physical and mental tests that would determine if he became an officer candidate.

Staff Sergeant Douglas Trapnell was assigned the bunk below his. He lay with hands folded behind his head, apparently asleep. Al unpacked, storing his few clothing items in a footlocker. As he prepared to leap to the top bunk, a hand snaked out from the lower bunk and Trapnell greeted him in a backwoods North Carolina twang thick enough to be difficult for Al to follow.

"How y'all? I got in from Bitburg last night. Been waitin' for my Bunkie all this long day. Some of these boys not so friendly, you know. Name's Doug; Doug Trapnell."

Trapnell's eyes remained closed as he delivered the effusion. Al leaned under the top bunk to respond.

"Howdy, my name's Al. I came down from Atterbury this afternoon, just got in."

He paused, noticing that Trapnell's eyes were still closed, as if he had not heard. Feeling slightly put off, he continued.

"This whole thing is making me nervous, I'm not sure I want to take all these tests—and even if I pass, I'm not sure I want to be an officer. What do you think of this deal?"

The last comment seemed to energize Trapnell. He rose from the bunk in a single smooth motion and began circling Al.

"What the hell you talking about, boy? Sure you want to take these tests: sure you want to be an officer. You been riding the back of the bus awhile, this lets you ride up front. Now you can eat off of linen, fart through silk. No doubt about it. You're just nervous; forget about it. You stick with old Dougie, I'll make you a General."

Trapnell produced a winning smile and put a hand on Al's shoulder.

"You gonna be fine boy, just go on along with the program."

Al sat on the footlocker and looked up at his new friend: a short muscular frame, auburn hair, dark skin and piercing chestnut eyes; little feet that turned the toes of his shoes upward, pixie-like. His head appeared to be attached to his legs by a too-short string, causing a bird-like jerk with each step: an oversize pigeon. He looked older than most of the other candidates.

"How old are you Doug, you look a little old for this stuff."

"I'm 27, just made it under the age limit. Did crop dusting all over the South until I was 23, then they cancelled my draft deferment and put me in the Army, made me shoot a gun on a B-17. I shipped over after the war, re-enlisted, didn't want to come back here to the States. Been fixing airplane motors over in Germany until this deal came along. I guess I am a little old, but I got 2000 hours in dusters. Not much these boys are gonna teach me about flying."

He changed the subject abruptly.

"You smart, boy? I could use me some smart. Maybe we could be a team, if I can pass these here exams."

Al replied unselfconsciously.

"Yeah, I'm smart I guess; pretty smart. I always got top grades in high school. If we end up in the same place, maybe we could do each other some good."

Trapnell peered at the paper badge each candidate was required to wear and chuckled.

"L.A. Deforest, what's the L.A. for, Los Angeles?"

Al was embarrassed. His goddamned name again.

"It stands for Lockwood Allegro."

"Oh my! That's a bum moniker, boy. Your momma done hung a heavy burden on you."

"It was both of them. My Dad admired an artist fellow, Lockwood deForest, no relation. My Mom is a musician; plays string instruments, the cello and the viola. She thought I moved around pretty good when I was just born, so she threw in the Allegro: it means fast, brisk."

Trapnell shook his head solemnly.

"I see. Well, that's a shame."

"It gets worse. The Army makes you use your first name and middle initial. So my paperwork says Lockwood A. Deforest. If you think Allegro is bad, try Lockwood for a while."

Al was on the last part of the physical exam by late Friday afternoon, exhausted by four 10-hour days spent on a seemingly endless battery of mental tests; many of which didn't make much sense to him. Today was physical testing, and the test he was taking now seemed simple enough:

he was to focus on a wooden panel with paper instruments glued to it, simulating an airplane instrument panel, then look up on signal and peer into a 15 foot long darkened box. Two barely illuminated sticks stood upright at the end of the box, their position adjustable on tracks by means of pull strings. The idea was to align the sticks perfectly, so they were exactly side-by-side, thus showing an ability to change focus quickly from the inside of a cockpit to the world outside.

A technician measured the time required for each candidate to align the sticks, and Al was in trouble.

"Uh, let's try one more time, Corporal, that one was 15 seconds and the alignment wasn't very good."

Now Al was worried. In this instant he realized that he wanted to pass these tests, wanted this opportunity. His defensive lack of commitment faded away as he envisioned failure, and failure from a very simple test at that. He smiled encouragingly at the technician, wiping his damp forehead.

"Yeah. I'm sure it's just because my eyes are tired, it's been a long week; a lot of close work I'm not used to."

The technician raised his eyebrows noncommittally, switched off the light inside the box and pulled the strings to randomly misalign the pesky sticks.

"We'll try again. Do it right this time."

Al knew he hadn't done well as he watched the technician peer through a window in the side of the box: his heart sank. The man straightened and looked at him thoughtfully, then at the long line of candidates still to be tested. He made a decision.

"Fuck it, Corporal, I'm going to pass you. The alignment was OK this time, but you took 12 seconds: the cutoff is 9. I'm giving you a pass because I think you're tired, like you said. Now move along."

That evening Al called his girlfriend Amanda Piper, in Tillamook, Oregon. It was a long distance call, a major extravagance. He plugged an ear against the noisy din in the hangar. 350 candidates were shouting in the miserably hot enclosure, in various states of intoxication thanks to the Schlitz Brewing Company, sponsor of 'nickel beer night' every Friday evening. Moody Field had obligingly made the hangar available because the Enlisted Man's Club was far too small to accommodate the group. The CO wanted the boys to go back home happy. After several rings Mr. Piper answered, it was a disappointment to Al.

"It's Al, sir. Is Mandy around?"

After a short summary of his situation for Mr. Piper, a World War One veteran, Mandy came on.

"God, Al, I thought you were never going to call, what time is it back there?"

"Well, it's almost midnight Mandy, I'm sorry to be so late, but the Base threw a party for us before we go home tomorrow. I more or less had to attend, you know."

"It sounds like more rather than less. How did the testing go, do you think it was OK?"

"I think the mental stuff was OK. But I'm not so sure about the eye exam: I had some trouble. I hope it's all right. After a week down here I'm getting pretty excited about doing this; I've met some great guys and I'm not so nervous now. I hope it turns out. I go back to Atterbury tomorrow morning on the train. If it happens, I'll get a 10-day leave before I report. I can get home and see you. I love you."

Two thousand miles away Mandy's dark eyes flashed and she frowned. She had hoped Al would fail the tests, finish his enlistment and get out. He would have the GI Bill for college now, and he could do so much better in the civilian economy. The thought of a seven-year commitment appalled her.

"Don't worry about the tests Al, I'll be here for you no matter what; you know that. I just want us to be together now, it seems like you've been away forever."

A familiar sense of being both helpless and slightly defensive overcame him.

"I know sweetheart, but I wouldn't put you through the life I'm leading now, we wouldn't have a thing. If I can get through this program, be an officer, we'll get married right away."

Mandy decided to drop the subject for now.

"Just get yourself out here to me any way you can, darling; it's so lonely without you."

Al was her first and only love: from the moment they met as junior high school freshman in the fall of 1941. Mandy knew right then Al would be the man in her life and there would never be another. But she had no intention of seeing him waste his life in the military. In time, she would make him see things from her point of view. But for now she was going along, afraid she would lose him if she drew a line.

Two weeks later Col. Mendes called Al into his office. He was beaming.

"You did it Al; you passed. I knew you could. Look here, they rated you a 9 on Pilot, an 8 on Navigator, and a 9 on Bombardier. You can hardly do any better than that."

The Air Force was using the new STANINE system of test scoring now, 1 to 9, where a 9 represented the top few of those tested.

Al was alarmed.

"But sir, I don't want to be a navigator or bombardier, I want to be a pilot like you."

Mendes nodded enthusiastically.

"Yes sir, you're damn right, boy. You let me worry about where you get assigned. I have a few chits up there and I'll just call them in. A pilot, that's the thing to be all right."

# Chapter 8

Penrod Taylor sat dozing at the makeshift conference table they had cobbled together: four battered gray metal tables pushed together to provide room for the dozen civilian supervising engineers Wright Field had assigned to his problem. He could hear the men discussing complexities: the merit of this airplane versus that airplane for the intended mission. They had been going on like this for four days and no solution was at hand.

Taylor had presented the problem succinctly, devoid of detail to keep the meeting at a low level of security.

"We need an aircraft that can carry two men and 1200 pounds of payload 3700 miles: 1850 going in and 1850 returning. It's perfectly all right to fly at a high, cruise-efficient altitude for half the distance, but it has to drop down low 900 miles before reaching the target to avoid defenses. Then we need 45 minutes to maneuver in the target area, and 30 minutes of fuel reserve at the end of the mission for contingencies. There is no possibility of aerial refueling anywhere along the route. That's it."

He passed out a one-sheet summary to each attendee, stamped CONFIDENTIAL.

An excited buzz filled the room. This was the type of problem airplane performance engineers loved: finding something, anything, to do a very tough mission. The group quickly rejected the older combat bombers, the various cargo aircraft, and the fighters: all lacked the range to be useful on this very long mission. The P-38M had sufficient cruising range to do the job, but could carry only 400 pounds of payload. Taylor wanted to know about the new bomber, the graceful swept-wing B-47.

"If the P-38M can't carry my payload, how about the new jet bomber?"

One of the performance engineers swiveled toward him with a rueful shrug.

"Oh, man. I wish you hadn't asked. The jets are fast all right, but they just gulp fuel at low altitude. The B-47 uses as much fuel sitting on the ground idling as it does going 400 mph at 35,000 feet. It uses a third of its fuel just climbing up to cruising altitude. Forget about it, that sucker can barely get around the landing pattern."

Taylor held out for a 1200-pound payload. Congress was sold now on the idea of telephone intercepts and the new Hallicrafter communications intercept receiver/recorders weighed 800 pounds. Then there was another 400 pounds for the cameras. He was on shaky ground insisting on the heavy payload, but they had to do this one right. There would be no further authorizations if this program failed. He was becoming concerned. The engineers didn't seem to have an answer he could live with.

His bladder sent urgent signals: six cups of coffee since breakfast were calling for a way out. He excused himself and went directly to a bathroom down the hall. As he relieved himself, a young man in bowtie and shirtsleeves appeared at the next urinal.

"I know one that will work for your mission, but they won't let me talk about it."

Taylor was tempted to ask the kid how he knew about the mission, but thought better of it. Not enough details were included in his one-sheet summary to compromise the mission and the senior engineers weren't getting anywhere as far as he could see. He spoke over his shoulder on the way to the sink.

"You'd make me a happy man if you could solve our problem. Tell me what you're thinking."

"Well, you could use the P-61, it has the legs and it can carry your payload. There's a small problem though. You can't carry two pilots. You'd have to put a gas tank where the rear seat is to make the range."

Taylor shook his head slowly and a corner of his mouth twisted up.

"You mean that big ugly thing they called the Black Widow, the night fighter? We would need a bunch of them, son. I thought they were all cut up after the war."

"That's what every one else thinks, too. But some weren't cut up, some were buried: forty of them. And then there are eight still flying, they changed the fuselage a little and renamed it the F-15, but it's just a P-61 with a more streamlined body. It's a reconnaissance airplane, used for weather missions over in the South Pacific."

Taylor's heart sank; he had experienced hope for a moment. Concern slipped back to grip him.

"Not very many airplanes for what I have in mind, I'm afraid. Why hasn't this been discussed in the meeting? I asked for every conceivable idea…by the way, I'm Pen Taylor, what's your name son?"

"Evan Fogarty, sir, and I knew who you were. I think my boss didn't bring it up because he doesn't believe me about the buried ones. But I was over there last year and we dug one up; we wanted parts to repair a chase plane for the German jets we were testing. The one we dug up wasn't all that bad. It was buried in clean sand, apparently gently, because the airframe wasn't banged up much, and there was no corrosion. Of course they didn't have engines or flight instruments; those were salvaged. But we have plenty of both, that wouldn't be a problem. Just clean them up a little bit, fit engines and instruments, and they'd be fine."

Fogarty could see that his bait was being nudged. Now he would sink the hook with candor.

"The canopy was cracked on the one we dug up, and the fabric on the control surfaces was rotten too, but we could fix that easy."

"This is something awfully important, Evan; I don't know what to say. By the way, why were they buried, why weren't they brought back here and cut up for the aluminum salvagers?"

Fogarty continued, seeming to ignore the question.

"Just go back in the meeting and bring up the P-61; have them send a survey party over there to check my story, you'll see I'm right. You really don't have a choice Mr. Taylor, there isn't anything else…and they were buried because the Government didn't want to ship them home and didn't want the Philippine Communist guerillas to get them, and the farmers were all up in arms about setting them on fire. They had just been flown to a new air base in the jungle when the war ended. The bulldozers were already there, so they dug a hole and buried them."

Taylor brought up the subject of the P-61 when he rejoined the meeting, doubtful but wanting to hear about the technical aspects, to see if there was a mission match. One of the supervisors smiled and nodded.

"Evan found you, didn't he? He's a good kid, bright and energetic, but I think he's a little off base with this one."

Taylor persisted.

"If we had a bunch of new shiny P-61's, could they do my mission?"

The man bit his lip and drifted into hushed thought before speaking.

"With some modification, yes they could. We'd have to put fuel bladders where the radar and gun turret are located, and more in the rear pilot's seat. I think we'd be looking at 4200, 4300 miles on your mission, something like that. And we could hack the 1200-pound payload. But then you'd have only one pilot to fly the thing for 14 hours or more: that would be very hazardous. And we really can't count on those buried airplanes, they're probably wrecks. We only have a few F-15's left now, and they'll be retired next year. The whole concept is shaky, Pen; not practical."

Taylor's fingers clenched in his lap; this was an experienced supervisor he did not want to discourage.

"Well, you're probably right but what else do we have? As nearly as I can tell, nothing, so let's get a survey party out there, wherever it is, pronto."

He was suddenly sure he was on the right track. An expression of satisfaction showed in his eyes as a thought came to him.

"I seem to recall Lindbergh was able to stay awake for 33 hours."

# Chapter 9

"Come on, come on; come on. Oh, God…god, just do it now, now; now."

"I…I don't want to, I…oh shit!"

She shivered with delight.

"No, no sweetheart. It's fine. It's what I wanted. What I needed. Jesus."

Al rolled off her lean fine-tuned, heavy breasted body to lie sweating on the overripe hotel mattress. They both shivered on the backside of heavy orgasm, receding into an exhausted daze.

"Goddamn, how good can it get?"

Mandy giggled.

"I don't know; I never did this before. I don't see how it could get any better, though."

"We need to be careful sweetheart. Imagine if you got pregnant."

"Yeah, imagine."

"No, I'm serious. I can't get married now, they'd throw me out of the program."

"Well, I'm not pregnant, dummy, I'm hungry. Let's take a shower together and get out of this fleabag for a while. But not too long."

They were in Osceola, Arkansas. Al had just finished basic flight training. They ate at a small Lithuanian restaurant on the edge of the vast Osceola Swamp. Al ordered catfish, butter-bread, goulash and pickled beans for two, and a liter bottle of cheap red wine.

"I can never tell you how much I love you Mandy. I just don't have the words."

She couldn't pull off the witty-sophisticate image any longer. Her face crumpled.

"I want to be with you all the time now. How much longer? When does this end? I act like some goddamned whiny dependent and I don't like it. We should be together, Al. Even you can see that can't you?"

"Sure, baby, sure I can. I can see it and I can feel it. Not much longer now. One more phase, six more months, and I'll graduate. Then we'll have the money and we'll get married and begin a real life."

"Oh. Al, it's not a real life. It's a life dragging around to these piss-ant Army bases in the middle of Shitsville. Well, you know what? It's OK, I'll be glad to do it. You're worth it."

Al recognized the familiar attack. The last thing he wanted was some furious argument during the precious four days they had together. He tried to sidestep.

"No, you're the one who's worth it. You're the only one I'll ever want or need. I've never had an eye for another woman and I never will, Mandy. Just cool it. We'll be together forever in a matter of months. I promise you it'll be the best thing."

"How can I make you see? You could be so much more, Al. This is a strange little play-world you're living in. You may be good at it, but you'll never be rich and influential. We could do that if we were together on this, easy. Just you and me, beating the world."

"For Christ's sake Mandy, give it up. I don't want to sit in some office shuffling papers and dealing with nervous customers. I'm good at what I do here. I learn fast, I'm a good flyer. I know; I hear the instructors talking. In here, I'm somebody. I'm doing something I really enjoy."

"Round 6 goes to the champion by a wide margin! OK, drink your wine and pay up, Smilin' Jack, we have to get back to the hotel."

# Chapter 10

Taylor was finishing his status briefing.

"About 4 months to get the airplanes in shape, and in the meantime we can use surrogate aircraft for training while the P-61's are being rebuilt out at Clark. We'll use Martin B-26's as trainers; the engineers tell me they fly pretty much like the Northrop P-61. This means we can stop these costly B-29 missions within 6 months."

Secretary Day's eyebrows rose in approval, but only a fraction of an inch. He was thinking of the political issues to be resolved.

"You've done a fine job; far more than I dared to hope for. Still, I want to be very sure about these old airplanes before we take this program to the White House. Are we OK on that aspect, John?"

Air Force Chief of Staff John Stenzell was collapsed in his favorite well-worn chair in the corner, tunic unbuttoned; his ample belly hanging forth.

"Pen's done the right homework Abner, we'll be all right on the technical matters. I just wish we had a few more P-61's: you can never have too many airplanes, you know. The plan calls for a total of 100 missions. If we need to fly more, or the loss rate is higher than we think, there could be some difficulty. Within the ground rules though, we're OK."

Abner Day returned to Taylor.

"I'm giving you a new assistant. I want you to take over all the high-level government coordination on this project. Turn the other office work over to the new man."

Taylor nodded; he was pleased to remain a part of the exciting effort. He turned and headed for the door to continue his hectic morning. Day had a last word.

"Think of a name for this effort, we're going to have to start calling it something other than X."

Day was turning back to Stenzell as his secretary buzzed.

"The Vice President is calling. You need to get on the line before he does, sir."

Day picked up the phone and sat patiently, knowing Vice President Cameron Glendennan would make him wait. He occupied himself watching children playing on a heap of junk and scrap iron across Lee Highway, imagining he could hear their screams of delight as they rolled mechanical oddments down the large pile. Glendennan came on the line several minutes later.

"Good afternoon, Abner. I've been entrusted with management of one of your sensitive programs. The President prefers not to be associated with the effort, so I'll provide the direction I'm sure you need."

Day sighed: Glendennan was a fool and a bully who would never be cleared by the Air Force for complete access to any sensitive program. He had a history of drunk driving incidents and two arrests for misdemeanor assault. The New Jersey Highway Patrol had reluctantly expunged the arrest records from his file under heavy political pressure, but not before sending covert copies to the FBI.

On the other hand, Glendennan was also a man who had purchased half the dry-cleaning establishments in New Jersey back during the

Depression, then made them successful through his own shrewdness and hard work. He had been a heavy Democratic Party contributor for years and he held a number of key posts in the national apparatus. He was virtually unassailable.

Day would check with the President to be sure this wasn't an end-run, but he doubted it. He would have to live with the man. He set about defining the rules.

"We're happy to have you aboard Mr. Vice President, but you know we'll never be able to get complete program access for you. Not with your history. The Air Force refuses to accept political direction on security matters, so you'll just have to do the best you can with low-level information. And Cameron, you won't be directing anything. We'll welcome your views, but the Pentagon runs military operations, not the White House."

Glendennan felt a gut level antipathy for Day: instinctive blue-collar mistrust of a patrician. Dislike slipped out before the politician in him could prevent it. He rumbled in a primal way, the snarl of an animal preparing for combat.

"It's time to start preparing for the mid-term elections, Abner. I intend to use the success of this program to strengthen my position. And it's not too early to be considering the '52 contest, you know. The President has assigned me to this task and I won't have you getting in the way of my oversight, secret clearances or not. And you can't prevent me from claiming credit if the program is successful, as my rumor-mill tells me it will be. So get off your high-horse Mr. Secretary. I'm coming over next Tuesday and I want a complete overview available when I get there. After that, I'll want weekly reviews. Tell your Generals that. Go ahead and see what your Yale Law degree can do about it."

Day flinched and hung up. He turned to his visitor. A glance told him Stenzell had absorbed the meaning of the conversation.

"We'll have the Vice President as White House representative on this project. I had hoped for Peter Sumner, the President's Chief of Staff, he's a much more rational fellow. Well, I won't let Glendennan get me down. We'll do this correctly in spite of him. And the first step is to staff the top of the program: we need a skeleton crew right now."

He brought up a subject neither of them wanted to talk about.

"I assume you'll pick some very experienced people for the overseas part of the operation, John."

Stenzell scratched nervously at his forearm as silence loomed between them.

"What happens if this thing turns into a catastrophe Abner? Are we going to deny it?"

Day reddened visibly; he hated the messy sandwich formed by these questionable, extra-legal activities. He hated the occasional necessity to strand brave men who deserved the highest support from a grateful nation. Yet he was well aware that the 80th Congress was an amalgam of the right and left. There were members who saw peace through cooperative diplomacy as the highest calling. And there were others, a minority now that the war was over, who felt the national interest should be backed by necessary force wherever conflict occurred. Even the President's advisors were sorely divided on the methods for ensuring national security in this devastated postwar world: some saw a great opportunity for world dominance, and others saw an opportunity to build a world based on sharing and cooperation. The President, who liked black and white rather than shades of gray, made these uneasy alliances even more difficult.

Day seethed with an angry retort, but he checked it: John Stenzell was not the cause of this problem. He rolled his chair back and put his feet on the desk.

"If we lose men or equipment in a compromising position, something provable in the World Court, there will be hell to pay John. What I think doesn't matter, the President will make the final decision with as much advice as he can get. He won't duck this one because the thing is too explosive if it goes wrong. I'll be one voice among many. We need to plan the program to make deniability as easy as possible under the worst circumstances. It's God's own miracle the Russians or Chinese haven't paraded a B-29 crew before The Hague. We would never get that program authorized today: two years has made an enormous difference."

"You're not answering my question, Abner."

"Because I don't like the answer. All right here it is: the new program will need strong deniability to receive political approval. I'll do whatever is necessary to get authorization for these P-61 missions, John. If I'm not successful the B-29 program will continue with all its flaws—there are too many officials in the bag to stop it. Too much momentum built up."

Stenzell went to the large picture window looking out on the Pentagon east lawn, hating what he was about to say.

"Then I disagree with you about staffing, Abner. I think we should pick young men for the missions, men with no assignment history to be dug from unofficial sources by the press. I'll put top men in the supervisory positions, but young men will fly these missions and do the hazardous work. It's a familiar theme: old men do the bidding and young men do the bleeding."

He paused, still looking out at the shade-dappled lawn, his face a study in strength and sadness.

"Know this Abner: I'll pick our very best young men for this job. I want that to become an emotional burden for you, the heaviest sort of burden."

Day's face flickered with the pain of an old wound reopened.

"It will be. To make it worse, I don't believe the Administration will do much about it even if we prove the Chinese are manufacturing an atomic bomb. The voting public is delighted by our new prosperity, the best we've seen in 15 years. The priority for the government right now is support of the civilian economy, and I can't really disagree. So don't be surprised by official temporizing even if we prove our point."

"It's too important to ignore Abner, no matter what. We have to know what they're doing at that site."

# Chapter II

The world and its vexations had disappeared into faint background; his entire being was concentrated in the Bonsai. The magnificent three-foot cedar specimen was illuminated by a photographer's lamp imported specially from Seattle for his trimming activities. The tiny green leaves were rendered huge by a floor-mounted 22 cm magnifying glass. He thought carefully. He snipped. His respect for the plant was enormous. A light knock on the thick oak door interrupted his concentration and he closed his eyes, seeking stability before he carefully placed the stainless steel surgical shears on the table. Interruption at this point was a serious matter.

"What is it?"

"It is Xeng, General. Your father calls. On the short wave."

General Pemberton Yu stretched his remaining arm upward and took a huge draught of air into his barrel chest.

"Where is the truck?"

"In the alley off the quadrangle. With respect sir, remember to keep the conversation short. The radio localizers are too good now."

"I come."

Yu left the room and strode across a large empty bay in what had been, twenty-five years ago, The Catholic Sisters of Charity Provincial Hospital. He was a bull of a man, exceptional for a Chinese at almost two meters tall and 103 kilograms, but he skipped like a dancer down the four wooden stairs at the far end of the covered and screened veranda. He crossed the brick-paved quadrangle, ignoring the noisy proceedings at the far end, and entered the battered Kawasaki radio truck he had taken from the Japanese in 1940. The radio technician, perspiring heavily in the heat of the enclosed space, tapped his earphone gently: they are listening.

"Father. I am here."

"Can you speak?"

"No. I will set up the land-line. Call in thirty minutes."

He left the truck to stand in the shade of the alley for a minute, watching with distaste the trial being conducted across the quadrangle. In the days of his maximum power, he would have conducted a ten-minute military court and then shot the thieves himself. Now, with Mao such a powerful presence in the countryside, he felt obliged to conduct these farcical show trials for the benefit of the people. Seventy peasants sat in the sun before a plank table built on saw horses while a political commissar harangued the two accused. Yu was convinced that some of these wretched peasants would turn on him when the time came. He stubbed out his coarse cigarillo and returned to the hospital. He already knew the sentences. It would be an hour before he was required.

His concentration was gone; it would be disrespectful to return to the Bonsai now. He was mildly irritated by the call—they were coming almost daily now, a sign of the times. He sat by the phone until it rang.

"How is your spirit, my father?"

"Good, good. I call to tell you that Mao's forces are about to break through in Chengdu. It is a matter of days until they own the city."

"I know, my father. We listen to the tactical reports on the radio each evening. The Kunmintong put a pretty face on things, but it is clear they have been cut off for the better part of a month now. The fools in the West know only what the city newspapers print. They have no understanding of the country people. They have no understanding of Mao's strength now."

"Yes. More importantly, I have received a report from a member of Chou's Committee on Disposition of the Proletariat. They expect Chiang Kai Shek's entire city structure to collapse within six months. Then they will come after the provincial warlords. First on the list is Szechuan. Then you: Sinkiang. It has never been more serious for us. I see nothing to be done. These men are beyond bribery and they do not care if the sins of the past are exposed. They are that strong."

Yu sighed. He didn't want to hear this.

"We have four more tombs now. Zhang-Lei tells me they are Chou and Han Dynasty I don't see how I can fully exploit them in the time you speak of."

"You are my seed. My issue. I grow old. I worry. We are fully established in the archipelago now. I want you to consider terminating operations before next autumn, before things close in around you. We drove Mao from Shanghai in 1927 and he has a long memory. Things will be hard for you, and very soon now I think."

"As you wish. I will arrange shipments of the lesser goods now. I think I will hold back the precious stuff. I can bring those objects when I come out. My heart aches, father, there is still so much to be done here."

Yu sat in the cool empty hospital ward lost in reverie, going back to 1917 when he was young and strong. Thirty years of fighting, thirty years of pillaging would end now. He felt forlorn. He had never imagined these foolish zealots would come to power. Later, one of his company commanders summoned him.

"It is time for sentencing now."

Yu strode back across the paved common area and leaped up on the plank table to speak to the assembly. He did not bother to confer with the trial judges.

"Listen to me. We all know about thieves. Thieves steal your heart; they steal your blood, they steal your life. Thieves can rob us of our very survival in these times. Lt. Chen stole five wrought bronze coins from the Han Dynasty. They were found in his home and he has no credible defense. He will be hanged just now. Sgt. Pen-Wai hid a terra cotta figurine in his bedroll. Pen-Wai has been with me since the Shanghai battles and I am grieved at his perfidy. We will take his hand, his left hand."

Chen straightened stoically; he would meet his end with dignity. Pen-Wai fell in the dirt and howled in fear. Yu nodded and two men gripped Pen-Wai while a third slipped a leather thong over his left wrist. They would stretch the arm over a stump because no one wanted to try to hold the hand. Fingers had been lost to careless axe blows. The axe man did his work and Pen-Wai fell on the brick pavers shrieking, carefully holding the stump up to avoid contamination. Yu noticed with some interest that the arm skin hung down loosely when Pen-Wai held his hand up, like an unbuttoned shirtsleeve. He reckoned that without the weight and connection of a hand, the arm skin was indeed like a loose sleeve. Interesting. When the tar man came for him, Pen-Wai tried to run, scrabbling into the crowd as he bled. Yu leaped down from the table and closed the space, delivering a mighty blow to Pen-Wai's head that stunned him. Yu gripped the stump ferociously and jammed it into the pot of bubbling tar where it sizzled hotly. Pen-Wai was revived by the agony and stood moaning, walking in short circles.

Yu was pleased; he thought there would be no infection now. The man was a good fighter and he had taken only the left hand. He would still be useful. He would be needed soon enough.

# CHAPTER 12

The noisy foursome drifted toward Al. He growled in irritation, forced by their loudness to leave the warm Texas winter sun. He moved his rickety wooden chair around to the shady side of the old shack and carefully planted the chair legs so they could not slip in the deep sand. He tested the chair and sat down, leaning back against the weathered boards to resume his catnap.

The instructor and his three students remained on the other side of the building. A fourth student was aloft in the powerful new North American T-28 jet transition trainer, practicing landings. The instructor loudly pointed out the airborne student's good moves and his mistakes for the benefit of the three groundlings.

It was quieter on the other side of the shack and Al fell once again into semi-sleep. He was totally relaxed, almost at the end of flight training. The course had been a joy: a wonderful 14-months of classroom and flight instruction that now seemed as brief as an eye-blink.

In a few minutes a T-33 jet trainer would land and pull up to the parking area just beyond the shack. This would be his last flight as a student pilot, a check ride with an unfamiliar instructor. Air Force Pilot Training Class 48N would graduate next week and Al would become a 2d Lieutenant, an Air Force pilot, slated to move on to type rating in the new P-80 jet at Luke Air Force Base in Arizona.

He had muffed a simple instrument landing approach last week, and his conservative flight instructor was calling for an outside opinion before signing off on Al's instrument training. Today Al would ride with a stranger and finish this last assignment. He was untroubled, well aware that his flying skills were exceptional.

But the eye testing problem he encountered back at Moody Field had not been a fluke: his eyes were unusually slow to refocus from near to far, an important requirement when breaking out below low clouds close to the ground; shifting from his instrument panel to the runway ahead just before landing.

Al was faking it. He simply went to the weather officer before each instrument flight and got a forecast for cloud base elevation in the training area. Then, when the altimeter told him they were descending near the bottom of the cloud deck, he would look up from the instruments and focus on the tip of the aircraft nose, twenty feet forward. That way, he already had pretty good far focus when he emerged below the clouds and looked for the runway. Al stayed quiet about his makeshift technique. The Air Force would have been displeased with such unorthodoxy.

The shack he leaned against was located directly below the downwind leg of the landing pattern, at the position where the T-28's rolled into a steeply descending U-turn, rolling back to level again just over the runway threshold, ready to land. He was enjoying the satisfying crackling string of backfires as the pilots closed throttles just before entering the final turn.

An urgent voice brought him to his feet.

"Roll level, get some power now, come on. ROLL LEVEL. JESUS CHRIST! POWER, POWER, POWER!"

He looked up and a stab of fear went through him, the fear his primitive ancestors must have felt when being overtaken by something large and strong. The T-28 was directly above, falling out of the final turn, going far too slow with no flying speed and so close he could tell the engine was idling, not making power. It looked as if the machine would fall right on the shack and crush him and he wanted to run but he didn't know which way. He felt the hair on his scalp and along his backbone bristle in some ancient defensive act. Then he saw that the trajectory would carry the aircraft past the shack by two hundred yards.

Al, the instructor, and the three students from the other side of the shack were all running now, the steps were agonizingly slow as they moved unconsciously toward the inevitable crash. The T-28 made a curious ethereal moan as air traveled some unaccustomed path across the plummeting aircraft. Al looked up as he ran but he had lost sight of the aircraft above him. Panic tried to bloom again just as the T-28 slammed into the earth 75 yards in front of them, left wing first.

He felt the ground shake violently beneath his feet as the machine slammed into dry Texas soil in a cloud of dust. The sound was incongruously tinny, as if a thousand pots and pans had been dumped in a street. The winter sun made a halo through the spray of raw gasoline from ruptured tanks as the wreckage slid away from him through the dirt to a stop. It didn't go far, the descent was almost vertical.

Al was first, arriving before the dust settled. He hesitated and peered frantically through the haze, worried about fire. Then something told him there would be no fire and he ran to the shattered fuselage. The canopy had been opened as part of the pre-landing checklist and he could see the student pilot clearly. He was dead, his upper body noticeably shortened in the seat by compression fractures of spine and ribs. His neck was broken in a Z: the head grotesquely displaced to the rear of the spine as though another person was looking over his shoulder.

Al was strangely moved; he bent down to look at this newly dead face. The mouth was half-open in a secret smile, exposing perfect teeth. The clear blue eyes stared ahead, half-lidded. He wanted desperately to know what this young man had done, what he had been thinking just seconds ago. He wondered if the pilot had been afraid as he saw he could not recover from whatever had occurred. He wanted desperately to communicate with this person—to know. But that could not happen.

Al crouched on the wreckage transfixed, smelling hot oil and raw aviation gas, hearing the ticking of cooling engine parts, hearing the burbling chug of air entering leaking fuel tanks. He staggered back from the wreckage, shocked and sickened, feeling ill and weak as the event slowly became real.

Now the instructor was in front of him, gray-faced, yelling.

"Why didn't the stupid son of a bitch roll the wings level? He might have been all right. He could have done it. Did you see the dumb fuck? Did you see the goddamned ailerons? He never even tried to get it level. God almighty, why didn't he just try?"

The man squatted on his haunches in the dirt, tears in his eyes. The other students remained far back from the wreckage, not willing to see what had happened to their flying partner.

Al walked back to the shack and sat down again in his chair. He didn't blame the instructor; he knew the callous words were an attempt to rationalize the horror, to provide reassurance that a man could always save himself if he thought fast enough.

He noticed that his hands were shaking. He tried to talk to himself just to see if he had a voice. The words were trembling and high pitched, like a frightened child. He stopped talking, dissatisfied by the weakling voice, and simply looked at his shoes. One shoe was half full of sand and small rocks from his run across the desert, but he made no effort to empty it. He thought about the instructor and disagreed with him. Sometimes it didn't matter how fast you thought. Sometimes things happened too fast and you were just fucking dead. He had seen too many like this in the year past.

Much later, Al became aware that his own flight instructor was there, sitting beside him in the dirt, talking.

"Come on kid, my car's over there, I'll take you back to the barracks. I talked to Bailey, he thinks his student froze after he stalled it."

Al continued studying his shoes. His voice was flat.

"That doesn't make sense, sir. The kid must have had 300 hours or more in high performance aircraft. Why would he freeze, why would he stall the thing in the first place?"

The instructor looked up from his seat in the dirt, willing to go a long way for his exceptional student. But he had nothing: nothing intelligent to say.

"I can't tell you, Al. Don't think too much about this, OK? Sometimes we never find out what happened. We just don't. And that instrument ride you're supposed to take? Forget about it, you just graduated."

# Chapter 13

Upperclassmen were privileged to live in small, individual rooms rather than the communal barrack bays assigned to those more junior. The Cadet Officer of the Day stuck his head in Al's room Sunday afternoon at sundown.

"The Wing Commander is having a special meeting tomorrow morning at nine Lieutenant, in the Link Trainer classroom. You are to attend."

Al was irrationally pleased at being called Lieutenant; it would not be true until next week.

"What's the meeting about?"

The young man was already off down the hall, continuing to spread the word.

"I don't know. Eight guys invited, all upperclassmen."

A short-notice meeting with the Wing Commander was unheard of: strange. Was he in some trouble he had not been told of? He quickly decided he was not. The tailors had come up from San Antonio last month to measure each man for new uniforms. They were enterprising civilians who specialized in making uniforms for the new officer graduates, bidding against each other for the business.

Al had selected a mid-priced firm with a history of military tailoring going back almost 100 years to the Mexican-American War: $748 for a complete ensemble including shirts and hats. The money would be deducted from his officer pay over a two-year period. After the order was placed Al relaxed for the first time in 14 months: surely no one would flunk a student who had his new uniforms ordered.

He was the last person to join the meeting. He looked at the back of seven heads and his mind clicked instantly on the common thread: all were top students in some aspect of training; academics, flying skills, or high in the Cadet Officer Corps—good leaders. Some were excellent in more than one area. The room was silent and he noted strained grins: everyone was nervous, wondering what this was about. He walked over and sat next to Trapnell, who looked at him and merely grunted. After a moment he smiled.

"How'd you get in here? They're not very picky about who gets invited to these shindigs, are they."

A door in the front of the room opened at precisely 9:00 AM. The Wing Commander and a nondescript civilian stepped through. The civilian was an older man, maybe 40 or so, Al thought. The two moved to the single desk on an elevated platform at the front of the room. The civilian sat at a chair beside the desk and the Wing Commander seated himself on the desktop, scanning the 8 faces before him. The Wing Commander was a Brigadier General who vaguely resembled the actor Robert Taylor: the students called him Bob in private. Bob was doing the talking today.

"Gentlemen, the Air Force has a new and urgent requirement. A special operations squadron is being formed under Lt. Col Dick Tuck. Every training base in the country is seeking a few top volunteers to man this squadron: the duty will be hazardous. Those who decide to volunteer will leave tomorrow morning for an accelerated training program followed by overseas deployment. We estimate the assignment will last 18 months, after which you will be reassigned in the normal manner, according to the needs of the service. I want each of you to think about this. We'll meet here at 1600 hours this afternoon; I'll need a yes or no. If you have questions, brief questions, I'll try to answer."

Dave Rey's hand shot up immediately.

"What's the mission, sir?"

"Mission details are classified, I can't discuss them now. We'll say a little more this afternoon, after we have volunteers."

Trapnell spoke.

"What kind of airplanes will we be flying?"

"An abbreviated course in the P-80. Then something unusual."

Padraig Dwyer had a question that was on everyone's mind.

"Will we be officers? I mean, we haven't graduated yet, we aren't commissioned."

"Those who volunteer will be commissioned this evening. Those who don't will be commissioned next week with the rest of 48N."

Now the civilian stood and whispered in Bob's ear a moment. The General held up his hand.

"I have been reminded of two things: first, this conversation is classified SECRET, no discussions outside this room; second, if you choose not to volunteer your record will remain unblemished. Your careers are intact no matter what your decision. That's all gentlemen, we'll see you at four."

Al walked out of the tattered wooden building, a remnant of World War I, and lit a Lucky Strike, inhaling deeply, thinking in the crisp winter air. A moment later Padraig Dwyer emerged from the classroom. He dropped his chewing gum in a butt-can nailed to a wooden post, and lit up. Al walked over with a question.

"Pat, what do you think he meant by…"

"I don't think we should be talking, man; you heard him. We just have to noodle it, decide by ourselves. Not much to go on, though."

"Fuck it, Pat. We're talking about our careers here; this isn't some dipsy-doodle war movie. I just wish we knew what we're going to fly, I don't want to get stuck in some cargo hauler."

Dwyer shrugged and turned away.

Al returned to his room, turned up the steam radiator against winter chill, and fell on the well-made cot. He was enjoying the luxurious freedom from barracks inspection granted only to upperclassmen in the final month before graduation. He felt flattered by this unexpected attention, flattered to be among the small group offered an opportunity like this, but he was still concerned. What if this turned out to be a backwater operation, flying C-47's in some obscure hole; hauling the base laundry, out of sight and out of mind? On the other hand, if it was something glamorous, career enhancing, that was a very different matter. He hadn't endured all this training without considering a full career in the Air Force. The bosses seemed to like him, and he did the work about as well as anyone, so why not?

Then there was Mandy to think about; she had visited three times during his training, a different air base each time. They were lovers now, had been since his 10-day leave before training started. And it was great: mind-boggling. They were two healthy attractive kids, and she was highly sexed when with Al, sensitive to his glances almost as much as his caresses. She took him so deeply inside her that he had constant, nagging worries about pregnancy, but so far, nothing. At least nothing that he knew of. Still, in unguarded moments he got the feeling she would be happier if he busted out of the program; happier to have him with her at home living the severe, circumscribed life of Tillamook, Oregon.

There was a time when that would have been all right, but not now, not when he had a sniff of the good life. Well, it was a solvable problem: they would just get married right away and work out the rest on the fly. He smiled at the unintended pun.

He slept through lunch and awoke with his burden resolved: this had to be a premier assignment, why else would they use the General as point man and invoke all the secrecy stuff. He would trust to luck, just as he had when Doc Mendes recommended him for flight training.

Five of the eight candidates accepted the assignment that afternoon and Al was one of them. He sat in the chilly classroom surrounded by gaily-painted orange and blue Link trainers, wondering about the other three. How they had reasoned? Why not jump at this rare chance? There would be no answers and he was slightly put off not to know.

The meeting itself was anticlimactic: little new information came forth. The civilian accompanying Bob provided one piece of news—they were headed for Laughlin Field, Del Rio, Texas. Four brand new P-80 fighters, just delivered from the Lockheed plant in Burbank, awaited them. So did their new boss, Lt. Col. Tuck.

L. A. Deforest was commissioned near midnight December 11, 1948. A sleepy man from the Judge Advocates office, called away from home in the middle of the night, did the honors. It never occurred to the new Lieutenant that this mysterious assignment might endanger his life. He felt well trained and confident in his skills.

# Chapter 14

Lt. Colonel Richard Ivo Tuck stood on a tall ladder at the east end of the hanger in order to see and be seen by the 35 new pilots who would make up the heart of his command: the 337 Special Operations Wing. It was not really a Wing, just 25 aircraft once it came to operational reality. Normally the Air Force would call it a squadron, but the Pentagon planners granted the higher title to blur the organization's true purpose: the illegal violation of another nation's sovereign airspace in peacetime. In short—spying!

Tuck hoped his nervousness did not show. He was a poor speaker and knew it: he much preferred working with men in small groups. Now he held up his hand for a moment to bring the noisy clatter around him to silence; he had a few things to say.

"Welcome, welcome gentlemen, I am Lieutenant Colonel Dick Tuck, your CO. You have all been assembled here in haste, in what you might call a hasty manner, and I know you have questions about the new assignment: well, let me assure you it is an exciting assignment, one that will keep you well occupied for the foreseeable future."

Tuck went on at length, speaking in redundancies, jumping from topic to topic with non-linear thought, not bothering with intervening transitions. Some of the new pilots, trying to follow his exact exposition, were confused. Others, skimming for ideas, became bored and inattentive. Finally Tuck came to an understandable point.

"Over there in the corner behind you is a brand new P-80 from California, just off the manufacturing line last week. We have three more outside on the ramp. In the next 90 days each of you will complete a training syllabus in the aircraft: air combat tactics, low altitude formation flying, celestial navigation and gunnery."

The group turned to study the beautifully shiny new aircraft, squatting low and sleek in a far corner of the hangar. They were happy to see the machine, but not overly awed. Each had just completed 235 hours in the T-33: a P-80 with a three-foot plug in the fuselage to house a second seat for the instructor. They were all pretty good amateur engineers now: good enough to know the shiny airplane in the corner would perform and handle almost exactly like the T-33.

Now Tuck turned and pointed across to the opposite corner of the hangar.

"And over there, that's the other thing you're going to learn how to fly; fly in a correct military manner, I might like to add."

A buzz filled the room as the young men turned to the bomber parked across the hangar, it was cigar shaped, stub-winged and mean looking, resembling an evil duck. Two old-fashioned radial engines faced them, each with a huge 4-blade propeller extending almost to the hangar floor. They had assumed the old Martin B-26 was a base mascot: the Commanders personal aircraft, parked inside the hangar for convenience, or perhaps something to haul cases of beer up to high altitude for chilling in the late afternoon before Happy Hour.

Now they looked at each other in bewilderment as Tuck continued.

"It's not an operational airplane, not what you'll be assigned when we go overseas, but the handling is similar. Since the operational aircraft are not yet ready we'll use that one, and two more like it, to provide preliminary proficiency training. You'll get a feel for what's to come."

Hands shot up across the group. Tuck leaned forward on his ladder and squinted at the audience before pointing to a man at the rear of the group. The designee had a question on everyone's mind.

"What is the operational airplane, sir? I guess we all thought it would be a jet."

The Security Officer had warned Tuck not to reveal the P-61 because some of the pilots would be eliminated as training progressed. It would be best if they left the program unaware of the ultimate aircraft. If word leaked out, the Chinese might anticipate the use of low altitude approaches to the target area and prepare a lethal counter strategy. Tuck disagreed with his superiors, but he was constrained.

"I'm not at liberty to say just now, but you'll all know within a couple of months."

There was a disapproving murmur from the pilots. They expected candor from the new boss.

"Why are we learning celestial navigation; we're fighter pilots, we won't really use it, will we?"

Tuck again apologized,

"I'm sorry, I can't address your question now. You'll learn soon enough though."

Al heard a pilot behind him mutter *sotto voce.*

"Well, shit. What kind of Mickey-Mouse are we getting here? He ought to tell us what the hell we're supposed to be flying on this clap-trap mission."

Tuck was through for the evening.

"OK. That's enough for now, except for one more thing: the resolution circle. There are chairs stacked back there, so each and every one of you go over and get one and form a circle."

Al was at the front of the group, among the first to select a chair, maneuvering uncertainly as the other pilots tried to form a circle with much trial and error.

Al had time to study their new CO. Tuck was an older man, late thirties, Al thought, of middling height and weight. His shoulders and chest were thin and his hips were wide. He was almost chinless and he had huge feet, as if the growth that should have gone into his torso had been allocated to his feet. His eyes were wide-spaced and outward looking, like a pug dog. He wore the Pilot badge adorned by a star, denoting Senior Pilot, and displayed three ribbons: fewer than usual for a man of his rank. Al was too young, too used to the rigid discipline of officer training, to form a critical opinion of his superior, but it was difficult to be impressed by the physical persona of Lt. Col. Tuck.

Tuck brought his own chair to the resolution circle and sat down, peering around the faces, head bobbing in silent greeting before he spoke.

"OK. Well, one thing about the resolution circle is two things: I'm going to tell you two things about myself, one good and one not so good. Then we'll go around the circle and each of you will do the same. No critical comments from the group when a man speaks, please, and no supporting comments. This is how we'll get to know one another: it works and it's fast. We'll need both."

He launched into his own historical monologue; college, the Air Corps before the war, flew the charming little Boeing P-26 Peashooter in the mid-1930's, P-47 instructor in Maryland, not released for overseas duty until near the end of the war, finally wangled orders to England, only slim pickings left in the air, three kills before the war ended. He was silent a moment before continuing.

"That last kill, it was an 8-engine Blohm and Voss, a huge experimental transport. I found it down in south Germany by the Alps. I made several passes and filled it full of holes, you couldn't miss. Finally, when I knew I was almost out of ammo, I decided to concentrate on one spot. I shot up the right inboard engine until I ran out of bullets. I got so involved I almost collided with the big thing. I turned around to come back at it, and I thought I had missed: it was just going along up there. Then the engine I shot up started to smoke, but it was another ten minutes before it caught fire. I flew right beside it; I could see the pilots. One of them kept looking at me while they fought to keep it in the air. Finally it slowed down and the nose went up in the air. It fell off in a flat spin and the nose kept coming up and stalling again, like a little model airplane. I can recall wanting it to be a model airplane, *willing* it to be a model airplane so the men I saw in the cockpit wouldn't die. But it just kept going down slowly, like it was falling through molasses. Then it hit and exploded. The air intelligence guys told me later there were 170 infantry troops on the thing, some kind of a test they were doing. All dead. I killed them; they had no chance at all, no weapons on board or anything. I don't sleep very well now: I still see that huge thing going down. I'm ashamed of what I did that day. I wish I could take it back, but I can't."

When Al's turn came he was embarrassed, made a lame comment about how glad he was to be a pilot. Then, without knowing why, he blurted.

I'm a little bit ashamed about leading my girl Mandy down the garden path. She doesn't even know I'm here yet, thinks I'm graduating next week and coming home on a leave. She'll be pretty mad—she wants me to be a civilian."

Trapnell surprised everyone with a comment about wealth; he came from a family with large tobacco holdings in North Carolina, something he had never mentioned before. The circle continued, ending an hour later. Tuck dismissed them without comment.

Al thought about the resolution circle as he trudged back through the poorly lit streets to the Bachelor Officer barracks, tagging along with Trapnell. His rational mind rejected the proceeding: it had been corny and sentimental. But something deeper within him, something primitive, had been moved by the stories. He asked for Trapnell's opinion and got it.

"The man's a warrior Al. Don't look like one, don't act like one, don't talk like one, but that's sure enough what he is. He was trying to light a fire tonight, but that long rambling speech—well, his matchbook was a little soggy is all. The circle thing was good, though. Don't worry, he's gonna make you a tough son of a bitch, just wait and see. I'm surprised you couldn't figure that out tonight, boy. You need to wake up in these here meetings, pay attention. You might learn something."

Al returned to his room, grabbed a handful of change, and raced back down the barrack stairwell; the communal payphone installed at the first floor entrance was not in use, a rare occurrence. Mandy answered directly, relieving Al of spending 15 minutes bringing Mr. Piper up-to-date.

"It's so good to hear from you, darling. I didn't think you'd call until after graduation, when you had your next assignment."

They had agreed she would not come to Texas for the graduation ceremony. They were saving money for their honeymoon, firmly planned as soon as he could get leave, before he reported to his first duty station. Now he felt defensive and hangdog: how could he explain the extraordinary events of the past few days? He licked his lips and cleared his throat audibly.

"Something unusual has happened Mandy. This guy, a General, he came around and asked a few of us if we wanted a special assignment. Well, only a few were asked, and we had almost no time to make up our minds. We couldn't call our families or talk to anyone. So anyway, I had to think fast and I accepted the deal. I'm already commissioned, a 2d Lieutenant, and I'm down here at another base now, I can't say where: security, you know. But it's going to be fine, everything is all right. As soon as I'm out of here, I'll come home and we'll be married and have that honeymoon we've been looking forward to. So you shouldn't worry."

Mandy was stunned to silence, trying to absorb the confusing message. Then she felt unreasoning anger bubbling up: she didn't understand all he had just told her, but it was clear that there would be another delay before they could be married; a delay caused by his unilateral decision to pursue a so-called career. She smoldered a moment, furious, before speaking.

"Goddamn you, you just went off selfishly and did what the hell ever you wanted to do. You never gave me a thought, never even gave me a chance to say anything. I guess I'll always be your second choice, won't I? I'll be the person you come to after you've decided what pleases you. Well, I don't have to put up with this, Al. I love you, I guess I always will, but I refuse to be a good little housewife doing her masters bidding, chasing you around from one shabby base to another, dropping babies. If you want to waste your life being a soldier, being some little titmouse in a second rate organization, you can count me out. I could never be proud of you; there's so much more you could do if you had the guts, if I could get you to wake up."

She hung up.

He was devastated, angry. He had damn near killed himself to take advantage of these opportunities. He had done well, better than 99 percent of the men he knew could have done. He was someone now; an officer, and she demeaned his accomplishment. He was mad and underneath he was scared, unable to see a life without Mandy.

# Chapter 15

Al sat in the contraption, exhausted, every muscle in his body shrieking for relief. He wasn't supposed to know how long he had been at his task; there was no clock. But he had been able to hear quiet conversation between the three Flight Surgeons monitoring his performance. The eleventh hour was nearing completion; there were three more to go after that. Several times he had thought of throwing in the towel, just quitting and getting out of the damned machine. But something kept him going; stubbornness he thought.

He sat in a sawed-off section of a P-80 cockpit, something salvaged from a wreck last year down south of the base. The section was mounted on three makeshift pneumatic jacks so it could be shaken and jounced to provide a crude simulation of flight in rough air. Most of the flight instruments had been taped over, but an altimeter, airspeed indicator, and a magnetic compass remained in view.

His task was to keep the three instruments steady on a set of assigned values, which the Flight Surgeons changed every few hours by calling in new numbers over his helmet intercom. Al had been placed in the simulator this morning with two quarts of bottled water, a small sandwich, and a relief tube. His task was simple enough; keep the heading, altitude and airspeed reasonably steady by manipulating the throttle, control stick and rudder pedals. Success required continuing for 14 hours without falling sleep or giving up. A heart rate monitor and blood pressure cuff were installed for reference, but the Flight Surgeons expected wild vital signs; the real business was endurance.

He finished at eight that evening. He tried to lift himself from the cockpit but could not; his trembling, partially paralyzed musculature would not respond. There was a winch above the test set up for just this occasion. A technician appeared and Al's parachute harness was attached to the device. He was lifted from the cockpit and set upon the floor.

The three doctors appeared from behind a curtain walling off the test area. One doctor handed him a quart container of orange juice and four APC's: pills of aspirin, phenacetin and caffeine.

"Take these, they'll relieve the muscle pain in 15 minutes. Just sit there and move around a little on the floor. We'll get you up in a while and start you walking."

Al experimented. He could roll over, rise to his hands and knees, and crawl: a wonderful feeling. He asked the big question.

"Did I pass?"

Another doctor flashed a grin.

"Absolutely, Lieutenant. No problem. But you did something we haven't seen before. Smart; we'll use it in the training syllabus."

Now it was Al's turn to grin.

"You mean rolling that thing up on its side?"

The doctor nodded.

"You kept all the instruments centered by side slipping along. No one else has done that. It was unconventional—but OK. Actually, it's a great way to relieve some of the muscle strain."

Al shook his head.

"I don't think I would have made it any other way. Rolling the wings over and then holding course with the opposite rudder pedal sort of put me on my side, like changing position in a bed. It really took the load off for a while; my ass was paralyzed. Incidentally, it would really help if you could mold a soft support to fit inside that aluminum seat, the parachute pack isn't very comfortable after a couple of hours. It started feeling like a sack full of rocks."

The three exchanged significant glances: not a bad idea.

Al had three days off while the Flight Surgeons finished endurance testing for the rest of the pilots. He napped most of the first day, exhausted and sore in every fiber.

Tuck called a meeting in the hangar on the fourth day, ascending his now familiar ladder to address the group.

"OK. You gentlemen here have passed the endurance tests, so we begin P-80 qualification this afternoon. We have eight Instructors down from Nellis to help out, and fifteen more P-80's were delivered yesterday. We're going to change the plan a little; push through the training syllabus in 60 days instead of 90. We'll log four flying hours per day, six days a week, if the airplanes hold up. Flying will be 5:00 a.m. to noon. Two hours off for lunch and a break, then ground school from 2:00 until 8:00 p.m."

He paused a moment, allowing the muttering to subside before continuing.

"You may have noticed we are a smaller group today; five of our gentlemen were eliminated in endurance testing. Don't let that bother you; the endurance test was the worst thing you'll see in this program. From now on it's flying and ground school; things you all know about, things you're good at."

Al, Dave Rey, and Padraig Dwyer were in the air that afternoon, flying formation with one of the Nellis instructors. They flew down the Mexican border for an hour as the instructor pointed out local terrain features. Al heard the instructors voice on his intercom, tinny and faint on the low power link.

"We're going down now, follow me in trail." The instructor rolled upside down and pulled into a vertical dive, headed for the ground, his students strung out in a ragged line behind. He pulled out of the dive by the narrowest of margins, just 200 feet above the ground, and the group returned to Laughlin at 530 mph. Ragged clusters of mesquite and chaparral rolled in at them long and lazy, like waves getting ready to curl and break on a sandy beach.

Al was pleased as he parked the aircraft; the P-80 flew almost exactly like a T-33. That meant this would be an easy program. He started to shrug out of his parachute harness as they walked away from the parking area. The instructor, a wrinkled little guy who looked older than his Captain's bars indicated, held up his hand.

"Leave them on, gentlemen, do not vacate your chutes. We're going up again for a night navigation hop as soon as the refueling crews get us gassed up."

The instructor used the word *vacate* precisely, speaking as if he possessed language skills not many people had. Al smiled helplessly at Padraig Dwyer; maybe things were not going to be as easy as he thought. Dave Rey shrugged and turned to the refueling crew.

"Let's do it. Fill mine up with Oxydol soap flakes and I'll blow bubbles all the way to Arizona."

The learning curve tilted upward the following week when they began flying the old B-26, a new and alarming experience for the young pilots.

They had flown various single engine propeller aircraft in training, but the old bomber was entirely different.

Tuck was helping two other multi-engine instructors with the flying—they were short of pilots who were qualified in the archaic bomber. Al would ride with him on his first twin-engine flight.

He stepped out of the operations building holding a mimeographed paper chit from the scheduler. The blanks were filled in for ' *1000* hours. Lt. *Deforest*. Local familiarization flight. Acft. B-26 *39-32541*. Instructor *Tuck*'. He flagged down one of the yellow FOLLOW ME jeeps and jumped in the front seat next to the driver, whose melamine badge said 'PFC Linakis'.

"Take me over to the B-26 parking revetment…uh, aircraft 541."

The PFC grinned slyly.

"Yes sir. We'll have to drive out through the boonies though; the taxiway is shut down today for repairs. This your first ride sir?"

Al was focused on the cold, a blue-northern was howling down from Canada. He wore only twill flying coveralls with nothing underneath. He needed his long johns.

"It is. What are you grinning about Linakis?"

"Well, sir, the other pilots have been a little shook up about those B-26's. I just wondered if you'd heard about that."

Al realized that he was being made sport of: the never-ending fun of ground crewmen with new pilots. He was an expert at this game after 14 months in flying school.

"No one mentioned anything to me. What's wrong with them?"

"Stuff goes wrong with them. They're pretty old and beat up. For instance, Col. Tuck and a student flew back up here from Eagle Pass last week with an engine on fire. It never did go out, they landed with the thing on fire. There it is down at the end of the revetment."

Al cupped his hands to his eyebrows, squinting against the morning sun and the clouds of blowing dust. He saw the B-26 sitting at the far end of the revetment. The left main gear was removed and a jack stand had been substituted. The left engine had been dismounted and the nacelle was scorched, burned through in a few places exposing underlying bulkheads and stringers, like a partially skinned skeleton.

"Oh yeah. I heard about that one. I don't see why that would make anyone nervous though. I'd just get out and run alongside and hold the wing up."

PFC Linakis got it: this guy was bouncing the ball with him. He liked that.

"That would be great, sir, that would be just the thing. Take some long legs though, to keep up."

"I don't know what the hell you're talking about Linakis."

The yellow jeep pulled up in front of one of the bombers. Al got out and extracted his parachute. He waved a casual goodbye to Linakis and went to sit on the nose wheel, waiting for Tuck to arrive. After a ten-minute wait he got up and went restlessly to the rear of the airplane, wondering when Tuck would emerge from the hangar complex across the airfield.

"Go ahead with the pre-flight, Lieutenant. If you decide the airplane is ready to fly, come back here and get me."

Al started at the unexpected sound and turned to see Tuck sitting on an upended oil drum far back in the sand and scrub brush behind the revetment. He was smoking a thin cigar. He was the regulation 150 feet from the gasoline-filled bomber.

"Yes sir. Don't you want to come and kind of follow through with me here? It's my first time you know."

"You a pilot?"

"Yes, sir."

"Then get on with it, you've passed ground school on the airplane. When you've made a decision, come and get me. It takes two of us to get the thing going. And if it isn't ready to fly, tell me why."

Al was vaguely put off: what the hell did he know about a B-26? He had read the manual, passed a brief ground school course, and passed the blindfold cockpit check. But these were minimal things: he had no experience, no feeling for check items that could bite him. He went through the pre-flight checklist and found several disturbing anomalies. He returned to Tuck on his oil barrel.

"Sir, I'm not sure that airplane is airworthy."

"Not sure about what?"

"Well, there's a lot of oil leaking out of the number one engine. Some leaking from two, too."

"I'll look at it with you, but these radial engines all leak oil. Some say the more they leak, the better they run. The important thing is to be sure we have a full ten gallons in each reserve oil tank. Wouldn't do to run out of oil in flight, would it?"

"No sir, then there's the Dzeus fasteners holding the left nacelle. They're so battered and worn I don't see how they can hold on. It looks like someone has been hitting them with a hammer to get them closed."

"Anything else?"

"Hydraulic fluid streaked all the way down the belly from the bomb bay. Something is leaking in there. I checked the hydraulic reservoir though, it's topped up."

"Well, are we going to fly it?"

Now Al realized Tuck was teaching him: holding him responsible for their safety. There was no better way to enforce a lesson quickly. He fretted a while, staring absently at Tuck's gargoyle face—the protruding eyes, the wet lips, the overbite. Tuck appeared monstrous to him, malformed and needy. Why would someone put this load on him?

"It's OK. Except I want you to look at number one engine with me."

Tuck's face remained expressionless. He bent over and carefully stubbed the cigar in sand.

"We'll look at that engine."

Al sat in the hot cramped co-pilot seat, bewildered by the vast array of gauges, switch panels, and controls. He smelled sweaty seat cushions, aviation gas, and burned oil. The seat cushion was crushed from years of use, it was pretty flat and uncomfortable. Already his bottom was sending an unwelcome message. Looking out the window, they seemed to sit insanely high above the ground; this was nothing like his little fighters. It was one thing to pass a blindfold test of instrument and control locations, but quite another to have a well-developed sense of their purpose. The schooling seemed to fly out of his head as he sat there, feeling overwhelmed and stupid, disconnected, weasel-like.

Tuck startled him from his fugue.

"I'll do most of the flying today Lieutenant; just a 45 minute hop to give you a sense of the airplane. I want you to follow me on the controls on takeoff, then when we get upstairs you can take it and try some slow-flight and cruise. OK?"

Al nodded dimly as Tuck's hands flew over switches and controls preparing for engine start. Tuck carefully consulted the pre-flight procedures card. He pointed at each item as his lips moved silently. He replaced the card in a holder on the center console and leaned out the left window.

"CLEAR AIRSCREWS!"

The crewman below looked around, making sure no one was near the propeller; then responded.

"Clear number one"

Tuck flipped the magneto switch to BOTH, pushed the engine-primer button momentarily and energized the starter. Eventually the giant engine coughed and fired, shaking the airframe violently and emitting a huge cloud of white smoke. When both engines were running at idle Al found himself nearly deafened by the sound level in the cockpit. Tuck jabbed his shoulder and patted his own headset. Al spent a bewildered moment before sheepishly realizing he had failed to don the padded earphones. He quickly removed them from a hook above his head and slipped them on. The sound level diminished greatly. Tuck signaled for the wheel chocks to be removed and expertly taxied out of the parking area. At the runway threshold he turned to Al.

"You handle the throttles on takeoff; come up to full power smoothly, nothing jerky. If you slam the throttles forward you can destabilize the superchargers, lose power. We don't want that, do we?"

Al nodded vacantly and moved the two levers forward in what he hoped was a smooth manner. The old bomber responded with an appalling racket and began a very sedate acceleration down the runway. Tuck was busy steering but he took a moment to tap the airspeed indicator.

"Call 80 mph for me, then call 100; we'll fly off at about 110. Follow me on the controls."

The bomber flew itself off the runway at 110 mph; no control movement was necessary. All the jet aircraft Al had flown required an exaggerated back-motion on the stick to get off the runway. He was speculating on this matter when Tuck yelled at him a second time.

"Gear up! Come on mister, wake up!"

He searched frantically for the landing gear handle and suddenly remembered his primary instructor yelling at him from the back seat of the T-6 trainer.

"Get your head out of your ass Deforest: wake up."

Al smiled faintly at the memory while still looking for the landing gear handle. Tuck turned again in exasperation.

"So are we going to just fly along with the landing gear hanging out there? Do something. Anything. Jesus weeps for us, dragging along here."

Finally Al located the gear handle, down low on the control pedestal, and slammed it to the up position. Tuck nodded in satisfaction but said no more as they climbed to cruising altitude. Al occupied himself trying to remember other important lessons about the ancient airplane but few came to him. Tuck turned to him when they reached cruising altitude.

"Take it. Just try different throttle settings and get a feel for the trim positions. Gentle turns."

Al maneuvered the airplane for twenty minutes, developing a feel for the controls. It was a world apart from the P-80. The little fighter responded almost to his thoughts, zipping off in whatever direction was desired like quicksilver. It was whisper quiet and smooth, producing only a thin high-pitched tone from the turbo-machinery of the jet engine. Here, the controls felt heavy and the big airplane was ponderous in both roll and pitch. The racket from engines and propellers seemed deafening.

He wondered about the god-awful racket. There was time for theorizing: the flying was undemanding, much like driving a car down a smooth road. Al had a hazy concept of acoustics, of the center of percussion: a hypothetical point in space where all the diverse noises emanating from a machine could be replaced with a single concentrated source that produced the same overall sound. He thought maybe the pilot of a single engine plane was near the center of percussion, and all the sound moved away, producing a quiet spot to sit in. But here, in this ponderous machine, he was seated between the engines, outside the center of percussion, and therefore smack in the middle of a heavy noise field. He nodded his head silently and decided to give Col. Tuck an acoustics test.

"I wonder why this airplane is so noisy in the cockpit, sir? Do you think it's because there are two engines?"

Tuck was watching a light plane approaching from their 11 o'clock position. He spoke without taking his eyes off the intruder.

"No, at least that isn't the main reason. You sit near the center of sound in a fighter, in a null, in a quiet spot. The sound moves away from you in all directions. In a two-engine airplane you sit away from the null, probably near a point where the sound from the engines reinforces itself, almost doubles."

Jeez. Al wondered if the boss was reading his mind.

Tuck wanted to teach him something new.

"Slow down to 100 mph and hold our altitude steady. You'll feel the stall coming on, the wing burble. Let it stall and watch the altimeter; we'll go down like a rock. Don't try to fight it, just drop the nose and get power up quickly. When we're flying again, level it out and check how much height we lost."

Al was appalled; they lost almost four thousand feet before he could recover.

Tuck noted the reaction, nodded.

"The thing is this; the B-26 like a duck; all heavy body and not much wing, so if you aren't going fast, you're going to go down. Remember, if you get a stall don't try to fight it, just dump the nose until you get some speed again. Most of all, don't let it slow down below 115 mph on the final approach or you'll find yourself sitting on the ground two miles short of the field."

When they returned to cruising speed Tuck tapped the airspeed indicator.

"Stall performance is the bad thing about having small wings. The good thing is we have lower drag everywhere else in the flight envelope. See here, we're going 290 mph with only 60 percent power. If we had a big wing out there, something that handled well at low speed, we'd only be doing about 220 mph. That's 70 mph extra, pretty good for getting somewhere fast, don't you think?"

Al nodded to show he understood. Tuck smiled encouragement.

"Now let's go home. You're going to land, I'll help with the landing checklist."

Al thought about the flight that evening in his room, alone in the darkness and slightly nervous in the quiet of evening. He had seen a new facet of Richard Tuck today: he had seen a direct and unpretentious man, calm and capable, an excellent teacher. Now the flight seemed weird, full of high and low contrasts that he was only beginning to understand. But one thing he did know: if you got past Tuck's unattractive exterior, there was a good man inside there. He could see this.

And he wondered again why they were flying the noisy, crude old bomber. What in the world were they preparing for?

# Chapter 16

Penrod Taylor was bringing Secretary Day up-to-date on *Project Heat Lightning*. It was not going well.

"Good God, Pen, are you telling me we don't have enough airplanes? We've made the deepest commitment with the White House and Congress. We've assured them our program is properly planned. I don't like the sound of this."

Taylor knew when his boss was agitated: his mouth formed a silent 'eek' and he plucked his suspenders. He was doing both.

"No sir, that's not what I'm telling you. All I'm reporting here is that Operations Analysis has modeled our penetration paths and come up with a 6% loss rate per mission: 1% from mechanical failures and 5% from enemy action. They modeled the Chinese air defenses along the lines of the German air defenses in the Balkans at the height of the war. I'm convinced they give far too much credit to the Chinese."

Day moved about the office, lips moving silently, plucking his suspenders, which he referred to as 'braces'.

"I'm not sure your individual opinion will carry much weight with our detractors, my boy. They'll use the official Operation Analysis as evidence we should scrap this project and take our chances about Chinese intentions."

"Sir, I was around for the Balkans show. I flew a B-24 on the first Ploesti mission in 1943. We took our lumps right at the target, but in and out was easy, a piece of cake. The same OA guys predicted 14% losses on those runs."

"That's an anecdote, Pen, not solid analysis."

"Here's our argument: the Chinese have never had a solid air defense because they didn't need it. Their inland targets have always been too remote for enemy aircraft. They're poorly organized and poorly equipped. They have to defend fourteen separate telephone links and they'll never know which one we're going to hit. They'll be spread very thin. It's nothing like the German situation."

"Then why didn't the OA folks make an adjustment?"

Taylor expelled a frustrated breath, shaking his head.

"I can't tell you. I think they're just being extremely conservative, covering their ass."

"Thin soup, Pen. Do we have any more P-61's available?"

"No sir. We've scraped up every P-61 in the world at this point. For instance, we found 2 more this month. They were parked out at Davis-Monthan in Arizona. Their paperwork indicated they had been scrapped. But somehow they didn't make it to the scrap man back in '46. They were just sitting there, intact."

"So we may need to expose our pilots to more attrition than we had thought, is that it?"

"If you go by the OA studies, yes. I just don't believe they're correct. In the end, though, none of it matters: the P-61 is all we have. If we want intelligence data from Hotan, we use the airplane. It's that simple."

"What sort of losses?"

Taylor was uncomfortable with his answer.

"We're estimating 100 missions are required to gather the intelligence. If OA is right about the defenses, we might be looking at sixty percent losses."

"The Air Force has never kept a unit in combat beyond thirty percent losses, Pen."

"I know. If OA is correct, we would be setting a new precedent."

"Well, at this point I can only pray you're right and they're wrong about the attrition, Pen. We're committed."

"I'm sure I'm right, sir.

Day nodded, no longer listening closely, responding more to Taylor's tone of voice than the facts. He switched to a new topic, hoping for better news.

"What do you think of Colonel Tuck now that you've spent a few months with him?"

"I think General Stenzell made a very wise choice. Tuck is dedicated to the mission and supportive when it comes to the men. I've, uh, spent a few nights in the Officers Club down there; to get a sense of morale you understand. Tuck says very little on his own behalf, but the pilots think the world of him. He's pitched in wherever they were shorthanded. He served as an Instructor Pilot on the B-26 because we were short-handed and the last time I was down there he was teaching the mechanics how to troubleshoot the new Bendix Automatic Mixture Control Carburetor; the one they're retrofitting on all the P-61's. I found him at a hangar workbench, in coveralls, showing the men how to troubleshoot. I liked what I saw; there was no sense of rank, just a group of men doing a job. And he has some theatre in him: he's arranged the equivalent of a major studio preview for those two P-61's. They'll be flown in at night next week and towed over to the hangar from the far side of the field so no one knows they've arrived. The maintenance men have built a frame to surround them in the hangar; they're going to hide behind a curtain. Then Tuck will get all the pilots in for an unveiling. He's as excited as a kid."

Taylor paused, uncomfortable.

"There's just one thing. Since we won't let him fly the actual missions, I'm a little worried he'll become overprotective of the men. If OA is correct, the average pilot lifetime will be 16 missions. We have a lot of flying scheduled sir, I don't want him to become defensive and start pulling punches when things get rough."

Abner Day sat up in his chair now, alert.

"His job is to get the intelligence we've specified. Can he do it, Pen? I need a straight answer."

"He'll be fine, I'm sure sir."

Taylor had more difficulties.

"I was on the Hill Tuesday, talking with staffers from the Senate Armed Service Committee. They want you to know that Senator Meyer will be over to see you next week. He finds the B-29 losses unacceptable now, he'll insist on a halt within the month. After that, it's the P-61 or nothing. We have no other aircraft even remotely capable of these missions."

# Chapter 17

All the pilots were gathered in the hangar, milling about and noisy, making sly jokes about the polished chromium helmets worn by two Air Policemen guarding whatever lay behind an extensive black curtain drawn across a corner of the hangar.

Tuck ascended his ladder and waved an arm at the noisy men.

"You've all wondered what the ultimate airplane would be, our mission airplane. Well, tonight you'll see it and I think you'll agree with me that we're all privileged to be going into dangerous country in this fine machine."

He swept the room with his eyes, looking for smiles, looking for enthusiasm. The men were guarded, glancing at each other and wondering what he was talking about.

"I know there has been some disappointment in our B-26 program and I'm sorry we couldn't be more open with you about our final training. Well, now we can. All right, here it is, the moment we have all waited for, a modern miracle."

He signaled to the Air Policemen to draw back the black curtain. Trapnell leaned toward Pat Dwyer.

"Hooray for Hollywood. If old Tuck don't shut up and show us something, I'm gonna die of old age standing here waiting on his miracle."

Al whispered from behind them.

"Yeah, and if you don't shut up old Tuck will see you die of old age flying the B-26."

Trapnell half-turned his head.

"It's lonely at the top, Al. Those of us who are superior need to do a little communicating with the lesser endowed."

They had to be impressed by the display. Standing before them were two very large, strange looking twin-engine aircraft, dramatically illuminated from above by flood lights. Both had long tail booms that ran back from the engines to a twin tail, and a central pod for the pilot. They stood far above the ground on tricycle landing gear: huge things, as big as a bomber. The two were clearly variations on the same basic airframe. The one on the left was highly polished silver and the pilot pod was a pleasing canoe shape, crowned by a clear bubble canopy. The one on the right was all black and the crew pod was an ugly misshapen thing, starting from a blunt nose and sweeping back through the pilot's seat to an unshapely, bulbous rear end. Turrets and plexiglass windows sprouted at unaesthetic locations. The black one had a large black widow spider painted on the nose, she perched in an elaborate web, her red hourglass showing clearly. The name *Shady Lady* was painted below the spider in cartoon print.

The spider captured the airplane's look perfectly. The huge black airplane reminded Al of an overgrown, lumpish P-38; the one the Germans had called the Gabelschwanz Teufel, the fork-tail devil. He tried hard to remain objective, to be a neutral professional, but he found himself nodding enthusiastically. A smile crept onto his face; the ungainly thing seemed pretty good to him, pretty interesting. He looked forward to flying the monster.

Bob McMurtry sidled up behind Trapnell.

"Look at those guns, Doug, eight of them. I'm going to get real good with that bird and sneak up behind you in your little pissant P-80 and blow you out of the water."

Trapnell grunted.

"Well, it could happen…if I'm in a coma."

Tuck looked out across the faces and he could see that he had them now. He beamed and his head bobbed in approval.

"All right now! Not bad, what do you say gentlemen? This is the P-61D, the ultimate interceptor of WW2, designed from a 1940 Army Requirement for a very fast high altitude airplane, a night interceptor, really a night fighter if you want to look at it that way. We'll get 32 of them, all fresh from a factory overhaul. They have the very latest Pratt and Whitney R-2800-77 engines installed, and the General Electric CH-5 turbocharger. With these engines we can…"

A commotion in the back of the group caused heads to turn.

"SNAKE!"

A group of enlisted ground crewmen behind the pilots watched passively. Some turned their heads away in apparent unconcern. They had removed the hibernating rattlesnake from its rocky den above the gun calibration range yesterday and warmed it overnight to provide extra excitement for Col. Tuck's big meeting.

The pilots nearest the snake moved back rapidly as it took a defensive posture: coiled, looking about, and striking feebly at those who came near. The base Security Officer left his position below Tuck's ladder, picked up a shovel standing by a workbench, and advanced on the reptile. Al saw what would happen. He shouldered his way through the pilots and confronted the man.

"No, no, no. Give me that thing, don't hit it."

He turned the shovel and expertly inserted the handle beneath the snake at mid-body, then lifted the creature and made for an exit, snarling at the man nearest the door.

"Open the goddamned door so I can get this fellow back out where he belongs."

Tuck's pug-dog eyes were turned to the encounter, but he said nothing. He saw Deforest's moral courage, but he wondered if the young man would have the constitution for what was ahead.

"All right, all right. Very funny, what if the snake had bitten one of you. Where would we be then?"

He pointed to the crewmen in the rear.

"I'm talking to you men back there; you bunch of stupes. You're not putting one over on anybody, not on anybody at all."

When Al returned he continued.

"As I was saying, these engines allow us to go extremely fast in level flight. And we can climb up to over 50,000 feet at half fuel load. That puts us over a mile above the enemy fighters we're going to encounter. And you know what? Well, these airplanes, the ones you are looking at right there in front of you, they can go 4650 miles without refueling, isn't that something? Of course that's with wing tanks, those four tanks you can see there on the black one. The one on the left, the silver one, that's a variant. They cut the bulb off the back end, smoothed up the center pod and put a nice clear bubble canopy on it. It's supposed to be for reconnaissance, but we'll use it as a gunship. It will be for protection mostly, but we might cause a little diversionary excitement where we're going. Every one of these airplanes has four 50-caliber machine guns and four 20mm cannon. That's a tremendous amount of firepower;

we'll use it all on some of the missions. Now, what do you think? Let's have some questions here."

Dave Rey lifted his arm.

"How fast?"

Tuck looked at his notes and then looked up with a wide smile.

"Well, with the new engines we've just installed, she'll do 465 mph at Maximum Cruise power and 525mph at War Emergency power. The fastest propeller-driven airplane in the world."

Doug Trapnell had a crop-duster's question.

"How come it's got them great big tires? It looks like a swamp buggy."

Tuck knew the answer without notes.

"It was designed to land and take off from rough unprepared fields; wheat fields, coral airstrips and the like; a real front-line airplane. And when we all walk over there underneath it, you'll see full-span flaps. They're big as a barn door, we can land at only 80 mph."

Tuck was happy, the men were responding well to the strange machines.

"We've received permission to personalize our airplanes, so you can come up with a name and nose-art for these planes."

The men looked at each other approvingly. They liked the idea of naming an airplane, just like the WW2 guys had done. They all looked up to the WW2 guys. Tomorrow they would scratch up a few artists from the ground crews and get going. They knew the real missions were going to be rough; they would be working against a stacked deck. Nose art would give them powerful JuJu.

Pat Dwyer wanted to know when the real missions would begin. A hush fell over the room as Tuck answered.

"Starting tomorrow you will all be accessed to a new level of security, and we'll begin daily status briefings on *Project Heat Lightning*; that's the name of our program. Then, you'll know as much about our operational date as I do. The short answer is this: I expect us to be overseas and flying real missions in four months, sooner if we can do it."

Another question floated forward anonymously.

"What are we flying against?"

Tuck held up his hand to silence the murmurs.

"I can tell you this much, we're going to the Orient, we'll be flying somewhere in the Orient. And I can tell you that our mission is reconnaissance, not shooting at things. We'll only shoot to defend ourselves or to cause a diversion of attention. You'll get the details when we're closer to deployment."

Tuck took over again.

"OK. Let's walk on over to the black one, I've had scaffolding erected so you can get up there and take a look in the cockpit. You'll be flying that big brute before you can blink an eye."

# Chapter 18

After breakfast the following morning the pilots were transported to an isolated warehouse across the base. They filed into a well-lit room containing metal chairs, a Magic Lantern view graph projector, a large green chalkboard and a small conference table at the front. The windows had been crudely painted over in flat black for security. Today they would learn details of *Project Heat Lightning*.

Tuck and the nondescript civilian, the one Al had seen back at his training base when General Bob was soliciting volunteers, were sitting at the table in front. Tuck stood and motioned to a large coffee service at the rear door.

"Good morning. You can go get coffee any time you feel like it. But don't turn your mind off while you're doing it, we won't repeat the information in these briefings. I'll introduce our guest in a minute, but first I'd like to review where we stand in the program, how far we've come, you might say. We started with thirty-five men and now we're down to twenty-two: five were eliminated in the 14-hour endurance test, four asked to be reassigned, and four have been eliminated with various flying difficulties. But all of you are now qualified in the P-80, and you've completed the B-26 syllabus satisfactorily. In my judgment there will be no more eliminations, you gentlemen right here in this room have made the grade, and I'm pleased to say we're all moving on to the real thing now. We're going ahead as a combat unit."

He paused to get their attention.

"There will be no more re-assignments for convenience, gentlemen. If you elect to hear our story today, you will not be allowed to leave the program voluntarily unless I say so. And I won't, you can believe that. So let's take a five-minute break here and you can talk among yourselves, then I'll ask you to affirm your position. I suppose you remember the session when you volunteered: there will be no career prejudice if you decide to drop out now. But after this you can't get out, it's that simple."

Dave Rey looked over at Al as the pilots began to talk among themselves.

"Man, I don't know about this. Al Storr talked to me before he quit, he thought Tuck was nuts. They had an engine fire in that old B-26 down by Eagle Pass and the nacelle extinguisher couldn't put it out. Tuck just sat there and told him to fly the thing back here, told him there was no way he was going to lose a valuable airplane. They landed with the engine still burning. What kind of a guy is that to be leading you anywhere?"

Trapnell sat behind them and now he leaned forward, pointing a finger at Rey.

"He's the right kind, that's what kind, Dave. I talked to Storr, too. Did he tell you that Tuck just sat there, never once tried to take control of the thing? The way I see it, the man risked his ass to let a rookie carry him home, tried to show some confidence in his student. You all do what you want, I'm stickin' with the old Dick Tuck: he's sure enough got some sand in him. Never you mind what he looks like, he's OK."

The five-minute break became twenty-five minutes before Tuck decided to call them to order.

"All right. All right now you gentlemen, I need to know where you stand. I want you all with me, let's be clear about that. But if you don't feel right about things, don't see your way clear, you can just stand up now and exit. The bus will take you back to the barracks and you'll be out of here in two hours. And it's not bad if you do; I mean wrong if you do, I think we have made that plain enough. All right, now what do you want to do, gentlemen?"

The pilots looked around the room: they were worried, filled half with anticipation and half with dread. They wanted to see what everyone else had decided. Silent minutes passed and no one left the room. They were all in.

Tuck was deeply gratified; all his boys would stay with him.

"Well, I'm pleased. Now we'll pass out some forms for you to sign, these forms state that you can never in your lifetime discuss what we are doing. If you do, you can be charged with treason. I've already signed mine and now I want you to do the same."

As the completed forms were being passed to the front of the room Tuck stood again. Now I'd like to introduce Mr. Penrod Taylor, an Assistant Secretary in the War Department…I mean the Defense Department. It's hard to keep up with these things you know. Well, Mr. Taylor has been in charge of the higher-level elements of *Heat Lightning* since the very beginning, and now he will stand right up here where I am and tell you all about it. That is, he'll tell you what he can for right now…oh, and I also want to add that Mr. Taylor was a B-24 pilot over in Europe during the war, so he's really one of us, a person who can understand what we're faced with."

The young men liked to hear that; it was reassuring in some vague way, a lift after the upsetting announcement about having one last chance.

Taylor stood, smiled, and nervously patted his hair.

"Congratulations gentlemen; you've all done well. Col. Tuck has asked me fill you in on what will be happening as you move closer to operational status. First, the airplanes; we are finishing the refurbishment of 32 P-61C's and D's, airplanes that were left over in the Philippines after the war. We started with 40, and we've cannibalized some for the parts to fix the remaining 32. Eight more F-15's, that's a variant of the P-61, are in the hold of a freighter right now, on their way here from Guam. They will be in Los Angeles later this week. They'll go to the Northrop plant at Hawthorne to be reassembled and then they'll be flown down here for your use in training. We'll have plenty of airplanes right here in about two weeks."

Someone in the back of the hangar whistled and shouted.

"That's great. Where are we going with them?"

Taylor surprised them with a straight answer.

"You'll be flying from Isla Mattoon, a small island in the Indian Ocean. A runway is being bulldozed out of the coral right now. It's a little primitive; you'll live in tents. As far as transportation, most of you will go overseas by troop transport out of San Francisco. But ten of you, drawn at random, will fly our training planes, the F-15's, across the pond. By the time you finish the training syllabus here, you will all be capable of successful transoceanic flight."

Al leaned forward to Dwyer and whispered.

"I'm glad he put the word successful in there."

"And here's something else you can look forward to; a polar flight. Near the end of training each of you will fly up to the North Pole and back without refueling. You'll use dead reckoning and celestial navigation: a dry run for the real thing. I can't talk about targets yet; you'll be briefed once you're aboard ship and on your way. Now let's take a few minutes for your questions, at least the ones I can answer."

Hands shot up everywhere; Taylor took one from the rear of the room.

"Col. Tuck said we'd fly reconnaissance only. No shooting unless we're shot at. Will we have guns in all the airplanes?"

"No. The P-61's will be unarmed. There is no room for guns once the payload and extra fuel are added. But the F-15 versions carry their original war complement; four 50 caliber machine guns and four 20 millimeter cannons in a belly pod. All the early missions will be done in three's: two recce birds and a gunship. Later, if we find no resistance along the flight routes, we have the option to convert the F-15 versions to pure reconnaissance."

He paused and looked at Dick Tuck.

"The planners wanted to make all reconnaissance aircraft. Colonel Tuck said no; he wanted guns on some of them to protect his men. So you can thank the Colonel for the armament that will go along with you."

The questions continued, but Al only half-listened. He was deeply moved by the drama of their situation. He lost himself in a Hollywood daydream of a great air battle in which he triumphed over the enemy after strenuous, heroic, deeds. If that happened, then Mandy would have to pay attention, she would have to respect him.

# Chapter 19

Al tapped on Trapnell's door that evening. A grunt came from within. Trapnell was lying on his iron cot reading a thick volume.

"What's up, boy?"

Al sat in the room's only chair.

"What are they getting us ready for, Doug?"

Trapnell put his book aside and sat up.

"Well, let's see; a long range airplane, celestial navigation, polar flying from all the way down here in Texas. Seems to me we're gonna go and bother some people we don't have no business bothering, seein' as how this is peacetime and all."

"That's what I was thinking. Do you think we're going to do something illegal? Something that isn't right, I mean."

Trapnell pointed to the book on his bed: H.G. Wells' tome, The Outline of History.

"See this work here? The man tries to sum up how we got where we are here in the world today. It's ponderous reading, I'll tell you that."

He paused and rubbed his face, preparing a short explanation for the entirety of history.

"Mostly the womenfolk don't want no trouble: oh, they like to pick at each other and all that, but they don't want bloodshed, for justice or not. Nope, it's the men been troublesome; always wanting to go and straighten the other fellow out, correct his ways. And if they have to kick his ass, bloody him, to make him see the light, well that's OK. It's OK because these right-thinking fellows got a mission to help that poor cuss, get him won over to their way, the right way. So legal don't matter, Al; legal ain't even in it from an overall perspective. It's more a case of who has the horsepower to lead the way rather than who's got the right, legal or moral or otherwise."

He saw that Al was confused and tried to particularize the lesson.

"The way I see it, you and me need to think about whether we like what we do, and not spend too much time on this legal and moral business. Take me for example; I could go have a good life working my Daddy's tobacco farms, maybe inherit the whole deal some day. Or, I could go down there to the Panhandle and do the same thing on my Uncle's peanut farm. Well, I don't want to do that: I'd be bored shitless. What I do want to do is get my enjoys flying fancy airplanes. I could get out of this outfit and go back to dusting in a Stearman or maybe one of them Boeing's. Or I could go down to Chile and fly Fords or Fokkers on some hick transport route over the Andes. But that ain't nearly the fun of flying these big powerful airplanes. And the only place I can do that is right here in the Army, so this is the place for me: at least for now. I ain't gonna trouble myself about any of this do-unto-others stuff, no sir. I'll be a good boy and do what my bosses tell me to do, long as they don't land me up in Leavenworth."

He grinned and pointed to his thick book.

"I believe that's what men been doin' for about the last ten thousand years, Al. And sad to say, those boys been having a lot of fun doin' it. 'Course you got to have the good sense to be on the winning side in these dust-ups: them's the ones that write the history and give out all the medals and such. No sir, boy, you just ask yourself if you like what you're doing. If the answer is yes, then you leave the heavy thinking to Tuck and all these fine-feathered Generals who keep coming around here, nodding their heads at us like they're smart or something."

He squinted to see Al's face, hidden in the glare of a gooseneck reading lamp on the small desk.

"Well boy, you feel better now that old Doug's shown you the way?"

"No."

# Chapter 20

He sat on the taxiway at Alameda Naval Air Station on the eastern shore of San Francisco Bay, holding short of the runway, awaiting a green light from the tower before takeoff. They were trying to pass through the West Coast in low profile, but already their aircraft had caused comment and drawn crowds of Navy people. Nine more F-15's sat idling on the taxiway behind him, looking like an orderly flock of two-tailed silver dragonflies. They would take off at ten-minute intervals and proceed independently to Kaneohe Naval Air Station on Oahu for refueling, then on to Wake Island.

Al was full of nervous energy; this was their first long range over-water flight. His ship *MoonDancer* was fueled for 2800 miles, enough to get there against headwinds with two hours of reserve. He squinted through the haze as the tower operator aimed his 'biscuit gun' and flashed a green light. He opened the throttles slightly, but the heavy airplane squatted and would not move. Some wag in the waiting line saw the airplane's stubbornness and broke radio silence.

"You got gas in the hack and your laundry is back. Go man, go."

Now he goosed the engines and rolled forward. He aligned with the runway carefully, stopped, and looked at the F-15 next in line on the taxiway. Dave Rey, unrecognizable in helmet and oxygen mask, nodded and waggled his middle finger at him. A hand waved from the fourth airplane but it was too far away to tell who was waving; maybe Paidrig

Dwyer, but he couldn't be sure. Tuck was somewhere in the pack, flying with them but not exerting command, allowing his pilots the maximum learning experience.

Al had a ritual dance for these long flights: he rotated his head and shook arms and hands loosely while his feet wiggled the rudder pedals. He would not have this luxury again for almost 11 hours. He set the brakes and opened the throttles carefully, knowing that jerky throttle movement could de-stabilize the turbo-chargers and make him abort his takeoff, causing a humiliating short exit from the runway in front of his friends. The engine power came up smoothly to 44 inches of manifold pressure, and then jumped quickly to 66 inches as the turbochargers kicked in.

The long nose in front of him danced and jittered with 4800 deafening horsepower: a greyhound in the starting gate. He turned his attention to runway alignment because the airplane was heavy with fuel; it would be a squirrelly handful until he had enough speed for natural aerodynamic stability to become his ally. With a last shake of his head, he released the brakes and rolled. The runway unwound past the nose slowly, he had time to admire the silver F-15's sitting in a line on the taxiway, posed like birds of a feather, and then his speed picked up and the runway became a blur. He stabbed rudder pedals as the heavy, waddling machine tried to leave the centerline. At 85 mph he glanced at the manifold pressure gauges and saw a steady 66 inches on both engines: good turbo-chargers, there would be no abort on this takeoff. Now he was getting light and the controls felt like an airplane. At 125 mph he eased the control yoke back, felt the airplane wanting to fly, then heard the thump as his wheels left the ground and the landing struts extended to their lower limit. He slapped the gear handle up and quickly corrected a drift toward the left side of the runway as a breakwater flashed past below him. Suddenly he was hurtling over the eastern part of San

Francisco Bay, climbing slowly, headed toward downtown buildings across the bay.

He would cruise-climb, something they had been trained to do for the upcoming operational missions. He reduced the throttles below normal climbing power, then all the way down to cruising power: 36 inches. He felt a distressing sinking sensation as the engines slowed and the takeoff thrust decreased. He knew his brain was tricking him, reading the slight deceleration as a descent when it was not. But it felt like falling. He checked the vertical speed indicator, saw a reassuring positive climb rate, and waited for the big plane to pick up to the desired cruise-climb speed. The airspeed indicator slowly passed through 150 mph, then 200, then 225. At 245 mph he expertly rolled in trim tabs until the control wheel forces were neutralized. Now the ship was flying on its own and climbing steadily and making a beeline for San Francisco.

He was ascending at 300 feet per minute, a paltry figure but exactly what he wanted. He remembered routinely climbing 6000 feet per minute in the P-80 jet, and grinned at this snail-like progress upstairs. A glance forward showed he was already halfway across the Bay, just north of the Oakland Bridge. He turned left, altering his course southward toward Monterey, following strict instructions to avoid the city and other populated areas where curious citizens might wonder and gossip about the strange aircraft.

Low coastal foothills south of the Bay, rain drenched and verdant from winter rain, came rushing toward him. He would barely clear them. A large flock of sheep on the green hills, spooked by the roar of engines only a few hundred feet above them, darted left and right of his ground path like spilled cream. The hills dropped away, yielding to rich farmland south of Watsonville planted in neat rows of strawberry and artichoke. He saw fishing boats scattered outside Monterey Harbor, the tiny faces of crewmen looking up at him.

He picked out a single boat and watched the men on deck as he passed over. The faces turned up to him, squinting in afternoon sunlight, trying to identify the noisy airplane. He thought suddenly of how comforting it would be to change places with one of the tiny men down there. Then he would be safe aboard a cozy boat close to shore and another man would be tackling the daunting task of navigating this huge machine halfway across the Pacific.

The rugged coastline disappeared and there was only the white-capped Pacific Ocean stretching endlessly before him in afternoon sunlight. Thirty minutes later the Farallon Islands passed beneath his right wing, obscured in fog. There would be no land now until he sighted the Hawaiian Island chain tomorrow morning. This was the pucker line, his last reassurance of safety.

He remembered a retired Pan American Airways Master Navigator who had lectured them on over-water flying. The man posed a simple question for his students: would you rather fly from Honolulu to San Francisco, or the reverse? He called for a show of hands. The pilots looked at each other, not sure why it made any difference at all, and the show of hands was roughly even for each trip. The man smiled.

"Well, gentlemen, if you go from Honolulu to San Francisco you can sleep all the way and not miss a landfall. Think about it, if you wander off-course by 1000 miles you'll still hit land in Canada or Mexico and be relatively safe. Going the other way, if you miss the Islands by 50 miles you'll never see them at all. It's much harder to navigate from a continent to an island, because there isn't much land for you to find."

The Master Navigator had their undivided attention for the rest of the class.

Al turned to a heading of 256 degrees. He would hold this course until nightfall, and then get a star sighting and make a celestial position fix.

The engines purred smoothly and all instruments were in the normal range. The pucker line had not affected him—yet. He turned on the autopilot and selected Heading Hold from the Mode Panel, freeing himself from routine flying chores. He turned on the Automatic Direction Finder and fiddled with the tuning knob until he found a radio station playing Big Band music.

This was his favorite music, and he would have at least 45 minutes before the signal became too weak to receive. Modern jazz was sweeping popular music to the sidelines these days, but Al couldn't buy it. The jazz seemed thin and dispassionate to him, too cool to warm his heart. He vastly preferred the romantic lyrics and danceable rhythms of the swing tunes, the scat and the power of Louis Armstrong and King Oliver doing blues. Now Helen O'Connell and Bob Eberly were singing Green Eyes, and his feet danced on the rudder pedals, swinging the long aircraft nose in time with the music.

He removed a spiral-bound leather notebook from his breast pocket as darkness fell. Tuck had allowed each pilot to prepare his own navigation plan, then paid from his own pocket to have them professionally printed and leather-bound. Al remembered his plan in detail, but it was comforting to see everything printed neatly before him. The small leather-bound notebook gave him a reassuring sense of permanence and security for the long flight ahead. Somehow, Tuck had known that it would.

A simplified star map was printed on page six and he used it to locate the North Star, Polaris, off his right wing. He removed a sextant from his navigation case and carefully centered the star in the sextant eyepiece. A knurled thumbwheel cranked the star image down until it coalesced with a bubble horizon at the bottom of the eyepiece. He read the star's elevation angle from an angular sector at the bottom of the instrument and made a note on the small writing pad strapped to his thigh. He repeated the process for the star Theta-Eridani and noted the time from his instrument panel clock.

Page eight in his plan book was a foldout, a rendering of the ultra-new Weems Star Altitude Curves. Here, he found the lines for Polaris and Theta-Eridani and used their intersection to read his position: Latitude 36 degrees 34.7 minutes North, Longitude 136 degrees 12.9 minutes West. He plotted the position on his ground track map. He was 14 miles south of his planned ground track and 22 miles further out to sea than he had predicted. He smiled in broad approval and felt a bloom of pride and confidence: his first celestial position fix was completed. He corrected for the unanticipated wind drift and turned to his reflection, grossly distorted in the darkened plexi-glass canopy.

"Pretty damn good navigating, Christopher Colombus."

Now he had done it when it counted. He knew that a man sitting in a tiny airplane over the vast ocean in the blackness of night could find his position with a simple optical instrument, a good clock, and a few pieces of paper: it was a miracle. He had done it in the classroom and on training flights, but this was the real thing; his life depended on it.

He took a flask of coffee from its mooring on the cockpit sidewall and poured a cup, then contorted until he could reach a pack strapped to the back of the seat. He pulled out a pastrami-gorgonzola-on-rye sandwich and had dinner. He watched his new 300-gallon rubber fuel bladder in the rear view mirror as he ate. The bladder had replaced the original rear pilots' seat. It was made of a gray-green rubberized cloth and flexed lewdly as he bounced in mildly turbulent air, looking like an evil bag of Jello. Al wondered what would happen if it suddenly burst. Then he forced the thought away; it was better not to dwell on that sort of thing.

Nothing was required now until his next star fix. He set his wristwatch to the buzz-alarm function, selected two hours, and settled back for a nap. Sleeping while piloting a military airplane was outrageously against orders, but he didn't care. He had been taught to fly the Army way and mostly, he flew the Army way. He even understood that the Army techniques had been prepared by panels of senior pilots with years of experience, far beyond his own. But he had a rebellious streak, and on occasion, when he felt his own home grown technique was better, he abandoned orthodoxy and derived considerable satisfaction from doing so. Now, eight hundred miles at sea in the black of night, he saw no reason to stay awake. If something happened to the aircraft he would be the first to know.

As sleep closed in he thought of his telephone call to Mandy yesterday, the first since their breakup three months ago. The Security Officer had sternly warned the pilots about personal calls and the dangers of lapsed security, but Al needed desperately to speak with her before going overseas. Mandy answered on the second ring, flustering Al; he had hoped to warm up with Mr. Piper.

"Uh…yeah: it's Al, Mandy. I'm here on the west coast and I just needed to talk with you."

"I don't know if this is a good idea, Al. I've said everything to you—unless you've changed your mind about the military. I'm seeing other boys now—well, men really."

He shriveled miserably. He was about to risk his life and she was dating other guys. He bridled momentarily at her lack of understanding and then stuffed the anger down inside.

"Well, I really haven't had a chance to think about changing my mind, Mandy. We've been pretty busy you know, getting ready to go overseas and all. Even if I did that—changed my mind, they still have me for seven more years. I won't be able to get out until 1956, and that's a long time. You know I love you, and you'll never fool me; I know you still love me. C'mon Mandy, have a heart, for Christ sake."

He heard choked sobs, then a long silence before she answered.

"This has never been about who I love, Al. This is about the kind of life I wanted with you, the kind we both deserve. You've wrecked things now. I don't see how you can ever get out of the mess you've made. You're better than you think you are, Al. You never understood that, you've settled for peanuts. You never gave me a chance to show what we could have been together. If I have to find another man, then that's what I'll do. I'll have a good life no matter what. Don't call me again Al, this is just too hard."

He sat on the hard telephone booth stool; overheated and perspiring in the afternoon sunlight. He counted eight deep breaths before he could trust himself not to break down. She was going out on him. He was a fool; he was a mud lark in love with a cruel swan. He didn't know what he could do now.

\*       \*       \*

Suddenly he was belted from deep sleep, thrown hard against his shoulder straps by violent turbulence. His sleepy mind heard the roaring tinny din of hail lashing the canopy and metal structure around him. He tried to look forward over the nose but there was thick cloud ahead, he could see nothing. The cockpit was illuminated by a greenish glow from basketball-sized luminescent balls of static electricity that danced off the propellers and walked slowly across the wings. Lightning flashes close-by spoiled his night vision. Groggy and befuddled, he looked at his watch and saw that he had been asleep almost two hours.

The instrument panel told a shocking story; he was reasonably level, but the vertical speed indicator was pegged upward at 5000 feet per minute and the airspeed was zero. He grabbed the control yoke in desperation, felt resistance, and lost precious seconds in confusion before realizing the autopilot was turned on; he was fighting the autopilot. The airplane was taking a terrible beating, shivering and banging upward when he flew into updrafts, then slammed down into a free-fall seconds later. He shut off the overwhelmed autopilot and tried to make appropriate corrective actions, but the violence was far beyond his capability. At times the turbulence was so severe he could not read the instruments as they danced crazily in their shock-mounts. He was sick with helplessness. He was losing and he knew it. His mind shrieked outrage at the brutal foe that had overtaken it. He kept thinking, no, no, wait a minute—let's go back and start this over, let's be calm, let's think about this. But the storm was implacable. There would be no pause, no reprieve.

An obscure ground school lesson came to him suddenly: in severe thunderstorm turbulence normal instrument techniques were not enough. Forget airspeed and altitude and heading control. Fly attitude alone: watch the little airplane in the artificial horizon instrument and do what was necessary to keep the wings level and just pray you could pass through the turbulence before the airplane disintegrated. He also remembered the instructors' strong warning: never penetrate a violent cold front, always fly around it. Al regretted his nap greatly.

Hours seemed to pass as he fought the storm. He was tiring now, getting behind the action, not responding well, not sure he could prevail against this powerful predator. The de-icers were on but they weren't helping. He could see ice building on the wings.

He was going down now; he knew it even if he couldn't read the instruments, the engines were losing power. Stark fear jolted him from lethargy as he suddenly realized he had not turned on the carburetor heat controls—the engines were choking on ice. He slammed both heat controls full on.

*MoonDancer* had been at 29,000 feet when he went to sleep and now, as nearly as he could tell from the erratic altimeter, she was down to 14,000 feet and sinking fast. He wanted to live so much but a growing numbness blocked his actions. He felt himself folding, accepting his fate. He would be in the water three miles below in just minutes. It didn't seem to matter much.

The violence was over as suddenly as it had begun. He was back in smooth air and the airplane was no longer staggering under hammerblows, now it responded normally. Fear and apathy remained, but now there was a hot and awful joy flowering slowly within him; there was a chance he would survive this night. He glanced at the wings and saw chunks of ice beginning to separate from the wing leading edges, responding properly to cyclic inflation and deflation of the rubber de-icing boots.

*MoonDancer* was down to 3700 feet now, but she was level and picking up airspeed. He removed his oxygen mask and rubbed a gloved hand wearily over his face, trying to think what to do. He wanted altitude, wanted altitude right now. He pushed the throttles forward to maximum climb power and saw a gratifying climb rate of 2400 feet per minute. To hell with cruise-climb, to hell with fuel economy, he needed to be upstairs.

Al had time now to feel a surge of anger toward the Alameda Weather prediction: calm and cloudless skies for the entire flight. He remembered the exact words; a strengthening high pressure cell south of Kamchatka would drive the usual mid-Pacific low pressure cell ashore just south of Seattle, guaranteeing fair weather for the entire Eastern Pacific region.

Then he remembered standard flight instruction. Weather advisors are just that: advisors. They cannot know what will actually occur en-route on any flight. Responsibility for a successful flight always resides with the pilot in command. There was some sort of lesson here, but he was too tired to grasp it.

He wondered if his peril had been communicated to Mandy by some telepathic process. She would mourn him if he fell from the sky, he was sure of that. He was almost sure.

Near dawn now, the rising sun behind him illuminated a flat band of silver clouds and the sea was purple-red with reflected light. He was bone-weary and another life-threatening emergency was developing. The sky had been solidly overcast since he passed through the front. He had been unable to locate stars for a navigation fix. Except for the crudity of dead reckoning, he had no way to know where he was, and soon he would be coming abreast of the Hawaiian Islands. He had fuel for only four more flight hours, if he missed landfall he would be forced to ditch in the open ocean. The F-15 flight manual predicted 11 seconds afloat, and then *MoonDancer* would sink.

Figuring airspeed and approximate heading, he should be somewhere south of the Hawaiian Island chain. The low-pressure system associated with the violent cold front would have driven him south, he thought. On the other hand, any number of other wind factors might have come into play. In the final analysis, he just didn't know, he could be north or south of the Island chain. He felt tiny and helpless, almost unwilling to make the effort to find out.

Tuck had persuaded the Navy to broadcast an emergency message from the high power Kaneohe non-directional radio beacon beginning at 3:00 AM local time, the earliest any of the pilots would be within range. The message was a Morse signal on 589.7 kilocycles; K-N-H, repeated every 30 seconds. His ADF antenna would be able to get a line of position to the beacon, but it could not tell him whether he was proceeding toward the station and safety, or heading away toward disaster. He would get just a line. He needed a heading.

Al tuned to 589.7 kc and heard only the awful hiss of static. His radio mechanic background told him Kaneohe was not broadcasting. Even without the K-N-H modulation, the broadcast carrier wave alone would have silenced the static. It was almost 5:00 AM now, what the hell was going on here? The station should have been broadcasting for two hours. He decided to abandon the Kaneohe beacon and try for a Honolulu commercial station. After twenty minutes of tuning he came on a faint, fading signal on 818.3 kilocycles. Eventually, during periods when the signal was up, he could recognize music and his heart soared: the signal must be from Oahu or one of the other islands; at this point he didn't care which.

He waited to see if the signal strengthened. When the signal reached its maximum strength he would know he was directly abeam the transmitter. He throttled back to reduce the engine racket and pressed the headset against his ears in total concentration. The signal was so weak he really couldn't tell if it was strengthening: half the time he heard only static. Eventually he lost the signal entirely and turned around to backtrack, losing another thirty minutes before he was able to reacquire. Now he realized he was so far from the station the ADF unit was unreliable: he would never be able to accurately determine station strength.

He looked down at the ocean, still an odd maroon color from dawn light reflected off the clouds. He was in the turbulent air that trails behind a weather front and he saw whitecaps on the waves below. They were being blown to froth by the strong wind. He closed his eyes and tried not to think about a water landing: a seed of panic wanted to blossom within him.

He waited a few moments and read the direction needle on the ADF—it told him the station was in a direction 75 degrees off his nose, or 255 degrees, the opposite direction. One or the other; the ADF could reveal no more. He felt sure he was south of the Islands so he chose the 75-degree heading and turned to the north. If he had guessed correctly he was closing on the station and the signal would now increase.

But it did not; within ten minutes the scratchy music was entirely gone. Now he had to make a desperate choice: he could turn around to 255 degrees and head south, or believe what his heart was telling him and hold the present course. He was so sure about being south of the Islands—it was hard to even contemplate turning around. Being wrong meant being dead. He switched on the autopilot and settled back with eyes closed, doing his best to calm himself. Finally his training as a radio mechanic training won out. Against shrieking inner warnings he turned the aircraft around and headed south. He closed his eyes again and hid inside himself, preferring not to know what was ahead.

In ten minutes he thought the erratic broadcast maximums were slightly stronger and the fades were getting shorter. Twenty minutes later he had a steady weak signal and he heard an announcer at the station break, identifying KKHP in Honolulu. He remained anxious and unconvinced, but moments later he spotted a small patch of cumulus clouds barely above the horizon to his south—right where his nose was pointed. Al knew these small formations occurred directly over islands as land-heated air moved upward in the morning sunlight. Now, for the first time in hours, he felt cautiously optimistic.

The tension began to drain from him, leaving a bone-deep weariness that made logical thought too great an effort. He needed to look up the Kaneohe Air Station landing approach radio frequency and also, just to be safe, review his ditching procedure. He was on the inboard wing tanks now, the last ones with gas, about 40 minutes of flight left. But the fuel gauges were notoriously inaccurate near the empty reading and he did not trust them. He needed to be ready to ditch. He turned to page 12 in his flight book to find the frequency of the Kaneohe search radar, tuned his radar transponder to 927.6 megacycles, and switched the unit on at the highest power setting. Seconds later the most wonderful voice he had heard in his life boomed through his headset.

"Unidentified aircraft, this is Kaneohe Naval Air Station Search Radar, we have you at 86 miles bearing 035 degrees at 31,000 feet. Squawk IFF now."

Al had no identification transponder; they had been removed from all the aircraft for security reasons. He silenced his microphone and practiced three times before he found an acceptable voice.

"This is MUSKRAT FOUR DOG, Kaneohe."

The wonderful voice was there again for him.

"Roger, MUSKRAT FOUR DOG. Start a maximum rate descent now, hold present heading. Tune 112.3 KC in five minutes for landing instructions. Welcome home, we've been looking for you. Do you require assistance?"

"I have two low fuel lights. You can put a crash boat in the Bay on my flare path, but I think I can make it. Thank you."

*MoonDancer's* right engine coughed and quit on the taxiway, but Al continued to the transient parking area on the left engine. Ground crews would probe the fuel tanks later to find 7 gallons in the right tank and 22 gallons in the left. He had started with 2400 gallons. Before he could finish the shutdown procedure a Navy man climbed the interior wheel-well ladder and poked his head through a hatch in the cockpit floor.

"God Almighty sir, we thought we'd lost you. There was a helluva storm out there; we got four of your aircraft down at little bitty County Airports all over the Islands. Two more are still missing. We have some PBY's out right now, searching, but those guys are almost out of time. You're the last we're gonna find, I guess."

Al slowly disconnected his oxygen, radio and intercom connecters, then removed his helmet and gloves, carefully stowing each and trying to gather the strength to get out of his seat. But the strength was not there. He turned to the Navy man.

"I guess I'll need some help to get out of this thing."

It took two ground crewmen to get him down the ladder. He was tippy: his legs felt like nerveless columns of Jello supporting a load of brick. He asked to be put down. They sat him on the nose-wheel tire beneath the aircraft and he gulped the fresh breeze blowing in off the Pacific. He fumbled in the flight suit pocket for his Lucky Strikes, lit up, and pulled down the first quarter of the cigarette in one drag. Smoking near the airplane was strictly against regulations, but he didn't give a shit. After what he had been through, he was bulletproof. A few drops of rain spattered on his face. He noted three other F-15's parked around the area, but was too tired to be much interested.

Later he was able to stand and limp to the FOLLOW ME Jeep for a ride to Base Operations. Doug Trapnell and Dave Rey were standing outside the Operations building when Al's Jeep pulled up. Trapnell rushed over, talking so fast in his backwoods accent that Al's sluggish mind did not comprehend. Eventually, he tuned in to the running harangue.

"Jesus Christ, boy, I leave you alone for five minutes and you poop in your pants. Well, I'll tell you this, you and I are going to fly on over to Wake Island together, I can't trust you out of my goddamned sight."

Al saw the look of terrible concern on Trapnell's face and stifled an angry response. He turned away, ashamed that he might break down in front of his friends. When he could trust himself, he pointed to the cluster of F-15's in the distance.

"Those yours out there?"

Dave Rey nodded and grinned.

"Mine is there, the second one. Trapnell's is sitting on a 3000-foot dirt airstrip over on Molokai. He fueled out right over the island and dead-sticked it in: great flyer, lousy navigator. They don't know how the hell they're going to get it out of there."

Trapnell smiled and raised his eyebrows.

"Perfect landing, not a scratch on it. I had to walk a ways, though."

Now Al felt anger replacing the bone-deep fatigue.

"What the hell happened to the Kaneohe locator beacon? You know, the one that was supposed to save us if we got lost. I tried to raise it for an hour and the goddamn thing was off the air. I was 250 miles north of the Islands and didn't know where I was. I damn near kept going north—and that would have been the end of me somewhere up in the Aleutians."

Dave Rey had asked the same question when he landed two hours ago.

'They tell me the power tubes in the transmitter failed when they tried a test at two o'clock this morning. They had one spare set, but they failed too. They couldn't get on the air and they had no way to tell us."

Al, who had maintained radio beacons as an enlisted man, snorted in disgust.

"When I did that work, we never had less than two-gross of those tubes on hand. That's 288 tubes, gents. The things are so unreliable you have to replace them like chewing gum."

It slowly occurred to Al that he was in a touchy business. Well intentioned but ineffective actions by others could kill you. Yes sir, they could.

# Chapter 21

Tuck was scribbling notes to the encryption technician, who was typing secure radio Teletype signals to the basement of the Pentagon where Penrod Taylor waited anxiously. His scribbling came to the hard part.

'I have reviewed the prudence of this flight in my mind, and I stand by my decision. My young men have all come through the worst Pacific storm in 50 years unharmed. The aircraft are safe, although it will be two more days before they can be gathered and transported here to Oahu. I intend to hold an all-pilots meeting this afternoon to get opinions on the advisability of continuing our next flight leg. If I am supported, as I believe I will be, we will continue to Wake Island by this weekend. The men have learned greatly from this difficult experience and I have full confidence in our ability to continue. I also know we were perilously close to disaster yesterday. If you wish to relieve me of this command, I will understand.'

It was several tense minutes before Taylor's reply came through.

"I need to speak with Gen. Stenzell before responding. Please be available nine hundred hours your time for reply."

Taylor called Stenzell's formidable secretary. She wasn't hopeful.

"The General is booked solid all day, Mr. Taylor. I'll try, but it may be evening before he can see you."

Stenzell called back in ten minutes.

"Pen? Come on over, I've been hearing rumors."

Stenzell listened to the story without comment, then leaned back in his chair, closed his eyes and put his feet on the desk.

"What do you want to do?"

"We're saving 45 days of ship transport by flying across the Pacific, that was the whole idea and I was in full agreement. We'll be operational 45 days sooner. So I guess Dick Tuck was just doing his job. The weather-guessers didn't see that big thing coming; happens all the time, unfortunately. I know Hollywood would never cast Tuck in the role, but I think the man's a fine Wing Commander. Courageous. The men see all that too. They trust him. I wouldn't want to even consider replacing him."

Stenzell smiled faintly but did not open his eyes.

"Dick's a good officer. He's never had an early promotion because we keep giving him the hardest jobs, but I believe he's on his way to becoming one of our generals. If he survives, that is. OK, he stays. By the way, you can tell him for me he's a full Colonel now. His promotion came through last Saturday. I jiggered the system a little bit. He'll receive a formal message in about a week. And tell him I like his style. Are you going to tell them about this flight over on the Hill?"

"Secretary Day is in Israel, that deal is heating up again too. I'll need to talk to him about it. My recommendation will be to speak with them, we can't manage this news."

The next day Taylor spent his lunch hour in the Pentagon Crypto-room. He scribbled a short message and watched a clerk encode it on the keyboard of a refrigerator-sized machine, then push a transmit button. The brief message required almost ten minutes to send over the old-fashioned radio Teletype link. Tuck was waiting at Fort Shafter in Honolulu; the only secure radio facility available to transient pilots.

"General Stenzell and I fully support your command. Continue flight operations at your discretion. Am hoping you can arrive Clark by Wednesday next week. P-61's loaded aboard ship in Manila Harbor now and awaiting your F-15's. Good luck and Godspeed. Gen. Stenzell informs you of promotion to full Colonel effective date April 27, 1949, paperwork to follow. Our sincere congratulations on this deserved promotion. Inform ASAP scheduled flight dates, times. Taylor, DOD."

*   *   *

Senator Evan Meyer beckoned Taylor back into the small meeting room shortly after midnight.

"Come on in, Pen, I'm sorry we kept you out in the hall so long, but your story poses some delicate issues for us and we needed time for debate."

He smiled, wanting to be friendly.

"That's what we do you know; debate things. Let me get you a brandy and give you our position."

He walked to the small bar, poured a snifter of 80-year old brandy, and introduced his colleagues.

"Secretary Taylor, let me introduce Congressman Levi Jones of Iowa, Senator Bartholomew Schiller of Mississippi, and Congressman Alton LaMotta of Wyoming."

The three nodded silently. Meyer would do the talking.

"This Congress is a melting-pot of differing opinions, Pen. A coalition of elected officials, who I shall not name, has called for a halt to the B-29 program because it is provocative and flies in the face of world peace. They have the muscle to kill the program if they choose to do so. We've kept them at bay this year by promises that *Project Heat Lightning* would soon supplant the B-29 missions and end these terrible losses. Now, we find that questionable judgment has threatened the project's very existence. We know you were trying to save time, to get in the air earlier with these P-61 missions. We also understand that you were successful—this time. But a catastrophe would, in our judgment, end *Project Heat Lightning* and in all likelihood end the B-29 Program also. Believe me, if the naysayers threaten to go public with these unauthorized shenanigans, the present Administration will be only too happy to bury whatever needs to be buried—and they won't think twice about it. Then we would be left with no reconnaissance program at all; an unthinkable situation to those here in this room,"

Meyer paused to light a cigar and ingest a deep sip of brandy.

"So here's the word, Pen: we'll tell our colleagues about yesterday's narrow escape and we'll use our own muscle to see that nothing adverse comes from it. But know this; one more of these…uh, difficulties and we may lose both programs. We won't be able to prevent it. So I'll say no more for the moment, but the burden falls directly on you to ensure a smooth program. We have confidence in you and we believe you can handle this responsibility. But if we have another setback before there are hard intelligence results to defend the program, we will hold you personally accountable. We won't hold Secretary Day accountable, or the Man in the Moon, but you, young man. Is that sufficiently clear?"

Taylor wanted the approval of these men. A part of him quavered under the stern warning. But he also understood they were playing hardball here; it was his job to see there were no more hairsbreadth escapes.

"Thank you sir, let me affirm that the responsibility is mine alone for successful prosecution of this program. There will be no more cause for concern, I assure you."

He considered offering his resignation if there were further troubles, but decided that would smack of weakness.

He left the room feeling old and inadequate; there were no guarantees in this high-risk affair. But if there were no further difficulties at Wake Island, the airplanes should arrive at Clark Air Base in the Philippines by Tuesday, a day ahead of schedule.

Taylor smiled to himself, they were getting close to operations in spite of these razor-thin escapes: they were living The Perils of Pauline.

# Chapter 22

The Navy volunteered a classroom for Tuck's resolution circle meeting, right on the beach at Kaneohe Bay. He assembled his nine pilots in a circle to dissect yesterday's flight. As usual, Tuck was the first. He had seen the impressive line of lightning ahead and detoured south, hoping to circumnavigate the storm. But after 400 miles with no end to the massive formations he turned and penetrated the storm. He landed at the County Airport in Kona with less than 30 minutes fuel. He confessed to questionable judgment in subjecting his inexperienced pilots to the dangers of a stormy Pacific flight.

Bob McMurtry was next.

"Actually, it wasn't so bad. I found Oahu without much trouble, and got in here with two hours of fuel left."

He paused.

"Well, I did have one problem. You know that big hole in the floorboards between the rudder tracks? My flight book caught on a pencil when I tried to get it out of my breast pocket. I fumbled and it fell through that crack down into the bottom of the fuselage. I could see it down there, so I un-strapped, and ducked my head under the control wheel to reach it. But my arm wasn't long enough, so I got my flashlight and poked at it, but I couldn't get it. I got back in my seat and rolled upside down to get it to fall up on the canopy. What I got was a shower of muddy water and some old 1942 assembly sheets from when the airplane was built. I was out of Alameda six hours and I didn't want to go back, so I just knocked three degrees off the straight-line course to Hawaii, for wind you know, and kept going. I went through the storm, but it wasn't so bad where I was. Come morning there I was, with Oahu right in front of me. How about that?"

They all laughed. One of the pilots snorted.

"How about shit-house luck, Bobbie-boy?"

Tuck made no comment, holding to the ground-rules, but his face showed disapproval of McMurtrys' dumb-luck approach to flying.

Al managed the news a bit when his turn came.

"Well, I had a good star fix about twenty minutes before I hit the front, so I know I was almost on course. But then I guess I dozed off a bit, and the next thing I knew I was in the shit."

Heads nodded understandingly around the circle. Al wasn't sure Tuck bought it, though.

The afternoon was devoted to a discussion of the proper way to proceed to Wake Island. No one was in favor of more solo flying. Many opinions were put forward. Tuck felt they should all proceed as a group, in a loose gaggle together.

They put it to a vote at four in the afternoon. They would fly in pairs, each pilot confirming the others navigation. Tuck didn't think it was the best way, but he agreed. He wanted his young men to take responsibility; they would need the experience soon enough.

They also voted to send a radio message to Wake Island ensuring an adequate spare parts inventory for their locator beacon. Al suggested they hold firm for a minimum of 20 tubes and the others agreed, knowing he had been a radio mechanic.

They would rest tomorrow and the next day while 20 Northrop mechanics, specially flown to Hickam Air Force Base across the island, came over and checked each aircraft thoroughly.

Tuck located an airborne radio-Teletype receiver in Navy inventory at Pearl Harbor and was having it installed in his plane so he could receive weather reports en-route. He would fly in the lead and radio weather news back through the following pairs. All in all, Tuck was pleased. His men had experienced a dangerous flight, and now they had worked together put effective safeguards in place. If all went well they would be able to leave by Thursday and arrive at Clark Air Force Base in the Phillippines by Monday, two days ahead of schedule.

In a few short weeks these young men would be flying thousands of miles into hostile territory. He suppressed the thought. He would try to have them ready.

\*     \*     \*

Al was on the runway now, in the lead position. Trapnell insisted on being paired with Al for the flight to Wake Island so he could look after him, and Al had no objections. He craned his neck to look back to Trapnell, sitting idling on the runway 50 yards behind, and clicked his transmitter button twice. Two clicks came right back, but no words. The flight to Wake was 2200 miles, slightly shorter than their first leg, but they carried an extra 200 gallons of gas for insurance. They were heavy today, but they would be heavier still on mission operations. Al wondered what the airplane would feel like at maximum weight with even more fuel aboard.

The Kaneohe runway had just been extended to a length of 12,000 feet in preparation for the new Navy jets that would be coming soon. *MoonDancer* lifted nicely at 130 mph with plenty of runway still ahead. Trapnell quickly pulled up on his right.

"OK, boy. We're off to see the Wizard. This time put your thinking cap on."

The pair thundered low across the Diamondhead crater and set a course due west as the sun was setting. Al felt pretty good about this flight; it seemed like old stuff now.

Tuck was radioing weather reports back through the formation every hour, reducing the apprehension they all felt after their near disaster getting to Kaneohe.

There was little to do between celestial navigation fixes. Al found himself compelled to talk of the troubles he was having with Mandy. He pressed the intercom button and raised Trapnell flying a few hundred feet off his right wing. After an hour of overly lurid details, he had it all out.

"…I just don't get it. What does she want? I've already done more with my life than my Dad and hers put together and it still isn't enough. I don't know what to do."

Silence. Al called Trapnell again.

"You there, Doug? Did you hear me?"

"Yeah, I heard you. Be quiet a minute, I'm formulating a thought."

Formulating a thought? Eventually Trapnell spoke.

"Al, here's the thing about the man-woman deal. When a man looks at an attractive woman, he thinks about his dick, and when a woman looks at an attractive man, she thinks about her standard of living. And that's it, the whole thing."

Trapnell cackled, pleased to capture the essence of the elusive relationship. Al didn't think so.

"That's it? That isn't anything, Doug. We aren't even talking about the same thing, you didn't answer my question at all."

"I gave you a tool, Al. You can use that tool in a thousand situations and come up with the right answer. You know, give a man a fish and you feed him for a day, teach a man to fish and he can eat for a lifetime. That's what I done for you."

"Well, I don't see how to use what you said. It doesn't apply to my situation."

"Sure it does, you're just not working at it hard enough. Do you remember geometry? You had your theorems and your corollaries. The theorems were the general ones. You applied them to specific problems and that gave you the corollaries. You just need to work on the corollaries."

Al still didn't get it, but he was impressed by the philosophy. He had not known of Trapnell's profundity.

They raised the Wake locator beacon at five thirty the next morning, but didn't need it. They could see the island easily in the dawn light.

Al suggested a formation landing, knowing the other pilots would be watching. The thick undisturbed morning air felt like heavy syrup as they glided smoothly down the runway approach locked in formation, landing in precise tandem just ten minutes off the predicted arrival time.

2200 miles of over-water flight and Al was quietly pleased. He'd seen the Wizard.

# CHAPTER 23

## Troopship USS Benjamin Harrison

They were in the bowels of the ancient vessel and Al thought he was getting seasick. The penetrating stench of diesel fuel was everywhere and he felt as if he was in motion. Looking about the shabby airless briefing room he could detect not the slightest movement, but sweat was forming on his forehead and he felt a seed of queasiness near his stomach. They were all together now; the remainder of the 337 Special Operations Wing had joined the F-15 pilots at Clark. Half the wing aircraft complement, 15 P-61's and the 5 of theover-water F-15's, were stowed in the cargo hold below them, outer wing panels removed for compact storage. The other aircraft had gone ahead on a cargo ship to be unloaded before the Pilots arrived at Isla Mattoon.

Tuck stood at the front of the room, conferring with an unknown Major over a stack of viewing transparencies. The men were all gabbing noisily when Tuck held up his hand for silence.

"I want to introduce Major Mack Feeny, who has been in charge of preparing our operational base. Believe it or not, well, actually just believe it, Major Feeny has been working on our base for almost a year. Most of you were starting flying training when he went out there and just got to work as hard as he could, hogging a runway out of mud and coral, building your quarters, building maintenance facilities, and things of that sort. The Major will speak to us here in a moment, but first I think we should show appreciation for his efforts with a round of applause."

No one saw why a man should be applauded for doing his job, there was tepid clapping and a few whistles as Major Feeny took a position behind the battered podium and the lights went down. Al wished the lights would go back up; the darkness seemed to increase his queasiness.

"Our destination is Isla Mattoon Island, 40 miles off Chittagong, India in the Indian Ocean. Special arrangements have been made with the Government of India to allow occupancy, and we'll be far enough from the mainland to ensure reasonable freedom from observation. Col. Tuck will describe security details and mission destinations in a few minutes, but right now I'd like to tell you a little bit about your new home."

He switched on the Magic Lantern projector and placed a transparent photograph on the platen showing a runway of pinkish beige coral cut from lush jungle. Hills crowded the left side of the runway, but to the right the land sloped gently downhill to a white-sand beach. The turquoise water of a lagoon stretched to the right. A line of surf farther out indicated a coral reef. Palm trees grew up the hillside. Feeny nodded at the approving looks from his audience.

"Yes, it's beautiful out there. You'll need to be careful about those hills on the left side of the runway. The runway is presently 8200 feet long. We plan to extend to 10, 000 feet, but that's for later. We'll begin operations with what we have."

He exchanged transparencies to show a medium-sized hangar, four Quonset huts, and a large city of tents. The structures were backed into revetments carved from the jungle.

We live in the tents you see there; they're pretty nice, wooden floors and all. Days are very hot and humid. The nights are just hot and humid, so the tents will give you more air. We have a Flight Surgeon and three medics, so you will be well taken care of."

There were only a few questions, and Major Feeny yielded to Tuck. The men wanted to hear from Tuck. Where would they be flying?

"We'll be flying against targets on the Tibetan high plains in Western China. There are Atomic Assembly Plants near Hotan, Kashi, and Aksu, China. All these cities, well they're really just towns, are scattered around the edge of the Takli Makan desert, now under Maoist control. Those are the Communists, you know. We'll be photographing some large installations up there, factories that are suspected of making atomic bomb parts. Now here's the exciting part, we're going to fly right down near the ground and get inside the microwave beams that send telephone traffic to and from the seat of government at Chengdu. In addition to recon cameras, you'll be carrying a brand new payload, the Hallicrafter HSP65 communications intercept unit. It records the voice traffic on over one thousand telephone channels. Think of the fun the analysts back in Washington will have with those tapes. You can imagine how important our mission will be, and by God, gentlemen, we're going to have a big time up there, getting into as much mischief as we can. OK, that's all I have now. Let's try some questions."

Al's hand shot up along with a dozen others, his seasickness forgotten.

"When's the first mission. Who will fly it?"

"We dock at Isla Mattoon on May 11th. The plan calls for a mission on May 14th. That's tight, but we can do it. As for who flies first, I haven't decided. But on that score don't worry, there's plenty for all. I expect every one of you will have a first mission under your belt before June. The idea is to hit these guys hard and fast, get what we need before they can respond."

Padraig Dwyer shouted from the back of the room before anyone could raise a hand.

"How many of us on each mission. What's the range—the route?"

"We'll start with two P-61 reconnaissance aircraft and one F-15 gunship on each mission. The P-61's will hit different microwave links at the same time; gather as much data as we can before they get smart and encode the links to protect them. The F-15 will ride shotgun. We'll come in low for the last 700 miles or so, throw those Chinamen way off, they won't know where we're going until the last minute. We'll go in along the India-Burma border to the Himalayas, and then cross into China at Chengdu. Make a hard left at Chengdu and fly up the northern flank of the Himalayas to the target. Then, when we're still several hundred miles away, we'll go down low and drop off their radar screens.

Trapnell had the next question.

"What's the opposition look like?"

"Well, the B-29 fellows are getting high altitude flak, pretty well aimed flak. The photos show dense gun emplacements around the sites. But the biggest problem there has been the YAK's. The Russians loaned a bunch of their old beaters to the Chinese Communists back in '46: YAK 3's and 9's. It's not a bad airplane, sort of a poor man's P-51, but the Chinese don't seem to be flying them very well. Not enough training I guess. Lately though, our aircrews have seen better flying on occasion; they think maybe a few Russians have come down to the desert to help out their friends. And then there have been a few sightings of the new Russian jet, the MIG 15. But of course that's not confirmed, it could be a mistaken identification."

Tuck let that thought trail away.

# Chapter 24

Al was cleaning his gun on an old cardboard box when Trapnell stuck his head in the tent.

"How y'all? Just thought I'd come by and see what the boys on the high ground are doing."

He was dressed in olive drab boxer shorts, sweat-stained t-shirt, and GI boots. The boots were covered with thick clots of red clay. Paidrig Dwyer rolled up from his cot, sweating and miserable in the heat, irritable.

"Killer look, Doug. You going to the Academy Awards? Doing Hooray for Hollywood?"

"I am going to my morning ablution."

"Ablution? What the hell does that mean? And how do you think we're doing in this tent? It's not the Waldorf-Astoria you know. Look at these fucking mosquito nets. They don't keep the bugs out and they don't let the air in. I'll be dead of exhaustion in a week. I'm applying for medical retirement. And don't come in here with those muddy boots, I just swept the place out."

"Ablution means to take a shower and get clean, Pat. Something a dumb Mick like you wouldn't know about. Ever hear of reading, my man? Books? You start to read and it's like a dung beetle rolling that little ball around; your IQ just gets bigger and bigger. You're what, Pat, 21 or so? Well, start reading and you might get your IQ up to 21 before you die.

You think it's bad in this here smelly tent? At least you boys got a wooden floor. Down there in the hollow we got sand. Rained all night and my cot sunk down to the mattress; smells like a wet dog today."

He turned his attention to Al's pistol, lying in pieces on the cardboard surface.

"I aint'a gonna take that thing along with me, no sir. Shoot a Chinaman with that and you won't even raise a welt. Looks like some fairy's gun, Al; or something a woman keeps under her skirt. Needs some nickel plating and mother-of-pearl handles to be just right, though. You boys got no pride, I can see that. Me, I'll just take my .45 pop-gun along, get a little respect when I shoot me some of them folks."

Al had to defend the .32ACP 'Agent's Pistol' they had been issued along with flak vests and steel helmets.

"The OSS used these during the war when they parachuted into Europe, behind the lines. There were tests, Doug, scientific tests. This little gun won out. It's light, the clips are small, and it won't dig a hole in your chest under the shoulder straps on these long flights."

"Surely, professor. Do tell. Well, why don't you just put that thing back together and see if you can kill a few of these here mosquitoes tonight after the lantern goes out. You might help a bit with our mission. And don't worry about us boys down there in the swamp when you shoot, that bullet will fall down on the ground before it gets halfway there. It'll just lay there, saying Howdy to our enemies."

Dwyer scratched at his mosquito bites.

"I'm volunteering to test-fly every one of these planes when they get their wings back on, at least it's cool up there."

Al laughed.

"That'd be great, Pat. Maybe you should do the afternoon beer-chilling flight too."

Dwyer stood and scratched his crotch, where a fungal infection was forming after just one week on the island. The salve Doc handed out didn't seem to be doing anything.

"To think I volunteered when old Bob came and told us about this dangerous mission. The only danger here is sweating to death, or those big land crabs you can hear shuffling around on the floor at night. Jesus. Did you see McMurtry's fingernails? He climbed a palm tree down by the runway and got the fungus in them: they're falling off. Doc gave him some blue shit to put on them, but it isn't doing anything."

A lemur poked its nose from beneath Al's bunk; her golden eyes regarded the assembly with high hope. Al had passed the animal every morning on his way back to the tent after breakfast. It sat in the hollow of a huge tree regarding the strange invaders with no sign of fear. One morning he approached it with a tin of blueberries. He spoke in soothing low tones and offered the can up toward the branch it sat on. The lemur reached down carefully and accepted the gift. It plucked a berry and tasted, then cleaned up the entire contents in minutes. Now it came each morning to the tent for a treat and stayed to sleep through most of the day. It was a nocturnal hunter, disappearing each night at dusk. Al thought the cat-like creature resembled his mother and named her Violet. Dwyer looked down at the furry creature.

"You'd think Violet would stick around and eat these ugly crabs, but no, she has to go out there and bust her ass getting stuff in the jungle."

Violet understood that no food was being offered. She disappeared back under the bunk.

Trapnell snorted.

"You think a land crab bitin' you on the ass is as bad as it gets? Wait 'til you take one of them airplanes up to China and they start shootin' those 88's and 105's at you Pat; then you'll know what the hurt locker is all about. I know about it, they had me shootin a gun on those B-17's over there in Europe during the war. You'd see those little fighters coming at you like gnats, and then them gun ports would start winkin at you real friendly-like. But you didn't know where them bullets were going. It was worrisome. I got hemorrhoids from it I was so clutched up. Only 23 years old and them Germans gave me hemorrhoids—a damn shame. Now you may not get em Pat, but there's things worse. When you get back from one of these trips, them Malays over at the laundry ain't gonna award you no medals boy. They're gonna be saying: Pat Dwyer, wings of silver, shorts of brown."

Al finished his pistol reassembly and stabbed the small black gun into a shoulder holster hanging from the tent frame.

"They're almost through putting the planes back together and I haven't seen Tuck all week, when are we going to get the word?"

Dwyer tried to lean back on his bed against the mosquito netting hanging from the tent ceiling but the flimsy material would not support him.

"Christ, is there no way to have a little comfort around here? I talked with the Exec yesterday out at the maintenance tent, he thinks we'll be having some mission briefings in the next day or two; old Tuck's down in Rangoon now talking on the secure Teletype. They're finishing up target selection is what I think. I bet we'll fly in the next week or so. I asked if we get to pick out our own airplanes, but the Exec claims we won't, we'll be assigned whatever the maintenance boys have ready to go. I flew *Joker's Wild* over here and she's a great ship, a lucky ship. That's the one I want to go in, by God. When Tuck has his big meeting I'm going to speak up about it. You guy's should too."

Trapnell's chestnut eyes studied Dwyer, he wondered if the kid was complaining too much, wondered if he was going to be all right.

"Oh, we'll be rolling along like Hannibal's Map here pretty soon, I guess. And I'll be happy to raise my hand for you about the airplanes, but I don't really care, they're just big hunks of metal and gas to me. If the mechanic says OK, and I say OK, then that's it."

He thought a moment.

"On the other hand, I always favored *MoonFly* come to think of it. She took me up there to the North Pole as pretty as you could ask. Maybe I'll make a fuss about that. What about you, Al?"

"That's easy. I'll take *EyeCatcher* whenever she's available. That'll bring me some luck."

# Chapter 25

Tuck held his all-hands meeting in the locked, airless mission briefing room: twenty-two pilots and the Executive Officer sat sweating as he stood and waved a wooden pointer to get their attention. Before them, a large map of Southeast Asia and Western China was stapled to a wall. The Tibetan towns of Hotan, Aksu and Kashi had been circled in green grease pencil. Yellow tape marked the flight route to each city: a 700 mile haul from Isla Mattoon up the Burma-India border to China, then a sharp dogleg to the left extending 1100 miles across two thirds of Southern China to the three cities. Several areas along the route had been hashed with diagonal red lines, for which there was no map legend.

Tuck had a stack of old ammunition cases as a podium. He wanted an air of professionalism. He banged on the rickety structure with his wooden pointer.

"All right you men, all right there. Let's quiet down now and cut the chatter. I have something to say here and it behooves you to listen, to gain a little knowledge maybe. Right up here on the wall you can see our targets near those cities circled in green."

He paused as perspiration stung his eye and then addressed the Executive Officer.

"John, go out there and find us a fan or two. We need some fans in here. Bad."

He returned to the map.

"A simple enough job. We fly up these yellow lines, slip into the microwave links serving our targets and do some recording. If we have time, we'll go on over and try for some low angle photography of the construction. Then we turn around and come back home; all safe and sound."

He pointed next to a thick blue line of tape that traveled from the center of the three-city area down across India to Karachi.

"If there's trouble, and trouble can happen to anyone you know, we have a route to be used by damaged aircraft that might not be able to get back here to Isla Mattoon. The route to Karachi is 600 miles shorter than a flight back home. Now I want you to read these signs and memorize them. They just might save your life."

His pointer indicated a sign in large black letters taped near the center of the map *'Escape route in emergencies only! Average compass reading from target area 192 degrees. Distance 1150 miles. Flight Time 3.8 hours.'*

He gave the group a moment to read and continued.

"The Government of India has agreed, with economic persuasion, to allow use of a jungle airstrip 30 miles from Karachi. Landings will be strictly limited to combat damaged aircraft, and a representative of the Indian Government will be on hand at all times for verification of such damage. And we have another hole card here. There are three Marine Reconnaissance teams operating with Chang Kai-Sheks' Kunmintong guerilla forces down in southern China. The 337th Intelligence Officer is in communication with these teams, and approximate locations will be given to individual pilots just before takeoff. If you're forced down up there, try to get somewhere near these fellows before bailing out. They can help you. It's an extra chance we'll have."

Every man in the room recognized how slim this extra chance was, but at least it was a chance. Morale perked up.

He allowed the buzz to die, then pointed to the second crudely lettered sign *'Do not fight below 300 mph. Dive away!'*

"This is for the F-15 pilot's, it summarizes everything we learned in Air Combat Maneuvering training. We can't dogfight with the YAK-9; they're too maneuverable. If you have to fight, sneak up behind and hammer them, or do diving attacks and get away. We can out-dive those things by almost 150 mph, but we can't out-turn them. You fellows keep that in mind and that might save your life too."

A voice in the rear of the room spoke up.

"What are the red hash marks for?"

Tuck squinted through cigarette smoke to identify the man.

"Well Trumbauer, those marks show where we think the Chinese ground defenses are. Antiaircraft guns mostly, maybe a few fighters. We'll avoid those areas when we can. You'll have plenty of warning if we come across a flak site. I remember during the war you could hear the flak radars in your earphones: they buzzed, some hummed, some drove you to distraction warbling. It won't be any different this time, you'll know when you're getting near a defended area."

Dwyer spoke up.

"Some of us have been talking, sir, and we'd like to fly individual ships; our favorite ships. It would make us feel better. *Joker's Wild* has always been the best flyer for me, for instance."

Tuck was aware of the role superstition played with combat pilots.

"That's OK with me, provided the plane isn't down for maintenance. If that's the case you'll fly whatever the Executive Officer tells you to fly."

He paused, remembering impassioned pilot arguments over a particular aircraft from his P-47 days.

"And no squabbling. If any one of you decides to argue about a plane and cause a problem with the other pilots, I'll call the whole thing off and let the Exec make assignments."

Tuck's final announcement was a blockbuster.

"You will notice on this chart right here that I have not made assignments for the first mission."

He poked at the chart as if the men could not see the blank spaces.

"Well, that mission, the first one, will be flown by Trapnell, Deforest, and myself. The target will be two of the telephone links serving the atomic assembly plant northeast of Hotan. Trapnell and I will fly the P-61's. We'll make two thirty-minute passes up and down the microwave links designated here as T4 and T7. The objective is to record as much voice traffic as possible. Then we'll go over and get some low-angle photography before we exit the area. Deforest will fly the F-15 gunship; he'll orbit at 5 thousand feet about ten miles south of us, over the Tan Lun mountains. He'll provide cover; he'll watch out for us, and he'll come in to help if we get in trouble."

There was a startled murmur through the room. Dwyer blurted out.

"Sir, you're not supposed to fly operational missions. We know that, we heard that guy Taylor say so."

Tuck's chinless face broke into a rare grin.

"Keep that among us schoolboys, will you Dwyer? I wouldn't be much of a leader if I didn't know what I was sending you fellows into, would I? Besides, I wasn't listening very closely when he covered that topic."

Al was lost in thought; he had tuned the room out. When Tuck announced his name it was like a physical blow. Suddenly it all became startlingly real: the work, the training, and the mission exercises were over, now he must perform. Now he must sing for his supper.

He sat sandwiched among the other young men, sweating in the tropical heat, trying to examine his feelings. What he felt was a mixture of pride, excitement, curiosity, and the tingle of raw fear. The mixture of emotions was odd and unfamiliar, an unsettling experience. This would be combat flying even if he didn't fire a shot: his first experience. He felt sweat in his armpits rolling down his ribs and hoped desperately he would be adequate.

*       *       *

Al sat on the taxiway, watching the two black fat-bodied P-61's idling on the coral runway ahead of him. The grotesque bulb at the rear of the fuselage that had once housed an electric gun turret and a radar operator station was now filled with fuel. All told, in drop tanks, wing tanks and the gray-green rubber tanks in the fuselage, each plane carried 3800 gallons of high-octane gas. They were dangerously above the maximum weight allowed for takeoff, but they would fly anyway. Tucks' voice came over the intercom, rendered tinny by the crude low-power link.

"CEMENT LEADER to CEMENT TWO and THREE, check water injection pump pressure."

The big, reliable Pratt and Whitney engines were being deliberately run with lean fuel charges, far leaner than factory specification. The lean condition gave the best cruising economy. It also made the engines cranky on takeoff, where maximum power was needed to lift the overloaded aircraft from the coral strip. Water had to be sprayed into the cylinders along with fuel to avoid combustion detonation, a kind of super-ping that could destroy an engine in seconds.

Al looked at the instrument panel.

"CEMENT THREE. Water injection on; pump pressure 70 pounds."

He heard Trapnell repeat the message; then Tuck kicked the football.

"Rolling now."

The two black aircraft waddled sluggishly down the coral runway, throwing dust high in their wake. Al could see nothing; he waited in frustration to see if they were off the ground safely. Minutes later he heard Tucks' voice on the radio.

"Gear up."

Trapnell repeated the message seconds later and he relaxed. Heavy takeoffs were a bitch; they used up almost all the 8200-foot airstrip. The handbook performance charts showed a 6200-foot takeoff distance, but it wasn't true. The coral gravel seemed to add wheel drag. They had tested yesterday with *GoogleEyes,* the best airplane in the Wing, making several takeoffs. The average takeoff roll was 7100 feet. That seemed to leave a comforting distance to spare, but Al knew the extra 1100 feet would be covered in an eye blink at their lift-off speed of 135 mph.

Now he aligned with the runway, still unable to see Tuck and Trapnell because of the slowly drifting dust cloud. Seconds later a soldier standing in the back of a Jeep halfway down the runway, aimed his 'biscuit-gun' and shot a green light. He started the takeoff roll. Al sat high above the runway and he was fifty feet ahead of his own dust cloud and he could see better now. Far down the strip, end markers were appearing as the coral dust blew off to the left, up the hillside.

He broke ground with very little runway left and flashed across the beach, noting the piles of steel runway planking stacked neatly below, awaiting installation later in the month. Tuck had chosen to start flying missions now rather than wait on the construction process.

Al caught the P-61's 75 miles north of the base. Tuck looked over, nodded, and returned to his navigating. It was perfectly safe to use their low-power intercom links for communication; they were undetectable beyond a quarter-mile. But Tuck was an experienced combat pilot, he knew the life-saving value of discipline and intended to communicate this to his young men, even in small matters. They flew northeast for two hours, covering the jungle over the India-Burma border at a steady 250 mph.

They began to hear the massive air surveillance radar at Chengdu while still two hundred miles from the border. At first the sound was a tiny note, barely audible. Then the note rose to a strong fluctuating warble until it saturated their earphones with a doomsday hum. Tuck said something Al could not hear because of the ominous hum.

"Say again."

"We're crossing into China now. Keep a sharp eye from here on in."

Al felt the thrill a burglar feels entering a darkened home. He started the search drill they had learned: right wing; look high, level, low. Nose; high, level, low. Left wing, high, level, low. Rear-mirror; high, level, low. It was boring work, but he was tremendously excited. They were finally doing something that really mattered; they were in hostile territory. A few moments later Tuck spoke again.

"Turning left now, we'll by-pass Zayi."

Al leaned his head against the right side of the bubble canopy and craned to see the mid-sized agricultural center, a smear of criss-crossed medieval roads and huts with a few multi-story buildings in the downtown area. The countryside was gray-silver and barren, wearing its winter mantle. He could see to the horizon without a hint of haze or dust, it was a perfectly clear day; there would be no hiding in the clouds on this mission. He wondered what the citizens of Zayi would say if he parachuted down to land in the city square. He was an Occidental; he would be a Martian in this ancient land.

Tuck was holding radio silence now; they were deep in enemy territory. He got their attention with a waved arm and gestured at the ground. Al watched Tuck's black P-61 roll upside down, and then the nose fell through to a steep circling dive. Al followed automatically in loose formation, 200 feet out, keeping his eyes on Tuck's airplane and maintaining station, never looking at the ground, never looking away from the black airplane as it circled down and down. They leveled just a few hundred feet above the barren Tibetan steppes and began the long final run. Now they thundered past occasional herds of wooly musk ox, tended by men on horses who looked up at them and pointed. Al could see their faces, he wondered if they had a way to communicate with the government. He guessed not. He concentrated on low-altitude flying chores, needing to back up Tuck's navigation.

Two hours later they left the rolling steppe country, moving away from the protective flanks of the Himalayan Mountains, approaching the flat, arid high desert south of Hotan. Al was tired; they had been in the air for almost five hours, he didn't see how he would be able to do anything heroic up here. He wanted a nap. He wondered if Mandy would somehow know of his dramatic situation: some kind of telepathy.

Tuck waved them both in close; the local tracking radars were searching for them now, making a din in their headsets. He wanted to be heard.

"OK, that's the plant site northeast of the city, five miles or so. Cement Two can you see the microwave towers for the northern link, the T7 link?"

Trapnell, normally relaxed in the air, came back in an excited voice.

"Yes sir, I see that little tower up on the sand hill, and then the far one way off there; on that red mountain. I got it, just like the briefing photos."

"Verify power to the Hallicrafter payload. Verify headset switched to payload output."

It took Trapnell a moment to reconfigure the various switches involved in activating the receiver/recorders and tuning his headset to listen to the Chinese voices on the telephone link. Listening in was a final check to ensure they got the voice recordings they had come for.

"Roger both. Shall I go down now?"

Al saw Tucks' head swiveling around, looking for enemy air activity.

"No. Hold one minute. Cement THREE; you get upstairs to your orbit. Keep a sharp eye; we won't be able to do anything but fly the links. If you get flak, weave; don't break off. We're here to gather an hour of recording, not to run home like...like a bunch of scaredy-pants. Sing out if you see enemy aircraft so we can take evasive action. It's 7 minutes past the hour now; we'll rally at 500 feet on the edge of the desert due south of Hotan in one hour. If there's a fight, you're on your own. Let's go."

Al watched the two black airplanes peel away from him, heading north toward the massive dry-lakes of Hotan. He would miss them now, he felt unspeakably lonely.

He climbed to 5000 feet, feeling creepy, as if someone were behind him watching. He worried about the P-61's, so dangerously exposed to anti-aircraft guns around the microwave links. The intelligence analysts felt the enemy gunners, who were used to B-29's, would experience difficulty getting the correct low altitude range. But the analysts were back in the office looking through optical readers at photography, and CEMENT flight was up here: fat targets for the gunners. He banked in a steep circle to check for trailing aircraft, looked above and below, saw nothing. Newly-formed, scattered cumulus clouds obscured his view of the microwave links. Occasionally he could glimpse Tuck and Trapnell through the breaks: tiny flying insects plodding slowly across the flat alkaline desert floor.

Then, from a group of trucks parked near the T4 link, a series of flashes followed seconds later by black puffs in the vicinity of Tuck, but far above him. Black puffs were 105's and gray puffs were 88's, they had learned that. The volume of fire surprised Al: only a few 105 flak guns had been predicted up here. They all seemed to be shooting at Tuck.

He heard a garbled radio transmission before Tuck's voice came through clearly.

"All right, Lieutenant. I agree, we're too slow; we're wallowing in and out of the links at this speed. Let's take it up to 160 mph and see if that's better."

Al smiled to himself. When the chips were down Tuck did what he had to do. Forget about radio silence.

He was totally concentrated on the situation in the T4 and T7 links, not clearing himself adequately, when a flight of three dark green aircraft appeared a thousand feet below flying exactly on his course. They had flown right up under him on the same heading, but evidently had not seen him. How could they have missed him? He shook his head savagely; dumb luck, not skill, had saved him.

"CEMENT LEADER and THREE, bogeys five miles out on your ten o'clock position: about 4000 feet above the terrain. I don't think they see you yet. Attacking now."

Al rolled upside down and pulled into a shallow dive, approaching the three green aircraft from the rear. Still out of range, he leaned forward to find the rearmost aircraft in his gun sight and saw only blackness. He had forgotten to turn on electric power to the sight. The gunsight took five minutes to warm up; too long, he would just have to look out the window and shoot. Now he could see that his approach was too fast, way too fast: he was overrunning his targets by 100 mph or more. Still, he could get in a quick burst before he dove past them. He aimed and pressed the firing button on the control yoke. Nothing. He had failed to power the pneumatic gun-chargers; there was no ammunition in the firing chambers.

Jesus Christ, what else? He broke off the attack, still upside down, and pulled the nose through to make a broad looping circle back up to his starting point.

He executed the delinquent pre-firing routine: guns, gun-sight and camera now all powered. He selected the four deadly 20mm cannons housed in the belly-pod, fired a short burst, and smiled: he was finally getting it right. At the top of the climb he rolled upright, searched the sky, and relocated the enemy flight. The three were about a mile ahead of him now, still flying level on a constant heading. He had not been seen.

He took several deep breaths, fighting for calm, and began a shallow dive: right side up this time. The gun-sight was still sightless: not enough warm-up time. He would shoot visually. This time the approach speed was right; he was slowly overtaking the formation. He lowered the nose below the last plane, estimated an aim point, and fired a spotting burst. A short chain of 20mm shells floated away from him, the tiny incandescent flares in the base of every third round looked like cheery Christmas lights. The shots fell beneath the last plane, just as he had expected. Now he was ready. He checked the turn and bank instrument to be sure he was not unconsciously skidding the airplane, throwing his aim off, and then pulled the nose up slightly and loosed a fairly long burst. This time the tracers floated slightly below the green fighter, then they seemed magically to rise up and pepper the fuselage and right wing. He saw dozens of white flashes as cannon shells vaporized the aluminum structure. Nothing happened and Al felt sharp disappointment: they had all been solid hits.

Then the enemy airplane slowed and the right wing folded upward. It rolled violently, the nose dropped, and the right wing separated from the fuselage. Al was too close; he felt small jolts and heard clanks as he collided with debris. He slammed the control yoke hard right and turned away from the two surviving aircraft, certain they would attack him now. He searched his rear view mirror and saw the survivors plodding ahead on the same course, apparently unaware of the attack. He craned his neck in all directions as the turn continued, but saw no other aircraft in the area. Apparently the aircraft were not acting as decoys.

Confidence surged as he renewed the attack. His gun sight worked now, but decided to ignore the instrument and shoot visually. He picked the fighter on the right and loosed a burst at 900 feet, near maximum range. The tracers floated out past the nose of his victim, then the rearmost rounds in the long burst slammed into the fuselage and propeller. White vapor streamed from the nose, probably engine coolant. The canopy blew off and he saw a body hurtle into the slipstream: a bailout.

He broke off, feeling very tired now, wanting to be elsewhere. He scanned for other aircraft: still there was nothing. He opened the throttles and climbed steeply, certain the last fighter would finally engage him. He circled back and saw the sole survivor continuing in a gentle turn, but not taking evasive action. He was wary now, ill at ease: this must be a trap. He scanned again, saw nothing behind or above, and dove at the green aircraft. Now he was overconfident and loosed the cannons at too great a range; the pretty orange dots moved away, separated and flashed around the airplane. He couldn't tell; probably all misses.

He closed the throttles for engine braking, slammed out the speed brakes, and S-turned to avoid overrunning. Now he was right behind, just 200 yards aft of the green fighter. The victim continued in a gentle turn to the left, still not taking evasive action. Al wondered if the pilot was trying to surrender, or if was he oblivious to the danger. Had the pilot not seen the tracers, not seen his friends go down? It seemed impossible.

No time for worrying about it: he fired a long burst at point blank range. Now there were no beautiful floating tracers, the ammunition slashed almost instantly into the tail and fuselage of the green aircraft. He was considering a touch of rudder to bring fire onto the other side of his target when there was an orange flash and tremendous explosion ahead.

No chance for avoidance; he was in the dangerous wreckage before he could think about it. He felt a heavy double impact as he flew through the debris field. A thick film of oil spray covered the windshield and leaked back along the canopy. He could smell burnt rubber. He went on instruments to maintain control, wondering where the burned rubber had come from.

He felt a slight roughness in the right engine and the control column vibrated gently in his hand, indicating unseen damage. Now the 400 mph air stream was clearing the oil from his canopy and he could see through spots in the smudge. After a careful sweep for other attackers, he looked across at the right engine and saw nothing. He checked to the left and saw a deep dent in the wing leading edge. The metal bulged above the normal wing surface. Uneven airflow over the aileron was causing the vibration he could feel in the controls: not too serious. He leaned his head back until he was in the rotational plane of the propellers on the right engine. Something was out of track; one or more propeller tips had been bent back by debris impact. But the engine was running reasonably well and he could do nothing about the bent propeller.

He scanned across the desert floor: CEMENT ONE and THREE were not in sight. The antiaircraft guns were no longer firing and he saw no sign of smoke or wreckage in the area. Trapnell and Tuck must have successfully exited the area. He looked at the instrument panel clock: nine minutes past the hour. The fight had lasted less than fifteen minutes. He shook his head, it seemed as if a year had passed.

Al headed south across the lakebed for the rally point, looking desperately above and below his position, hoping to see the two P-61's. They were gone. He flew due south until he was in foothills, then turned east to begin the trip home, hugging the hills with only 200 feet clearance. He was in Nepal now, and shouldn't have been, but somehow it seemed safer. He felt vague and wispy, as if some part of his soul had escaped, leaving a large empty spot inside.

Seven hours later, near two in the morning, he made a rough, bouncy landing at Isla Mattoon. He noticed glaring lights as he approached the parking revetment. A large crowd had gathered, standing on top of the anti-bomb embankments; it looked like the entire Wing. No one attempted to climb the nose wheel ladder as he went through the shutdown procedure. He was irritated: he had been through enough, now he wanted help.

He carefully unplugged the oxygen, intercom and radio connections to his flight suit. As he removed his helmet he could hear clapping and he peered into the glare: three hundred men were giving him an ovation. His face crumpled and he felt hot tears start and he furiously brushed them away; he was too tired for this.

He slowly opened the canopy, reached for the windshield handholds and levered himself to a shaky upright position. He squinted in the glare of the overhead lights and motioned for the 20-foot wheeled ladder to be brought forward to the side of the fuselage. He scooted his way down the steps bottom-first, holding the handrails for support, the descent of an old man.

Now there were people all around pushing and shouting questions. He looked at them stupidly and could think of nothing to say. Trapnell's face appeared in front of him.

"Pretty good scootin, boy. They had to carry me down."

Tuck reached around Trapnell and silently shook Al's hand. He turned away and gestured for his staff car, a beat-up old Chevrolet carryall. After Al was loaded Tuck stood on the running board and waved for silence.

"We'll have a pilots' resolution circle tomorrow morning at nine. The Exec will split the rest of you into two groups for summary briefings on the mission: one at eleven and one at two. Go to bed now."

The intelligence officer had generous glasses of bourbon waiting: the three men downed triple-hits before going through their stories. Both Tuck and Trapnell had experienced difficulty staying in the narrow microwave beams, they had been flying near stalling airspeed to maximize the intercept time. The airplanes were so sluggish at that low speed they had drifted in and out of the beam haphazardly. Even so, Trapnell had 40 minutes of good recording and Tuck had 30: plenty of fodder for the Washington analysts. Both Tuck and Trapnell had experienced flak toward the end of the mission but never close enough to prompt evasive flying.

Al told his tale but neither of his companions had seen the enemy aircraft or his attacks and they could not verify his story. The Intelligence Officer took notes, then shrugged: confirmation of Al's kills must await the development of his gun camera film. No one could think of a reason for the peculiarly docile behavior of the Chinese pilots. They had been like gunnery targets, like the canvas sleeves they shot at in training.

He was awake most of the short night, too stimulated for sleep, deeply grateful just to be there. He thought of the men in the green airplanes, knowing he had killed at least one of them, perhaps all three.

For some reason he thought of countless dreary evenings during the Depression when he had gone to bed hungry, with nothing more in his stomach than a half-helping of beans and rice. He knew about life's difficult times, how they began and how they ended. He wondered how this one would end.

He felt nothing at all for the young men he had killed today. It had been like shooting clay pigeons.

# Chapter 26

The Executive Officer stuck his head in the door.

"The Green Hornet wants permission to land,"

Tuck looked up from his desk to see the man's head poking through his office door.

"Why?"

The reply was unwelcome.

"An elephant aboard, to see you personally."

He clutched at a straw.

"How do you know it's the Green Hornet? No one ever stops here without formal approval."

"Sorry, sir, the IFF code is correct. It's the Green Hornet all right. They want you to meet the airplane."

Tuck was standing on the roughly prepared area that served as transient parking when the battered old C-47 taxied up looking the worse for wear in a coat of faded green jungle camouflage from WW2. The transport served the State Department, bringing Government employees up the long chain of Eastern Pacific Islands from Australia once a month. They paid the Air Force a fortune to operate the service. It was a bargain compared to arranging commercial transportation.

The crew chief threw open one side of the cargo doors and a metal stairway clattered out, followed by a rumpled Brigadier General who sniffed the stench of leafy jungle decay in the humid air before he cautiously descended the rickety stairs. The crew chief threw a leather briefcase and an overnight bag to the ground and closed the cargo door. The Green Hornet blasted around in a circle and headed back to the runway, showering everyone with coral gravel. Tuck stood at attention and saluted the squatty unshaven figure appearing through the dust.

"Colonel Richard Tuck, sir. Commanding."

The man smiled and held out a hand, not returning the salute.

"Bob Overdorf, Colonel. Let's get out of this mess. We need to have a little talk."

In the office Tuck asked if he would like to shower and clean up. Overdorf shook his head.

"Let's do what we need to do here, I'll clean up later. The shuttle won't be back for two days. You got a drink around here? Jesus, it's hot in this little closet, can you do something about that? What the hell are those things doing?"

Tuck walked over to the large floor fan and turned it on; it made the room a little better, but not much. He didn't notice the heat any longer. He was puzzled by Overdorf's last comment, then realized the man was referring to the land crabs shuffling about the office floor.

"Those are land crabs, General, we have a lot of them; they're mating now. We shot them for a while, but there were too many. Then the Exec put out poisoned bait. That got a howl from the pilots: they keep a lemur down in tent city and they were afraid she'd be poisoned. Now we just tolerate them."

Tuck produced a bottle of government-issue bourbon, Old Fedcal the label said, and poured two half-tumblers. Overdorf eyed the bottle suspiciously then threw down the entire contents of his glass.

"Ooh. Goddamn. That's good whiskey, where do you get it?"

Tuck smiled edgily.

"It's actually Wild Turkey, sir. Packaged for overseas use at government facilities."

Overdorf's red eyes stared at Tuck a moment as he rubbed a stubbled cheek.

"Well. Let's cut to the chase here. We intercepted some radio traffic up at Hotan the other day. The boys in the back room say one of the voices was yours. Was it?"

Tuck sat silently, considering possible replies. How the hell could they read his radio transmissions from ten thousands miles away? No matter, nothing cute was going to work here. He told the truth.

"Yes sir, it was. I went up there with two of my kids. A first mission, General, you know how they go. I just wanted to be sure they did all right."

"Did they?"

"They did. One of them nailed three YAKs, and it was his first time in combat. The other one stayed with it through bad flak. We got what we went after."

Overdorf shook his head.

"Your orders are pretty clear Colonel. You are to avoid flying in any region where you might be captured by a foreign government: anytime, anywhere. Ever. So what did you think you were doing?"

Tuck stumbled over his explanation.

"I was leading sir. I was doing what I should be doing, setting an example. These missions we're flying here, they're going to be the longest, the worst, you or I have ever seen. If a kid goes down up there we'll never get him back. Even in Burma or India or Nepal, where we have influence with the governments, there are no rescue facilities. Seven hours in, an hour at the target, seven hours out. Any hiccup, whether it's a flak gun or bad spark plugs, and we've lost one forever. I reassured them by taking the first mission. Do you think they want to take orders from some fat-ass sitting behind a desk making reports to the Pentagon? Do you think my being a Colonel means a thing to them out here? Well, it doesn't. They need some leadership, something to take the scare off. I was just doing my job. You've led men in combat I'm sure, sir. Tell me I was wrong."

Overdorf put his feet on a wooden crate stenciled, 'Rations, C, beef with gravy, potato pancakes, carrots, apple dumpling'. This sad-sack looking Colonel was right, he had commanded squadrons and groups in North Africa and Italy. Eventually they had relieved him for being too protective of his pilots. There had been a fine medal, but then he was on staff and out of it. Stenzell sent him out here because he knew the pain that came from being relieved of command. He wished to Christ he wasn't here delivering this stinking message.

"OK I'll tell you; you were wrong Colonel. Never mind what the book says. What you do out here cannot be compromised by a show trial with you as the star performer: a bedraggled old man they captured, an old man with an easily verified past. We've made your pilots anonymous now, all their records are in special storage and they won't see the light of day until long after the two of us are floating around up there in heaven. If you fuck things up out here, we'll lose political support overnight and we won't have the information you're supposed to get:

information we can all agree is vital to the interests of the United States."

He leaned over and extracted a paper from the leather briefcase.

"Here. This is something you need to think about."

Tuck took the paper and read: Orders relieving him of command of the 337$^{th}$ Special Operations Wing and appointing a man he did not know.

"There's no effective date on these orders. What is this?"

"A warning. Keep playing Errol Flynn and you'll end up in charge of nuts and bolts at Maxwell Field, Alabama. Or you might get court-martialed. There are plenty of officers who'd kill for this job, me among them."

Tuck sat thinking in the wretched tropical heat. He loved the Army, or the Air Force as it was now called. He had completed just over seventeen years of service. He counted on finishing with honor and distinction, but he needed another ten years to achieve that goal. And there weren't too many jobs out there in the civilian world for a middle-aged fighter pilot. There was no choice for him, not really.

"All right. I understand. I'll stop flying missions now, and I'll do the best I can for these pilots. They need it. They deserve it. But it's a piss-poor way to run a railroad, General."

Overdorf studied the stiffly erect figure across the desk a long moment, making sure he wasn't being woofed by this unorthodox man. He smiled cautiously.

"That's the spirit. You know, General Stenzell will be mighty relieved to hear this. He thinks a great deal of you, expects you to keep climbing the ladder. And so forth."

He nodded to himself.

"OK, that's what I came for. I guess I'd like a shower and a bed now."

He turned as the Exec came to escort him out.

"No backsliding now, Colonel. Believe me, it would be fatal."

# Chapter 27

Len Toa headed the brief investigation, and now he spoke for the Peoples Republic of China.

"The Devils came and they photographed our most precious resource. They did other damaging things we have not yet evaluated. They raped the Peoples Republic at a time when we struggle with the KunMintong, when we can ill afford exposure such as this. And you…you kissed them gently and sent them on their way unharmed. You have failed in your work, you have allowed grave damage to occur, and you have failed the people. What can you tell this Court that would bring mercy to our hearts?"

General Sun Po Lee looked at the small group arrayed at the table before him: a group of Party Committeemen and the Russian. This was bad, the very worst. He might have had a chance with a military court. He knew his fate, now he could only hope to spare his family and aging parents from official wrath.

"It is true that my forces could not stop these Americans with their new airplanes. I take entire responsibility for the failure. But in doing so, I would fail to an even higher degree if I did not point out the many things I have needed and not received. The radar at Chengdu was not working properly again; we had no warning. We must have warning to be properly prepared. The Soviets have supplied us with fine new airplanes but our young men are barely trained, actually just students, and they were not equal to the enemy in maneuvering skill. Before, with the B-29's, we had Russian pilots and the big bombers could not maneuver. That is not the case now; these fellows fly lighter, more maneuverable aircraft. Given time, our young pilots will improve and be effective. And our ammunition is unreliable, the fuses often fail and we don't know why. We need technical assistance, technical training."

The Russian registered comprehension. The Committeemen were impassive. General Po saw how it would be. He had a final comment.

"But these things were all within my area of responsibility and I was unable to make the necessary improvements before these people came with their new airplanes and their treacherous low altitude approach to our heartland. Now I can only ask you to remember how well my forces have done against the B-29's. Our performance took time, took months of study and drill. I ask you to remember all this and to spare my family. That is all."

Len Toa looked left and right along the table.

"The Committee will witness punishment."

Lee's elbows were bound tight behind his back with a rawhide string. He was seized by the hair and dragged outside to kneel in the dirt, ringed by militiamen to his rear and the Committee members to his front. He stared passively at the dusty clay before him, his mind moving away from reality. He had no power here; there was no way to stop the proceeding. Toa nodded to the militia Captain. A soldier behind Lee stepped forward and bayoneted the kneeling man in the back.

Sun Po Lee had interviewed male and female survivors of the Nanking Occupation in 1937: the Japanese had used many of them for bayonet practice. Some reported no pain at the initial thrust; they said the pain came later. Lee had believed them, but now he found it was not true, he felt agony stab at his kidney and up into his lungs. A thick oak club came down on the top of his head and the pain ended.

Major Abram Karpov watched the execution impassively, but he was horrified. An officer convicted of this sort of dereliction in the Russian Army would have been shot in private, with some minimal level of dignity.

Now he was in charge of the Air Defenses protecting this goddamned barren facility, at the end of a very long supply line. He was in need of exactly the things Lee had mentioned. A knot of fear and disgust churned his intestines as he wondered how long he would have before the investigators came looking for him with charges of ineffectiveness. He would do his best, but in the end he would never allow himself to fall victim to this sort of barbarous inhumanity.

# Chapter 28

Abner Day summarized his material and suggested a next step.

"Gentlemen, five different sets of first generation Chinese-Americans, each from a different ethnic background, each fluent in a different dialect, have analyzed these tapes. Your own Science Advisor has been involved. There can be no question that the Hotan facility is meant to assemble lightweight atomic weapons suitable for use by intercontinental range aircraft. Opinions vary as to an initial operational date, but the latest date is in the early summer of 1951, two years from now. The CIA is supporting an earlier date sometime in 1950. With this remarkable intelligence coup at hand, I can unhesitatingly recommend an end to the B-29 program. I refer to an immediate conclusion of the flight operations. We should dismantle the program and return the aircraft to their parent squadrons now. We need not lose another life in these outmoded machines."

Heads nodded. He was emboldened and played his other card.

"The P-61 program should also be discontinued. It has yielded rich dividends, but now we gather only corroborative material, nothing new. I have conferred with General Stenzell and we agree the training of new P-61 pilots here in the United States should be discontinued now. The overseas Wing should cease operations as soon as practicable."

The Vice President squinted his eyes theatrically.

"You're half-right, Abner."

This was something Day did not want to hear. He paused a moment to regroup, his mind working overtime. There was a note of disapproval in his voice when he continued.

"Finally, gentlemen, we must now address the financial requirements for an extension of the DEW line southward from Anchorage to San Diego. Cost estimates for this extension are being prepared now, but the program will add approximately 175 billion dollars to the presently authorized budget. Unfortunately the bulk of those funds will be required in Fiscal Year 1950 and we must amend the budget just sent over to the Hill for Authorization. Stringent changes are required, changes that may precipitate unrest within the Administration, Congress, and perhaps even the voting public. That's it, gentlemen, I await your guidance."

Day sat back, removed a stenographers' notebook from his briefcase and drew a gold pen from his breast pocket. He looked to the Vice President. Sunlight from the window at his back made him look like nothing but a shadow.

Glendennan slouched in a high-backed chair across the table, his hand on his chin, index finger aligned with his lips. He raised his eyebrows and spoke through the finger.

"You tell him, Peter."

Peter Sumner, White House Chief of Staff, swept a leather case up from the floor and plopped it loudly on the desk, then rummaged and pulled out a paper. His eyes remained fixed on the paper as he read.

"We, the Vice President and the White House Chief of Staff, contest the findings of the Hotan ad-hoc Intelligence Committee, finding them unsupportable with the present level of raw intelligence data. The Administration believes that a great deal of additional data and analysis will be required before reprogramming funds for Fiscal Years 1950, 51, and 52. You are directed to continue the gathering and refinement of intelligence data on the Hotan facility and its associated sites, presenting such information to the Administration as additional significant, supportable conclusions become apparent."

Day was appalled.

"Peter, let me remind you that I am a member of the Administration you so blithely quote in your statement, not the enemy. Let me further remind you that General Stenzell and I have been appearing regularly in this room with a unified message for the Office of the President: keep some funding flexibility in the out-years in case this thing should come out badly—as it has."

He looked in his project notebook, frowning at the heavy silence in the room but resolved to plow forward.

"Our first appearance was July 1948 and our financial message was the same then as now—keep your options open on this thing. We no longer gather new information, we are repeating ourselves. Continuing *Project Heat Lightning* at this point is an obscenity. I demand a better explanation than yours before we continue to risk the lives of those young men."

Glendennan rose from his slouch and tapped the blue flesh beneath his jaw with the top of his hand. He had a late fund-raiser this evening and still hoped for an afternoon nap. He did not relish opposing Abner Day, a legal scholar and a man the public found highly credible.

"Abner, let me put it this way, off the record: Fiscal '50 is wrapped up, there will be no changes. Fiscal '51 will be a pre-election year and the last thing we want is a disruptive new war program stirring up the voters. So you need to go away and very carefully consider options to cope with this Hotan thing: inexpensive options. We simply do not want a funding revolt over this very speculative new issue."

He turned to Stenzell and his face was defiant; he was enjoying the contest. He knew who would win.

"John, get us a program of early research into the remote interception of off-shore attackers, something academic like that Bell Telephone Laboratories thing, the Nike series of anti-aircraft missiles."

Stenzell shook his head.

"The new Nike Ajax interceptor is still in Advanced Development; hardly a reality. And even if it were available in large numbers, the radius of action is too short. The maximum range for an aircraft intercept is only 15 miles, less than the damage circle for a medium sized atomic bomb. An explosion 15 miles from a coastal city would be devastating. There would be hundreds of thousands of casualties. No sir, the only dependable defense against airborne atomic attack from the Pacific is long-range radar and interceptor aircraft. The situation will not change for a dozen years, if ever."

Sumner was stuffing papers in his briefcase, not listening. Glendennan rose from his chair.

"Thank you for a most compelling meeting, gentlemen. The intelligence is outstanding. Keep working. This meeting is over."

# Chapter 29

Al had gunship duty today in the F-15. He was flying *DarkHorse*, orbiting over the Tan Lun Mountains watching Trapnell and Dave Rey as they plodded down the microwave link designated T9. He had been up here a dozen times in P-61's now and he knew the score. He was alert and edgy and determined not to repeat the addled performance on his first F-15 mission. The guns were armed, the gun sight was warmed up and he had jettisoned the near-empty external wing tanks for better maneuverability. If the strangely docile green fighters came after the P-61's today he would be ready.

Almost an hour at the target now and it was time to go—past time. He wanted to give them a call and suggest an exit, but he knew he wouldn't. They were veterans now, too. They knew their business; they would break off when they were finished. Moments later he saw Trapnell turn and accelerate across the desert floor. Rey followed an instant later and Al began to relax, they would all be out of here in minutes.

Al turned to the exit heading and slowed to get behind and cover them. His eye caught a flicker where the grasslands ended at the edge of the desert just as the left wing blocked the view. He rolled up to the vertical and saw four YAKs moving across the desert floor on a course that would intercept Rey.

"DIESEL TWO three bandits your ten o'clock high, take evasive action. DIESEL LEADER continue exit you are not threatened."

Al rolled into a diving turn and leaned into the gun sight, maneuvering until the enemy aircraft were centered in the three concentric glowing orange circles. The inner circle was a series of dots that would flash when he was in range. He looked up, sweeping the empty sky for other aircraft and once again felt a floating-away sensation. Things were turning too fast and he needed to get ahead of the action. Something inside him retreated and he understood that his civilized mind was taking refuge in a safe place.

The YAKs were lighter and more maneuverable than his heavy F-15. He would not dogfight with them. But he was faster and he would use that advantage in a single high-speed firing pass and climbing exit. He remembered the hand-lettered sign on the briefing room blackboard: NEVER FIGHT BELOW 300 MPH!

Only one of the YAKs was there when he got back to his gun sight. The other three had disappeared. He guessed they were coming for him, doubted they would be able to get into a firing position even if they were climbing toward him. The remaining YAK was firing at DIESEL TWO now but the tracers were going wide, still out of range. He glanced at the airspeed indicator: 550 mph, far above the maximum permissible airspeed. He believed in airspeed limits, he had always felt nervous near the redline airspeed. In his mind he saw the airplane disintegrating into bright aluminum fragments that showered down to the desert floor below as his body hurtled through on its final trip. But Rey needed him badly; *DarkHorse* would just have to hold together.

Nearly in range now and he fired a short burst, hoping to unsettle the attacker. The rounds floated out and separated around the green airplane, but they were ignored. The enemy airplane kept firing short bursts at Rey.

He closed at a tremendous rate and now the YAK was about to pass under his nose. He rolled upside down and pulled hard on the control yoke, but the controls were very heavy at this speed and he could not generate much nose movement. His hand went to the elevator trim tab and he cranked hard up-elevator. Now the nose moved nicely toward the target, but the heavy acceleration pressed him down and his vision dimmed to a small cone. Al knew about g-forces; he could dial up the size of his visual cone by controlling the g forces. More elevator trim made his visual cone small, less elevator trim opened the cone up until his vision returned to normal.

Now the green airplane crossed his narrow field of view, climbing sharply as the pilot broke off his attack. Al rolled and matched the climb, totally concentrated, not looking behind for the other attackers. The YAK pilot commenced wing-rocking aileron turns: a scissors maneuver designed to cause Al to overrun and get ahead of the YAK so the pursuer would become the victim. Al felt a growing alarm—these were not the passive pilots he had encountered in back in May, these guys knew what they were doing.

He chopped the throttles to stay behind and managed to turn with the YAK for an instant. Now the fighter came across his nose and he fired a burst and saw solid hits: several panels flew off the machine before it rolled hard right and disappeared.

Al turned to clear the area and a second YAK was head-on right in front of him, 400 yards out, its guns winking brightly at him as they fired. The aircraft passed twenty feet above him and he glimpsed an elaborate heraldic shield painted on the fuselage just aft of the canopy and immediately felt a hard aerodynamic bump as he flew through its wake.

He turned and dived after the YAK he had hit, hoping it was sufficiently crippled for him to catch up. He tried to understand how the second YAK had maneuvered to a firing position, but could not. Things were not going well. He found his victim in a steep dive two thousand feet below and slammed the throttles open in pursuit. Something was wrong, the pilot made no attempt to pull up as they approached the desert floor. When Al was sure the fighter could not avoid ground impact he loosed a long cannon burst, not to hit the machine but to record the impact on his gun camera film.

As he pulled up, there was a din in the cockpit, like hail, and he felt a terrific jolt on his right foot as something flashed past him outside on the right; going up. Al slammed into a vertical turn and lifted his numb leg. He watched reluctantly as his foot appeared above the gloom in the lower cockpit. He was relieved to see he still had the foot: the heel of his flying boot had been shot off. Fear knotted his insides as he numbly looked at holes in the side of the cockpit and saw the badly bent rudder pedal.

Now he wanted to be away from these unpredictable aircraft, he had no desire to continue this uneven engagement. He pulled up in a maximum performance climb, panicked, wanting only to be away from the danger, not clearing behind for enemy aircraft.

He thought maybe he was out of danger as he reached 18,000 feet. He banked sharply several times and there were no aircraft below him. He didn't think it was possible for either of the planes to be above him now. He reached 25,000 feet and that was high enough: he set a course due south. He would try to get across the border into Indian airspace before heading back to Burma, staying parallel to the border. Hopefully these voracious hunters would not enter neutral airspace.

He was turned backward checking the tail boom for damage when orange slashes of tracer ammunition came at him again. The attack ended before Al could react, and seconds later a second green fighter appeared off his left wing, at his altitude and on a crossing course. Where the fuck was the other one?

He was being herded back toward China. For a moment he was paralyzed by unreasoning fright, his mouth tasted like copper and he could tell his breath was foul. He bored straight ahead, taking no evasive action. The fighter closed from the left slowly and Al could see the same heraldic shield on the fuselage. Somehow, the pilot had climbed with him, stayed with him for miles and now he would attack. Al felt as light as smoke; so light he wanted to laugh and he wanted to live. He collected himself and checked the cockpit: the gun switch was still on; he had never thought to turn it off.

Now the green fighter was flying parallel several hundred yards off his wing, no longer trying to close with him. Al looked across and he could see the pilot. He seemed larger than the pilots he had downed in May, perhaps a person of European descent. The man held a camera, apparently trying for a picture of *DarkHorse.* Without thought Al turned into the little fighter, on a collision course. *DarkHorse's* nose came to bear on the green airplane and he fired a cannon burst and saw hits; blue-white flashes of vaporized aluminum. His guns stopped firing and he heard the empty chuffing of the pneumatic charging system. He was out of ammunition. The mindless wheezing cycling was a dirge; the loneliest sound in the world. He rolled upside down and pulled the nose through while slamming both throttles forward, breaking the lead seals that marked War Emergency power, a power level that would damage the engines in minutes. He could goddamn well outrun this guy in a dive. He was pretty sure he could anyway. Maybe.

Twenty minutes later the sky around him was empty and now he was sure it was over. The tension started to come off and his body let him down: he became dopey and his mind ached for sleep, his fingers trembled from an excess of adrenalin as he moved the controls. He turned to the southeast: he would cut across India to intercept the Burmese border halfway home, taking five hundred miles off the return trip. Strictly against orders, but he didn't care. Enough was enough.

Two hours later he crossed into Burma at Mt. Berteau, angling toward two contrails high above him in the afternoon sky. He came level with the black aircraft three hundred yards off their left side and clicked his transmitter button three times in greeting. The pilots looked at him and nodded. Rey motioned for him to come over and join up.

Trapnell had a surprise for them as they flew across the coastline south of Chittagong.

"DIESEL LEADER has low hydraulic pressure. I guess one of them shooters up there nicked a line somewhere. Come over and take a look, DIESEL 2."

Al maneuvered under *MoonFly* and inspected the belly.

"I can see a bunch of small holes aft of the left engine cowling on the outboard side, and there's a pretty big tear in the fuselage right by the wing trailing edge. Looks like red hydraulic fluid stains all along the engine nacelle. I guess you just pumped out all the juice. You want to go on in and land now?"

"I still have 300 gallons in the fuselage tanks. I think I'll try to get the gear down, then fly around out here a while to lighten up. Can you stay with me?"

"I'm down to 150 gallons, the fight took me down pretty good. Tell you what, I'll stay up here another 30 minutes until we can check your gear, then I have to land. OK?"

"Yep. Y'all stay behind me there while I try to pump up the emergency hydraulic system. DIESEL 3 you go on in now, no sense in all of us being up here."

They orbited together five miles off the island, making lazy circles in the afternoon sky. Finally Trapnell had to give up.

"No hydraulic pressure Al, must of holed the emergency system too. I'm going to put the gear handle down now and see if I can jerk them into place."

Al moved out to the side and watched the three wheels descend slightly below the aircraft and then hang up.

"They're out, Doug, but they're not down."

*MoonFly* suddenly zoomed skyward and Al followed him up 500 feet.

"OK, the nosewheel looks locked down now, and the right main wheel too, but the left is still hung up. Try some skids."

Trapnell went off down the sky skidding violently left and right. The left main landing gear appeared to extend as Al flew underneath again.

"Hold still now, Doug, I'm right underneath you. I'm looking up into your wheel well. It's too dark in there, start a left turn so the sunlight gets up there."

He watched as Trapnell's wings banked up and sunlight illuminated the wheel well.

"There's shrapnel damage, the lock pin is smashed. I don't think it'll ever go in the hole. And the tire's flat: you're going to need to land real gently and hold it absolutely straight or that left gear will fold up like spaghetti. You won't have brakes, so drag it in on the flaps as slow as you can. Maybe you ought to think about bailing out."

"Roger all that. No parachutes today, I should be able to get down OK. Thanks for the help, you better go down there now and land. If I cream this thing I'll block the runway."

Al landed and raced *DarkHorse* back up the taxiway far too fast at 50 mph. He carelessly nosed the plane into the first parking revetment, shut the fuel off and killed the master switch, not bothering with a shutdown procedure. He was down the nose gear ladder in seconds, sprinting for the runway threshold, limping on his heelless boot. The crash crew and medics were already there, lights flashing. Al climbed into the fire engine cab to listen to the radio traffic. He could see *MoonFly* circling lazily a mile off the surf line, like an oversized flying insect, its feet hanging down in the breeze. Trapnell had to give up his fuel burning orbit at 6:00 PM, there were only minutes of daylight left.

"OK, that's it, I'm coming in now."

Al watched and worried. Trapnell was the best there was, but it would be a tricky thing. The big ship came around in a slow descending turn and the setting sun glinted off the canopy as he slowed and deployed the huge barn-door flaps. Al thought he was a little low, but then realized he was trying for a touchdown right at the threshold to utilize the entire runway for slowing without brakes.

*MoonFly* flashed across the runway threshold and the two rescue vehicles bolted down the runway behind, intent on the closest possible chase. The touchdown was perfect; the nose rose ever so gently and the main gear kissed softly onto the crushed coral. Trapnell was holding the nose high and utilizing wing drag to help slow down. It looked perfect to Al. Then, halfway down the runway, without warning, the damaged left gear collapsed inward and the plane fell heavily onto the engine nacelle.

A cloud of coral dust erupted and continued, thick billows of creamy pink dust arching into the sky as the plane skidded down the strip barely slowing as it floated across the gravel. Al's peripheral vision caught motion at the edge of the cloud and his fighter pilot's eye was able to track the peculiar boomerang-like motion of two broken propeller blades as they ascended from the cloud flying skyward. The blades traveled far out over the lagoon and then turned and started back toward land. One fell in the lagoon and the second buried itself upright in sand at the tide line, looking like Merlin's sword. Now his attention returned to the skidding aircraft as the fire truck charged down the runway a half-mile behind the dust cloud. Al didn't think he could be more tired, his mouth felt like cotton and he knew his eyes were blood red. He prayed there would be no fire.

*MoonFly* skidded slowly off the runway at the 7000-foot mark, sliding down a boulder-lined berm to end tail-high in the palmetto scrub just above the beach line. There was no fire. Al's heart lifted; it looked pretty good. The fire engine braked to a stop on the runway above the wreckage a minute later and he was first out of the truck scrambling down the runway embankment, headed around the tail of the airplane to help get Trapnell out. Maybe he was unharmed; maybe he wouldn't need any help. Al heard the sharp crack of a pistol as he neared the pilot pod and saw the three medics who had been in the ambulance ahead of the fire truck. They were standing in front of wreckage, but not moving in.

The nose of the aircraft was severed cleanly just forward of the pilots seat. Trapnell sat firmly strapped in, pointing a pistol at the medics. His face was ashen beneath the powdery coral dust that covered everything. He looked peaceful and sleepy, like a mime covered in white powder. Except for the red ovals where his legs had been. His legs were gone, severed just above the knee.

One of the medics moved forward cautiously.

"Aw, Jesus Christ sir, let us help you. We can help you now, we've got to stop the bleeding."

Trapnell shook the pistol at the medic and turned to Al.

"Propeller blade did it, Al, came right through the cockpit and cut the airplane in two. Cut me in two. Ain't that the goddamned luck?"

Al moved forward without thought and Trapnell fired again, the bullet passed Al's neck with a puff of air.

"Doug, I'm your friend. You're not going to shoot me, I'm coming in there right now."

Trapnell leveled the gun and Al looked into the wide muzzle.

"No you're not, boy. You're like a brother to me, but I'll sure enough kill you. I ainta goin' home thisaway: a fucking cripple. Y'all just stand there 'til the clock runs out."

Trapnell spoke in a childlike voice, one Al had never heard before.

The senior medic turned to his associates, " Get your ass up there and get five units of whole blood and get back here. Move it."

Al looked at the medic and saw hopelessness.

"Doug, at least let this guy come in and give you a shot."

Trapnell's eyes had been at half-mast, now they opened and regarded Al calmly.

"Don't need no shot, can't feel a thing. I'm just lightheaded, sort of in a dream. Oh, I know what happened, I can see it. But it's like it happened in…another time. Not bad at all."

They watched Trapnell bleed for several minutes before his head fell forward on his chest. Al was on him in an instant, pulling the gun from limp fingers. The senior medic was right there too, struggling to apply tourniquets to the stumps. They lifted the unconscious pilot and carried him through wreckage to a spot of grassy cover. His ashen face looked serene in the dying light.

Al sat in the dusty saw grass waiting for the medics to bring a stretcher, listening to Trapnell's soft unconscious moans. He wondered how it had all come to this. They were just kids, no one ever imagined something like this could happen. They had been so excited by the opportunity to fly, to learn new things; and now this nightmare. For Doug it would be a lifetime of nightmares, it would be never-ending.

Soon the ambulance came bumping down the rocky runway berm toward them. Al's hands moved lightly across the saw grass, drawing comfort from the roughness. He looked at Trapnell and he looked at the massive wrecked airplane looming behind them in the tropical twilight. He felt like a poorly prepared actor in a surreal melodrama. His mind would not grip the horror. He felt ill and feverish and thought he must be getting the flu.

Al found one of the legs as he trudged back up to the runway. It was trapped in a palmetto bush and the shoe end was up. He was glad he didn't have to look at the cut end. The boot was neatly tied with a double knot. He ran his finger over the toe and saw that it was well polished under the dust: Trapnell was neat and orderly. He tugged the leg free of the bush and turned back for the ambulance. It was surprisingly heavy and he was sickened that a thing this massive could be detached from the man he knew so well, from his friend.

He watched the ancient faded blue Dodge ambulance jounce up the runway side to the top. The siren sounded as the vehicle accelerated back down the runway. He remembered his mother saying 'You can't ever go back in time, Al, that's what memories are for'. Still, he wondered if there was a way to stop time and go back thirty minutes and play the thing differently. He wondered if anything in the world was worth the price Douglas Trapnell had just paid.

Underneath the horror he felt a terrible fear that he too might be maimed before this was over. Given a choice, he would a thousand times prefer death. But he knew he would not be given a choice.

## Chapter 30

Rudenko moved the phone away and shook his head, unwilling to take more abuse.

"My dear Abram-Ilyich, you really must stop cursing. We are comrades in the great Soviet march to equality, that is certain. But until we arrive at our destination, I am a General and you are a Major. Your vituperation discourages me and reduces my eagerness to help you in the troubles you describe. Summarize, please."

1500 miles away, Karpov closed his eyes. He wanted to scream at this sluggish bureaucrat, this container full of nothing but air. Instead, he breathed deeply and centered himself.

"As you wish, General Rudenko. First let me express my deep gratitude at the shipment of new YAK-9M's. While there are only four, and I requested twelve, I must tell you we will make effective use of them against these goddamned Americans. You ask what else I need? Well, I am in desperate need of twenty ZSU23-4's on tracked mounts so we can move them through the desert. Hopefully they will be the radar-directed kind. You are perhaps aware we have only the old Bofors40-4's, left over from the war before last. They are dangerously unreliable, my dear General. They should be junked. And I need 2000 rounds of proximity-fused 105mm anti-aircraft shells that will actually burst near an airplane. These fucking things we use here can be fired into a mountain without exploding. And I need 4000 rounds of 88mm, for the same reason. That is all."

A long silence ensued. Karpov could hear something being tapped. He thought it might be a bunch of keys banging on a desktop. He hoped this briefcase-dragging functionary would get off his ass and do something for him. He needed help desperately.

"That was better Karpov. Not perfect, but better. I am responsible for the five largest air defense sectors in the East. Do you know how many of these unpleasant conversations I endure? Do you know of the shortages plaguing the Eastern Supply Administration?"

"I am sure your challenges are without limit, comrade. As you know, I must send a report on the efficiency of our logistic support to Leningrad Headquarters each Quarter. I am preparing the Third-Quarter Report now. What shall I say of the Eastern Supply Administration?"

"Now, now, my man; let us not be viperish. I will send you six ZSU23-4's. I will send you 300 rounds of 105mm ammunition. I will send you 1100 rounds of 88mm ammunition. That is all I can do."

"Agreed."

"And because you have been such a good fellow, I will send you four new graduates of the ZSU Radar Gunnery course."

"I weep for joy."

# Chapter 31

"LIME 6, take the runway. Take the runway now."

The call jolted Al awake; he had fallen asleep on the taxiway awaiting clearance for takeoff. The F-15 had been idling for almost ten minutes, waiting for his hand like a patient horse. Al sat slumped in the seat harness, head on his chest. Fortunately he had locked the brakes or *CalamityJane* would now be off in deep sand at the end of the taxiway. Try explaining that to the flight surgeon, he thought grimly. Panicked and embarrassed, he considered skipping the takeoff checklist.

Common sense kicked in. He took a deep breath, closed his eyes for a moment to clear the confusion of sleep and started a careful execution of the checklist. Finally he read the last item, Cowl Flaps Full Open, and he depressed a small switch on the left console while watching an instrument that contained a tiny rendition of a cowl flap.

"LIME 6 rolling. Call departure at Bandong Non Directional Beacon."

Tuck had planted runway markers at 1000-foot intervals down the runway. Al pulled the control yoke back smartly at marker 6 and the nose came up, but *CalamityJane* was shockingly overweight and she would not lift. His hands went to the throttle quadrant, ready to push up to War Emergency power if necessary. He tried again at marker 7 and she reluctantly lifted, touched down again, and started a sluggish climb. The airspeed indicator showed 138 mph. Al grimaced as he selected more wing flap extension; marker 8 was the end of the runway and blowouts were a growing menace at these high liftoff speeds. *CalamityJane* was 3800 pounds above the maximum weight allowed by her designers: every ounce was needed for his heavy ammunition load and the extra fuel to orbit in the target area. He would stay longer in the target area than the P-61's. He would be on-station before the first P-61 arrived at the target and would not leave until the last was safely away.

Northrop factory engineers had been consulted about the overweight condition. They were a serious, whispering, head-shaking group who eventually guessed that the overweight was tolerable if the landing gear and wing structure were inspected for cracks after every flight. They delivered the final report verbally: no one was willing to author a written report. The pilots heard the report and agreed, but they were not reassured.

He watched anxiously until the vertical speed indicator settled on 300 feet per minute-up and then slammed the gear handle up. Both engines thundered at maximum takeoff power, shooting thirty-five feet of orange-blue flame from the exhaust stacks back along the underside of the wing to disappear in the blackness behind. The fiery exhaust reflected off the inboard aspect of both engine nacelles to produce bright light in the cockpit, spoiling his night vision. He made the first power reduction as he climbed through 1000 feet. Most of the orange glare disappeared, leaving him squinting in the cockpit darkness to read the instruments.

Moments later a yellow light at the top of the instrument panel winked on for a few seconds and then off. The light indicated he had passed over a radio beacon floating in the sea five miles off the end of the runway, a marker for alignment with the runway on instrument departures. He pressed the transmitter button.

"LIME 6 Bandong Marker.1600 feet climbing on course."

Unless there was an emergency he would not use the radio again for fifteen hours.

The navigation light on his right wingtip was a greenish halo. He was in thick clouds now and he would remain on instruments for several hours. It was mid-October, far past the height of the summer monsoon season throughout India and Southeast Asia. But a stubbornly persistent high pressure cell in the ocean southwest of India continued to drive thick wet air into South Central China to prolong the three-month rainy season. Later, in the high desert of the Takli Makan, the air would be clear; moisture was a rarity in the target area.

He watched the airspeed increase to 275 mph as he adjusted power. He knew *CalamityJane* so well he could guess at the proper power setting. Early on he had sawed at the throttle a dozen times before getting the proper combination of airspeed and climb rate. Now he would cruise-climb for three hours, ascending to 23,000 feet as he reached the Chinese border.

He drowsed for an hour, and then took radio bearings on Vientane, Mandalay, and Hai Phong to plot a ground position. He was about 20 miles inside the Indian border, but unconcerned because India had never registered a protest over airspace violations. He reached to a dial on the autopilot panel and changed heading from 032 to 035 degrees. He would be back on course in 30 minutes.

Al was bored and strangely nervous now. He tried for music on the ADF but received only static. He watched with vacant interest as the autopilot made tiny random corrections; the rudder pedals moved slightly, the control column moved forward and aft, and the control wheel turned. The autopilot was a box of vacuum tubes, resistors, switches and coils sitting just forward of his seat under the floorboards. It was a magical device: somehow the inanimate collection of parts kept him on course and level. He opened the detent on his shoulder harness and leaned forward to place his hands on the floor and absorb the warmth that radiated up from the unit: the autopilot was his comforting friend. He was here. Isla Matton was far in the past and he could not know what lay ahead. Here, the autopilot was his friend, the only thing helping him. It was all very sad and his eyes filled with tears. He took a deep ragged breath and sniffed. Jesus; he was losing his sanity, falling down the hole.

He poked nervously at the controls to provoke the autopilot, first jabbing the rudder pedals to swing the nose, then slapping the control yoke with the flat of his hand, causing *CalamityJane* to porpoise. He mentally measured the period of the oscillation and arrived at 23 seconds. This was pleasing; the flight manual listed a pitch oscillation time of 19 seconds under nominal conditions but he was still heavy with fuel and flying in thin high altitude air; two factors that would account for the extra four seconds.

The flat early morning sunlight highlighted dust motes floating lazily about the F-15 cockpit. He smiled to himself; he would never see a dust mote in the drafty P-61. The odd clumsy three-level greenhouse of the P-61 was a mass of unsealed leaks that allowed chill air and rain to pour in. But the problem had been solved in the F-15. The designers shaved the bulbous top off the fuselage and fitted a pleasingly sealed bubble canopy.

He was still bored and there was yet thirty minutes to pitch-over and the low altitude approach. He occupied himself reading words silkscreened on the instruments and controls: labels, instructions, warnings, and military nomenclature: NO AUTOPILOT BELOW 150MPH, PROPELLER CONTROL FORWARD MAX RPM, RADIO FUSE BOX, MANIFOLD PRESSURE MAX LIMIT 66 INCHES MERCURY.

Al loved nomenclature for its ability to classify even the most obscure items. He craned his neck around awkwardly to see the base of the gun sight mounted above the instrument panel. There, affixed by four rivets, was a brass plate summarizing the complex unit: GUNSIGHT, AN43, INCANDESCENT FILAMENT, DEFLECTION COMPUTING, SPERRY. He smiled to himself; there in seven simple words was everything Uncle Sam needed to know about the gun sight, everything a supply officer needed to find the proper warehouse niche for the unit.

Suddenly and without warning his chest constricted and he felt vague and featherweight and remote, as if his head was swooping upward out of the airplane. He could not breathe. The awful fear that came now in unguarded moments attacked him and he had no defense. His face and armpits broke out in heavy sweat; he smelled the stink of fear and tasted copper in his dry mouth.

Panicked, without thought, he reached into the map case and scrabbled open a map of India. His fingers ran across coordinate lines. Yes, there it was: the 3200-foot airstrip at Patna, India. If he turned due south now he could cross Nepal and be down and safe in less than two hours.

Then, suddenly and miraculously, he would be out of it. Out of this awful contest that could only end one way. Out of reading the weekly postings of missing pilots. Out of the terrible fear of maiming that had claimed him so often since Doug Trapnell went home legless. Out of the awful soulless mechanical briefings that consigned each of them to hell once a week. Free of the faceless bureaucrats, safe in Washington, whose demands grew and grew as the pilot complement dwindled toward nothing. Out of the sleepless nights that more and more sapped his strength and courage. Out of the relentless need for alcohol and the hangovers on flying days that slowed him and could easily kill him. Out of the fear of going down in the jungle and dying slowly in the endless green tropical forest that stretched for a thousand miles.

He would land and surrender himself, confess to war crimes and take his chances with an Oriental system of justice. He would hope the Indians did not turn him over to the United States for that would certainly be the end of him. His honor would be gone. His brothers would turn away, embarrassed by his cowardice. But he would live. God Almighty, he would live.

He reached for the control yoke to start the turn, then hugged his arms to his chest and sobbed in fear and pity.

For the first dozen missions he had been sustained by invincibility: he saw others die, but surely they had made grave mistakes. He was better; he would not make their mistakes. Then, when the Russian almost killed him back in August, that thin tissue tore away. He was left to fly on raw courage, but his courage withered before the awful reality of the missions. Then he continued because he could not let down his fellow pilots, his brothers. Now he flew because it seemed he had always flown and there was nothing else to be done.

Somewhere along this terrible path he had accepted death. He would die out here doing the best he could and he would never go home, never see Mandy again. But his body did not accept death. It failed him with primitive cunning. Doc House, the Wing Flight Surgeon, saw through his act. Doc had already recommended that he be relieved of combat flying. In the end Tuck overruled the Flight Surgeon: he needed Al right here flying, he didn't think things were all that bad, and he bought Al's argument, at least for the time being. But there would be more, Al knew that.

Almost an hour passed in his shattered apprehensive retreat from reality. He slowly became aware of his situation. He had flown past the low altitude descent point by more than a hundred miles. He folded the map of India and replaced it in the map case, then gulped in a deep shuddering breath. He turned off the autopilot and pushed the controls forward.

He would carry on, he did not know what else to do.

*     *     *

He concentrated on executing absolutely perfect circles now. It was something to do while he waited. He was just low enough to be shielded from the Hotan Acquisition Radar by the Kun Lun Mountains, yet close enough to the T3 and T6 links to get in fast if he was needed. The panic was gone now and he was deeply, mortally ashamed. He knew there would be more attacks in the future and he hoped for the strength to suppress them.

The unexpected call startled him.

"LIME 2 hit, going down near Qira. LIME 6 can you assist?"

LIME 2 was his roommate in Primary flight training, Art Trumbauer.

# Chapter 32

Mandy was trying to get out more, to be social. She reluctantly accepted a dinner date with Roger Beemis, a student in her evening bookkeeping class. She drove her own car and met him at the restaurant. There had been a strained ten-minute silence while they waited for service. She smiled encouragingly. He finally spoke.

"So where did you say you work, Mandy?"

"I work for Mr. Barlow at the funeral home. He says I'm his bookkeeper, but I really just collect the invoices and charge slips and send them to our accountant at the end of the month. And I answer the phone and take dictation. But I'm learning more so I can be truly useful. What do you do, Roger?"

The waitress arrived and Roger turned to Mandy.

"What?"

"Just a glass of wine, please. Something light."

"OK. A glass of white wine and a triple Jack, water back. Where were we? Oh yeah, I work over at Pittsburgh Grainery. We store wheat and hops, and we mill the grain. I'm second shift foreman, the youngest foreman ever. I work hard, I want to amount to something."

"It's wonderful that you're so ambitious. How did you get to be the youngest foreman?"

"It's easy. Work hard and do more than they expect you to do, work the twenty-hour day. You live alone?"

They were in a log-cabin steakhouse: sawdust on the floor, checkered tablecloths, and a four-piece western band. Not knowing, she had worn a rose-satin sheath and heels. She leaned forward to answer, straining to be heard above the band.

"No, I live with my folks over on South Second."

"Oh. Well I guess that's pretty good. Me, I have an apartment over in Bay City, got it the first year out of high school. Two bedrooms and a kitchen, the whole shot. Of course I'm not there much when I work, just in and out. It gets a workout on date-nights, though, I can tell you that."

The sunburned face grinned hugely at her. She struggled for a new topic. The waitress arrived again.

"You folks ready to order?"

Roger looked at Mandy's drink.

"Ooh, not going down very fast, is it? Well, hit me one more time. We'll order later."

Mandy signaled the waitress a half-hour later and ordered dinner for both of them. Roger was shouting at her above the band, something about his brothers and football. She smiled.

"How do you like the class? I really struggle with the homework, but I know I'm learning. I like Mr. Butterworth, he's a pretty good teacher; don't you think so?"

"Butterworth? Mr.Cary Butterworth? Isn't that a hell of a name, I ask you? Well, I tell you, I don't get some of it. But I don't have to, I just want to scrape by and get the course on my employment record. PG is paying and I don't get reimbursed if I flunk."

Mandy finished her dinner and turned to Roger. He was on his fifth bourbon. His dinner sat untouched.

"Can you drive home?"

"Drive home, why would I drive home? I haven't had my dinner yet. You're sorta rushing things aren't you?"

"Well, it's getting late and I have work tomorrow."

"OK. Let's go. We can take my car."

"I'm concerned about you driving. You've had a lot to drink."

"Well, shit. We don't have to drive anywhere. We'll just go get in my car for a while."

"I don't think so, Roger. You look like you're going to pass out."

He giggled and paid the bill. They walked to the parking lot and Mandy turned silently to her car.

"Wait a minute sweetface; what do you think you're doing?"

He came up behind and pressed her into a parked car, swaying drunkenly.

"Got to pay the Piper, darlin."

Mandy was strong. She half-stepped away and swung her hip hard into his legs. He staggered the length of the car and fell in the gravel. She moved forward gripping her purse, ready to slam him in the head if he moved. Roger looked up dizzily; he had no appetite for combat.

"Goddamn cunt. You're a dry socket. Took my money, too."

She thought of her mother as she drove home, telling her she had to get out and meet men. Mom said there was no sense wishing Al was any different, because he wasn't—and he wasn't here anyhow.

Tomorrow she would tell her Mom—there were worse things than sitting home.

# Chapter 33

Suddenly Al felt better, he had a job: something immediate and important and he could do it. The doubt and erosion of courage were swept away. He would help his friend. He switched the radio to high power knowing he would alert the defense forces for a hundred miles around the target area.

"LIME 6 on the way. Can you bail out?"

LIME 2 was low now and the mountains blocked his radio call, it was maddeningly garbled.

"…low. Trying for…bed…east of…"

Al understood where LIME 2 was headed.

"Got it LIME 2. Take your walkie-talkie when you exit the aircraft, I'll need to talk to you. Your transmission was garbled; I think you're trying for the dry lake east of Qira, call again if you're not; just click your transmitter button and I'll know you're somewhere else. Hold on about ten minutes."

Now he had given the enemy everything they needed to know. He had no choice.

He selected the 20mm cannons, watched the gun-ready light go green, and fired a short burst. A few beautifully orange incandescent tracer rounds slashed out in front and floated lazily away. He switched to the 50 caliber guns and did the same just as *CalamityJane* cleared a mountain pass south of Qira. LIME 2 was somewhere on the clear grayish lakebed fifteen miles ahead but he was still too far away to see. As the distance closed he saw two armored columns raising dust clouds as they headed through desert brush toward the lakebed. Across the dry lakebed a beginning column of black smoke was rising from the dry brush just at the edge of the alkali surface. If the smoke was LIME 2 burning he would arrive almost simultaneously with the nearest of the racing vehicles. It would be a close thing.

Al suppressed a deep and very human desire for high speed. He slowed to 250 mph, the best speed for shooting, and turned to the nearest dust column. He had to stop them; he would look for Art after he stopped them. He opened fire with the 20's while still a mile away from the column, far out of effective gun range but wanting to get their attention. Now return fire started from somewhere in the middle of the dust cloud. A glance told him it was not accurate and he continued the attack as the platoon of six tracked vehicles slowed to a halt. He dropped to only feet above the lakebed and opened fire on the lead vehicle. Dust spurted two hundred yards right of his target and he banked slightly to walk the fire in, quickly registering solid hits. There was a low-order explosion aboard the vehicle and he saw a single man jump down before a violent explosion tore the entire machine apart. He turned to the second vehicle, very close now. He would only get in a quick burst prior to passing over it. Before he could shoot he heard the tinny pock-tat-pock sound of hits somewhere on his aircraft. Then the stuttering noise rose in a crescendo like summer hail and he broke upward to escape the heavy and accurate fire.

He watched the two columns in his rear-view mirror as he climbed. Two vehicles in the lead column were turning around and moving away from the burning aircraft. The second column was stopped about a mile away, only four vehicles in that one. He flew to the western edge of the lake and dropped into a ravine angling to the south before doubling back toward the enemy columns, hidden now by intervening low hills. Al smiled grimly as he glanced in the rear view mirror. Clumps of sage were flying in the air from his prop wash. He was skimming inches above the desert floor, too low to be tracked.

Seconds later he broke above the intervening hills at the rear of the four-vehicle column and immediately shoved the nose down in firing position. His maneuvering had paid off, the column was directly in front of him and he poured fire into the closest vehicles. No explosions this time, but the near vehicle erupted in fire and he saw crewmen abandoning the second.

No time for more shooting as he flashed above the small group and turned for the original column. It was easy to spot: the desert flamed around the wreckage of the first weapons carrier. The second and third vehicles were turning now; they had heard his attack and were preparing to shoot. Again Al dropped to the desert floor and opened fire while out of range, sending ricochets flying wildly around the sky, hoping to unnerve the gunners. In range now, he poured fire into the third vehicle, saw solid hits and got a few rounds into the second vehicle before passing above them. No return fire this time.

Al headed for the wrecked aircraft. Now he could see the black P-61 down on one wing and burning in the brush a few miles ahead. He glimpsed a figure standing in sage and scrub oak a quarter mile from the wreckage, waving frantically. Amazed by his calmness, Al dug the mission briefing-book from his flight suit, looked up the walkie-talkie frequency, and dialed the numbers into the low-powered intercom transmitter. No time for radio procedure now.

"Art, was that you down there. I thought I saw you."

"Yeah. I'm all right. You really knocked the shit out of those guys. No one else close by, we ought to have a few minutes before reinforcements can get here. Do you think you can land on the lakebed and pick me up? You're all I've got, pal."

"Can I get in on the lakebed? I haven't had time to look and I won't take time now. Did you set the destruct charge on the Hallicrafter payload?"

"I landed on the lakebed. It's OK. No brakes or steering and I ran into the desert and the gear collapsed. Shit, I didn't set the charge. The nose isn't burning yet; I'll go over and do it now. Taxi up to the edge by my plane, I'll be waiting."

Al flew down the lakebed, planning to make his approach into the wind, from the east. As he began the turn into a final approach he again heard his ship taking hits, then saw tracers flashing down from above and kicking up fountains of dirt ahead of him. An instant later a green YAK-9 flashed past him and began a level turn, maneuvering for a second attack. Al knew his abrupt turn for the landing approach had saved him.

Now he had no choice, he must engage the YAK; there could be no landing with an enemy aircraft overhead. He slammed the throttles open and turned outside and slightly below the YAK, hoping to remain in its blind spot until he could close the distance and open fire. The YAK continued a circuit around the lakebed looking for Al, failing to note the silver F-15 closing from behind and moving within firing range. Al knew he was wasting precious time but still he was careful to remain in the blind spot. The YAK made abrupt turns twice, looking for Al to his rear. Each time Al's powerful hydraulic-boosted ailerons outperformed the YAK's mechanical ailerons and he was able to stay out of sight. On the second circuit around the bed Al closed the gap to a few hundred yards and he was ready to fire. He turned in on the tail of the green aircraft and was instantly spotted. The pilot must have been highly experienced, he started a turn to the left and then did a difficult cross-control maneuver unexpectedly back to the right. Al turned upside down, cross-controlled also, and opened fire. The green aircraft dove sharply into the lakebed in a cloud of dust and debris. Al flew down the debris path upside down, fascinated to see the plane's heavy engine rolling and skipping down the flat dry earth, keeping pace with him for most of a mile.

Now he was entirely out of position for a normal landing into the wind. He chose to make a fast downwind landing and save the precious minutes required to maneuver back up the lakebed. He rolled upright, turned for the lake and lowered the landing flaps all at once. As speed bled off and he concentrated on the landing Trumbauer's voice erupted in his ear.

"Gear, Al, gear! Get the gear down!"

Jesus Christ! His hand slapped the gear handle down. He had forgotten the landing gear in all the chaos.

The landing was smooth and very fast, the wind adding to his groundspeed rather than reducing it. He steered for the wreckage as soon as he could, stopping a hundred yards out from the sagebrush as Trumbauer ran toward him. The downed pilot clambered up the nose gear ladder and grabbed Al's seat from behind, panting and sweating and red in the face.

"Go right now. I saw a tracked vehicle coming out of the brush across the lake, about two miles away, he'll be in range before long."

Al had a different idea, he swiveled the aircraft around in a tight circle, stopping when he saw the tracked vehicle moving across the lakebed toward them. He opened fire without aiming, saw dust clouds fly up from the desert floor short of the vehicle. Then the firing ceased abruptly: he was out of 20 mm ammunition. He opened the throttles without pausing, snapped the gun selector from 20mm to the 50 caliber setting and started a takeoff run directly at the enemy, presenting the smallest possible target to the gunners. Tracers flew above him as he neared flying speed and he delayed the takeoff to fire a short burst at the armored vehicle. No hits, but the enemy firing stopped for the briefest moment, then continued. He hauled the control yoke back and broke free of the lakebed just as a heavy thud slammed *CalamityJane*. The right engine faltered and then resumed full power as he flew directly above the vehicle, looking down from fifty feet at the reptilian thing, its turret swiveling in a vain attempt to track him. No time now to look for damage; he concentrated on holding the aircraft just above the lakebed as he flew away. He was low, slow and vulnerable. His head swiveled frantically looking for other aircraft in the area and he yelled above the engine roar.

"Check behind, Art. If there's another one up there we're dead meat."

Seconds later they crossed into desert terrain south of the lakebed at 195 mph and he used the speed to zoom in a climbing turn. Now he glanced at the right engine and was shocked to see the entire cowling missing. The beautiful flower-petal arrangement of 18 finned cylinders was fully exposed and seemed at first to be intact. Then he saw that one entire cylinder head was missing and a thin stream of oil was pumping back in the slipstream. He turned again to Art.

"See if you can crawl back over the fuel bladder and look for leaks and wing damage."

Trumbauer punched his shoulder and disappeared over the flexing olive-green fuel bladder. He was back moments later, " No fuel leaks. The nacelle is chewed up but the wing looks OK. If the engine holds we should make it. God Bless Pratt and Whitney."

This most reliable of aviation engines was famous for continuing to run with battle damage.

Al trimmed the aircraft for hands-off flight and thought about their situation. After a moment he turned in his seat.

"What do you want to do?"

"I think we should head for Nepal and cut across India to get home. Illegal as hell, but it takes almost 600 miles off the trip. Leave the engines at climbing power until we get high enough to cross the Himalayas."

Al nodded agreement and added a thought.

"Once we're on the other side I think I can feather Number 2 and get us home on one engine. A long trip, but we should be able to get back if nothing else happens. What do you think, Art."

Trumbauer leaned forward and shouted above the din.

"Do it. You'll have to share oxygen with me until we can get down on the other side of the mountains. I'd appreciate not having to bail out, I left my parachute back there in the brush."

In low foothills several miles south of the lakebed Gunnery Sergeant Augustus Omer Quinn, USMC, stepped back from his spotting scope. He had watched the entire action. Quinn fought in Nicaragua in 1928 and all through the Pacific Island campaigns of the war, and he had never seen anything like this bizarre event.

He was advisor to a platoon of Nationalist Chinese infantry gathering intelligence in Sinkiang province. He turned to the Chinese Captain leading the unit with a puzzled grin.

"Man that was something; I never saw anything quite like it. I don't know what the hell it was about, but I think we'd better call it in with tonight's radio report."

\* \* \*

Al sat with his debriefing officer in a small cubicle. He had been separated from Art Trumbauer to allow an independent check of their narratives. Al answered the questions dully and mechanically, not being helpful, not reconstructing the action, making only short declarative statements. The routine triple-shot of bourbon that came at the end of every combat mission sat warmly in his stomach. He wanted more. He wanted sleep.

Finally the Intelligence Officer wound down and stopped. He sat studying his handwritten report for several minutes, shaking his head. The whole thing was incredible, almost unbelievable: it would need to be checked against the other pilot's report. On the other hand, Deforest had definitely landed with Trumbauer aboard his aircraft and it was hard to see any other way the transfer could have happened. They would have the gun camera film developed tomorrow; that would tell the story for sure.

Colonel Tuck needed to see these notes right away. He carefully stapled his hand-written pages and attached with a paperclip Air Force Form 39-62, Airframe Survey and Report. The maintenance officer had completed a preliminary survey of the F-15 in 30 minutes. It didn't take a genius to see that *CalamityJane*, Aircraft 42-33835, would be retired in place. She was beyond economical repair with over 400 bullet, shell, and shrapnel penetrations.

The man sighed; now they were down to only four F-15's and seventeen P-61's. They started with ten F-15's and thirty P-61's: nineteen aircraft lost in seven months.

In seven months, they would be down to no airplanes at this rate. He wondered where it would end.

# Chapter 34

Doc House was getting angry now because Tuck wasn't listening. Or he wasn't hearing.

"You can't treat this as some sort of boyish prank. They're all drinking now, and I think Deforest is the ringleader. He doesn't seem to know it, but he influences the way the other pilots act. Most of them do what he does, so that just makes it worse."

"Well, I understand most of what you say here, Doc, but pilots do drink you know. You should have seen my P-47 squadron over in Europe. And we were near the end then, the worst of it had occurred the year before."

"Deforest is a…a gentle personality. I think you're giving him too much gunship duty, sir. And I think he should go on a less intense mission schedule for a month or so. He'll recover. Otherwise, I just don't know, we may lose him. And then there are the flying regulations, you know. I'm looking the other way for now, but I can't continue forever."

Tuck understood Al's gentle side, the exquisite vulnerability. Al had never made the connection between his combat victories and killing people: he thought he was shooting clay pigeons. If he ever made the real connection it would bring him dreadful emotional trouble.

And he liked Doc House: he knew Doc was doing his Flight Surgeon's duty. But he had a job to do here and he wished to Christ a few of these people would just forget the details and help him with what they were here to do.

"Deforest is a very capable officer, Doc; I have great hopes for him in the long term. I know he has a gentle side, I can see it too. But believe me; it disappears when he's flying. I assign him to the gun ships because I know he'll bore in when there's trouble, and the record shows he does exactly that. All our kids are exceptional, but Deforest keeps thinking in the worst of it. He's intelligent and cool, never impulsive when things get rough. That's rare. That's valuable."

Doc's face clouded with uneasiness. Somehow Tuck was dancing this conversation around on him. He would try something else.

"All right. I see you're not convinced. Let's get Deforest over here and let me show you what I mean."

Tuck yelled to his Exec through the closed door.

"Find Deforest and get him over here now.

Ten minutes later Al knocked on the flimsy door and entered. Right away he could see he was in the soup and the unreasoning fury boiled up again. The anger was always there now, just below the surface. He'd been ratted out. He didn't salute, merely nodded to Tuck.

Tuck sat stiffly behind his desk, staring at Al. Major Ray House sat in a chair by the small window fiddling with a paper in his lap, not looking at anything. Tuck opened his mouth to speak and was drowned out as a P-61 engine ran up to full power in the maintenance area. He started to shout, thought better of it, and simply motioned for Al to take a chair.

Eventually the noise died away. Tuck shook his head and his Neanderthal brow furrowed.

"Dr. House thinks you're drinking too much to be flying safely. He tells me you're taking sleeping pills constantly now. He's…uh, concerned, thinks you may need some time off from flying duties; perhaps more than a little time. I just don't know; this is a bit of a surprise to me. I'd like to hear what you think, Lieutenant."

Al knew Doc House was on his case, so the meeting wasn't that surprising. Still, he had hoped Doc would keep quiet about the drinking. Now he needed to say something convincing.

"The mechanics make a very fine coconut drink, actually something like a sweet wine, an aperitif sort of. They have a still out there behind the ammunition bunker. Everyone drinks it. We sit around the tents at night and have a whack or two. We drink that shine and talk about things. It's really very helpful to morale, sir. I don't drink any more than the other pilots. We're a little exposed here you know. And of course I don't drink the night before I fly."

He looked at Tuck and thought about stopping. No, he needed to go on.

"And the pills, well I don't think you could find a single pilot out there who isn't taking Doc's sleeping pills. It's important to get enough sleep. These missions, sir: they're not getting any easier. And we hear things from the analyst staff about our tape recordings. There's talk going around that we just keep gathering the same information, that we're not getting anything new. The pilots wonder why we're taking losses when nothing new is coming in. It's not a good situation. We're flying now because we don't want to let each other down, not because we're doing anything important. It gets hard doing these missions Colonel—you know what it takes. It isn't exactly digging potatoes, you know. So I drink, they drink; we all drink. It makes it easier. I can fly just fine, I don't need anyone grounding me here; I'm not nuts. And where would a replacement come from? There aren't any replacements. I'm pulling my weight around here, the combat reports show that. I'd be letting my friends down. You'd shame me, sir. Don't do that."

Tuck put his feet on the desk, evaluating. Al had flown 18 missions now; all the kids were up around that number. There had been close calls; a few times Al almost didn't get home. He acted jittery, but they were all jittery now. These young men were finding out the truth about combat flying: survival is one part skill and one part luck. Well, Al was no worse off than the others, and he damn sure couldn't spare any pilots at this point.

He looked at House and shook his head.

"I'm not going to ground him, Doc. He's right you know; he's not crazy. Not anything like that. I want you to start seeing him the day after missions, talk with him. Have a talk with any of the other pilots who seem…uh, a little worn out."

Major House wasn't buying it.

"This is more than being worn out sir. He's trying to rationalize flying the morning after heavy alcohol use, and pills too. He's flying hung over; a gross violation of safety regulations—common sense, too. This is something I'll have to report sir, I can't ignore it."

Tuck was tired of the wrangling; there was a job to do here. Instead of pitching in, his people were quoting nit-picking regulations. He wondered how much longer before there was real trouble, a collapse?

Doc House glared at Al.

"Do you see the trouble we have here? The trouble you're causing? If I were you I'd think about making amends, son. The sooner the better."

It slipped out before Al could think.

"You bet Doc. I'll take up Zen, stop ruining my nerves with Demon Rum."

Tuck snapped at him.

"It's not like you to have a smart mouth, Al. I don't like to hear that talk. Get out of here."

Al knew he had won an easy battle: the Wing was below half complement now. They were far too shorthanded to spare him from flying duties. He felt fine, Doc was wrong about his nerves.

# Chapter 35

Al tumbled from the crew lorry and tramped through the humid tropical darkness to his aircraft. He was supposed to begin the pre-flight check, but he sat on the nose wheel tire first, breathing deeply. He couldn't quite catch his breath. Eventually he felt well enough to start the pre-flight check. When he reached the tail and moved his flashlight upward to check the giant fins, nausea came and he stepped into the jungle to vomit. The ground crew was used to it, they averted their eyes. As Al retched up the last of his breakfast the Crew Chief came over with a clean rag and canteen of water.

"The armorer gave you ball, A/P and tracer for the ammo load, sir: 1/3 of each. That's the 20's and the 50 caliber too. That OK?"

Al looked up dully, wiping saliva from his chin. He wanted to see a star, to feel some connection to the universe right at this moment. He wanted to turn his eyes from the reality of what he must do. A deck of marine clouds had moved in overnight, obscuring the sky. He turned to the crew chief and studied him with sad eyes, unmindful of the man's words.

"Fuck."

The Sergeant ignored the smell of vomit.

"I know, sir. Here you are, just go ahead and clean up, I'll finish the pre-flight for you."

Al nodded and rinsed his mouth; strangely unembarrassed. He felt no fear, but the vomiting made that a lie. The conflict puzzled him. He paused in a crouch, hands on his knees, dizzy and faint and struggling for a deep breath. When his breathing was even again he moved to the nose wheel ladder and climbed up to the cockpit twenty feet above.

Ten minutes later he was at the runway threshold watching for the green light. It was pitch black and he could not see the runway controller, only the double string of low-power sodium runway lamps marking the takeoff path. Seconds later a green light blinked. He moved the throttles to Takeoff Power.

They had a real runway now. Tuck had finally shut down flight operations for ten days to pave the coral airstrip with steel landing mat. The difference was clearly evident in the extra acceleration Al felt as the propellers bit deeply and pulled him forward: a small pleasure. He scanned the instruments at 95 mph and all was normal. Seconds later, feeling the aircraft getting light, he was startled by a loud bang. The cockpit was illuminated by an orange glow from the right engine.

A glance at the instrument panel told the story: no water injection pressure on the right pump. Without the cooling effect of water in the fuel mixture the engine was destroying itself. He snatched both throttles back, glanced at the airspeed and cursed—108 mph and above refusal speed. There was insufficient runway left to stop now, he would be a fireball in the palmetto scrub off the runway end. He slammed both throttles ahead again, hoping the dying engine would hold until he could get into the air, regretting greatly the momentary loss of acceleration.

Now there were only a few dozen runway lights before blackness at the end of the airstrip; he hauled the yoke full back and the overweight machine lifted sluggishly as the runway end flashed past. The engine folded up on him with a low order explosion, a crump, and he looked over to see the entire inboard wing on fire. With no other choice he pulled power back on the dead engine, moved the mixture control to the cut-off position, slammed down the NOMEX fire extinguisher handle and felt the big plane begin to roll to the right. He cranked in maximum rudder trim and still his leg strained to counter the strong one-sided torque from the remaining engine.

He looked up from the instrument panel and struggled to focus the vital outside images he desperately needed to prepare for ditching. He saw a blur: his old eye accommodation problem. Far to the right, surf phosphorescence outside the lagoon was a woozy line. It began to tip crazily. He tried to will his eyes to long-distance focus. Suddenly he was overwhelmed; problems were piling onto problems. More problems than he wanted to deal with.

And he gave up.

Unthinkably, he sat back in his seat and made no further effort to save himself. It was just too goddamned much: these awful wringing missions, Mandy's rejection, and the friends now gone forever. He sat and felt the weight of life lifting mercifully from him and it was wonderful: an honorable way to leave the human race behind. No one would know what he had done and in a moment the burdens would be gone.

He remembered Trapnell sitting legless in his broken aircraft.

"Not bad at all."

Seconds later there was a gentle jerk to the right, then a violent impact, then nothing.

# Chapter 36

A dozen riders clattered into the courtyard of The Catholic Sisters Hospital and dismounted. Yu dismounted carefully, he was gravely sore and stiff from 900 miles of riding, Chengdu to Kunming and return. Fifty-two years old he was, almost forty of them spent fighting and running. It seemed like more. One of his Lieutenants, still mounted, inquired after him, concerned. Yu kept walking, simply waving the man away. He pushed through entryway screen doors and sat in a rattan porch chair on the covered veranda, breathing heavily. After a time, he slapped on the wall with his riding crop. A soldier appeared.

"Sir?"

"Get me the radio-telephone. Set it up here next to me. Bring me quinine water and ice."

"Sir, uh, it is not advisable. They listen now to all communications. Even the land lines."

"Shut up. Do as I say."

Yu removed his eye-patch and rubbed the empty socket. It itched now, sore and infected by fungus from the hot, dusty trip. He would need more of the special salve, but it was a week away in Quindao. It might as well have been on the moon. His lower spine ached sharply when he moved. His kidneys burned. Three times his small group had barely avoided large elements of Communist cavalry. Once, on a whim, he had chosen to avoid a narrow canyon and take a difficult trail along the mountainside. Halfway across the mountains he had looked down on a regiment of cavalry traversing the canyon. He would not have survived the encounter. The countryside was alive with Maoists now; his traveling would need to be curtailed—was curtailed. The trip had startled him, he was used to being in charge, to controlling the province. Now he had become a fugitive. Even worse trials were ahead. The time had arrived: his operations were ended.

Three technicians struggled around the corner of the building carrying the field telephone and a battery pack. Yu watched idly as they set up the unit. One of the technicians put a voltmeter across the battery terminals and nodded at the 28-volt reading. He plugged in the battery and handed the telephone to Yu. The men stepped back but did not leave. They wanted to know what was going on. Yu glared at them.

"You, where does your family live?"

The man stiffened, Yu had been misunderstood.

"No, no. I mean you no harm. I need a diversion. I want you to call your poor parents on this telephone to create confusion."

He pointed to another technician.

"Find my servant, U-Ping. Tell him to call his parents also, on the landline. More confusion."

He stood and headed for his horse, still standing in the quadrangle outside. He addressed the small group on his way out.

"Do not try to follow me, if I find you following, or if I find you listening, you will have more woes than a lifetime should give to any man."

In spite of his soreness, in spite of his horse's exhaustion, he cantered eight miles to the next small village with a telephone. An old peasant woman who made calls on behalf of the villagers tended the single telephone. He stormed into her small hut.

"Out, I will need your telephone. Come back in thirty minutes."

He dialed the Baoshan long-distance operator from memory. It would take at least ten minutes for the listeners to patch into this obscure exchange, assuming they were not deceived by his multiple phone contacts. It would be enough.

"Get me the Singapore operator, I will speak to anyone at 52-8739."

He timed the call: it took four minutes before the phone rang. His father answered after several rings.

"It is me, father. Do not talk. Listen. Take notes. Can I start?"

"Yes, yes. I have a pad and pencil here."

"I am at the hospital now. I will pay the men this afternoon and leave tonight with three of my bodyguards. We have all the objects. Forty-seven of them are secreted at the locations we know as M, and P. I have twelve with me. I intend to hide three at W. I will have nine with me when I proceed to B. I will stay at or near B for the next sixty days, or until you contact me. Use channel 9 on even days of the month, channel 27 on odd days of the month. Use the appointed hour. Do you understand this?"

"It is clear, my son. I have the notes. I pray the Gods will ride with you on this perilous journey. Is there anything more I can do to ease your burden?"

"No, father. Goodbye."

# Chapter 37

Someone was calling, and now he was mentally swimming upward from a dark place, reeling with confusion, compelled to find the voice. Time had passed: he knew that. He was stuck somewhere in the dark and he was disoriented, sunlight came from below him instead of above. Something burned his throat and lungs and breathing was an exhausting effort. Panic was near. Now the voice was understandable.

"If you're in there, tap on the fuselage. Say something."

It took time to think of something to say.

"I…I'm here. I can't breathe. Cut a hole. Need air."

"OK, OK, sir, we'll get you. We…we can't cut a hole. We think the air you're in is all that's keeping the plane afloat. A diver, a frogman is coming. He'll swim down and come in below you with an extra air tank. Can you hold on?"

Al didn't think so.

"Not much longer. Hurry."

As he waited the predicament became clear: he was wedged in the rear of the pilots pod, between the giant fuel bladder and the aft fuselage wall. Apparently the wreckage was afloat with the nose down deep underwater and the tail pointing skyward above. His hands moved across objects in the water below and he found he was out of his seat. He wondered how that had happened.

Slowly he understood that the peculiar light in his airspace was sunlight reflecting off the white lagoon bottom sand thirty feet below, coming up through the opening where the nose had been, producing a strange limpid green illumination in his small airspace. Al forced his mind to study scallop patterns in the bottom sand caused by lagoon currents. He could have read a newspaper sitting down there, the water was so clear.

The pilot's seat and parts of the shattered nose came slowly into his downward watery view. The wreckage lay still and peaceful on the bottom sand, passing slowly from right to left as he drifted over it. Then he could see only sand again. He was sailing around the lagoon in his makeshift boat. He chuckled; this was fun.

His mind seized upon the question of drift speed. After a time he figured about two knots. Apparently he had drifted away from the crash site and now he was drifting back across the debris field due to tides or winds or he knew not what complicated forces. He remembered takeoff time, five twelve in the morning darkness. He must have been here more than an hour. Amazing.

Roiling bubbles suddenly disrupted his space and a mask appeared a few inches away. A hand removed the mask and he saw a young face.

"Jesus, the fuel stink in here is really bad. I have an air bottle here. Put the mouthpiece in your mouth and start breathing. Hold your nose, we'll get you out of these vapors. Are you hurt, do you think you can swim up to the surface if I pull you out of here?"

A lot of questions were being asked. Al had to think a while.

"Arm. I should be OK. How do I get out?"

"I'll swim down to the hole now, then reach up and pull you down by your legs until we're both clear. Don't struggle; don't try to fight me. When we're clear, I'll jab you twice with my finger. That means you should swim to the surface, swim toward the light. Do you understand me?"

Al nodded, the air bottle prevented conversation. Somehow the crash had a pleasing quality. It was almost a happy event.

# Chapter 38

Violet 'Birdie' Deforest went to answer the doorbell. The front door was old-fashioned, the kind with a large oval glass in the center, and she could see the man standing there. She thought he was a deliveryman and opened the door with an expectant smile as the man took off his cap and brushed down thinning blonde hair.

"Good afternoon, ma'm; I'm Captain Axel Berge, down here from McChord Field. That's in Washington State."

Birdie didn't understand; the man's khaki uniform with blue tie and belt confused her, she thought he was Western Union or something. She didn't know about the new Air Force uniform. Al had always worn regular khaki, like the Army boys did—with an Army Air Force shoulder patch. Anyway, Al was overseas now and she had never heard of McChord Field; what did any of that have to do with her son? Captain Berge bobbed his head deferentially.

"May I come in? I have some information about your son."

Birdie stepped back and silently motioned the man in, still confused, but unworried. The man turned as soon as he entered the parlor.

"I'm sorry ma'm…well, the Air Force is sorry, to tell you that your son has been hurt in an aircraft accident. He's alive, we know he's alive, and he's been evacuated to another location for treatment. As more information becomes available we'll keep you informed."

Birdie realized she was being slow about this, even stupid, but somehow her mind could not grasp what the man was saying or why he was here.

"Al? Do you mean my son Al? Why he's overseas, he's not up in Washington State, not anywhere near there. And besides, Al is very careful; I know he wouldn't hurt himself in one of those things. He told us how careful he was going to be. No sir, you must have made a mistake."

But now a slow and terrible awareness came creeping, and she called for her husband.

"Curtis, can you come in here? There's someone here, I don't understand what he's saying. You'd better come right now"

Captain Berge was about to continue his explanation but he thought better of it. He looked down at his feet and awaited the father. Presently Curtis Deforest emerged from a basement stairwell off the foyer, tucking reading glasses into a sweater pocket.

"I'm Al's father, is there something wrong?"

"Well, yes sir, there is. I'm afraid your son has been hurt in an aircraft accident overseas."

Deforest looked between Birdie and the Captain, seeking understanding.

"Al is hurt? How badly is he hurt? We want to see him. Can you arrange that?"

Berge saw he was making a muddle of the explanation and decided to slow down and speak carefully.

"Well, we were informed of this by Headquarters USAF, from back east, just two hours ago. They decided we were closest to you, and that it would be better to speak to you in person: better than a telegram. So I'm here to do that. There isn't much detail just now sir, we know your son was taking off from an overseas location; a base, and something happened to the engine and he crashed. He went down in the water and they rescued him as soon as they could. He was treated at the site, but apparently he needs additional care and now he's being evacuated to a larger hospital. That's all happened overseas, sir."

Deforest shook his head, anguish spreading slowly within him.

"When did this happen? We want to see him; go to him right now."

Berge shifted uncomfortably, not in the least liking any of this.

"The message indicated a crash at 1117 Zulu, that would be about midnight last night in terms of local time, your time here. And folks, your son is part of a highly classified operation, I'm afraid we won't be able to take you to him. Of course we'll arrange for a call from his doctor as soon as possible. And hopefully, he'll be able to call you himself before too long. I'm just very sorry about this. I wish I could do more."

Curtis Deforest looked at the hapless Captain.

"I tell you mister, we may be poor, but we're not without influence. If you can't help us see our son, our son injured doing your goddamned bidding, then I'll take the matter to our Congressman. And I'll also call the Portland Examiner and tell them about this affair. I'm sure they'd like to know how you treat your men, and their families. We just want to see our boy; he's what we have. He's all we have"

Tears formed in his eyes and he looked at the floor, nonplussed and angry.

Berge wondered why he had drawn this assignment instead of someone from the Base Information Office. But he felt sympathy for these good people.

"I'll ask you not to do that sir, in the interest of national security. Please give me a few hours, let me see what can be arranged."

Deforest walked to the front door and opened it, gesturing impatiently.

"Please leave us. If we have not heard from our son in two hours, or from someone treating our son, I'll do exactly what I just said."

He turned back to Birdie as the Captain made his way out, distressed to see her sitting on the sofa, dry-eyed, anxiously twisting a handkerchief as she looked up at him.

"I don't understand; how could Al be hurt? He told us he would be safe flying those things."

He nodded, knowing her so well, and spoke quietly.

"Yes you do understand, Birdie. It's just that it's difficult for you, hard to accept that something may have happened. You don't want to believe it, dear. Neither do I, but I fear it may be true."

Toward evening, Birdie decided that Mandy had to know. There had been a terrible spat, she knew Mandy was seeing other men now, but she had never doubted the love between them, never doubted they would be together when Al got through all this. Now she called the Piper residence and Mr. Piper answered.

"Bob? This is Birdie; I need to talk to Mandy. Al's been hurt."

She reflected on her voice as she waited, pleased; it had been a strong voice, the voice of a strong mother. She needed to be strong now, for Al and for Mandy too. Seconds later Mandy came on.

"Birdie, what's happened, what's happened to Al?"

She took a breath, wanting to start well.

"Mandy, Al has been in an aircraft accident and he's hurt. We don't know how bad it is yet, we just received…"

Her voice broke in sobs as she tried to continue.

"…and, well, we just don't know. Curtis is trying to find out more, we hope to know more soon. That man from the base, he said he would try to help us,…dear God I pray my boy is safe, let him be safe…"

She could not continue.

Mandy stood in the front hallway holding the old two-piece stem telephone tightly, shocked, and she spoke more to herself than to Birdie.

"I knew something would happen. I did this; I caused this—my ugly temper. I can't lose him now; he can't go away. I won't have anything at all."

She put the telephone down and sat on the hall floor, her back against the stairwell wall, comforting herself by rocking, repeatedly slamming her back. The blows felt good, like a penance. Four months ago, angry and embittered by Al's wrong-headedness, she had traveled to Portland and aborted her child: Al's child. If he didn't come home there would be nothing left for her now, nothing but the memories: her awful bittersweet memories. The other men: the ones since she broke with Al, she didn't care about them. She had tried to expand, to be a more worldly person; she had accepted dates, the calls had come in steadily as the town found out about her break with Al.

At first it seemed good; she was showing her independence, showing that she didn't need him. But the weeks went by and so many of them were jerks or fools. And the ones who weren't jerks seemed without personality: cardboard people. She came to realize there would be no others, that no one would take his place. Ever. She had made the mistake of a lifetime and she didn't know how to correct it. Now this.

Later she became aware of her mother crouching on the hallway floor in front of her, saying something. She had not heard; her mind was repeating oh,oh,oh…so rapidly she had shut out the external world. Now she heard her mother's frantic voice.

"Mandy, speak to me, speak to me now. What's happened, what's wrong?"

She blinked and saw her mother through tears, but said nothing. She picked up the phone and called Birdie, not responding to her mother's frantic questions. When Birdie answered Mandy had a single question.

"Where is he? I have to know."

Birdie had only begun to speak when the call was interrupted.

"This is the long distance operator. I have an urgent overseas call for anyone in the Deforest residence."

Mandy's telephone line went dead as Birdie accepted the call. Birdie heard a strange voice, distorted considerably by the poor quality of long distance telephone communication.

"Who is this please? I'm Col. Richard Tuck, I'm Al's Commanding Officer."

"This is Al's mother. Oh please tell us he's all right. He has to be all right."

"Well, m'am, I don't think it's all that bad. Al has some cuts, and his arm is broken. The worrisome thing would be about his lungs, you see: he was underwater for some time, trapped in an air pocket underwater. There was gasoline in there with him too, high-octane aviation gas. It burned his skin some, chemical burns don't you know; not fire, and he breathed the fumes before we could get him out. So we sent him to a larger hospital where he can get better respiratory care, ma'am. A doctor and a flight nurse went with him; he's in very good hands. His plane should be landing down there just about now, so we hope to hear something very soon."

Birdie was terribly alarmed.

"He's only just arriving now? How can that be? They told us the accident was hours and hours ago."

Dick Tuck took a deep breath before giving his careful answer.

"Yes ma'm: we're a long way from civilization out here, I'm afraid."

# Chapter 39

Roberta Fowler happened to be gazing out the front window when the staff car pulled up: a Buick, she noted, not the usual Chevy. Then she remembered yesterday's conversation with her sister, an Embassy secretary.

"Oh Bobby, we're getting a hush-hush visitor. Some Army guy from up north, no one knows where. He was hurt; the Ambassador got a call from Washington, direct. He's going to the Expatriate Hospital, we're supposed to look after him while he's here."

The driver door opened and a paunchy middle-aged civilian emerged. She recognized him as one of the lifetime State Department types, a Third Secretary or something. He went around to the passenger door and helped the man out. A boy really, she thought. She was disappointed; this must be the older man's teen-aged son, not the mystery visitor. Roberta was between husbands, and the mystery man had sounded interesting. She was in charge of the Embassy Clinic: two treatment rooms downstairs, two small rooms upstairs for recovering patients. The Malaysian Government provided a small office building for the Embassy downtown, for the main diplomatic function, but her clinic was located far away in an upper middle class suburb for lack of room at the main facility.

The Embassy employee pushed through the front door without knocking.

"Morning Mrs. Fowler. The Ambassador would like you to keep track of our guest here for a week or so; lung injury, broken arm, cuts. Just routine rehabilitation, then he'll be gone. Oh…I forgot. Nurse Fowler, this is Lieutenant Deforest."

Wide-set green eyes in a rosy-cheeked face turned to her blankly. All the sorrow in the world looked out at her from the solemn face. Now she took in details of this strange boy: curly black hair, tall, good looking, clutching a small valise like a stricken child. She brushed all that aside and took on her nurses role.

"We welcome you, Lieutenant. Do you have a medical record with you, something from the hospital?"

Nothing. The blank stare continued. She shook her hair lightly, unconsciously.

"I see. Well, let's get you settled in upstairs. Please follow me."

As she ascended the stairs with Al dutifully in tow, the man called after her.

"I'm leaving now Mrs. Fowler, I think you'll hear from the Ambassador this afternoon."

She selected the room on the left at the top of the stairs, and turned to him after they entered. Someone had tried to dress him as a civilian, but it was painfully apparent he was a military person: the khaki trousers, blue belt with silver buckle, black service-issue shoes and khaki windbreaker were only lightly moderated by a cheap sport shirt of garish tropical design. She took the valise and opened it: shaving kit, socks, underwear, extra trousers and another of those hideous tropical shirts—and the missing medical records. She sat in the room's only chair and skimmed: Greenstick fracture left ulna. 89 stitches shoulder, buttocks, and neck. Pulmonary edema. Penicillin required six times a day for five days. Twenty-day rehabilitation recommended. Favorable prognosis.

Not much of a problem here, she thought; just keep him moving out in the fresh air.

She looked up.

"What happened to you?"

He sat on the bed staring at the floor, disengaged, not present. The green eyes turned to her, and tears were forming.

"I lost my ship. I couldn't hold it, and I just gave up. I didn't care."

He shook his head, disapproving of the destruction he had caused.

"They have names you know, like people. She was *MoonDancer*. Now she's gone."

She was up without thought, moving to him, cradling his head on her breast, unaware that her tears were mixing with his own.

He was asleep when the Ambassador called in the late afternoon.

"Bobby? Al Sherman here. I've received a call about that young man in your care, a call from up north…I need to be careful about what I say. He's part of something very important going on up there. I've had a long talk with the Flight Surgeon who brought him to us, and I just now got off the phone with his Commanding Officer. Apparently, he's been brave for a very long time and now the Flight Surgeon thinks he's broken down; combat fatigue or the like I guess you could call it. The doctor wants him shipped home, thinks he's about finished. But the Commander doesn't agree, he wants him back. He says he needs him badly to help finish their work. I told him we'd do our best down here, our best to help out. I'm no psychiatrist, Bobby, but I think we should just try to get him out every day somewhere here in Singapore, get him interested in the world again. I'll send a staff car over with an itinerary; we'll give him some activities: cultural, exercise, sightseeing, that sort of thing. I'm counting on you to see he gets proper health care and exercise while he's recovering. Can you do that for me, please?"

"I've already started, Mr. Ambassador."

There was a long pause.

"Bobby, I don't suppose there's any harm in telling you: that youngster is an air ace. Some way or other that boy has managed 12 air victories up there, doing God knows what. The Commander says he's a warrior, that he's very fierce. Can you believe it? He looks like a high school freshman to me."

Roberta Fowler went to Al that night and gave him the ancient caring comfort he so desperately needed.

# Chapter 40

Al thought they were having a wonderful time. Bobby sat quietly in the booth beside him, a warm and comforting presence. Her hand rested lightly, possessively, on his forearm. He felt at peace. She gave him a sense of belonging and security.

Huge eight-foot electric fans moved air just fast enough to keep perspiration from forming as they watched sampans maneuver in the opaque green water of the River Batu Phat below the balcony at the Narrow Gauge Restaurant. Hours ago they had finished an excellent dinner of Kobe steamed beef, noodles with pepper and celery in an excellent mystery sauce, and candied plums.

Now Al was on his fourth brandy—or was it his fifth. No matter, he felt terrific. So terrific that he shouted at the other diners.

"DUCK! BE QUICK! NOT BAD AT ALL!"

At first the diners had been amused. Now they were becoming annoyed.

An ancient withered Chinese man appeared at their booth, tolerant and apologetic, but hoping that Al would restrain himself.

"I am Atherton Yu, owner of this restaurant. I wonder if our food and service have been satisfactory to you sir? You seem disturbed."

Al squinted through his cigarette smoke.

"Atherton? What kind of name is that for a Chinaman?"

Yu's face was suddenly frozen.

"Do not speak down to me, Lieutenant. I was born in Atherton, California: the product of an American mining engineer and a lovely Chinese woman who had immigrated to Sumatra, where they met. I am a graduate of the University of California at Berkeley, Class of '08. My father did not see fit to give me his name but he gave me every other advantage. I am quite certain I know more of this world than you do."

Even Al knew he had just heard a shockingly personal account from this patrician man. An account no oriental would give a stranger. He tried to appear sober.

"I meant no offense. We were having dinner—an excellent dinner. I was probably carried away. We'll pay now, and leave your restaurant sir."

Yu suddenly sat in the booth.

"But I don't want you to leave Lieutenant Deforest. I wish to speak with you, perhaps suggest something that may be to our mutual advantage, to our benefit."

Al sobered slightly and his guard came up.

"You know my name? How do you know my name? No one here knows my name."

Yu rose and slipped a card from a small holder.

"I know many things about you. May I suggest a meeting tomorrow, say at ten?"

He wrote an address on the card, handed it to Al, and retreated with a cursory bow. Bobby looked at her young charge.

"And what was that about?"

Al shook his head. He didn't know or care; he felt the beginnings of a sick stomach.

The next morning he took a pedi-cab to the address on the card: a large city park. Uncertain about where the meeting was to occur, Al wandered the ten-acre facility for a half-hour before finding Yu sitting on a bench in the shade of a giant banyan. The old man did not look up as Al sat down. He was quietly smoking a cigarette, holding it between thumb and forefinger in the European manner. Uncertainty made Al angry, and he was angry now, but also too curious to let the matter lie without an explanation.

"I'd like to know how you knew my name last night. Until I know that, you're the enemy."

Yu sat smoking and did not respond to Al's question.

"Are you acquainted with a Lieutenant Dwyer? Padraig Dwyer is his name I believe: a curious use of the ancient Irish."

Al sensed something ominous in Yu.

"I know the man. Or I did know him, he's gone now."

Yu nodded and a smile closed his eyes to slits. He was pleased.

"Gone but not dead, Lieutenant. In fact, he is being held by my son in Sinkiang Province."

"Held? Held by your son? I thought you were an American citizen."

Yu turned to him and smiled gently.

"You ask reasonable questions Lieutenant. I see you are coming around to my view of things. The short answer is that I hold dual citizenship. But let us not waste our time with word games. Lieutenant Dwyer will be released to the Indian border authorities tomorrow morning at

Brahmaputra. There will be difficulties, diplomatic difficulties, but he should rejoin your unit within a week or so, I imagine. And now I suppose you wish to know why an old man would perform this generous act, do you not?"

Al was far behind, dumbfounded.

"Well of course I do. That is, if what you say is really true and not some sort of a confidence game."

Yu stood and carefully shredded his cigarette, walking about and scattering the tobacco to leave no unsightly litter.

"I want something from you. This is my gesture of goodwill. In addition to my restaurant businesses I am a dealer in antiquities. In fact, antiquities have provided my principle income for many years. When I was young I traveled the Western Provinces, looking for sites where our illustrious ancestors buried their family members, and their family valuables. I mentioned UC Berkeley to you last evening; my degree is in Geology and I found this background most helpful in my quests. I would pay the peasants to dig for me, and leave my young son in charge while I continued on, always looking for more."

He chuckled over some private memory.

"Even in youth my son was a harsh man; he tolerated no pilfering. Violations were swiftly dealt with. We became a very successful team and our wealth increased as the years passed. Finally, before the Japanese occupation, I was able to purchase a Generalship in the southwestern region of Sinkiang Province. You might say I bought a franchise to pillage the entire Province. Money did many interesting things in the old China, but now we have reformers battling to run the country: Mao and Chiang Kai-Shek conducting their destructive Civil War. I care not a whit for either, but I make occasional alliances with both. My son, Pemberton Yu, remains the Sinkiang warlord to this day, fighting sometimes on one side and sometimes on the other: it is a matter of his survival you see. Unfortunately, Maoist forces now control all my routes out of China and I find it increasingly difficult to arrange transport for my treasures. My son advises that Mao will win the war in a few months now—then our business will wither."

Al's eyes had begun to droop, partly due to his hangover but mostly because he was finding the conversation unbelievable. Yu saw the dazed look and clapped his hands loudly.

"LISTEN TO ME! Through the years we have exported thousands of objects, but I have always held back the very best; an insurance policy, you might say. And now we come to your role, Lieutenant: I want you to land your machine at an airstrip controlled by my son, pick up some small objects, and fly them back to your base. There will be no need to dissemble with your superiors: you may fly a normal mission, I ask only that you to stop a few moments on your way home. When you are home, the objects will be removed from the airplane by others; you need never be directly involved in the handling. In that way, you may salve your conscience if you wish. The rewards are great, my friend; the risks small."

Yu folded his arms and stared straight ahead, seemingly unaware of Al's presence.

Yu's proposal was clear enough. Al was furious: angry at being taken for a traitor and a fool. But a seed of interest bloomed somewhere inside, and now he had questions.

"How do I know you're not with some American Intelligence Service, checking on us?"

"You do not."

Al didn't care for the answer but he continued.

"Why me?"

"A simple answer; because you are above suspicion. Are you aware that your Colonel Richard Ivo Tuck has submitted a nomination for the Medal of Honor?"

"That's bullshit. I haven't done anything to deserve that, and Tuck would certainly talk to me first if he thought I had."

Yu nodded, amused by the attack.

"Oh, but he certainly has. I have copies of the paperwork. An action on October 22, I believe. There is doubt of course; your man Trumbauer has gone missing and now there are no other eyewitnesses. But the Colonel is hopeful that the Marine Reconnaissance unit operating near Qira that day may be able to provide corroboration. If they survive, that is."

Al shrugged to hide his confusion. How could this tiny, withered man know these things? Everything Yu mentioned was classified Top Secret. He chewed his lip furiously, trying to make sense of this affair, looking for a safe path. Fuck it, he wouldn't take the chance.

"Get this, Mr. Yu: I reject your proposal. I'll have nothing to do with you: you're either a very clever confidence man or some kind of Federal security agent. Take a hike, mister."

"Do you have Government life insurance, Lieutenant?"

"Of course; ten thousand dollars. Every soldier has it."

Yu rummaged in his tunic for a pen and paper.

"Write the name of your bank for me. Tomorrow your account will have an additional ten thousand dollars. If I were a Government agent, that action would amount to entrapment, invalidating my case. Then, after I have received my goods from your airplane, I will deposit an additional two hundred thousand in any account you name. I suggest the use of an overseas bank. No confidence man would do that, don't you agree?"

Al sat down and waved irritably.

"I need to think."

An hour later he was still rooted to the bench, staring at his feet. He felt an off-the-ground feeling. Things were rolling too fast; he could never calculate all the odds, never know the ways of this devious man. He was probably overlooking something important. But he stayed and he thought: angry and confused and intrigued. This was a way to strike back at his powerlessness, at the daily insanity he was enduring.

"This is just outrageous Mr. Yu. It's probably treason. I could be shot for what you suggest, or I could spend my life in Leavenworth Prison. I guess I'm insulted too, what do you take me for? And how did you know I would be down here in Singapore, no one could know that ahead of time? I ought to just report you and let the authorities handle this."

Yu had left the bench again, sitting with his legs crossed and back braced against the banyan tree ten feet away, being patient.

"If you report me, it would be an inconvenience, no more."

He meant to go on, but his shoulders began to shake and he emitted a wheezing croak. Al thought it was an asthma attack of some kind and he stood, ready to help. Yu held up his hand. The features of his face had disappeared in wrinkles and his eyes were dancing. He was laughing—at Al.

"And you would support those who feel you are suffering combat fatigue. They would send you to the proverbial flak home where you could talk to the rubber walls."

The croaking subsided and he went on.

"Even if by some meager chance you were believed, I would never be arrested here in Singapore. You wonder what I take you for? You are a brave and determined man, Lieutenant. Probably more brave than you realize. I would not propose this scheme to a lesser man. And what have you to be insulted about? I do not propose a defection or a dereliction of your duty, just some business: some unusual business. As to our meeting here in Singapore, it is merely propitious. I had selected you several weeks ago, knowing nothing of your trip to Singapore."

Al wanted to see inside this little man.

"What exactly are these objects you want me to carry?"

"I suppose there is no harm in your knowing. You will carry nine figurines: small statues. Two are Terra Cotta, from the Ch'in dynasty. Four are solid gold, with silver inlays. And two, my most precious, are jade with gold inlays. They are all virtually priceless in the open market."

"Why not have your son bring them out when he comes? If he's as good as you say, he should be able to protect them."

"A good question. I have thought of this, but I cannot take the risk. He must pass through a dozen other provincial warlords on his way to the coast, and he is...distinctive in appearance. He intends to come alone; a large force would be discovered. He has waited too long now. He will be lucky to escape with his life, even with my money easing the way. No, you are my best chance young man. I tire of your evasions now: will you do this for me?"

There are a handful of moments in life when a person knows things will never be the same and time will divide irrevocably into two parts: before and after. There was no conscious decision, no particular rationale to ease the way, the words just popped out of him.

"I intend to document this meeting and place the papers with someone who will turn them over to U.S. Intelligence if I should meet with an accident."

Al thought a moment. He was angry and scared and he wanted to scold the old man with the same energy he would use to step on a scorpion moving toward his bedroll.

"Or if your payment should fail to appear after the shipment is completed."

He ended on a lame note.

"Now what do we do?"

"You will be contacted at your base when the time is appropriate; there are arrangements yet to make. Good luck to you in the meantime."

Al started away down the shady, macadam-topped path, and then returned once again to the strange man.

"How can you know these things? It just isn't possible, we have top-notch security everywhere."

Yu snorted.

"You have an Occidental's version of security: ego-centric security. You have little rooms with locks, you have guards, and you have secret meetings. You think the 337th Special Operations Wing is invisible. But you talk, Lieutenant: you talk at meals, you talk at your showers, and in your latrines. You talk at your movie shows and you talk on the flight line. And you think that no one hears you. You think the little brown men who unload your ships, and cook your meals, and clean your clothes, and handle your recorders and ammunition are sub-humans. You think them incapable of understanding your fancy, advanced, white-man's technical language. I assure you they are not. Money speaks with these men—as it has spoken with you, Lieutenant."

Al left the park by a different route. He passed through the zoo section, bought a handful of corn and fed a small herd of Ibis. He was calm now; he was doing something to strike back. The mood stayed with him on the walk back to the clinic. He could not know that the eventful afternoon was a defining moment in his life, a watershed that would shape his future forever.

The next morning Al sat slumped in a hard-backed wooden chair at the Military Transport Terminal on the far side of Singapore International Airport. He was killing time, trying to doze, waiting for his ride. Yesterday's bizarre encounter seemed an impossible strange dream.

But inside he was oddly at peace, feeling sentimental about his fuck-ups. By tomorrow, the dream would fade and be gone.

# Chapter 41

Lt. Col. Roy "Doc" Mendes pushed the dinner plate away and leaned back in his chair with a sigh.

"That was a mighty handsome meal, Mrs. Deforest, we don't get too many like that in my line of work."

Birdie Deforest wanted to impress this man; she had prepared chicken and dumplings, her home made sauerkraut, zucchini squash in lemon-butter from the garden in back, and plum duff. Now he would pay for his supper. Mandy began the questioning.

"We need to know where Al is. I want to see him, the Deforests want to see him. We're just desperate, Colonel. We've called the telephone number the Air Force provided and a man reads things about Al from a sheet of paper. We're not allowed to speak with him. I've written—we've written letters to his APO address. Until this accident, the Deforests received replies from Al, heavily censored replies, but now they get nothing. I…I've had a disagreement with him. I haven't written lately. But that's all over now and I need to see him. When can we see him? Please, will you help us?"

She tried to remember any other action she might cite, wanting to appear aggressive and involved, not passive.

"Oh, and we also sent a letter to the Inspector General; a complaint. He wrote back, but it was just gobbledygook: mumbling. We'll get no assistance there."

Mendes was about to retire from the Air Force; he had completed twenty-two years of active duty since his enlistment in 1917, with a decade out between the wars. Now he was receiving pressure, light pressure, from above. The Air Force had been severely downsized at the end of the war and the stringency was continuing. He had gone very slowly with all this because he loved the service life. But he had decided now: he would make way for younger men.

He was arranging his next life. He passed the Washington State Board of Medical Examiners reciprocity exam last August and now he was licensed to practice medicine again. He would join a colleague in general practice in Wenatchee, Washington upon retirement in May. It would be a wonderful way to start the second half of the twentieth century.

Mandy had prodded and poked until Birdie called him back in Indiana, believing Birdie was a better match for a middle-aged man. Mendes had listened carefully, grunting noncommittally at appropriate intervals, unable to satisfy her about Al.

Finally, against his better judgment, he agreed to this meeting in late November as part of his resettlement to Wenatchee. He knew Al's situation: he knew of his combat record, he knew Al was back on flying status now, he knew of the appalling losses that had decimated the Wing, he knew of the ambiguous, waffling guidance coming from the special office in Secretary Day's organization. All this he knew from his well-tended grapevine.

He looked across the remains of an excellent meal at the young woman who was clearly the leader here: mid-sized with a sturdy athletic build, deep brown eyes slightly narrow-set in a square face, a generous mouth and a too-strong jaw line, a curly cap of chestnut hair cut boyishly short in the latest fashion. She was a lovely, strong, intense young woman. He could see that she cared deeply for Al. Doc Mendes sighed, he didn't want to be on the wrong side of these fine people, but he didn't see how to avoid breaking their hearts.

"I know of Al's situation generally, but there is very little I can disclose without getting my tail caught in the Mixmaster. It's about military security, you know. But I tell you what, if you just ask me questions, I'll try to give yes-or-no answers. Provided, of course, you all agree to keep my name out of this affair."

They would use him ruthlessly to advance their cause, and he knew it. This was a feeble maneuver to cover his tracks. He could not in good conscience leave them in their present state. Mandy was on him in a flash.

"We all agree to confidentiality. Where is Al now, is he in Europe?"

He shook his head no. She tried again.

"Is he in Japan, the Orient?"

Only the second question and already he was breaking his own rules.

"In the orient."

Mandy again.

"Is he all right, have they lied to us about his injuries?"

"They have not. He is recovered now."

Curtis Deforest had a question.

"When will Al come home?"

"I have no idea, but I would expect his organization to cease operations within a few months."

Mandy's hand flew to her mouth.

"What do you mean by 'cease operations'? Do you mean Al is coming home then?"

It was getting harder for him.

"I don't know if Al will be coming home then, no."

Birdie gasped.

"Is he in danger, are you telling us he's in danger?"

Mendes looked at the three stricken faces, wishing he were elsewhere.

"I'm sorry. In my opinion he is in mortal danger."

Mandy's face crumpled and she looked down at her lap, the Deforests looked stunned and uncomprehending. Birdie spoke finally in an odd far-away voice.

"He…he promised us. He promised us those machines wouldn't be dangerous, and now they are. What can we do?"

Doc Mendes would tell the truth, he had no way to alter the outcome for Al.

"Pray to your God. Miracles occur. But you must prepare yourselves for an unfavorable outcome."

Mandy bolted from the table, scattering Birdie's bone china and silverware on the floor. Her leg caught in the chair and she staggered across the small dining room, then she was gone. The others sat silently.

Late that night she poured her heart out in a letter to Al.

*Dear Al,*

*I have so much to say to you. But let me start with I love you. I've loved you since that day we met so long ago. Just now I read what I wrote in my diary that fall evening in 1941.*

*' Today I saw the boy I will spend my life with. I was climbing the main stairwell and I glanced up. There he was, tall and green-eyed, cute and shy. He looked at me too, and I know he felt the same thing but he didn't speak. His mouth opened and I hoped he would say something. Then he looked at his feet and continued on. I can't tell Mom, she'll say I'm only fourteen and being stupid. But I'm not. He will be my man'.*

*Well, I can't say it any better now, my love.*

*The past year has been so full of mistakes, mine mostly, but I think you have made a few too. It doesn't matter. This letter tells you that I want to share your life no matter what you choose to be. There will be no other man for me no matter what. I know that now.*

*I had dinner tonight with Dr. Mendes and your parents. He will retire soon and practice medicine again up in Wenatchee. He tries to be gruff, but I see his good heart. He thinks the world of you Al. He thinks you will be a great man in the military. I agree, but I still feel you [we] could be so much more here in the real world!*

*Then he stabbed my heart with a knife of ice. He told us you are in mortal danger. I try not to believe it, but I think he knows the truth. I can only pray every night that God will turn his mercy to us and see you home with me and safe again. I'm in shock; I can't understand how this has happened.*

*Please, please be as safe as you can. Come home to me. I will always love you.*

*Mandy*

*P.S. I didn't want to write this part, but now there is something I must say, something for only you to see. If God has turned his face away from me, and you are gone, then very soon I will be gone too. There is not enough in this life without you.*

She reread the letter. It said what she wanted him to know. She would mail it in the morning. Somehow things seemed better now: surely he would be alive and he would read the letter.

But he would never see what she had written.

# Chapter 42

Tuck sat alone at a battered gray metal desk beside the briefers podium, studying the seven men who remained to fly his airplanes. He listened carefully, trying hard not to be critical of their startling proposal. David Rey was the spokesman, finishing up now.

"…you appeared before a special session of the Senate Armed Services Committee last week, sir. All we ask is that you make an inquiry; make an appeal to them. We know we're not engineers, but we've been gathering this stuff for eight months now, and it all seems to be the same; we fly the same links, we hear the same voices, we take the same photographs. And it's getting damned rough up there, they know our tricks now; we're not fooling them very often. Just talk to them, sir, see if something can't be done to end this. We're willing to go where you ask us to go if there's new information, but we're repeating the same mission over and over."

Tuck rubbed his chin, cheek, and eyes in a slow circular sweep. He was weary of all this: heartsick over sending these young men out week after week while the losses rose steadily. He thought of the fifteen men who were not here in the room: missing and presumed dead. He thought of Padraig Dwyer's miraculous escape. Now he was gone too, for the second and probably last time. And he thought of Douglas Trapnell, legless, lying in a rehabilitation hospital near death, still refusing to cooperate in saving his own life.

He felt like getting up and walking out of this pathetic gathering, just disappearing somewhere by himself. But he had a job to do and he could not.

"I hope you fellows know that if we were at war, what you're saying could be thought of as a mutiny, or desertion, or failure to follow a lawful order. And then, there you'd be, sitting in a cell in somebody's prison somewhere. And I hope you know that even if that didn't happen, the whole Air Force would know what we did—that we folded in a tough situation: that we crapped out. I hope you know all that, and you've thought about that before you came in here and confronted me."

He knew these young men were correct, from their own narrow viewpoint. He suspected something was terribly wrong in his chain of command. They should have folded this show three months ago. But he was a soldier and he would follow his orders, at least to a degree. He was tempted to explain all this to these young men, but he would not; he would put a cork in it and do the best he could for all sides.

"For the moment I'm going to pretend I haven't heard you—pretend this meeting never took place. The monsoon is gone now. We have pretty fair flying weather. That's OK, I can cobble up a weather report that says something else and I can act on it. So I'm halting flight operations for the next three days; you're all grounded due to bad weather. I want you to think this through during the next three days. I'm going to take a ship down to Bangkok and use the secure radio. I'll talk to Mr. Taylor in the project office and see what can be done. Now mind you, I can't promise a thing."

He looked at them to assess the impact of his words. Maybe he had them going in another direction, at least for the moment.

He called Al in later.

"Our world can't work if people just do as they please, Al. Men will always be asked to do terrible hard things. Are you a part of this thing?"

Al sat looking at his feet.

"I'll go on flying for a while, but it needs to end, sir. We're down to thirty percent strength now. Dave did some reading; there's never been a military unit with casualties like this, ever. What the hell are we doing? And they shut down the replacements. There's no end. We've done our job, we need to quit now."

∗          ∗          ∗

Abner Day listened to Stenzell's story. He had to agree with the pilots.

"They're right you know, John; we're not getting anything new. I should have seen this and acted earlier. They've given us more data than we ever hoped for. I must do something."

Stenzell's feet rested comfortably in an opened desk drawer.

"Dick Tuck is doing a dance on this one. He doesn't want me getting into the details. I suspect the men have put an ultimatum to him. That's unacceptable: I should crack down on the whole outfit. On the other hand, they've given us more and better information than we dared dream of. And the individual performance is magnificent: I have nominations for a Medal of Honor and two Air Force Crosses from the unit. The Medals Board has done a preliminary review; they'll probably be accepted. We ought to shut it down now, Abner. It will be a tough sell: Dr. Jackson over at CIA is in hog-heaven proving all the points he's been ridiculed for in the past, and the White House will try to use him as an excuse to continue, you know."

"I've already talked with Jackson. He thinks the Chinese are managing those links now, discussing routine information most of the time. He wants one more raid: a feint with an exit, and then we send more aircraft in to surprise them. I've promised him that much in exchange for his support on closing this thing out. We're covered there."

"Jackson is only an analyst. Your bosses are in the White House, you can't just defy them."

"I intend to shut this operation down. I'll try for support, but I'll do it unilaterally if I must. The President wants to stay out of the entire issue so he won't be a problem—Glendennan is the problem. *Heat Lightning* is a success story and he doesn't want it to go away. He wants to use it in the '52 campaign. But none of that matters John; the operation is finished. I'll take the whipping for shutting it down, I really can't do less."

"It could be the end of your Government service, you know. They could dismiss you."

"There are worse things, John. I'll tell Glendennan after the fact, when there's nothing he can do about it. He's too smart to try leaking to the press at these security levels. If we go face to face, I have enough backing on the Hill to stare him down. Prepare the shutdown orders, I'll countersign tomorrow."

Glendennan heard the next day and he was seething. He summoned Day to his office and glared at him with eyes that raked like talons. He meant to be polite, but anger hissed from him like a broken steam pipe.

"Last night I received word that you ordered Project Heat Lightning shut down. Is my information correct?"

"Yes it is, Mr. Vice President. There will be one more mission and that is the end. I counter-signed the field order yesterday afternoon. I intended to inform you today, it seems you beat me to the punch."

Glendennan wanted to control the meeting, but Day's cool tone aroused and infuriated him.

"By God, you had no authority to do that. I'm running the project, and I don't want it shut down. You will reverse the order today. And if I find you sneaking around, trying to sabotage my direction, I'll fire you."

"I won't reverse the order. You have no jurisdiction in military affairs. I report to the President, not to you.

"I represent the President in this matter, Mr. Secretary. Go along with this, or plan on finding a new occupation."

Day had hoped it wouldn't come to this.

"We are sacrificing lives for no substantial purpose now. I'm ashamed to have allowed you this much latitude, Mr. Vice President. *Project Heat Lightning* is finished. Go ahead and try for the President's support. If you get it, which I doubt, I'll be over on the Hill within the hour. I have the backing necessary to sustain the shutdown and you don't. And if you lose that fight don't count on the Party for a nomination in '52, you're not that well thought of. If you think you can fire me, go ahead. Frankly, you don't have the horsepower."

"I won't tolerate your insubordination, Day. Get on board here or I'll run right over you."

"Think for a moment of these young men Mr. Vice President. From this small unit we have a Medal of Honor nominee, two Air Force Crosses, two Silver Stars and God knows how many DFC's. And we have almost seventy percent casualties now. They've done their job; they really can't give us more, there's not a shadow of a doubt about Hotan now. So you aren't going to do anything. It would be morally wrong to block this, and I don't think you have the political courage to fight me. Let it end now or expect a nasty fight, one you won't win."

# Chapter 43

Tuck radioed ahead thirty minutes out, he wanted a pilot's meeting as soon as he landed. A half-mile from the runway he was close enough to see a small group standing in the coral gravel beside the threshold. His gargoyle face softened under the oxygen mask: his boys had come to greet him. He pulled the big P-61 up on its props and dragged it across the surf to set down only feet inside the runway surface.

He flashed past the pilots soundlessly except for the deadly whik-whik-whik of propeller tips slashing air. Bob McMurtry, standing with eyes squinted against the glare off the surf and hands folded across his chest, turned to the others.

"Pretty great landing for an old man."

They drifted to Tuck's parking revetment and waited impatiently. Tuck smiled wordlessly as he stepped to the ground, pointing to the Quonset hut that served as an Operations Building.

"No talk out here, gentlemen, let's get in the briefing room."

Tuck scooped a Coke from an ice-filled tub in the briefing room and smiled at the pilots.

"We will receive orders tomorrow for an all-out mission. The orders will also authorize shut down of this operation immediately upon your return. One more effort, fellows, and we can all go home."

He waited patiently through the din of cheering and questions before continuing.

"We'll put up two raids. The first target will be Aksu. The second will be one hour later at Quiemo. We know they manage telephone traffic now so the first mission will be a feint. We hope to catch them unguarded and speaking openly on the second. You can speed up in the microwave links this time: 225 mph. That will put you in and out fast. We can prepare for the raids by Sunday. We'll fly Monday. When you're back we'll start shutting down the base. I've requested a C-54 in here next Friday. Every one of you will be on your way home then. I'll stay out here with a small crew for two more months to finish things."

He paused to clear his throat loudly.

"We'll start rehearsing mission details tomorrow. Get with your crew chiefs now: be sure we're ready to go on Monday. It has been a privilege to fly with you. God bless you, gentlemen."

Tuck was saying what they wanted to hear. They looked at each other, excited, not really listening to his details—they would catch all that later.

They would survive this nightmare; they would live.

## Chapter 44

The seventh aircraft thundered across the surf line outside the reef. The small man in his sampan knew there could be no more. The entire pilot complement of the 337th Special Operations Wing was now aloft.

He spoke briefly on a mobile radio. Ten minutes later Atherton Yu received a call at his home in Singapore; it was 14 minutes past midnight. Yu arose from his bed and padded down the hall to his night operations office in the high-rise building he owned. He spoke to the Night Manager briefly. The Night Manager placed an overseas call to his Uncle in Chengdu, China.

Yu returned to his bed, pleased. The Maoist dimwits had a time and a place now, even they should be able to capitalize on the opportunity. A quiet smile rearranged his wrinkled face: this would be a tidy end to a rewarding piece of business. He had his artifacts and now he would destroy the man who had delivered them. And he would destroy a few others along with him.

\* \* \*

Karpov came up slowly from deep sleep, aware that his liaison officer was there, chattering excitedly. He sat up, ignoring the man and fumbling for the old wind-up clock on his nightstand. It was a present from his dear Mother, purchased with pennies from the tea-tin she kept in her cupboard. It was 1:15 AM. He held the clock comfortingly against his chest and listened to the man's heavily accented Russian.

"They have put the whole force up, seven aircraft, all they can fly. The first wave took off at ten thirty, the second at twelve fifteen. The first wave should arrive just after sun-up. It is unusual. I suspect they will try for two different links. A fake first, and then the real strikes."

"Thank you, now sit down and be quiet. I must think of the deployment."

He had changed things greatly since the unfortunate Po met his death. There was every reason to believe they would do well today, perhaps even deal a deathblow to the remainder of the $337^{th}$ Special Operations Wing.

He had removed all defenses from links T1 through T5, links that had never been violated by the Americans. Karpov was guessing, betting his life, that they never would be. Now 136 more tracked air defense vehicles were available to him, parked in the desert south of Hotan. They could be deployed to any of the remaining links within two hours, long before the Americans would arrive. And he had replaced some of the unreliable 88mm ammunition with new shells just received from Vladivostok. He was expecting the first new 105mm fuses next week, but that would not help him now. And he had wrenched control of the eleven YAK fighters in his area from the bungling Chinese Air Group Commander. They sat on the small airfield at Zangguy, serviced and ready to fly.

Karpov looked at Djarmen Cheng sitting quietly in the corner and he liked what he saw: Cheng was young and smart and tough. He had done brilliant analysis of the American attack patterns. If they survived this never-ending ordeal he would arrange a transfer to the Soviet Self Defense Force. Cheng would do well.

"So Djarmen, how do we use our pitiful little Army?"

Cheng's impassive face revealed nothing of the size of the bet they were about to make.

"We have analyzed their attacks. They never go for links near the actual facilities, probably thinking they are heavily defended. So scratch T9 through T14. They know we are managing traffic in the T links now; therefore they will surely try for one of the new B links. B3 is in the middle and I think they will go for it. They will believe it is the least defended. So I say go very heavy on T7, T8 and B3. Scatter the rest around, just in case. And the best guns should be placed right at the towers, not out to the side where deflection shooting lowers their effectiveness. The Americans always enter at mid-link and fly right up to the towers, where the signal strength is best, so we should be shooting almost point-blank as they approach. Then we have the airplanes. We should not allow the YAKs off the ground until the invaders are nearby: they have fuel for only ninety minutes. We have lost many opportunities because they land for fuel during engagements. Instruct the ground gunners to use the good ammunition first. That should do it."

They knew so much more now, yet there remained a large element of guesswork.

"You're sure?"

"No Major, I am not sure. It is my best guess. If it seems more comfortable, spread another 50 gun units to the remainder links. I really believe they will hit B3, though."

"If we guess wrong, there will be…consequences."

"I understand that."

"All right. We will place 60 guns under the towers at T7, T8, and B3. The old Bofors four-barrels can be out to the side; I don't care. The fucking things will probably blow up anyway. Keep three of the new YAKs at

Hotan. Divide the others between Qira and Pulu. All crews on full alert right now. If the first wave attacks the T links, we hold back a 60% reserve for the second wave. Oh, what about those new MIG's?"

"They are both down with contaminated fuel controls. It's not so bad, they haven't done well at low altitude."

"No one flies until I give the order. Anything else?"

"An order to the gunners: no firing until the targets are within 1000 meters."

"Make it so."

Karpov sat on his rumpled bed later, wide-awake, peering through gloom relieved only by a single 15-watt light bulb. He had just done all within his power to prevent the goddamned Americans from stealing more information. Somehow the situation amused him; all his war years, all his years in the many schools of the Soviet Army, and they came down to this moment and a handful of decisions. Imperfect decisions based on fractional knowledge.

He would shower now and get over to the Surveillance Center. He hoped God was on his side, if there was a God.

# Chapter 45

*EyeCatcher* lifted heavily from the runway. Al watched for a positive climb rate and snatched the gear handle up. His eyes flicked to the engine water injection pressure, 70 pounds, a normal reading. Since his crash the other pilots kidded him about Pavlov's dog: hold up a water injector and Al would drool. He was the last off tonight; there were six ahead of him. Dave Rey was first in the F-15 *FlakHound*; he would fly combat cover and coordinate raid timing for the P-61's.

The lights of Chittagong passed beneath his left wing and jungle blackness stretched ahead for 700 miles; there was nothing to do for almost three hours. Al tuned the ADF, hoping to find music. Mandalay, Rangoon and Vientane stations came in perfectly, but the music was oriental. He didn't care for the tone or rhythm, and the lyrics were strange.

Roberta Fowler had introduced him to the new program director for station WNZN in Singapore. Al was delighted to discover the man shared his passion for American popular music from the first third of the century. Now he remembered the frequency: 606.6 kilocycles. Suddenly, delightfully, Al Jolson's notable 1914 recording of You Made Me Love You was there in his ears, as strong as a good Portland station from his youth. Al sang along, doing his best to follow the singing, cajoling, talking, whistling entertainer: the man had more octaves than an octopus. His feet danced on the rudder pedals, but *EyeCatcher* could not follow the tricky, syncopated rhythm. He needed a smaller airplane to do the tune justice.

The next selection was Isham Jones' 1930 recording of Stardust. Something jagged and painful stabbed him as he remembered dancing with Mandy in the high school gymnasium to that very recording, gliding smoothly across the hardwood floor. The haunting violin solo brought her face to him now and hot tears blinded his eyes. He willed them away but they would not stop. He took off his gloves and wiped angrily. Suddenly, desperately, he wanted to be home, he wanted to make amends. Less than a week now and he would be on his way.

At dawn he glanced at the terrain and instantly recognized his position. This was his $23^{rd}$ mission and he knew every granite formation, every clearing, along the 700 mile Burmese border as well as he knew the road system around Tillamook, Oregon. The day promised to be relatively cloudless, just some patchy cumulus and a thin overcast—fine flying weather. Far ahead he could just see the coppery sheen of the Mekong River against the rising sun.

He thought back on the months of high hazard flying; he thought of pilots who were still here and pilots who were not. There had never been confirmation of a single death. The aircraft simply failed to return from a mission and they had no way to know what had happened. Somehow it comforted him to think they had all been damaged in the target area and wandered into the jungle to crash. Maybe they were still alive, since the Chinese were such poor shots. But they were getting better. The Intelligence weenies claimed there were lots of Russians active in Sinkiang Province now. He unconsciously shook his head: when all the analytic chit-chat was over and done with, there remained a large element of luck in his survival. He had come so far now. He just needed that same luck to continue through the day that dawned across the terrain ahead of him.

He heard the familiar ominous hum of the Chengdu Surveillance radar as he crossed into China. He impulsively chopped the throttles, rolled upside down and pulled the control yoke back into his lap. *EyeCatcher* entered a steep spiraling dive, nearly a spin, losing 7000 feet per minute. Al loved the feeling of near-disaster, as he shot through layers of cloud in the crazy circular descent. He entered the Mekong River Gorge and dropped to the river bottom. This was not a stealthy maneuver; he simply enjoyed looking at the abundant wildlife along the river edge. He had flown around a rocky outcrop on this part of the river and surprised two Panda's with a baby lolling on a grassy slope at the edge of the forest a few weeks ago. Deer were plentiful, and there was a good chance of seeing wolves and elk. Every sighting was a small reward for the dangerous business he would undertake in a few short hours.

Al arrived on his assigned orbit station at 8:23. He dropped low and circled a group of nomadic herdsmen at 250 mph. The oriental men on their tiny ponies looked up at him, hands shielding their eyes, squinting into the morning sun. Two of the men waved at him, and Al waved back, pleased to make human contact. He went through the payload checklist then turned the entire setup off with a master switch. Once in the link, a flip of the master switch would begin his recording. He trimmed for hands-off flying and sat back in his seat stretching the kinks out. He would wait now for word from Dave Rey; flying at 47,000 feet forty miles to the northwest.

Twenty minutes later Dave Rey's voice boomed through his headset.

"YOKE to CACTUS. Be advised BUTTON is encountering heavy resistance. Use caution."

Rey sounded uncharacteristically excited. Al was confused, unsure if he had been given clearance to proceed. Dave said nothing about proceeding. He listened for five minutes and then tried to contact YOKE.

"YOKE from CACTUS THREE. Am I clear to proceed?"

Nothing. No answer. Something was happening at Hotan: something that distracted Dave enough to prevent a call. Well, fuck it. He wasn't going to sit around here waving at the locals all day, doing diddly-do. He couldn't worry about it; he was going in. He rolled out of the holding pattern heading toward the mountains. The horsemen waved goodbye but Al did not wave back. His mind had moved ahead.

He crossed the Altun Mountain summit with feet to spare, glanced left and right, then dove down a canyon on his left that spilled out on the desert floor five miles ahead. He exited the canyon on a broad alluvial fan and now he could see the series of microwave repeater towers marching across the desert floor at thirty-mile intervals. He glanced at the airspeed indicator and it showed 460 mph. He nodded in satisfaction, wanting to cross the desert and get into the microwave links as quickly as possible. At this speed he would be there in ten minutes.

His head swiveled frantically searching for ground defenses and fighters. He carried neither guns nor ammunition. He would be helpless in event of a fighter attack. Only speed was on his side. Al did not slow as the nearest microwave tower approached, he planned to enter the link at high speed, throttle back, jump over the nearest tower and begin recording in the link next down the chain, away from Qiemo. He banked vertically and pulled enough g-force to dim his vision as he aligned with the link, then throttled back and almost immediately had to pull up to clear the 300 feet tower nearest him.

He turned on the payload master switch and concentrated on aligning with the microwave transmitters towers and slowing to 225 mph. Moments later the audio power needle jumped from zero to 44 decibels and he could hear Chinese voices in his earphones: he was solidly in the link and getting good voice data. *EyeCatcher* settled nicely on 225 mph and he trimmed for exact level flight. At this speed he would remain in the link for five minutes before encountering the next tower. The payload signal strength meter stayed solidly in the recording range.

He turned his attention to the desert floor ahead. As usual, his eyes were slow to focus for the distant landscape. A sudden jolt of fear went through his insides as the next tower came into clear view. Several heavy vehicles were parked beneath and around the tower. Seconds later he saw a flash from beneath the tower, then two more from vehicles near the tower feet.

Now he understood what had happened to Button flight: the Chinese had aligned flak guns with the links and no longer needed worry about angles, about deflection shooting. They were firing straight down the links, hoping he would run into a shell, or come close enough to trigger a proximity-fuse. He choked the fear down and concentrated on staying solidly in the link, recording voice traffic as he was supposed to. He could do nothing about the flak guns except trust that his luck would hold.

He had been through this so many times now and come through OK. Just a few more minutes and he would be safely away. The flashes stopped as he neared the tower. He jumped the 300-foot tower and looked down. Men in green drab uniforms were turning the vehicles around to shoot at him as he flew away. Somehow, the idea of being shot at while going away was comforting: not nearly as bad as head-on shooting. There were guns at the next tower also, but he was not fired upon. He flew across the tower: the guns were manned all right, but no one was shooting.

Al nodded: he could feel his luck in play. Then a moment of unreasoning panic swept him: he wanted out right now, he would just make a left turn and get the hell out of this mess. He could be over the mountains and safe in ten minutes. But he did not turn. He pushed down the ugly knotted fear and kept flying down the link.

It was Pvt. Dymtry Ivanovitch Kalekian who changed Al's life. The nineteen year-old Soviet Armenian had been sent to the ZSU factory school on rapid-fire anti aircraft guns after basic training. The training concentrated on radar directed guns and in this area he was quite competent. But the radar on his gun had failed last week. When the emergency order came his Captain assigned him to an ancient pre-war Bofors four-barrel gun with an optical sight. Most of the battalion had been deployed under the huge towers, but the Captain assigned Dymytry's tracked vehicle to a spot almost a kilometer off the microwave line. He had nervously argued: he was not used to an optical sight and he would do much better if allowed to shoot from under the towers. But the Captain was firm, and here he was: far, far from the track of the enemy.

He had been allowed to fire a spotting burst earlier, and the result was appalling. One of the four barrels on his cannon was worn so badly that the shells did not spin up to rotational stability. Instead, they came out of the barrel tumbling and spewed dangerously off the line of fire. Dymytry protested, concerned about hitting his own men over at the tower. Again the Captain was firm: shoot the goddamned gun. He was being paid to shoot when the airplane appeared, never mind the rest of it.

And now the airplane approached: a big odd black thing, appearing to be very slow indeed. Dymytry aligned the airplane with the front and rear sights as best he could and fired a short burst. Shells from the three good barrels floated out toward the airplane, but seemed to rise above it at the last minute. Shells from the bad barrel went everywhere: some curved and skittered up vertically, some slammed into the desert floor not two hundred meters from his location, and some curved over toward the tower.

This was too dangerous. Dymytry decided to aim far above his target. He would fire one more burst and then secure the old gun. He fidgeted, undecided, until the airplane went past the point of closest approach and was headed away. Then he fired a long burst aimed so far above the craft that his companions at the tower would not be endangered. He watched the tracer shells float away down range far above the strange craft. Then, to his astonishment, the big ship lurched out of alignment with the towers and climbed steeply to the south. For a moment it appeared that the flock of floating shells might have intercepted the target, but nothing happened. The aircraft continued to climb and appeared to be leaving the area. Dymytry heaved a sigh of relief that he had not killed his own people. He set about securing the weapon.

Al had almost eighteen minutes of good recording now, and things were getting hot. As he approached the fourth tower in line he could see even more muzzle flashes than at the previous towers. Close-by there was a sudden orange flash and smoke and the aircraft rocked. His instructors said if you could see the flash, you were way too close. That was enough: it was time to go. He hauled *EyeCatcher* up into a steep left-hand climbing turn, certain the heavy flak guns at the tower ahead could not follow his abrupt movement.

Almost clear, and then he flew directly into Kalekian's burst of light cannon shells. A single 40mm shell flashed across the tail boom and entered the rear of the pilot pod. A five-second timer had shorted the fuse as the shell slowed near maximum range. Now it was an inert half-pound of lead and steel, but it still traveled at 1100 feet per second and still contained lethal kinetic energy. The shell barely missed the auxiliary fuel tank and smashed into the armor plate behind Al's seat. The armor was only designed to stop .50-caliber ammunition and it could not stop this much heavier round. The shell broached going through the armor and split in several pieces. One piece went through Al's chest and spent itself in the instrument panel. A second piece flew upward, passed beneath his helmet, and shattered his skull.

He knew none of this: one moment he was in a hard climbing turn, the next moment he was gone.

## Chapter 46

Mandy was sorting the monthly collection of bills and receivables for Mr. Barlow. She had been hired three years ago as a secretary-receptionist, but her quick mind and initiative impressed Barlow. Last month he promoted her to Assistant Treasurer. The title was lofty; Mandy really just collected all the utility bills and invoices and organized them in manila envelopes that she turned over to the accounting firm at the end of each month. And she still did the secretary-receptionist job. Barlow's strength was in customer relations. He hated paperwork and had gladly delegated the burdensome chores: just running the Clatsop County Funeral Home kept him sufficiently occupied.

She was about to make coffee when the terror struck and she knew something awful had happened to Al. The thought slammed her with the impact of a hard blow. Her face drained white and she felt torn inside in some vital place. She panted and icy cold spread through her body as panic rioted within her. She shook her head like a punch-drunk fighter, trying to deny the knowledge. Her mind remained clear, but she lost control of her body; it sagged forward until her head rested on the desk. It was as if she was paralyzed, but aware. She willed her mind away from the awful premonition, but nothing helped. She wanted rational thoughts: Al was recovered from his crash and back on flying duty now. He was all right; this shocking feeling made no sense.

Finally she came to the only thought that offered comfort: surely God would not do this to them twice.

But the knowledge was there and it would not be defeated: Al was gone. She huddled down in the chair and pushed her head hard into the desk. She was sick to her stomach and her heart pounded frighteningly. She shook her head angrily and thought how stupid this all was. She felt consciousness slipping away. She lay still, afraid to move: the thing would get worse if she moved.

Mr. Barlow came into her office from the embalming room some time later. A terrible bus accident had forced both the day and night crews to work overtime and he refused to leave the facility until all the victims were prepared for viewing. But he was old and exhausted and seeing Mandy lying across her desk, eyes shut, in deep pallor, caused him to flinch. Illogically, he thought she might be dead. He leaned over her and whispered.

"Mandy, can you hear me? It's Mr. Barlow, talk to me please. What has happened here?"

She spoke in a weak tiny voice.

"Al: something has happened to Al. I'm afraid. I don't want to get up. I don't want to know."

Barlow knew immediately this was some dreadful business.

"Has someone called you? How do you know?"

"No one. I feel it."

He sat in the chair beside her desk, trying to decide what to do. He was sensitive to things occult.

"Mandy, I'm going to call my wife now, she'll come right on over here and be with you, she'll help you. I don't quite understand, but…but I respect your feeling. I guess maybe something has happened at that. Can you tell me what else I should do?"

There was a long pause before she responded.

"Can you take me to the Deforests? I need to be with them now."

Barlow shouldered the Deforest front door open without knocking and struggled inside, supporting Mandy under her arms. He placed her on the living room sofa and turned on the lights as Curtis Deforest entered the room in pajamas.

"What in heavens name is going on here? Barlow? Mandy? What are you doing?"

Mandy looked up dully but said nothing. Barlow knew of the agony Mandy and the Deforests had been through a few months ago. He searched for a plausible explanation, but there wasn't one. He spoke uneasily.

"Well, Curtis, Mandy has had a premonition or something. It's about Al. She's afraid. I…I think we need Birdie in here."

Barlow knew about death and he had seen more than one crystal clear example of telepathy. He was afraid Mandy might be absolutely right and he didn't have the heart for what was to come. Moments later Deforest brought Birdie into the room; she had been sound asleep. Her hand flew to her mouth when she saw Mandy. She sat beside her immediately.

"What is it child? Do you know something? Is there something we should hear?"

"I felt it. It hit me hard, like a truck hit me. Something happened to Al, something not long ago, only an hour. I don't know. I'm afraid. We need to find out, but I don't want to know."

Birdie believed something terrible had happened to Mandy, but she was not prepared to believe that Al was hurt—again.

"Curtis, you call the Air Force, someone in the Air Force, right now. See how scared the child is? We need to put this awful feeling of hers to rest. But I think it will turn out all right, sweetheart. Al couldn't be hurt again; I just know it in my bones. You go call, Curtis."

As Curtis Deforest walked to the hallway telephone he remembered a fall day in 1945. The three of them had driven to Portland to put young Al on the bus for a faraway training base. He had no fear for his young son's safety, the war was nearly over and he would come to no harm. Deforest hated war; he only wanted an education for Al, the GI Bill.

Now their house was full of people in the middle of the night and they might never see their son again.

# Chapter 47

Sometimes he could see a portion of the instrument panel, but mostly he saw a gray haze. He had no idea what he was doing here, even though some part of him knew he was in an airplane. Something was wrong with his chest, but he didn't believe it was too bad—whatever it was. The thing with his head was bothersome, though. He could feel shattered fragments on the helmet he wore, and once he had probed behind his left ear. There was an unnatural softness there, and loose pieces of bone held on by scalp tissue. Just thinking about the injury terrified him. He decided to leave that spot alone for a while.

At first there had been no feeling at all, but now increasing waves of pain and sickness rolled through him. He thought it wouldn't be too bad, that he could ignore the pain. There were minutes when he felt no pain at all, and then a wave of agony would start above his left eye and tramp brutally back through his skull to his neck, building to a nauseating crescendo in his broken skull before receding again to nothingness. He knew he had to be brave; to not cry out or lose hope, but it was getting harder. He wondered if there was a way to summon help, but nothing came to mind.

Finally, without conscious thought, he needed to end it. He reached forward and rolled the pitch trim wheel nose-down, sending *EyeCatcher* into a dive. It would be over in a few minutes now: he would be released from this agony and uncertainty. The thought of sweet rest to come made his pain bearable.

Now someone called. He could hear a faint voice in the good earphone, the one on the right side of his helmet, but there was wind noise from a hole in the canopy above his head; he couldn't understand. He concentrated and finally caught the meaning after several repetitions.

"It's Dave, Al. Roll the pitch trim back up. I know what you're doing. Roll the trim up right now."

He was happier, someone was telling him what to do, helping him. He rolled the trim wheel back up and felt himself pressed into the seat as *EyeCatcher* recovered from the dive. Now what? He heard the voice again and slowly understood the words.

"I can see you're hurt. Can you fly? Can you answer me?"

Al didn't know what to do; he didn't think he could talk and it hurt terribly to turn his head. Eventually he raised his right hand in hope of some sort of communication. Now the voice came to him again.

"OK, Al. That's good. I understand you can't talk. You're flying in circles. The reason I found you is you're flying in circles, making big contrails. We need to stop that. We need to get you on the escape heading. I want you to turn to 165 degrees magnetic. Remember 165 Al, that's the escape heading. Turn now."

Al didn't know what it meant to turn now, so he sat still, hoping for a better instruction. The voice came back.

"Can't you see? There's a head wound, I see a head wound. If you can't see, raise your hand again."

Al could do this; it was easy. He raised his hand. The voice helped again.

"All right. Here's what we'll do: I'll tell you when we come up on the escape heading. Then I want you to roll in some right rudder trim, get straightened out. Put your hand on the rudder trim control to show me you know where it is."

Al put his hand on the trim control without thought.

"Good. We have about two minutes yet. I want you to put your hand on the fuel selectors now. Show me the fuel selectors there on the left console."

Again Al could do this without thinking, he reached over to the console, being careful to keep his injured head level.

"Turn all three handles so the pointers are down, that will put you on ALL: you'll feed all the tanks into the pump and get every drop available. You're going to need it. Turn all of them down now, Al."

Al was quite pleased; he understood that he was talking to Dave Rey. He was being helped. This was what he'd needed all along. Dave spoke again a few minutes later.

"We're coming around to 165 degrees now. When I say Mark, I want you to rotate the rudder trim wheel about two inches forward, toward the nose. That'll straighten you out."

Time passed. Al was unclear.

"Al, reach over to the autopilot panel now and punch the heading-hold button. You'll fly right on out across French Indo-China. You'll get to the South China Sea at Hai' phong. Keep going to Hainan Island and then turn on your IFF beacon. The Navy has BON HOMME RICHARD out there: it's the closest friend we have, about three hours away. You don't have enough fuel now to get back to base. Remember the IFF beacon. If you understand, hold up your hand."

Al felt pretty good, the words were clear enough. He held up his hand. Dave Rey had a devastating final comment.

"I have to leave you now, Al. Low on fuel. I took some hits, my tanks are leaking. I can't get out with you, so I'll try for the Burmese border and bail out over the jungle down there. Do you remember that my folks live in San Francisco? If I don't make it back, be sure to see them. San Francisco, Al. Remember."

Some time during the long transit over Indo-China Al's vision partially returned. He could see the instrument panel clearly with his left eye, and his far vision was sufficient to make out ground features: the horizon and clouds. The right eye wasn't very good, he could see light and dark, and make out large objects close at hand, but that was about it.

His head wound was still bleeding and he felt well enough to try to do something about it. First he withdrew a map from the case alongside his seat, tore it into quarters, and balled up a section. His idea was to stuff the paper into the hole behind his ear and stop the bleeding. But as he placed the paper against his sensitive wound it felt far too stiff and harsh. He dropped the paper and lost interest in bandaging himself.

Later he remembered the first aid kit strapped to the rear of his seat. After several moments of painful movement he was able to disengage the kit and get it into his lap. He made a wad of gauze and stuffed it gently behind his ear, relying on the remains of his helmet to keep it in place. Two squeezable metal syringes of morphine were taped to a cardboard at the top of the kit. Al thought taking morphine might not be such a good idea, since he was supposed to be flying the airplane. After a moment's reflection, he pulled a syringe from the cardboard and jabbed through the flight suit into his thigh and squeezed the metal tube empty. In less than a minute he felt his entire body relax. Well-being swept over him. He fell asleep as the wound continued to bleed.

He awoke later and the first-aid kit was still sitting in his lap: that was good, encouraging. He could remember the struggle involved in freeing the kit from the rear of his seat. He was making progress. He leaned forward to read fuel gauges; about an hour of fuel left in the main wing tanks, none in the auxiliaries. *EyeCatcher* had climbed somehow and she was struggling at her service ceiling of 51,000 feet. He felt this rather than knew it. The exhaust sound had changed from a full-bodied roar to feeble pings as the cylinders struggled for oxygen in the thin air. The engines sounded like sewing machines. He was floating down the sky in a strange bubble where the laws of physics seemed suspended: no thrust and no drag, no lift and no weight. The controls were loose and unresponsive. He was way too high, he needed to get down; get down slowly and gently.

Now he was leaving a land mass and proceeding out over a large body of water. A large island jutted up far ahead, maybe a hundred miles ahead. Someone had told him to do something here but he couldn't recall the action he was to take. His hand reached out for the throttle quadrant and retarded both throttles evenly and the nose fell and the aircraft started down. The action amazed Al; it happened without any thought or effort on his part, as if another person was in here with him controlling the airplane. He fell asleep again.

Now another voice came to bother him. He came slowly up to consciousness and tried hard to understand this new voice coming through his right earphone. It was a little easier this time, he remembered from the other voice. He had learned something from the other voice and that was good. Finally the words registered.

"Aircraft off my starboard wing, identify yourself: talk, turn on an IFF beacon, wave your hand, anything." He turned his head left gently, but his shattered skull sent points of pain. He stopped. No use trying to see to the right, that eye didn't work. He thought a while and finally raised his right hand. The voice spoke to someone else.

"PEACHTREE 4 to OCTAVE. It's ours, but no markings except some nose-art: *EyeCatcher*. Old. One of those Army night-fighters I think.

Some damage, flak damage it looks like. The pilot's hurt, he seems to be out of it. What do you want me to do?"

He waited now, hoping for the voice again. It came.

"What's your fuel situation, how much gas do you have?"

Once he had known what the words meant but now he didn't. He sat very still.

"Gas! How much gas? Look at your fuel gauges. Hold up a finger for every hour of fuel you have left."

He leaned forward without conscious thought and studied the six gauges, then made a zero with thumb and index finger. The voice was alarmed now, he could tell.

"OK, OK. I can escort you over to Hai' phong and you can land at the airport, but they'll intern you…and the medical care isn't going to be good. I know you're American, or I guess you're American. The other thing we can do is get you to the carrier and you can ditch. We have helicopters there; they can save you. Either way, you have to buck up and start flying the airplane. If you want to try for Hai' phong, hold up one finger. If you want to ditch, hold up two. Al was perking up now; he knew what to do. He held up two fingers, but he had no intention of going into the water. He knew he wouldn't survive a water landing.

"I'll get you down; we'll put you in the water. Something…someone will be there for you, don't worry. But listen pal, you have to wake up and fly the thing, I can't do it for you."

The two aircraft maneuvered in descending turns for fifteen minutes, finally breaking through a marine cloud layer at 2500 feet. The ocean was flat gray slate with silver flecks as far as the eye could see. Al could see the aircraft carrier ahead on the right. It looked far too small for an airplane to land on. The voice came to him again.

"Fly wing on me. I'm going to take you down the approach path, but we'll go short of the deck. I'll put you down right into the wake behind the ship—at the stern, the back end: it's smooth water, and our helicopter is ready to help you. I'm pulling around on your port side now—your left. You seem to see better from that side. Stay on my wing, put your flaps full down. We'll slow to 95 mph. Can you go that slow?"

Al knew he could go even slower with the huge full-span flaps out, he held his hand up.

He aimed for the front edge of the flight deck. It was still discouragingly tiny. The voice yelled at him as they approached the carrier.

"Reduce power, you're too high, you'll hit the back of the ship. You're long; YOU'RE LONG!"

And another voice was yelling at him now.

"Aircraft on final approach, BREAK OFF, BREAK OFF. POWER NOW, NOW, NOW!"

Al didn't trouble himself with the voices now: all his faculties were concentrated on flying onto the front edge of the flight deck. He paid no attention to speed or flight attitude or possible obstructions on the deck: he simply aimed. He watched with intense satisfaction as the tiny deck become larger. There was nothing left in his small world but the flat surface ahead. Some other being was manipulating the controls as he sat in fascination, wondering if it was possible to run right into that tiny spot.

Now he saw a few figures standing on some kind of platform to the left of the flight deck. One of the figures was waving yellow paddles frantically. He turned his attention back to the deck: it was approaching at a frightening speed. Something within him sensed that he was too low or the deck was too high: maybe pitching up instead of remaining where he wanted it to be. Now he was clearly too low, and he pulled the control yoke right back as far as it would go and the nose responded sluggishly, rising until the deck was blotted out. His task was finished now. He could do no more to save himself.

*EyeCatcher* hit right at the edge of the deck, tail low. Both tail booms were severed and fell to the ship's wake far below before disappearing. Al felt a gentle jerk as the tails came off, then he was racing up the deck on the airplane's belly. He was a passenger now, along for the ride. He saw a wire barrier and felt another jerk. Now the massive carrier island structure was racing at him. He hoped this blow would be gentle, too. He didn't think his head would survive another hard hit.

*   *   *

"I'm a doctor son, we're going to put an IV in your arm now: a little stick is all. You're kind of caught in there, but the rescue boys will have you out in a few minutes."

Al felt the man reaching inside his flight suit, extracting his dog tags. The man studied the tags a moment.

"There's no name here, or serial number. O positive blood, that's good. And you're a Protestant son. We'll have the Padre here quickly. Just hold on."

He didn't want last rites, he wanted to tell them about the Other One: the one who was going over to Burma to parachute from his crippled plane. He tried to talk, but there were no words now. He motioned as if writing. The man pulled a small tablet from his shirt pocket and handed Al a pencil. It was hard to write. After three tries he had written ' Other One in Burma. Bail out. Half-way up the border.'

Al was pleased: now he had done everything he could. Darkness descended.

# Chapter 48

The Commander Air Group closed the Captains cabin door politely enough, but anger lit his eyes. He turned to a passageway speakerphone connected to the bridge.

"This is the CAG, Commander Denbow. Get me the Exec."

"Yeah, what is it Joe?"

"We need to come about into the wind for a launch."

"Come about? There's a typhoon back there. I don't know about that."

"Me neither, but those are Captain's orders."

"Jesus. This is nuts."

"I don't know what it is. Do it now or explain yourself to the Captain."

Denbow made his way along the passage to the ready room and hooked a finger at Chief Petty Officer Walter Lendowsky who was playing whist at the card table.

"Let's go, Chief. We have a launch as soon as we can turn around."

Lendowsky stubbed his cigarette but made no move to get up from the table. His card companions gave Denbow a strange look.

"In this? We shouldn't be launching in this, we'll get someone killed."

"I keep hearing that. Stick a cork in it Chief. We got a job to do here."

The BON HOMME RICHARD had altered course in the night to run before the storm, but now that would change. The massive aircraft carrier would turn straight into the wind and buck the violent sea.

Thirty minutes later the maneuver was complete and the ship was pitching in long even waves, the bow alternately pointing above the horizon and then below in a sedate and predictable oscillation. But the side motion, the rolling motion, was wild; a response to the crossing confused sea. The giant ship would heel over to 15 degrees, stay at this perilous angle for a time, start to return, then unexpectedly roll back to the extreme angle before returning to level. It was jerky and unpredictable: an off-the-wall thing.

Chief Lendowsky, trousers whipping wildly and foul weather jacket inflated by the gusting 40 knot wind at his back, was experiencing great difficulty anticipating when the deck angle would be satisfactory for launching the old S2F sitting waiting on the catapult, engines at idle. In his opinion, the whole fucking attempt should be scrubbed until they got free of the typhoon. They were likely to kill that Spook and a fine Naval Aircrew to boot. Launching an aircraft in these conditions was just plain goofy. But Denbow told him the Old Man had ordered it: he wanted the plane on its way to Japan right now.

The S2F pilot sat slumped in his comfortable seat as wind gusts whipped the fuselage about violently. The windshield wipers were unable to keep up with sheets of near horizontal rain but that was OK, he could see well enough out the side windows. He had volunteered himself and the co-pilot and now he questioned his judgment. He turned to his cockpit companion with a falsely cheerful grin and spoke above the moaning howl of the wind.

"Billy, why the hell did you volunteer me for this?"

Billy Louder was nervous too, but the remark broke the tension and he got out a good belly laugh.

"Ain't this awful? I guess I wanted to leave a nice insurance check for my heirs and mendicants, sir."

In the cargo bay Nurse Lt. Jana Weymeyer looked out the small round window opposite her seat: she could see the dents and scorch marks on the carrier island where the young man in the litter had crashed his peculiar aircraft attempting a landing: an attempt made in spite stern warnings to the contrary. The ship anti-aircraft weapons had been ready to fire as the crippled machine made a clumsy approach to their flight deck.

The Captain tried desperately to contact Pacific Fleet Headquarters in the short critical period before the aircraft came aboard, but there was no response. Out of time, the Captain risked his naval career: he ordered the ship's weapons to stand down and gave permission for the landing attempt, if you could even call it that.

Nurse Wallace frowned involuntarily as she studied the gravely injured young man. The CAG told her that the Captain had been talking to Washington for most of the morning. He said the young man had somehow managed to fly his damaged aircraft for hours to get out of hostile territory after being ambushed and wounded. The stranger had an in-and-out chest wound and a shattered skull. He had been semi-conscious yesterday while the rescue crew cut him free from wreckage, but now he was in a coma.

She wondered at the CAG's choice of words: hostile territory, ambushed. The United States was not at war; why had he used those terms?

Her thoughts returned to the litter patient: he was unstable now; she did not expect him to live much longer.

Finally Chief Lendowsky liked what he saw. He was planning ahead, anticipating the orientation of the deck in about one minute. He was making an artful and experienced judgment. He twirled his signal flag. The S2F pilot nodded agreement at the signal: the deck angle was looking good to him, too. The engines barked out a full power roar and the pilot gave the ready salute. As the 900-foot flight deck came level, the launch officer fell forward on a knee and gave the signal. A steam-powered catapult pulled the S2F forward violently and flung it from the deck.

Almost instantly a gusting downburst of wind pushed the aircraft toward the monstrous waves so sharply the pilot had to slam the controls full nose up to prevent a crash. For long seconds the issue was in doubt as the machine struggled forward just above the wave tops. Finally the powerful engines broke the stalemate. The massive paddle-blade propellers, straining under maximum power, began to lift the S2F from the sea in a staggering nose-high attitude.

Aboard the BON HOMME RICHARD, dozens of long-held breaths were slowly expelled as the aircraft recovered from its stumble and assumed a sluggish climb angle. It was soon swallowed in the fast moving scud of the storm.

# Chapter 49

Birdie tried to get up as soon as the airplane stopped, before the engines shut off, but Mandy restrained her in the seat. The big military transport was full of young men returning to their assignments after Christmas leave and Mandy thought the frail woman might be jostled in the rush to the door. Curtis Deforest stood and maneuvered from the window across the canvas-strapped seats to stand in the aisle, young men or not. The airplane loadmaster, a Sergeant, knew why they were aboard. He struggled forward to their seat row and stood up on the metal edge. He yelled for silence from the milling soldiers.

"LISTEN GODDAMNIT. We have parents here in this row. Their son is hurt and they need to get to him right now. You all step into the seat rows and make way. No one leaves this aircraft until I escort these people off."

A WAC PFC was waiting for them at the foot of the portable stairs, matronly in a tan seersucker uniform and sturdy walking shoes.

"Good afternoon folks, I'm Deborah Eaton from Patient Services. We didn't have a staff car available so we'll go in that cab."

She gestured toward an ancient lime-green Ford sitting on the tarmac fifty feet away. A sign on the cab door said 'Honolulu Transportation Co.'. They piled into the old cab as Private Eaton and the driver stowed luggage in the trunk. She spoke to the driver over the cab roof.

"1 Jarrett White Way. As fast as possible."

The cabbie nodded, he knew the address. It was the new Army Hospital up on Moanalua Ridge, a massive structure serving the entire Pacific Theater. The WAC was handing a slip of paper to the gate guard when Curtis Deforest spoke.

"Our son. How is our son, can you tell us anything? We've had no news since yesterday when we left San Francisco."

"I'm sorry. I really don't know anything. I'm only here to take you to the hospital. Dr. Prather is waiting; I'm sure he will answer your questions. We've made arrangements for you to stay in guest cottages right on the grounds…until we know more. Miss Piper is to have quarters also, separate quarters."

Birdie hugged herself and shivered in the tropical warmth, these had been the worst weeks of her life.

Wildly different stories had come to them in the days after Al's injury. First he was simply reported missing when the maximum flight time of his aircraft ran out. Then they were told he had crashed at sea and a search effort was underway. Finally, a heavily censored version of the truth was given to them; Al had crashed at a 'secure facility', was severely injured, and had been flown to Japan for emergency surgery.

Ten days passed in which they learned nothing new. They were scheduled to fly to Japan on two occasions only to have the flights cancelled pending 'resolution of patient's condition'. Finally, two days ago, Curtis Deforest had managed to pry the story loose with pressure from their Congressman. Al was still in Japan. He had improved after several days of dangerous instability and was being flown to Tripler Army Medical Center in Hawaii for specialized treatment. The parents were authorized to join him, but Mandy was not a dependent and therefore was not offered transportation.

Curtis Deforest contacted Dr. Mendes at his new family practice in Wenatchee. Mendes made sure Richard Tuck was aware of the situation. Tuck called Air Force Headquarters in a cold fury. Mandy had been cleared for the trip yesterday morning while they all sat waiting in the Military Transportation Terminal at Fairfield-Suisan Air Force Base. She had shrugged at the news, knowing Mr. Barlow would loan her the money for a ticket if it came to that.

PFC Eaton was out of the cab before it stopped rolling at the hospital entrance.

"Go straight into the lobby, an escort will be there for you. I'll see that your bags are sent to your quarters."

They were seated in a small consultation room off the lobby when Al's doctor strolled in. He was boyish in appearance with a thin pale face and unruly black hair. A melamine tag on his white laboratory smock identified Lewis B. Prather, M.D., Medical Corps. Mandy's heart sank; Al had been entrusted to a recent medical school graduate.

Prather sat opposite them across the small walnut conference table and smiled vaguely, speaking in the soft vowels of the upper class South.

"I'm Dr. Prather, Lew Prather, case manager for Lt. Deforest."

He paused and studied a chart attached to his clipboard for almost a minute before looking up.

"Your son has been wounded twice. Something, a bullet or a shell fragment, went entirely through his chest from the rear. Ribs were broken, but no nerves or blood vessels were damaged by the transit and we consider this to be a minor wound. He was also wounded in the back of the head, a wound that now threatens his life. The projectile struck the left occipital plate and excavated most of the bone. The fracture was communicated to neighboring skull plates as well. Although there are no shell fragments inside your son's brain, the impact removed a fair amount of the left occipital lobe. In addition to the direct injury, his brain suffered a major hydrodynamic shock causing laceration and swelling beyond the site of the direct injury."

He paused to see if they understood his explanation. Mandy hated him for what he was saying.

"He was operated on at the Obara Institute in Osaka, Japan to place a drain and one-way valve inside his skull to relieve pressure. Since his arrival we have found it necessary to open a large hole at the rear of his skull to give his brain room for the swelling that naturally follows an injury of this type. He's in a coma now, we have several life support measures instituted."

Curtis Deforest interrupted the monologue.

"Will he live? Will he be all right? How in God's name was he shot, there is no war now."

Prather nodded, understanding the question, knowing he did not have some of the answers.

"He's badly injured. We're doing everything that modern medicine knows to do for wounds of this type. I can only tell you that his medical situation is as serious as these things get. If we step back from the details and look to statistics, I would estimate just about even odds that he will survive. Don't allow this to shock or discourage you, remember he has an equal chance to live. He will need your support now. I believe he will sense your presence even though he cannot acknowledge it. It's important that you carry positive, hopeful thoughts into his room with you now as you visit."

He hugged the clipboard to his chest and suddenly looked older, careworn.

"He is heavily bandaged and his facial features are distorted. The facial distortion is temporary and will return to normal appearance with time. I can't tell you how he was injured Mr. Deforest. He was doing his duty in a heavily censored military operation. They don't tell us those things. If you follow me we will go to him now."

Mandy half-raised her hand to get his attention.

"Mentally? Will he be all right mentally? Are his faculties all right?"

Prather was out of his chair and leaving the room. He turned back.

"We can't predict the extent of his recovery; individual cases are so varied. I would guess, and I emphasize guess, he will suffer some weakness of his right arm and leg, possibly a vision problem, and there may well be personality alterations. All of these difficulties respond to therapy, and we have learned greatly from the war. If he survives I think there is every reason to hope for a functional life. Later, when you have the time, we'll schedule sessions with a Rehabilitation Technician so you can get details."

Mandy frowned.

"But he won't be the same, is that what you're saying?"

Prather nodded as he left the room.

Birdie gasped at the figure in the bed. Curtis assisted her to the room's only chair before turning to the bed. Al was unrecognizable: he was concealed by a mass of bandages and IV lines. The tube from an oxygen respirator was bandaged to his mouth. The only thing Deforest could see were his closed eyes, the right one was purple and swollen. Tears started down his cheeks and he choked. But he willed these things back and spoke to his son in reassurance.

"We're here with you now son. We won't leave you until this thing is right. We all love you and we know you'll pull through just fine. When this is over, when you're home with us, nothing will ever touch you or harm you again. I promise you that."

He left the room to search for two more chairs.

*     *     *

Somehow he became aware an orange glow through his eyelids. He was present now, somewhere, but there was nothing else for some time. Then he felt the need to clear his throat. He tried twice and nothing happened. The third time produced something between a cough and a rumble.

Mandy had drowsed off over her paperback novel. The three of them each took an eight-hour shift. The endless succession of days and nights had worn her to emotional and physical exhaustion, but now she was on her feet, fighting up through cobwebs of uneasy sleep. She took Al's hand, talking to him, praying.

"I heard you darling, I heard you. I know you're there, if you can hear me open your eyes. Please God hear me now. Your Mom and Dad are here too; we're all here helping you to get better."

He heard the sounds and knew understanding should come. Something urged action, but he did not know what to do. Someone he knew was here, someone he knew. He weakly squeezed the hand holding his.

"Bird."

"What sweetheart? I didn't understand."

"Bird…in…house. Angel."

"I'm here Al. I'll always be here. You're safe now."

"Broken bird,…broken…angel."

She sank to the floor still holding his hand, and the bitter angry thankful tears came. She thought of what they had done to this gentle man. She clenched her jaw to kill the sob in her throat and hoped someday she could hurt them, hurt them badly. But with the anger came hope, the tiniest seed of hope, and some part of her reveled in the knowledge that Al would be well someday. She knew it inside, the same way she had known the instant he was wounded. They had reached the bottom of this dark pit. They could start to build the life she had always wanted, the life delayed and denied to them all these years

Now she sensed that Al was gone again, but there was no fear. She knew he would be back. She went to a payphone down the hall with good news for the Deforests. It was about time.

"Birdie? Oh, he's here, he's back. He'll make it now: I know it. The same way I knew when he was hurt. Dear God, he tried to say a proverb we both remember, one he used to love: If a bird comes into your house it's an angel with a message from heaven. But he added something: the bird is broken now."

# Chapter 50

Al sat on a toilet seat in the motel bathroom as Mandy tugged and jerked the thick black hair into place with a coarse-tooth comb.

"J...Jesus H. Christ Mandy, you're p...pulling my head off."

She had resisted attending this damned award ceremony, but pressure from her parents and the Deforests won out. The parents were all in a small coffee shop at the front of the motel while she prepared Al for the event. He was dressed in the only Class A uniform he had left. The others, all brand-new, had mildewed while lying unworn in his duffel bag on that tropical island for ten months. There was no money for a new uniform, so this one would have to do.

"Stand up Al, let's have a look at you."

Al smiled brightly and stood, grateful for the attention.

"I...I bet I look pretty goddamned good, don't I?"

Mandy was crestfallen, her smile faded. The rehabilitation therapists had patiently explained that swearing was common in brain damage cases. The language center and the swearing center were in separate areas of the brain. Until speech therapy allowed the language center to resume dominance, there would be these unfortunate references.

"I've told you Al, don't use those bad words. Especially not today, for heaven's sake."

"Oh, I know that. You can c...c...rely on me."

She studied her tall handsome husband and could not suppress a giggle.

"Maybe I'm the only one darling, but I have to agree with you; you look pretty good. Now go out there and put on your jacket, or tunic, or whatever that thing is called. And don't sit down until the car comes, you'll spoil the crease."

Mandy had insisted the ceremony be completed by 9:00AM; Al became fatigued easily, then his speech slurred and he tended to be irritable.

She put the comb away and left the bathroom to stand at Al's side, gazing out the large window at the brilliant fall plumage on oaks, liquid ambers and dogwoods in the forest across the highway. At home the leaves simply turned brown and fell off in soggy clumps. It was different here in Virginia; there was a magnificent blaze of color.

And Al was different now, too. Testing indicated that his memory was normal, and his ability to write had not been damaged. In spite of months of therapy his speech still slurred when he was tired, and he tired easily. Most days he napped through the lunch hour. Then, when he awoke refreshed, the weakness in his right arm and leg were almost gone. By evening though, he would limp noticeably and have difficulty picking things up with his right hand.

The greatest difference was an unexpected and miraculous gift for Mandy. Before, Al tended to be self-centered and arbitrary. His old focus was on things mechanical and scientific. Somehow all that had been swept away by the brain injury. Now he was softer, more compliant, and his interests seemed to center in things artistic and sentimental.

Mandy's lips curved upward in a secret smile as she watched his eyes follow the motion of the brilliant red and yellow leaves fluttering in the fall wind. She knew he would stand there watching for hours unless she made him move on to another task. The doctors assured her that his intelligence was normal, but his intellectual interests had shifted. And she wasn't sorry about it, not a bit.

The door opened without a knock and Robert Piper stuck his head in.

"Come on, the driver just pulled in."

They left the room and walked up the cracked, weed-filled sidewalk toward the front, where a black limousine awaited them. The ceremony was in the Office of the Chief of Naval Operations, away from reporters and other curious eyes for reasons of security. A Chief Petty Officer waited, signaling for all to get in the long machine. Then he abruptly held up his hand.

"Oh, sir. Wait a minute. We need to fix your uniform; there'll be photographers and all."

He unpinned Al's wings from the right side of his blouse and affixed them to the left side over his medals where the device belonged. Mandy was chagrined, she had not known, and neither had their parents.

Mr. and Mrs. Piper exchanged excited chatter as the limousine cruised down the George Washington Parkway to the Pentagon: this was a great day for Al, a day of recognition for all he had done. Mandy was somber and reserved. She stared out at the muddy Potomac River making its way south almost as fast as their vehicle moved in the morning traffic jam. She noticed that Curtis Deforest was quiet too: they had never discussed Al's injury, but Mandy was certain he resented the Government, held them responsible for Al's terrible difficulties. The driver pointed out the Pentagon as they approached. Mandy thought it looked like a warehouse: the most ungainly building she had ever seen. She was happy when they drove down a ramp to the basement and she could no longer see it.

She took Al's hand in the elevator to reassure him. He looked down at her and smiled serenely, apparently quite at ease. The Navy man herded them from the elevator across a broad corridor through a frosted glass door into a large room that had been furnished for the occasion. Ten folding chairs had been arranged in front of a small podium, and a long table at the rear of the room held coffee and cakes. Mandy noticed that a bar was set up alongside the coffee table and she spoke softly to Al as they waited.

"No booze, brother. Remember what the doctors said."

Al turned to her after studying the interesting room arrangements.

"Yeah. No a…alcohol, or I might have a seizure. Don't w…worry, I'll stick to bread and water."

The hallway door opened and a patrician couple stepped through: the man lean and white-haired, the woman well dressed and wearing expensive jewelry. The gentleman turned to hold the door for a wild looking young man in a wheelchair. Mandy recoiled instinctively at the legless man. He searched the room with angry dark chestnut eyes, saw Al, and sped over.

"How ya'll doing, young Al. I heard they got you too."

Al looked down in bewilderment.

"W…what happened to your legs Doug? Jesus Christ."

Trapnell looked up at Mandy and shook his head.

"Well, goddamn. I guess we're the long and the short of it now, ain't we: no legs and no brains. What a combination. Your powerful government in action."

He exuded a strong odor of alcohol as he spoke. Mandy bristled.

"I know who you are, Mr. Trapnell, but you watch your mouth. There's nothing wrong with Al's brains. He's just had a head injury; it will be a while before he gets back to normal. There are some things he can't remember right now."

Trapnell glared at her as if about to attack, then his face softened.

"Oh man, excuse me. I get to feeling sorry for myself and this stuff just comes jumping out. Gettin' old and crotchety before my time, I guess. I'm Doug, and I guess you must be Mandy. Damned if you ain't a pretty one. Sparky, too."

The parents stepped in and introduced themselves, accustomed to breaking up Doug's social explosions.

"I'm Boland Trapnell, and this is my wife Lenore. We want to thank you for saving our son's life, Lt. Deforest. We know what you did. We're grateful even if he is not."

Al shook his head.

"Well, you're welcome, b…but I didn't save his life. I d…don't even know what happened to his g…goddamned legs. In fact, he probably saved my life: he flew down to Wake Island with me to make sure I didn't get lost. He looked after me that day."

Trapnell grinned hugely, enjoying the gaffe. People minced around him now, treading lightly.

Abner Day, John Stenzell, Richard Tuck and Penrod Taylor stepped into the room from the CNO's office. A Major and two photographers followed. As the confusion of greetings and introductions swirled about, Tuck disengaged and walked to Trapnell's wheelchair. He knelt and embraced the young man clumsily; there were no words.

Mandy watched the crazy chestnut eyes dart about and she braced for another explosion. But the eyes closed and Trapnell patted Brigadier General Richard Tuck on the back as if he was a baby.

"There now. There. Shush, just shush."

Tuck stood and walked to the rear of the room, dabbing his eyes with a handkerchief. Trapnell seemed calmer.

The Major moved among the group, politely requesting them to take seats. Then he called the group to order and began the ancient business of honoring warriors.

"Attention to orders! The United States Air Force is pleased to recognize today the accomplishments of Lockwood A. Deforest and Caleb D. Trapnell with awards of the Medal of Honor and the Air Force Cross respectively…"

The citation droned forward at considerable length, and Mandy's attention wandered.

The Air Force Liason officer at Sawtelle Veterans Hospital in West Los Angeles had approached Al last month. The Medal of Honor nomination Tuck submitted almost twelve months ago had finally been approved. The Marine Reconnaissance Team operating in Sinkiang Province had been extracted three months ago and the leader, a Gunnery Sergeant Quinn, provided a statement corroborating the gun camera film taken the day Al rescued Art Trumbauer.

Al brought the news home to Mandy that evening. He was excited and greatly surprised; he had absolutely no recollection of the events he was to be honored for.

Now Mandy watched him standing at attention in front of the group and she worried that he would become exhausted before the long-winded Major wound down. She waved at him discreetly and mouthed.

"Relax, it will take a while yet."

Al grinned, but he remained at attention.

She studied Trapnell; he was quiet now, sitting in his wheelchair beautifully dressed in a cashmere sport jacket and trousers of the finest flannel. The trousers were discreetly folded and pinned above the jacket skirt, where the pins would not show. Her heart broke for these two, and for the other young men she would never meet.

Abner Day moved among the group after the ceremony chatting and shaking hands. He smiled at Mandy and put out his hand.

"This must be a proud day for you, Mrs. Deforest."

Mandy crossed her arms and refused to take the extended hand.

"It is not a proud day for me. Can you look around this room and be proud? Look what you've done to these boys. Do you think a medal and a scrap of ribbon can make up for what they've lost? I don't. You should be ashamed."

Day lowered his hand.

"I'm sorry you feel that way. These are not the first young men to make a great sacrifice for their country. They have my greatest respect."

He meant the words he had spoken and he was not offended by her anger. With long practice he forced his mind ahead to the next events in his busy day and moved away from Mandy to the next group. He wrote in his diary that evening.

*November 21, 1950*

*Attended awards ceremony this a.m. Two young airmen from sensitive program, both grievously injured. Wife of one was young and strong and beautiful, not intimidated by high position of those in room. She attacked me furiously over husband's injuries. I listened but did not respond. She must think I am a cold one. I wonder how many policymakers are forced to look at the consequences of their actions at this close personal level. It was very hard.*

## Chapter 51

Mandy pulled to the curb at the bus stop and handed Al a slip of paper.

"Two interviews today, Al. The first one is an air-conditioning installer job. It's on Crenshaw just south of Olympic. Take the blue-line bus to Crenshaw, and then you can walk down to Olympic Boulevard. The second one is with Southern California Edison, reading electric meters. It's almost downtown, on Hoover. When you're through with the first man, walk back up to Olympic and wait for the orange-line bus, the one with the orange sign in the window. Get off at Hoover. Here's your lunch and put these addresses in your shirt pocket."

Al took the brown bag and waved goodbye. He sat on the bus bench and crossed his legs, keeping an eye out for the bus. He felt darn good today, the tiredness was almost gone now and his arm was quite strong: the VA had done a good job for him. Except the speech, of course: he still slurred a little in the evenings, and he slurred a lot when he was under pressure. He slurred when he had to do these job interviews, which he hated. He wanted to work; it would be a relief to have a job to go to, but he knew he didn't do the interviews well. The people were polite, but he could tell they were suspicious about his speech. Well, he just had to keep trying because they needed the money now. The Air Force stopped his disability pay three months ago: the letter said he was rehabilitated now.

They had been getting along pretty well before, Mandy made $107.50 a month as a VA secretary and he got $78.37 disability every month:

enough for their efficiency apartment in Santa Monica and some left over to pay for the old Plymouth they had purchased last year. Some weekends they went all the way up to Solvang and had a picnic; it was great.

But now they were having financial trouble and he could tell Mandy wanted to go home. He liked it here all right, except it was only May and already hot. The grassy winter hills were dessicated and brown already, nothing like the soft evergreen foliage they had grown up with.

He wrote a letter to his folks that Mandy didn't know about. He wanted work at home. They asked around, but Tillamook was a small town at the bottom of an economic cycle and there were no jobs. Mandy could go back to work for Mr. Barlow whenever she wanted to, but one job wouldn't provide a living for them. Situations like this used to bother him a lot, but it wasn't so bad now. Things would work out.

Mr. Paul Stein, owner of the Thermal Control Company, greeted Al for the first interview. Stein had a pale complexion and green milky eyes that looked to Al like boiled eggs. Stein waxed enthusiastic about the brand new field of air conditioning, and then he had the usual opening question.

"Can you give me your employment history? What was your last job?"

Al was used to the question, but it still made him nervous. He smiled and tried to look unconcerned.

"I was a radio mechanic in the A…Air Force. Then I was a pilot. I…I was injured. I can't do that work any more."

He slurred the last sentence badly and had to repeat it. Mr. Stein explained that his firm installed air conditioners in cars and in homes. In homes, the larger jobs required installing heavy compressors in cramped, superheated attics. He wondered if Al's injuries would prevent heavy lifting in that sort of heat. Al thought about it.

"Oh, I'm very strong. I think I could do the work. The heat w…would be OK, too."

When Al left Stein entered a note on the employment application, ' Do not hire. Drinking.'

Al thought he had done well as he walked to the bus stop; he could tell Mr. Stein liked him.

He got off the orange-line bus a few blocks early because he wanted to have his lunch in Westlake Park. There was a lake there and he liked to feed part of his sandwich to the ducks. It was a thrill to watch the ducks take off from the lake; the heavy bodied birds made a great commotion before entering the air, then sped upward at great speed, their small wings flapping energetically. It reminded Al of the takeoffs from Isla Mattoon. But he didn't miss that time anymore; he was happy here with Mandy. He was glad he had lived.

The interview at Southern California Edison was entirely different. Edison was a giant company and very well organized. Al stated his business and the receptionist handed him a standardized test on a single sheet of paper, directing Al into a small booth at the end of a long aisle. She explained the purpose of the test and the time limit. She would come for his paper in fifteen minutes.

Al sat down and studied the test. It was simple, really. A column of sixty fifteen-digit numbers ran down the left edge of the paper. Al was to copy the numbers in pencil on the right side of the paper. Pretty easy, he had always been good with numbers. He began, concentrating on the complex transpositions, and finished several minutes early. He proudly handed his test to the receptionist when she came. Later, in the personnel interview, the lady looked at Al's test and handed it back to him.

"Mr. Deforest, you've done very well on all the numbers you copied, not a single mistake. But you left out a sequence of ten numbers right there in the middle. Did you understand the instructions?"

Al looked at the test, convinced it was someone else's. There must have been a mix-up. But it was his test all right; he recognized the printing.

"Well, no. The girl said I had fifteen minutes and I finished early. I guess I just didn't see the ones in the middle. That's not so bad is it? I got all the others right."

He walked up Hoover Blvd to Wilshire to catch the green-line bus. That way he wouldn't have to transfer, he'd be able to go all the way out to the Sawtelle veteran's complex and meet Mandy at work. The Edison interview had not gone as he hoped: how the hell could he have missed all those numbers? At least he could tell Mandy how well he had done at the Thermal Control Company.

Mandy called her mother from work the next day. She tried to be calm and logical but it all came rushing out like toothpaste from a squeezed tube.

"Mom, we just can't be down here, I can't stand it. Al can't find work and we're behind with the bills. And I went to the doctor last week and I'm pregnant: talk about timing. The landlord said if we couldn't pay he was going to evict us. Al's tried and tried. No one says anything, but I know they won't hire him because of his poor speech. They don't see who he really is. We'll pack and leave this weekend. I don't care if we pick apples; we need to be near our families now. I want you to do something for me."

Her mother listened with love and sympathy and deep concern. They could take Mandy and Al for a time, but there just wasn't enough money to go around if the youngsters had to stay very long.

# Chapter 52

Alice Piper smoothed her skirt nervously and looked at her shoes. She was silently rehearsing before launching this important discussion. She willed the nervousness away: things would work out or they wouldn't. All she could do was to try.

"Howard, Mandy wants to come home. They're having a terrible time down there in Los Angeles. The government took Al's sick pay away. They just can't get by on what she makes, and Al can't find work because of his injuries."

That was good, she thought. She would get him on her side by mentioning Al. The whole town knew about Al.

Barlow shook his head.

"You didn't need to come all the way over here to tell me that, Alice. I've told Mandy time and again she can come back here whenever she wants to."

"Well, that's fine and we all appreciate your help. But Al needs work too, they can't get by up here either unless there's work for Al. I'm asking that you find a job for Al."

Barlow's brow furrowed, he had not expected this.

"Well, I don't know about that Alice. We're not supposed to know what Al did over there, but we all have a pretty good idea and we're proud of him, proud of our hometown boy. He's been doing such important work, Alice. What could I possibly offer him up here that would match what he's done? I'd be embarrassed."

Alice nodded, pleased.

"Al's very smart Howard, you remember that. His school grades were at the top. But he was hurt; his head was hurt badly, and all that military business is over with. Mandy says he's just as smart as ever, but he's different now: a gentle boy. I think he would appreciate any sort of work you could offer him."

Barlow twisted in his chair uncomfortably. Alice was leading him to something, but he couldn't see what.

"I know he was hurt Alice, but hurt or well, he's still mighty big in the eyes of our little town."

He paused to look out the window, calculating.

"Well, there is one thing that would help me around here. I just bought the funeral home over in Lake Oswego. We're short of embalmers over there. In fact I'm short of embalmers everywhere."

He looked at her for an uncertain moment, not sure he was doing anyone a favor.

"It's necessary work, Alice, honest work; but it's not the most pleasant thing in the world. The profession attracts some strange people: oddballs, drinkers, people who stay a time and then move on with no notice. If you think it might be suitable, I'd be willing to hire Al as a trainee embalmer for a small salary. Heck, I'll even send him to the school over in Eugene and get him certified. Then he could move up the ladder. But my god, Alice, that's not much of an offer for a hometown hero. I'd be ashamed. I'm not sure the City Council would be all that happy either."

Alice Piper was firm.

"They accept your offer, Howard; with gratitude. We'll all be so happy to get them back here with us where they belong. And you let Robert and I handle the City Council. I promise you we'll see each member and explain the situation. The City Council will never be a problem for you."

Al packed their belongings in the Plymouth that Saturday morning. The car was a business coupe, with an extra long trunk for salesmen's cases and the like. Everything they owned was packed in two small suitcases and two wooden vegetable crates. They looked tiny in there, and did not nearly fill the cavernous trunk.

They said goodbye to the young couple in the next-door apartment, checked again for overlooked items, and drove away from the only home of their married life. Mandy felt pleased and angry and deeply vindicated. She had nursed Al through the terrible, frightening recovery period in Hawaii. Then she helped him fight the goddamned government when he was denied a rehabilitation program. His year of rehabilitation at Sawtelle was ended now and he was well: mostly well.

They were on their way to start the life she had always hoped for, a life among friends and family at home—where they belonged.

Al wanted to drive up the California coast to Oregon, immersed in coastal beauty. He wanted to stop along the California Mission Chain. He wanted to see Cambria, San Simeon, Palo Alto, the Muir Forest and an endless list of tourist spots. He bubbled with anticipation: he wanted to stop and see them all. Mandy nixed the entire concept, she wanted to get home to Tillamook, get settled, and put in five solid months at work before taking maternity leave around Thanksgiving. They had lost time and it needed to be made up. His eyes rolled to her as he drove.

"Well s…shit Mandy, didn't y…you ever hear about gather ye' daisies while ye' may?"

A flash of humor crossed her face. She turned to him, hunched and trying to stifle a giggle. Then she threw back her head in a great peal of laughter.

"What a guy you are! OK, we'll split the difference. The Mission Chain and the Redwoods, then we hump it."

He smiled and turned back to the road. She suddenly thought how close they had come to missing all this and hot tears came before she could stop them. Al didn't understand.

"What's wrong?"

"Nothing dopey, just drive."

It was hot, slow going through Memorial Day weekend traffic in West Los Angeles, even worse in the San Fernando Valley. Traffic improved going over the Grapevine and almost evaporated in the San Joaquin Valley.

Finally, after eight hours with only two stops, they selected a motel in Modesto. Mandy protested the expense, but they went to dinner at a modest roadside diner and shared a birthday bottle of wine. Al's doctors warned him about alcohol, but the occasion demanded something special. They were both born on May 31, 1927: ten days after Lindbergh flew to Paris.

They were twenty-five years old now and they wanted to put the past behind them and they wanted to believe in the world ahead.

Al thought twenty-five years was a long time to have lived.

## Chapter 53

Eight years he had been with Barlow Services, Inc. now, and Al was overwhelmed with demand for his special personal touch at funerals. But he was just one person; he simply couldn't do it all. So increasingly he supervised, rather than participated in, the services. This distressing situation went through his mind as he was finishing Mrs. Waters.

The elderly matron's corpse lay in graceful composition; feet together, hands delicately crossed and resting upon the floral summer dress, right shoulder slightly down, head slightly elevated and turned toward those who would view her shortly. He had applied and removed three shades of blush, yet none presented the natural appearance he was striving for; none quite matched the foundation and eye shadow he had selected. He opened a theatrical makeup case and studied the selections, finally choosing a shade known in the trade as Rachel. The result pleased him. With the blush correct, he was very close to being satisfied with the presentation.

The Waters girls provided a dress, hat, shoes and handbag for the deceased. Al disapproved of the hat: it was not appropriate for the dress. But he always accepted family choices, so he had quietly praised the young women. Now he turned to open a second makeup case and searched for the correct eyeliner. Al owned four theatrical makeup cases and two mortuary make-up cases: expensive to purchase and expensive to maintain, but worth the cost. Relentless pursuit of perfection drove him to ever-higher levels of achievement. Economy had never been an option with Al, not in this business.

He applied the new eyeliner and stood back in sharply focused assessment. The color and blending were perfect now. Mrs. Waters looked, if not as she had in life, then at least in peaceful repose, prepared for her eternal journey.

The door opened behind him and embalmer Russell Peabody glided up silently behind him. He spoke in a hushed tone.

"Mr. Barlow would like to see you sometime today at your convenience."

Al nodded absently, his focus still on Mrs. Waters' appearance.

"Where is he?"

"He'll be at the Beaverton facility until noon, then he's going over to Salmonberry. He said he's going home early today."

It was an unusual request. Al roamed the five campuses of Barlow Services, Inc. freely, and Barlow was semi-retired now. Weeks could pass between meetings. He shrugged dismissively. He would find Mr. Barlow after the one-thirty service, over at the Salmonberry campus.

He returned to Mrs. Waters, a difficult case. She had been in the coroners vault for almost three days before shipment. Successful embalming was greatly aided by receiving the deceased within 12 hours of death. Two days post-mortem made her a Type III case, requiring stronger embalming solution than normal. The choice was critical; a solution too weak lead to putrefaction before burial, but a solution too strong caused tanning and wrinkling. Al felt he had made the correct decision here, but her hands were slightly shrunken, they required further effort. He loaded a syringe with collodion and injected through her palms to restore a natural appearance.

His goal was always to provide the bereaved with an eternal 'memory picture' of the loved one at rest and at peace: a pleasing mental image of the deceased that would last throughout their lifetime.

Al was licensed by the State of Oregon in Funeral Direction and Embalming Science and he held an Associate in Arts Degree in Mortuary Management from Beaverton Community College. He was very, very good at his trade, dedicated to providing the best possible experience for his clients. He viewed his work as a calling, not a craft.

Al was early for the service. He sat beside the podium watching as Mrs. Waters family and friends gathered. At one-thirty he stood and began reading his composition: 'In Memoriam—IV'. Through the years he had composed six services, each honed over and over again as he noted audience reaction. Mandy thought they were all excellent; she had obtained formal copyright protection. He finished in fifteen minutes, closed the leather-bound book softly and glanced at the clock. Then he turned to the small gathering: the faces looked at him, intensely concentrated.

"The family has requested the song 'As Time Goes By' to close our service."

Al launched the song with accompaniment from Mrs. Barlow on the chapel organ. His clear tenor voice reverberated strongly from the stained glass windows. As always, there were breakdowns in his audience, men and women weeping unashamedly. In the early years, when he was learning the business, the emotional displays were upsetting. They took something from his singing. Now he understood this deep need for tears and he was strengthened by the emotion.

He finished and walked to the rear of the chapel to receive the family and guests. He would not go to the graveside today. John Bigelow, the Episcopal minister from McMinnville, would lead the final ceremony.

Al was oversubscribed as a funeral director. Word of mouth kept him tightly, impossibly scheduled. He was by far the most requested member of the Oregon Funeral Directors Association. The organization knew; they kept track of such things. Al could not keep up because people somehow understood that he cared. And they saw the shadow across his heart that bonded them in grief.

Al was like a gatekeeper to eternity. He struggled prodigiously to understand the meaning of death. He owed his customers an explanation of the event that had devastated their lives. He read books from the public library, books with differing views on living and dying: Christianity, Judaism, Hinduism and Islam. He purchased by the dozens metaphysical texts on death. All these things made him more able to impart a sense of place for those left in life by a lost loved one.

Inside, he remained unsure there was a God available to him; a God of the type created by religionists. He felt personally indentured to a higher being, but the form remained obscure. And a bewildering voice sometimes poked through his haze of feelings, whispering there was nothing beyond. People just stopped, like an old worn-out watch. The darkness of eternal sleep might lie ahead, nothing more.

He pulled into the parking lot at the Salmonberry facility of Barlow Services, Inc. just after three in the afternoon. He saw Mr. Barlow's Pontiac parked at the rear of the lot, shielded from the afternoon sun by a giant maple. He entered the side door, proceeded through the chapel to the altar and opened an unmarked door behind the pulpit.

A shock of surprise brought Al to full attention. Barlow sat behind his desk, feet up, staring out at green forests to the north, a half-full tumbler of whiskey before him. Something was wrong: Howard Barlow never drank during the business day.

"Everything all right, Mr. Barlow?"

Barlow started visibly; his mind had been far away.

"Fine, Al, fine. Just sit down with me here for a while, we have some talking to do."

Barlow watched Al and felt a deep sense of good fortune. Eight years ago he had hired him as a favor, an act of charity. Now the reverse was true. Al was a natural in the service end of the business. He had helped to build a rock-solid, expanding business through all of Northwest Oregon. And Mandy was Treasurer now, doing the same solid work for the financial part of the business.

Today would be all the harder for their skill and loyalty and support. Barlow was nervous, unsure of a beginning.

"Drink, Al? It's OK, we're both through for the day now."

Al shook his head. He could drink now, there had been no seizure problems at all, but he wanted to be alert for whatever was coming.

"No thanks. I'll take a rain check."

Barlow swiveled his chair around to put his feet up on the now cold cast-iron radiator. He spoke with his back to Al.

"Do you miss the military Al; the flying I mean, all the excitement?"

Al was startled by the question, unprepared. He thought a minute before answering.

"I loved to fly, but that time is behind me now. I can't go back. I don't think I would want to go back. This is my life now, right here; as satisfying to me as flying ever was."

He resisted the temptation to ask what this was about. He trusted Barlow: a kind and generous man who put the needs of his employees first. He searched for a glint of humor.

"Besides, the flying I did was more terrifying than satisfying."

Barlow sat silent for a time, and then he spoke again.

"We received an offer to purchase the business Al; a good one, from a Dutch firm. I'm going to take it. Louella wants me to slow down. She tells me we've been doing this for almost 55 years now. I'm seventy-nine, I guess I'd like a little time for just the two of us before I become a client here."

He turned the chair around and his eyes were apprehensive.

"Don't worry; I'll see that you and Mandy are taken care of by the new owners. I plan to exempt five percent of the business from the sale and give it to you and Mandy. That's how I feel about the two of you."

Al's stutter was long gone but now it returned.

"W…w…wait a minute, Mr. Barlow. I…I want you to give Mandy and me a chance here."

"A chance Al; what do you mean? You know I'll be around, I'll see that you two are treated fairly."

Al and Mandy had talked about this lately; knowing his retirement must be close. Apprehension flickered through him. He needed to be clear here. He swallowed and took a deep breath.

"We want to buy the business. M…Mandy thinks we could get a loan. We've talked about selling the house if necessary. Just give us a chance."

Barlow stood to pace the room, this was even harder than he had imagined.

"Al, the offer is 1.1 million dollars. We both know the business will pencil-out about eight hundred thousand on profit or cash flow. They're offering me a three hundred thousand dollar premium. That's hard to ignore. And I doubt the bank will take a very liberal attitude about the premium when you talk to them about a loan. They'll chalk that extra up to goodwill and demand that it be paid off up front, or certainly within a year or two. I don't see how to get around that, unless I just turn down the offer. That would be pretty hard."

Al was scrambling now, weak and vulnerable.

"We both know part of that premium is because of what Mandy and I have done around here. Helping you, sir. I…I mean no disrespect."

"Louella and I love you two; you're like our own children. We would never hurt you."

"B…but you are hurting us. We always hoped you would give us a chance when you decided to retire. We just want a chance."

Barlow's gray eyes went flat. This was the dialogue he had hoped to avoid.

"What about your painting Al? It's been going so well, you'd have more time for your painting."

Years ago Al had had taken a few elementary art courses. The urge to express himself had come unbidden, but it would not be denied. Almost from the first his landscapes had been popular. He had been able to sell every piece. And his success compounded. The Mayor of Seaside, Oregon asked Al to do a family portrait after the death of his granddaughter Celeste. August Clementi owned two of Al's landscapes and he wanted a family portrait that included Celeste, done from a recent color photograph.

The work required six months to complete, evenings and weekends. Clementi was deeply moved; the portrait captured the essence of each family member, especially Celeste. He insisted on paying Al a full year's salary and he spread word through a network of influential friends. Al turned down most portrait requests these days and still he struggled with a three-year backlog.

Barlow returned to his desk chair and downed most of the whisky in his glass.

"OK Al, I'll stall these Dutchmen for two weeks. That gives you kids a chance to think this thing through. If you can come up with something that makes sense, sense for you and sense for me, I'll be inclined to go along. Fair enough?"

Al was not at all sure the proposition was fair enough, but he had no alternatives.

"Thank you, I'll talk to Mandy and we'll see what we can do."

As he stood to leave Barlow surprised him again.

"I've wondered all these years how you did those things overseas. It just seems…well, you're such a gentle person, the art and all. No one told us what happened, but we know about the medals. Louella and I are so close to you now, it just doesn't seem possible."

A muscle flicked in Al's jaw: here was another unexpected change of direction. The old fears and uncertainties came back as he searched for a plausible explanation.

"Well, I guess it was like being thrown into a river where it's wide and calm and you can swim safely. Then you go into a canyon and suddenly the river is so powerful you can't swim to shore. So you float along, always imagining you'll be OK in spite of the currents. You watch the shoreline and hope the currents will throw you into calmer waters where you can wade ashore safely."

He paused a moment. His stomach churned and once again he felt the awful dread.

"You float down the river with your friends and you stay a little longer than you should. Then some of them aren't there anymore but you keep on swimming and hoping because there's nothing else you can do. If the actual danger ever got into your mind you would just want to give up and go hide somewhere. I know I would, I'm no hero. But I never really thought I was in danger, at least in my conscious mind. I was just doing what I'd been trained to do, and I thought the bad things would always happen to someone else. Then finally the truth dawns: you can't hide any longer and it gets…terrible. It's a nightmare, only you're alive in it. In some ways, that time prepared me to do well here with you. Every funeral is a little ceremony for my friends, the ones who just disappeared and we never knew where they went."

Barlow sat wordlessly watching Al, weighing the structure of his complexity.

"I don't think I would have been able to do all that Al. Whatever happens now, I'm so pleased we've had these years together."

He shook his head in wonder.

"Amazing really, memorable. I've never heard the like."

# Chapter 54

They were at home talking quietly in the small den. Al finished his strong scotch and looked expectantly to Mandy, sitting bolt upright in his old lounger, sipping white wine from a long-stem crystal glass.

"It's a shock, I was sure Mr. Barlow would offer us a partnership or some form of equity in the firm. I never thought he would just sell out and leave us as employees."

She gave a sidelong glance through the pleasing transparency of her white wine. She was not smiling, but she was not as angry as Al expected.

"He's provided a good living Al, he's not obliged to continue taking care of us. Besides, I think this offer came at a perfect time. Howard is getting tired now. He feels his age. And Louella has been forceful about retirement. She wants him to disconnect, to take time for just the two of them and enjoy life while they have their health. He's almost eighty you know, there may not be that many years left. Are you angry, do you think he's being unfair to us?"

Al didn't know. His thoughts were dull and disquieting and he felt slightly dizzied by his strong drink.

"Not consciously unfair, he knows how we've helped the firm. But I just think he's rushing into this offer without opening his mind to all the possibilities. He has the right; it's his business, not ours. But he can't really need cash at this point; he's wealthy already. He's not giving us much time. I'm concerned that the banks won't really know what we've done for the firm, won't understand how we can continue to build the business. We don't have much to offer in the way of equity right now."

Mandy stood, shuddering inwardly at the thought of starting over.

"I've got to start dinner. Tonight we'll make up a proposal, a summary of you and me and our financial situation. We can add some material on growth, on our plans to keep the business growing. We'll make this into lemonade; you just watch Mr. Funeral Director and New Owner. We don't have much choice."

Al looked at her beautiful serious face. He saw the chestnut curls and the frown and the fierce courage he knew so well. He saw her strength.

"I know. We'll work together like we always have since I was hurt. I guess losing some brains wasn't all that bad, was it? And I love you. No one can ever take that from us, can they?"

She turned to leave the room, and then she turned back. Her eyes misted and two worry-lines appeared.

"They can't. Ever."

He touched his forehead in a mock salute.

Two weeks later they were in the office of Jack Quitman, First Vice President of Oregon Coastal Savings and Loan, making a third financial presentation in three days. Al presented the operational side of the business and now Mandy was finishing the financial aspects.

"...in summary Mr. Quitman, we are prepared to surrender our five percent equity in Barlow Services to the bank, mortgage our house for twenty seven thousand dollars, and pledge an income stream of ninety five thousand dollars a year from business operations. In addition, a group of Al's art customers have pledged a loan of forty three thousand dollars, to be subordinated to your loan. Except for small salaries, we'll take no profit from the firm until the loan is paid off. We want a loan of nine hundred fifty thousand dollars at prime rate, interest-only, for ten years and then all due. Our business plan shows an eight-year payback if we continue to grow as we have these past few years. We're solid business people, Mr. Quitman. We're lifelong members of this community, and we know how to run the business. All you need to do is say yes, we'll do the rest."

Quitman smiled a brief crooked smile and traced an invisible figure eight on the conference table. He was silent for several minutes before looking across the table.

"This will need to go to the loan committee, of course, and then to the board. I don't approve loans of this size; I simply represent them to the management."

His hands went in his pockets and he hunched forward.

"You're paying too much for the business in this proposal. There would be a matter of goodwill; sizeable goodwill that would need to be paid down on a schedule much tighter than your projection. In my opinion, amortizing the goodwill would represent a considerable strain on the profits of Barlow Services, even if you have the good fortune to grow the firm as projected in your business plan. The goodwill is a serious issue, one that may well dim the prospects of a loan from this institution."

Quitman floundered in a coughing fit. Then his big, beefy, good-natured face took on a kindly look.

"I've talked to Howard of course, I know what you're up against here and you have my sympathy. But the offer Howard has before you is really pretty generous if you think about it. After all, you would be five percent owners working for an offshore firm that will need to keep you as the principals. Having bosses who need you isn't so bad, and it could be a formula for success, even riches if you stay at it long enough. You would be much safer financially if you accepted Howard's offer. It's something to think about, the two of you."

Al's peripheral vision warned him that Mandy was preparing an outburst; he could see the furrowed brow and hardened eyes. He held up a hand to no one in particular and interjected.

"We appreciate your observation, Mr. Quitman, but the fact is we don't care to work for other people in this business. We've earned the right to participate as owners, not as hired hands. If we had to, I guess we would consider starting a small competing business and just see how things turn out in the end. We could start a smaller business, don't you agree?"

Quitman liked the Deforests; he didn't want any mistakes made.

"I suppose you could, particularly since you have backers from the business and from your art work. But think a moment: you would be starting from scratch and competing against a business you could partly own. Does that make good sense to you, to either of you?"

Mandy stood and began stuffing their presentation materials into a thin leather case.

"It isn't necessarily a matter of sense, it's a matter of heart for us. We've applied for a loan here. We'd like an answer from you within a week."

# Chapter 55

Theobald Christman was a mess: six days in the Coroners vault and there was little hope for a quality restoration. He was shrunken and salmon colored; a poor base for cosmetics. Al did his best and stood back from the worktable, nettled and unsatisfied. The muscles in his back tightened painfully as he leaned forward squinting and studying, searching for improvement. He smiled slightly: the problem was his eyes. The eye tissue had shrunk enough to give a gaunt, somewhat ghostly appearance.

He stepped to a multi-drawer steel chest holding the fixtures of his trade and opened the third drawer to a selection of cosmetic plastic eye-cups. He glanced at the corpse, selected a pair of #12 cups, and slipped them behind the eyelids using a silicone lubricant. He stepped back again as the telephone rang.

"Another rejection Al, this one from Portland Savings. They say the loan amount is more than they will consider for persons without a more substantial background in business. As if we don't run the damn place, you and me. That's the last of our applications."

It was a blow, but Al had an idea.

"We have friends all over Northwest Oregon. We'll pass the hat."

Mandy's heart refused to believe what her mind told her.

"Oh, Al we couldn't get a drop in the bucket if we passed the hat with every friend and acquaintance we have. It's too much. We may be forced to accept what Mr. Barlow is offering."

Time was running out. There were only days before Mr. Barlow would accept the Dutch proposal. Something bubbled up from his damaged memory.

"Do you still have my old letters from overseas? Did you throw them away?"

"Never. I've kept everything you ever wrote. Why? What do your old letters have to do with this mess?"

"Call the Pentagon Information Operator, see if you can find Dick Tuck. There may be one last move for us here. I'll be home early tonight, we need to talk."

They sat together at the kitchen table as soon as Al arrived home. Mandy had recovered a shoebox full of letters from the attic; everything he had written her from 1945 until the end. He looked at the pile helplessly.

"I never realized how much I wrote, this is quite a pile. We need to find a letter I wrote while I was convalescing in Singapore. That would have been about, oh, say November of 1949."

They divided the pile and searched. Mandy raised a wrinkled and yellowing envelope. It was unusual: civil post rather than overseas military mail. Al took the envelope silently and extracted the letter, reading carefully to the end.

"Did I ever mention the name Yu, Atherton Yu, while I was in the hospital in Hawaii?"

"I don't think so. You weren't making much sense then, but I'm sure I would remember a name that strange. Why, Al? What does that have to do with us?"

"Right now, just about everything. Read this paragraph"

Mandy read and looked up with a bark of humorless laughter, her face drawn with apprehension.

"I don't understand, Al. You seem to be hinting at…you seem to be saying something ominous."

He told what he could recall about the strange affair. She was stunned and unbelieving.

"God, Al, what did you do?"

\*     \*     \*

He searched the dark terrain below anxiously; ten more minutes and he would be at bingo on the fuel gauges, forced to leave. Maybe that was the best thing, what he was about to do was insane. The lights of Dukou reflected from the cloud base 80 miles to the east. Below was only darkness, relieved occasionally by the dim amber light of farmers burning wheat stubble in their arid mountain pastures. His eyes flicked across the rear view mirror just as a blue rocket ascended from the darkness twenty miles to his rear. His eye caught the motion instantly and he slammed *Lillie's Valley* up in a vertical bank just in time to see a parachute flare ignite and illuminate the mountains below.

He had been listening to music. Now, in spite of the desperate situation, he left the ADF on until Bing Crosby finished his famous 1937 Decca recording of *Sweet Leilani*, complete with tenor Lani McIntyre and powerful steel guitars as background. It was a crystal clear piece: a pioneering record made possible by a breakthrough in electronic amplifier technology the previous year, 1936. Worthwhile listening.

He carefully looked away from the bright light of the magnesium flare and watched the dimly lit terrain below the flare, hoping to retain some measure of his night vision. He was descending below mountain peaks in the immediate area in the dark of night unable to see ahead, using the flare as a crude guide. He closed on a string of dim flickering lights that defined a runway out there in the blackness. It looked discouragingly short for landing big heavy *Lillie*. He meant to make a direct approach in to the dirt airstrip, but now caution demanded that he fly down the illuminated path once to check for obstructions and be sure there was adequate length to take off again. He adjusted engine power, slowed to 180 mph and flew 200 feet above the terrain. Truck headlights illuminated the front and rear of the strip, but the middle was too dark to see anything. Small groups of men stood just outside the light from kerosene pots at the runway edge. No matter. He was committed. He was going in.

He banked off the far end of the airstrip in a wide low circle, praying there were no mountains ahead in the blackness. His hand snaked out and slapped the gear handle. He felt the turbulence and the familiar nose pitch-down as the gear doors opened and the landing gear descended. He trimmed the aircraft to continue the turn hands-off and reached into his mouth to unscrew the molar prosthesis fitted to all 337th pilots. He shook a small glass bead from the tooth cap and replaced the tooth, holding the glass cyanide ampoule lightly clenched in his rear teeth. If things went wrong, he would not be taken prisoner.

He took a white phosphorous grenade from a box below his seat and placed it in the outer leg pocket of his flying suit. He would burn the aircraft if he had to.

Now the nose was coming around to the landing approach path. He turned on landing lights and lowered the huge full-span wing flaps, slowing the aircraft below the recommended minimum approach speed of 85 mph until the airspeed indicator showed 75 mph and he could feel the wings burbling gently at the edge of a stall. The burbling rose to an alarming shaking. He slammed the throttles forward and pulled the nose far up in the air, exactly contrary to normal rules of flight. Now he was flying on propeller wash over the lift-starved wings: a peculiar odd-ball type of flight that almost wasn't. He was dragging it in on power alone. The slightest disturbance would send him out of control into the darkness immediately ahead.

But Al had over 900 hours in the P-61 now and that evened the long odds; *Lillie* was an extension of his arms and legs and eyes and he knew exactly what he could do with her and live. She responded to his daring direction patiently, like a draft horse. Gouts of exhaust flame from the roaring engines threatened his night vision as he craned his head to the left, tight up against the canopy to keep the dim oil pots that defined the runway in sight. If he lost them there was only blackness. His height didn't look right and for a stabbing second he thought he wouldn't remember how to land. Before the thought could take hold he passed above the truck at the forward edge of the dirt runway, cut power and pulled the control wheel smartly aft, all the way into his lap. *Lillie* simply stopped flying and dropped to the airstrip, her nose abnormally high in the air, swaying like a dangerous cobra.

He slammed on full brakes and felt the main wheels skidding and sliding dangerously. As speed decreased and the nose started down he released the brakes so the nose wheel would not skid and spoil steering when it touched the ground. The nose wheel bit into earth and now he could see the dim string of kerosene pots ahead, speeding to meet him at an alarming rate. He shoved down hard on the brakes again, felt them lock, and eased just enough to attain maximum braking action. The plane shook and rattled violently as it raced over the crudely prepared ground, threatening to disintegrate. But it had been designed to operate from forward airfields. Al knew the aircraft would take it: he would come to no harm. The sense of careening, of being on the edge of control, quickly disappeared and the aircraft slowed to a stop.

He set the parking brakes and looked down at his hands, shaking violently in the dim orange light from the instrument panel. There was nothing he could do now; he had delivered himself to the situation. He was suddenly helpless and in high danger. It was too late to worry about all that now; he was here and he couldn't leave until his business was finished.

Half a dozen figures quickly appeared ahead of the airplane, harsh in the landing lights. One of the men made a slashing motion at his throat. Al nodded understanding, but he was not about to cut the engines. If they would not restart he was a dead man. He opened the bomb bay doors, closed the throttles to idle and screwed in the throttle friction brake until the levers could not be moved. Now he could leave the plane without the hazard of creeping throttles. He released the seat harnesses, unplugged oxygen, radio and intercom connectors and removed the pistol from his shoulder holster. He jacked a round into the chamber, leaving the hammer on full cock, and then squeezed laboriously between the seat and fuselage wall to exit through the bomb bay ladder.

As he struggled rearward past his seat, an oriental face was staring at him just two feet away. He started violently and fear twisted his heart. Then he shrugged in resignation: friends or enemies, there was little he could do either way. The man tried to struggle up into the cockpit and Al slapped him harshly in the face, pointing down the ladder and yelling for the little man to get clear of the aircraft.

There was an instant when it could have gone either way. The man stared at him with a look of violence and fingered a pistol stuck loosely in his belt. Then his head shook a single time and he clambered back down the ladder. Al carefully de-cocked and holstered his pistol, but he did not snap the safety strap. He turned and backed to the ladder, reminding himself to be careful with the cyanide capsule clenched between his teeth. He felt a deep desire to stay right here in this cockpit, his friendly home for so many hundreds of hours this past year. He pushed back the primitive fear that threatened to overwhelm him and descended into the humid night, smelling the stench of human fertilizer and acrid smoke from the wheat stubble burning all around.

He reached plowed earth at the foot of the ladder and peered into a smoky gloom only slightly relieved by the P-61 landing lights. The kerosene flares along the runway edge tried to illuminate the scene, but they were a feeble help. Two-dozen Chinese, dressed in the blue cotton blouses and quilted pants of farmers, stood in a rough circle around the aircraft. The man he had slapped was gone. Al placed his right hand lightly on the butt of his pistol and held the other hand out in a gesture meant to convey: what now? There would be no talking here, even at idle the great engines thundered deafeningly and the propellers whipped furious dust clouds to the rear.

Two men on horseback appeared, apparently unbothered by the thick dusty propeller wash. They dismounted and came to Al. The taller man wore a patch over his right eye and a deep dent disfigured his brow, running from the eye socket up into his hairline. He extended his left hand and Al noticed the right sleeve was empty, pinned neatly at the shoulder of his high-collared military tunic. Al grasped the hand, leaned in, and shouted over the din of the idling engines.

"Al Deforest. Do you have the ladder?"

The man nodded and spoke in perfect American English.

"Yes, please shut down the engines so we can speak. I am General Yu."

Al shook his head and his mouth took on an unpleasant twist.

"Not a good idea. I might not be able to restart them. Bring the ladder and we can begin loading. Did you bring bungee?"

General Yu crooked a finger and walked out under the wing to the edge of the runway where speech was possible.

"We have the bungee. There are fifteen figurines now, not the nine we agreed on. Is that a problem?"

Al was concerned.

"How much weight?"

Yu turned to his companion and spoke in Chinese for an extended time.

"He says they weighed the original nine figurines at 82 kilograms. The added six are of roughly the same size and density. He thinks the total should be about 140 kilograms."

Al did some mental arithmetic: the whole load should be about 300 pounds. Placed at the rear of the fuselage, the load would move the airplane balance dangerously aft. Stability would be marginal at best. Even worse, the controls would be dangerously touchy on the maximum performance takeoff he must make from this short rough field. He stopped breathing and put his hands in his pockets to think the situation through. On the one hand, he could refuse to take the additional figurines. He had not bargained for the added load. On the other hand, he knew his aircraft intimately and thought he could handle the sensitive control issue now that he was aware of it. There could be no use of the autopilot on the 7 hours of flight remaining to Isla Mattoon. With stability so compromised, the autopilot would throw the aircraft out of control. And manual flying was distasteful: he was already exhausted from 11 hours of flight and the usual tension over the target. He did not relish paying close attention to the aircraft throughout a long dark night. Now he was breathing again but the breathing was going better than the thinking. He noodled the possibilities for several minutes and made a decision.

"I didn't bargain for this. The airplane will be dangerously unbalanced. What do I get out of the extra load?"

The scarred face smiled crookedly: Yu reveled in haggling. He laughed harshly.

"My father said you were no fool, Lieutenant. So, I offer you the original amount of cash and one extra figurine. You will have to trust my father's discretion in the selection of figurines, but I assure you he has every intention of providing you with one of the highest value. What do you say, my young friend?"

Al nodded.

"Let's get to loading, I can't waste any more gas sitting here. Tell them to stay clear of the propellers."

Yu spoke to his companion for several minutes and the man trotted back to the small cluster of men at the aft fuselage. He gestured into the dark and an attendant appeared with a silver tea service.

"Please take tea with me, young man. The loading will be done quickly now and you look as if you could do with sustenance."

Al sat with the General in dirt at the side of the airstrip and drank scalding hot heavily sugared delicious green tea. He felt the deep fatigue lifting as they chatted.

"This is easily the craziest thing I've ever done General. I don't even know why I am doing it. I never thought I would be capable of such a thing."

Yu turned his disfigured face to Al and the slightest smile appeared.

"Oh, I think I have an idea of your motivation, even if you do not. I have been where you are now."

He looked in his teacup for a long moment before continuing, remembering things that remained raw sores on his aching heart.

"Your personal sacrifice has gone beyond anything to be expected of a man. You're tired and angry. You want to hit back in some way that does not dishonor your sense of self and this is such a way. I have men like you under me. I know. And I have felt what you feel."

Al shook his head, numb, not wanting to think about the words. He looked silently at the dirt. After a time Yu added.

"It will all be over shortly, for you and for me too."

A man trotted out to the wingtip and gestured. Yu rose.

"You need to check the load now. It is time to go."

Al clambered up the crude ladder and looked into a small cargo space that had originally housed electronic units for the aircraft fire control radar. The figurines, cushioned in cotton and wrapped in burlap, had been carefully arranged along the floor. He reached in and tested the bungee cord that strapped them down to aluminum deck. It was absolutely taut. He nodded approvingly as he shut the hatch and screwed in the securing Dzeus fasteners with a coin. This cargo space was only opened at 300-hour inspections. No one would examine it for months.

Men were fastening ropes to the tie-down rings under the wings when Al descended the ladder. He made a turning motion and the men turned the aircraft around 180 degrees and pulled it backward a quarter mile to the end of the airstrip. Now Al turned to again Yu.

"I have to know the length of the strip and what lies beyond. Hills and such."

Yu came back with the answer after an unnervingly long discussion. Al was getting worried about fuel.

"The runway has been measured at 930 meters. Beyond, the ground falls away into a canyon. Across the canyon the ground is level for the next three kilometers. There are mountains on your right, but the left is clear. Good luck to you. I think we will meet again."

"Send one of your horsemen down to the end of the runway. Move that truck out of alignment with my takeoff path. Put it over to the side and let the lights shine at an angle."

Back in the cockpit Al carefully removed the tooth cap and reinserted the cyanide pill. He loosened the friction brake on the throttles and looked into the night. As far as he could see the runway was clear. He rubbed his tired eyes, did a ritualistic dance on the rudder pedals and shook his head back and forth, preparing for the ordeal. He stared out at the takeoff path and tried to imagine the canyon and mountains beyond, forming a mental image he would need when *Lillie's* long nose rose up and blocked his forward view.

Now Yu appeared forward of the left wing, barely within the illumination pattern of the landing lights. He waved casually. Al nodded and held up a hand in goodbye. He set the Directional Gyro to the runway heading and released the caging mechanism. The instrument would guide him after he left the runway and plunged into the darkened night ahead. He depressed the brake pedals strongly, set the flaps one quarter down, moved the propeller controls to Full Increase RPM, moved the fuel mixture controls to Automatic Rich and finally opened both throttles. He sat for a moment allowing power to build, feeling the satisfyingly violent thrashing as 4800 horsepower whipped the aircraft. He pushed the throttles forward even more, breaking lead seals that would mark the use of War Emergency power for maintenance crews so the engines could be changed. He risked combustion detonation and massive engine failure, but there was no choice. Now he had an extra thousand horsepower and that was it: there was no more. He released the brakes and began the most difficult takeoff of his life.

He divided his attention between the kerosene runway lights ahead and the airspeed indicator. At 60 mph he eased the control wheel back and waited for the big ship to lift. He had burned off more than half his fuel, he should lift off at 85 mph .The controls were exquisitely touchy with his new aft load and the nose came up almost before he was ready. The light controls were delightful and he unconsciously snickered; flying *Lillie* was almost like flying a Piper Cub. The truck headlights at the far end of the runway were rushing at him but the aircraft was still solidly on its wheels, not lifting yet. There was nothing to do now but wait and hope: he had done all he could.

He passed the last of the flares and entered solid darkness, feeling ground shocks as the wheels passed over unprepared terrain. There was a terrible jolt from below and he was flying, then he was settling. A second lighter shock, a sideways wrench, and then he was back in the air, flying sluggishly at 80 mph. The nose was very high and Lillie was doing her skittish horse routine again, struggling to gain altitude.

Now he concentrated on instruments, for there was nothing to be seen in the darkened night ahead. Slowly, slowly, the vertical speed meter came off zero and moved up to 100 feet per minute: appallingly little, and desperately needed. Now the instrument showed 250 feet per minute. He eased the nose down slightly and was shocked to see the vertical speed fall back to zero again. He quickly pulled the controls all the way back, into his lap. The nose came up again and he was climbing. A tap of right rudder and a glance at the Directional Gyro showed he was holding the runway heading. Now a climb rate of 400 feet per minute and the climb continued as he eased the nose down slightly. Now 95 mph and he knew he would live if the engines did not fail. At 110 mph he glanced at the manifold pressure gauges and was relieved to see 80 inches on both engines, he had not destroyed them—yet. He eased power back and trimmed the aircraft for a normal climb. He needed desperately to breathe and suddenly gasped for air and realized he had not taken a breath since the takeoff roll commenced almost two minutes ago.

Dawn found him halfway down the Burmese border, flying in a peculiar and unnerving cloud formation. He was between two thick slanting cloud layers that tilted down slightly from right to left as far as the eye could see. He shook his head at the sight and aligned the wings with the cloud layers. The instruments told him he was turning now, but his mind wanted to believe he was level. He watched the instruments carefully for a moment and rolled the airplane until the compass and turn indicator told him he was in straight and level flight. Now the massive straight cloud layers tilted eerily away to his left. He closed his eyes and told himself to just enjoy the odd illumination.

When he looked again the scene registered differently on his dizzied senses. He saw thick swirls in the tilted cloud layer above him and was reminded of homemade ice cream. He recalled vividly how Birdie would prepare the delicious batter of cream and eggs and sugar and vanilla while he and his father got the ice cream machine ready to go. First they packed the oak bucket with ice and salt, then placed the gleaming 2-quart container down into the ice mixture and capped the machine with its hand turned gear head and crank handle. Cranking was pretty easy at first, but it got much harder as the mixture began to freeze. Al would hold the oak bucket so it did not slip while his Dad labored with the crank. Then they would trade off until the freezing process was complete. Al was allowed to extract the container and take it to the kitchen where Birdie knocked the salt and ice off the exterior and opened the top. He could smell the vanilla and see the creamy swirls and taste their little long frozen drips as Birdie extracted the paddle blades and gave them to him to lick: chilly and rich in the summer heat.

And here he was in an ice cream sky: a vanilla sky. His grim tired face slowly became animated and buoyant. Surely this sky was a good sign. Surely things would turn for the better now.

Two hours later Al crossed the Burma coast into the Bay of Bengal. The odd band of clouds was far behind and the morning sun was well up on the horizon to his left. He pressed the radio transmitter button on the control wheel.

"BRICKYARD FOUR-FOUR abeam Chittagong, estimating your station at 27 past the hour. Landing instructions."

The bored voice was loud in his earphones.

"Roger BRICKYARD FOUR FOUR. Altimeter two niner eight eight. Wind one five from two seven zero. Use runway three one. There is no traffic, enter downwind leg. Use a right-hand pattern. Welcome back."

In the debriefing Al explained his notable lateness to the Intelligence Officer: he had encountered unexpected headwinds all the way down the Burmese border, apparently a residual of the eastern branch of the monsoon.

The Intelligence Officer's face twisted in a frowning half-smile: the monsoon had been over for six weeks and the weather forecaster was seldom this far wrong. But there had been no other aircraft aloft at the time so he could never know the truth. He wanted to believe. He wrote the mission report Al's way.

\*       \*       \*

Mandy stared wide-eyed at Al, her head shaking.

"You did that? God Almighty Al, what were you thinking of? They might have killed you. Our Government would kill you now if they knew...and you with all those medals."

Al pulled at a lock of graying hair, thinking.

"I don't know why I did it. I remember being tired, and mad, and disappointed that none of our officers had the sense to protest doing the same mission over and over. And I was mad at the goddamned government for the whole stupid thing. I told you what Yu said. Maybe he was right. Sometimes I think about it, but I really can't remember exactly what I thought."

He waited to see if more would come from her. Then he tugged his ear defiantly.

"I can tell you this, I'm not sorry I did it and I don't feel that I dishonored myself. See, you married a fraud and a criminal. What do you think of that?"

Mandy's dark eyes glowed with savage fire. She stared at him and he saw the frowning glare that preceded her famous attacks. Then her face softened and she leaned forward to place a hand at the back of his head and kiss him softly. Her eyes filled and she hugged herself as she leaned back.

"I think I love you. I've loved you from the moment I set eyes on you back in Junior High. You know how I hated what they did to you, the smug self-righteous bastards. Turning your head, making you a big man, then using you in the worst way they could. They're the criminals as far as I'm concerned, not you: the cock suckers."

Then she giggled.

"You were always so upstanding, such a Dudley DoRight. Now this. I don't know: it's funny and amazing, and improbable-just like you sweetheart. What a bag of tricks you have, Big Bad Wolf."

She stood and held out her hand, " Give me your glass. This calls for a couple more drinks, then the rest of the story."

She settled in again with replenished drinks and looked to Al.

"So?"

He shrugged matter-of-factly.

"I don't know."

"You mean the memory loss thing?"

"I think so. I didn't recall any of this until we started getting turned down by the banks. I've felt desperate. Then something bubbled up from down there where I don't think so well anymore, something that reminded me of old man Yu. I remembered about the letter. So here we are."

"But Al, this all happened before your last flight, maybe a month or two before then. I know you remember things from that period. Not everything, but the big stuff. Do you think it's there and you've just suppressed it—the way that government psychologist said you might do with the painful stuff?"

Al drew a blank.

"I don't know. I don't think that's what it is. I'm not ashamed: I never let my friends down. Nothing like that."

"So you may have a ton of money somewhere? You may have antique figures somewhere that you can't recall?"

"I guess so. And it isn't just mine, Mandy. It's ours. Unless you want us to go and tell Uncle Sam."

"Like hell we will. We need to pursue this right now. Did either of the Yu's tell you how much those figurines were worth?"

"I don't think so. I was just their transportation, a minor character. Necessary of course, but really just the cab driver."

Mandy sat staring at her light amber wine, deep in thought. Al brightened suddenly.

"Here's what we can do. First, you can start writing letters to places like the Better Business Bureau in Singapore—I'm sure they must have something like that. I'm going to find Dick Tuck. He's been moved over to Intelligence back there. I wouldn't need to tell him the whole story, just enough to see if he can get a trace on the Yu's."

He was silent for a moment, wondering if he should bring up a third possibility.

"Then there's that nurse who was there, Roberta Walker. She lived in Singapore and if she's still around she might know where old man Yu has gotten to."

Having said the words, he wondered at the wisdom of connecting Mandy and Bobby Walker. But they had to take chances now. Their future was at risk and time was too short.

Mandy wrote a letter to the Singapore Better Business Bureau that night. She addressed it care of General Delivery, not knowing what else to do. She also wrote a letter to the American Consulate in Singapore, requesting the whereabouts of one Roberta Walker, Nurse. She had watched Al's face as he mentioned the woman. She knew immediately, at least she had suspicions, but she put them aside: that was another time, another place and a different world entirely. She called the Pentagon Information Operator the following morning. She wrote Tuck's number on a scrap of paper and left it in Al's office.

After lunch Al walked around the corner to a Rexall Drug Store, changed a five-dollar bill and dialed the number from the store telephone booth. A young voice answered.

"Special Programs."

Al stammered a bit.

"I w…want to s…speak to General Tuck."

"He's not here sir; may I help you?"

Al didn't care to state a subject.

"No, I d…don't think so. Just tell him Al Deforest called. It's urgent."

He left a work and home telephone number with the noncommittal voice and hung up, unhappy. They needed to move on this thing right now.

# Chapter 56

Their six-year old daughter Mackenzie solemnly handed Al a message slip when he came home that evening.

"A man called this afternoon."

Al studied the childish scrawl, wondering why the babysitter had not taken the message.

"Did Sally let you take the call, Mac?"

"Oh yes, she lets me write down all the messages now. She says it's good practice for me. But she checks what I heard with what I write so there aren't mistakes, you know."

Al nodded, pleased. Mackenzie was a gifted child and he approved of her added responsibilities. The painfully printed note read ' Mr. Tuck said to call him anytime at Sycamore 7-8612, Washington Operator.'

Al cursed himself for stammering again when he contacted Tuck; he was supposed to be cured of all this stuff, why was it coming back?

"I…I…It's Al Deforest, General."

"You don't need to call me that now, Al, you're a civilian. How are you? How's that firecracker Mandy? The kids? What, two of them now as I recall?"

Al relaxed, the tone told him all he needed to know.

"We're pretty good, sir. Tolerable. And yes we have two kids now; Scott; he's eight and Mackenzie, our daughter; she's six."

"I had a long conversation with Mackenzie. She's a charmer, sounded older than six though. I was impressed."

Al always enjoyed bragging a little.

"Thank you. She looks j…just like Mandy. They tested her at school this year, in first grade. She's a gifted child. We're very proud."

Tuck, never a diplomat, got to the point.

"What's up?"

Al bit his lip uneasily and plunged.

"Mandy and I have an opportunity to b…buy the business out here. The owner Mr. Barlow wants to retire. We always thought he'd make it easy for us to buy in, but now some foreigners have come in with an offer for more than the business worth of the firm. Barlow wants to take it, and we can't interest the banks in loaning us money. I…I…we're desperate, we don't know where to turn."

Tuck broke in.

"I could loan you a little money Al, if it would help. I'd be glad to."

"Oh no, that's not what I want. But there was a man over in Singapore, when I was there on convalescent leave, and…"

"If it's from our time overseas Al, we can't talk on the telephone."

"It's OK, sir. I don't need to talk about that. I…I did a favor for a man while we were over there: just a business favor. He said he'd pay me for the work, but I can't remember if he ever did. You know, because of my head and all. I just don't remember. If he paid me, and the money is somewhere I don't know about, it might help us swing this purchase we're so worried about. So I need your help to locate this man."

There was a long silence. Al knew Tuck so well he could almost see the mental sorting going on before Tuck spoke.

"What's the man's name? How old? Where was this? When?"

"It all happened in Singapore, in 1949, when I was down there after I crashed. He was a businessman who called himself Atherton Yu: an oriental, probably Chinese, in his sixties I guess. He owned a restaurant there and perhaps other businesses. He might have had other names, too."

Al related what he could remember of Yu's background. There was another long silence before Tuck spoke.

"I'll be in Portland next Tuesday. Meet me there at the Diggers Claim. Eight o'clock. I'll try to have something for you, but that was more than ten years ago."

\* \* \*

Al showered, shaved for a second time and dressed in his best suit; carefully packed wrinkle-free for the occasion by Mandy. He spent nervous minutes in front of the bathroom mirror adjusting hair over the prominent scar that started above his ear and ran down across his head to the hairline before vanishing into his freshly starched shirt collar. Finally, after several false starts with the knot in his tie, he was out of time. He smiled at the image in the mirror, bought a fresh pack of Lucky Strikes in the hotel lobby and caught a cab to the Diggers Claim.

Tuck was seated in a booth when Al arrived, dressed casually in slacks and a sport shirt. He stood and studied Al's face for a long moment.

"You look pretty good Al: I didn't know what to expect. It's been ten years, and you had a rough time of it."

The waitress arrived for a drink order. Tuck smiled and turned to Al.

"What would you like?"

"Oh, I'm not much of a drinker these days. A tap beer I guess."

"Fine. I'll have a double Manhattan with extra Sweet Vermouth. Use Jack Daniels. We'll order later."

Tuck lit a Camel, inhaled deeply and sat looking out the window at dark currents on the Columbia River sweeping past below them, lit by floodlights on the restaurant dock. When he turned to Al there was uncertainty on his pug-dog face.

"You surprise me, Al. This fellow you asked me about turns out to be a very interesting character. After we finish, I'd like to hear how you met him."

"That would be fine, sir. I'm just pleased you could take the time to help me."

"If what I have is helpful, I don't want to know about it. I'm detached to the CIA now and this was never meant for sharing."

"Oh, well sure. I…I'll never mention it to anyone. Y…you know me. I never meant to use you this way, but things have happened. I guess it's fair to say that my future, Mandy's future, will swing on what you can tell me."

Tuck squinted at Al through the cigarette smoke curling up past his eye.

"You've dug up an interesting character. The man you know as Atherton Yu was born on a houseboat at Tungting Lake, China in 1878. His original name was Wei Jin-sheng and he never legally changed it, although he adopted various convenient aliases throughout his life. His father was an American mining engineer named Peter Atherton, and he sent the boy through Stanford, so that much of the story he told you is true."

Tuck puckered his lips. He looked irked.

"Talk about a charmed life: this guy was on every side of every revolution in China from 1912 until the Communists took over in 1949, the year the United States was thrown out. His Dad bought him a seat on the Shanghai City Council in 1912 and he used the position to assist the major drug smugglers in coastal China for years. He was rich and influential before he was 40. During that period he joined a secret society, the Ch'ing-Pang or Green Gang. Almost all the political and military leaders in China belonged to some form of secret society for their own protection back then. He got a big break in 1927: Chiang Kai-shek's Nationalist Party, the Kuomintong or KMT, used the Shanghai Green Gang to decimate Mao's Communists. That battle established the KMT as the ruling party in China for the next ten years. The KMT eliminated the local warlord in Sinkiang Province in 1933. For services rendered, the man you know as Atherton Yu was given the Military Governorship of the Province."

Al interrupted excitedly.

"Yeah. I remember now. He said he worked both sides of the street through that whole time period."

Tuck stubbed out his cigarette and pulled a small notebook from his pocket. His finger moved through handwritten notes until he found his place again.

"Well, he proceeded to loot tombs all over the province for the next 15 years, making deals with both the Communists and the Japanese Occupation forces as necessary to keep his business going. After the war he saw that resurgence of the Communists was inevitable, he knew his days in China were ending. He set up a string of businesses down the Malay Archipelago all the way to northern Australia. He gave the warlord job to his son P'eng Jin-sheng and left the country. Yu knew Mao intended to eliminate the wealthy power structure as soon as he conquered the KMT, so he was looking ahead, feathering his nest, getting while the getting was good."

Tuck signaled the waitress. It was time for dinner.

"Atherton Yu died peacefully in Brisbane, Australia in 1951. He left the estate to his son P'eng, who he called Pemberton for some reason known only to him. Pemberton controls the empire today from the old man's headquarters in Singapore. That's the story Al, I hope it helps you."

Al wasn't so sure.

"I met Atherton Yu in Singapore when I was recuperating in 1949. He promised me something and as far as I can tell, he never delivered. We have an opportunity now; we can make a good life after all these troubles. But it doesn't sound very good, does it? With the old man gone, do you think the son will feel obligated to meet his father's promise?"

Tuck looked at Al in silent censure, wondering and thinking. Al had been General Officer material: calm, methodical, a natural leader, brave and uncomplaining and a talented flyer. He was the type of young officer every Chief of Staff dreams of. And he thought of Douglas Trapnell, drinking himself to oblivion.

He was disappointed. Al seemed reduced now to a damaged, forgetful, anxious businessman working the angles for personal advantage. And it looked as if he may have had a hand in the sellout that killed his kids on the last mission. He shook his head silently and wrote Al off: you're breaking my goddamned heart, son.

"Al, I have pretty good information that Yu tipped off the air defense net around Hotan that day—the day I lost all my young men. The day you were wounded. I don't think you should rely on any sort of an honor system with men like that. The Yu's deal from strength; they're not charitable or honorable in any sense that you would be familiar with."

Tuck felt a flash of grief: his pleasure in the meeting vanished. He didn't want to ask, but he had to know.

"You weren't part of that sell-out were you Al? Christ, I'm not sure I even want an answer from you."

Al turned white-hot and leaned toward Tuck belligerently.

"H...How the hell could you even think a thing like that? Those guys w...were my brothers, all we went through. I'd die first. I almost did, for God's sake. No, this is about money; money they owe me for a favor, nothing to do with our mission. Nothing at all."

Tuck looked down in uneasy silence, sipping his brandy, debating. He teetered, eventually deciding in Al's favor.

"Would you say you risked your life for these men? Risked your honor?"

Al didn't need to think that one through at all.

"Goddamned right I did: a scary business. Yes sir, there's n...no doubt about that."

Tuck put a toothpick in his ear scratching an itch that never quite went away: a broken eardrum, a souvenir from his flying days.

"There is a way, a long shot. It may not work, but you'd have a chance. The Chinese secret societies never let go: once in, never out. Both the old man and the kid were members of the Green Gang: the Ch'ing Pang. Those folks won't abide someone who evades a debt of honor, at least their version of honor. If you risked your life, your honor as they define the term, they would want the Yu's to make good. The trick is to bring the matter to their attention. That's not an easy thing, there's no way for you to do it. An Occidental would not be believed; no, they wouldn't choose to believe an Occidental in a matter like this. Yu would lie for sure, assuming he even knows what the old man did."

Al was not ready to give up.

"I...I'd go there, sir. Wherever I had to go. We don't have much money, but I'd find a way. It's important."

Major General Richard Tuck scribbled a name on a napkin and handed it to Al.

"This fellow will call you. He owes me a favor."

Early the next morning, sleepless, Tuck sat up in bed. What had happened out there? It was a question he could not resolve to his satisfaction. God Almighty: a Medal of Honor winner. He winced at the thought.

He reached for the telephone and dialed the private number of the Air Force Inspector General.

# Chapter 57

Al pressed the buzzer, soiled by countless greasy hands. He tried to see through the fly-specked viewing port into the room beyond. Hopeless. He glanced down at Mandy as they stood in the malodorous hallway recking of cheap Muscatel and urine.

"God. I didn't think I'd be bringing you to a place like this."

Mandy waved a hand in dismissal. She was always up for an adventure.

"This is important. No one is going to hurt us. We haven't seen a soul in this building since we passed that bum asleep on the front steps."

The viewing port darkened and a voice issued from a ratty speaker beside the door.

"Kowloon-Pai-Chek Imports. What do you want?"

Al drew a blank. The need for success, the palpable pressure, caused his brain to misfire in the old way. Mandy looked at him anxiously for a moment. He remembered.

"I'm Al Deforest and t…this is my wife Mandy. We have an appointment with Robard Tun."

The viewing port lightened, they were left for five minutes. Al was about to knock again when a series of locks disengaged and the door opened. An oriental teen-ager, not above five feet tall, motioned for them to come in. She relocked the door and led them down a long dim hallway.

Mandy saw small offices on either side, about half of them occupied by workers bent over piles of paper at small writing desks. Telephones rang discordantly and she heard the constant chatter of several different Chinese dialects. A Teletype chugged rhythmically from the far end of the hall. The young girl stopped at an open door and silently gestured for them to go in.

They entered a classroom-sized space. Windows painted in flat industrial black spread across one wall. Frosted-glass transoms above the blackened windows allowed a moderate light level, but did not entirely lift the gloom. The room was empty except for a dozen six-foot stacks of file folders in boxes sitting loose on the floor and an old fashioned walnut desk centered on the window wall. Someone had scraped a circular hole in the window paint behind the desk for illumination, but it was not enough.

A reading lamp glowed on the left side of the desk showing a handsome young Chinese man sitting amid piles of paper. Five telephones sat on a small side table. Almond eyes regarded Al and Mandy for a long minute. The man stood and came around the desk, smoothing a fine brown silk jacket, cinching a brown silk tie. He made no move to shake hands or welcome them.

"Robard Tun."

Mandy spoke.

"We're the Deforests. A man made a bargain with my husband. We don't think he kept it. We need your help."

Tun put his hands in his jacket pocket, fished out a dented Zippo lighter and lit a cigarette, squinting at them through the flame.

"That's not much help. I need to hear more. The whole thing."

He went around the desk and sat down again, making no effort to accommodate them. Al snapped at him.

"Where are your manners? This is not the oriental way. Get some chairs in here for us."

Tun smiled faintly.

"I'm not an oriental. I was born in Kingman, Arizona and brought up here in San Francisco. I visit the Orient often, but the Orientals think of me as an American: Americanized. However, you are correct, I have been unmannerly."

He picked up a telephone and spoke a rapid burst of dialect. Presently the girl reappeared pushing two old wooden chairs into the room. She struggled them into position in front of Tun's desk, bowed, and left. Moments later she reappeared with a tea service and served delicious hot sweet tea. Tun's smooth face was side lighted by the old fashioned reading lamp as he questioned them.

"You say you don't think this man completed his agreement. Don't you know? How can you not know?"

Al went through the story of his bizarre nighttime encounter with Pemberton Yu, omitting his military mission and conveyance.

"Shortly after that, a few weeks after our meeting, I was injured: a head injury. There are things I no longer recall, areas where my thought processes are slower than they used to be. I remember both the father and son clearly; I can see them as we sit here. But I have no recollection of the weeks and months after I was hurt. It's possible I was compensated for my service, I don't know. But I don't think so. I was with young Yu in Sinkiang Province, hundreds of miles from the frontier. The Nationalist Government had collapsed three months before and Yu was a privateer, not loved by the Communists. He was on the run even then.

There was confusion and chaos over southern China and I don't even know if Yu got out alive. I'm not sure he reported my pickup to his father. I'm not even sure anyone collected the figurines from my airplane. We used different airplanes all the time. The one I used that night went missing on a mission in early November; no one knows what happened to it. It may still be in the jungle with the figurines in the rear for all I know. The point is this Mr. Tun; we are in desperate need of funds. We want you to help us find the money. If we were not paid, we want you to help us collect. If we were paid, we want to know where the money is."

Tun dragged deeply on his cigarette. He gently tapped a pack of Phillip Morris on the desk before him, neatly ordering the cigarettes.

"General Yu is a hero as far as I am concerned. While The United States dithered, he fought the enemies of the Chinese State with relentless ferocity. His guerilla raids from 1935 until the end of the war stalled Mao's Communists for years. If he had received the slightest help they might never have taken over. Even without assistance from the United States, he gave us a chance to escape to Taiwan with a semblance of government. There would be no Nationalist Taiwanese Government today without his leadership."

Al interrupted vehemently.

"H…He was a privateer. He made a…alliances with the Japanese and the Communists whenever it suited his personal goals. He and his father raped and pillaged the southern provinces for a generation, stealing cultural objects that are the essence of your civilization."

Tun shrugged noncommittally, choosing not to continue the debate.

"A tall tale Mr. Deforest, a tall order. Why do you think I can help you?"

Al leaned into the desk, exhaling cigarette smoke in Tun's direction as he spoke.

"Because General Tuck says you should; because you owe him a favor. We're here to collect, Mr. Tun, that's all."

Tun smirked and rolled his eyes upward lazily.

"I see. Well, I might be able to make inquiries in certain areas. I know nothing of this matter; it has never come to my attention. Interesting though, it has interesting possibilities."

Suddenly Tun's lips narrowed in anger. He snapped back in the chair and hissed at Al.

"You look like a frightened businessman. Are you willing to endanger yourself for this debt you say is owed to you? Are you willing to travel, perhaps a long journey? These are not inconsequential questions my insolent friend. I need a truthful statement from you. I will base my actions accordingly."

Al turned to Mandy and they looked at each other a silent moment, each feeling a crazy mixture of hope and fear.

"G…Goddamn right I'm ready to take risks."

Tun sat back in the chair and picked up a folder, turning his attention elsewhere.

"I can guarantee nothing. If my inquiries are fruitful I will be in touch."

He rang a metal bell on the desk, the kind with a plunger on top, and the girl reappeared.

"Maylee will see you to the door."

"Wait a minute, how long? I only have a few days now."

Tun's attention remained with the folder in his hands.

"Then I suggest you negotiate an extension, Mr. Deforest, shall we say a month?"

"I don't have a month, only a few more days. You must move faster."

Tun stiffened and snapped a cold look at Al.

"You come into my office and give me orders and expect me to hop for you? Were it not for Tuck, I would have you both beaten and thrown in the alley for your insolence. What I must do is not yours to determine. I owe Tuck, not you. I will investigate this distasteful matter, but not at a pace dictated by you. I do not care for you sir, do not burden me with your sweaty little business problems."

Al smiled grimly. At this point he was beyond intimidation.

"I'll do what I can, but you move it, Buster."

Tun sat quietly after they left, then called for Maylee.

"Get Sam on the phone."

Maylee placed calls throughout the southern hemisphere. She found Sam in Surabaya.

"He's on. He's not happy at being interrupted."

Tun colored in annoyance and his hand darted at the phone. It stopped. He sighed and shook his head. He needed to be pleasant; he couldn't push Sam around.

"How are you Sam, I had hoped to hear from you on the Chen matter before now."

Sam grumped.

"Leave me alone for a week and see the change: three new assignments this month and I can't get a single one to close. What do you want?"

"A Gaijin was here. He claims Pemberton Yu and his father made a deal with him back in 1949, an important deal. They welched…he thinks."

Sam was vexed. He dripped some acid on the conversation.

"Thinks? Doesn't he know? You're wasting time with loonies, Robard."

"He was injured after the deal was consummated; a head injury. Says he only just recalled the deal last month, eleven years after the fact. It sounds convenient."

Sam was in no mood for mysteries.

"I don't care if you waste your own time, but now you're wasting mine. You should blow this fellow off, or at least make him come up with something concrete. Yu is not a man to bait. You need facts, Robard, provable facts. Call me when you know what you're doing."

"Thank you. I know all that. The man was referred by Tuck; I can't ignore the problem. Therefore, neither can you. Put your current assignments on hold. Find Yu, but don't contact him. Let me know next week. This is important, get on it."

\*   \*   \*

Al and Mandy discussed strategies for delaying Mr. Barlow's business decision on the drive back to Tillamook. Mandy had one that would work.

"We have to lie, Al, convince him that we can secure the funds, that we have the collateral to swing a loan. I know it's terrible, but we need to phony up a bank letter of credit from some place that will be hard to investigate. We'll convince him a loan is in process: that we need a few months before we can get final approval. And we'll meet the price offered the Dutchmen, as high as it is."

"That's grand larceny, Mandy. If we can't pull it off, if Mr. Barlow loses the Dutchmen, we could go to jail. And we don't really have a way to stall a credit check on our supposed funds, do we?"

Mandy was driving. She turned and glared at Al, her dark eyes as hard as agates.

"It was fraud and worse when you stole those figurines, Al. We're just continuing the string here. If we get the money no one will know the difference, will they? We know how to run the business, how to grow it. And you're so good at the customer side. We can pay off the loan and be independent in ten years. We have to see Mr. Barlow tomorrow and convince him the money is coming. There's no other way."

Al stared out the car window at fallow Northern California farmland, bleak now in slanting winter sunlight.

"Jesus, Mandy, I don't know. Mr. Barlow is our friend, and he's no dummy. He's not going to throw the Dutchmen out on the strength of some phony-baloney story we come up with. It has to be good or we're dead."

But he silently agreed with her. They had to try; there would never be another opportunity like this. Not in their lifetime.

# Chapter 58

Maylee buzzed him on line 5.

"Sinjiang Lu is calling; says it's urgent."

Tun snuffed a cigarette and rubbed his eyes: it was 4:00 AM and he had not slept in two days. The Deforest affair was irritating, there seemed no bottom to the layers of deception he had encountered. But underneath he was excited by what he had learned. It had been a damned bold affair, the sort of boldness he rarely encountered.

"Good morning Sam, or I guess it's good night over there. How are you, what do you have for me?"

Sinjiang "Sam" Lu maintained an office in Libreville, Gabon. The sign outside his door said 'Private Investigator' and he spent time on investigations. He was also principal assassin for the Ko Lau Hui, the elder council of the Green Gang. All his considerable skill had been required to find Yu: he had tracked the elusive General for almost two weeks.

"Actually it's good afternoon. I'm in Madagascar and I've found Yu. He has citizenship here under the name Rashna BonsYuthar. He's been indicted for war crimes in Pakistan, Vietnam, and the Malay States. He bought citizenship here and he's safe, at least for the moment. His Lieutenants are running the business these days. He's like a Chairman of the Board, Emeritus. Heavy security: he'll be hard to get to if that's what you want to do."

Tun deflated, nothing was easy here.

"I only want to ask him a few questions for the moment, until I know more. Can you see him, talk to him?"

"I'll try. You need to tell me the whole story so I don't make a mistake with him. It could be very hard on me."

Sam Lu finished with Tun and placed a call to Ampahoni Enterprises, the shell corporation General Yu maintained in Madagascar. He spoke in the Cantonese dialect.

"I am Sinjiang Lu. I represent the Elders of the Green Gang. I have business with the General. Please arrange a meeting."

The female voice laughed; a delightfully high, tinkling sound.

"There is no General here, not even a private soldier. Give me your telephone number."

Lu was picked up in front of the Governors mansion in Antananarivo the next morning, blindfolded, and driven randomly through the countryside for hours before being released at the massive entry gate of a country estate. A long stone-paved drive led up a hill behind the gate, winding through dense low-growing tea bushes. Magnificent old Palmyra palms lined the drive as it wound out of sight over a hill. To the left of the drive a small cluster of female pickers in sunhats wandered slowly uphill as they expertly plucked green leaves and filled sacks slung across their bodies.

Lu sighed thickly as he looked up the long drive. It was hot and he intensely disliked walking. He crossed the macadam roadway and approached three men sitting indolently beside the gate.

"I am Lu. I have an appointment, let me pass."

One of the men stood wordlessly and held his arms out in an invitation for Lu to do the same so he could be searched. Lu swept the scene with a two-second glance as he was patted down. All three men wore side arms and the two who remained seated had automatic rifles at their side. The seated men watched him closely but made no move to stand. The searcher rapped out a short sentence and gestured for Lu to proceed. Lu thought the man spoke Tagolog, in the dialect of Southern Luzon, but he could not understand the words. He nodded and started up the long driveway.

Thirty minutes later he knocked on the heavy mahogany front door of a magnificent rambling field house built of coral block. He was perspiring and unhappy in his suit and tie. He understood that the long walk was a deliberate effort to be rude, to put him at a disadvantage. It was all right: he would be patient with these childish tricks.

The door opened silently and he entered a cool hall paved in polished basalt. The ancient female who greeted him gestured vaguely down the long hall, and then she turned and left. Lu wandered the hall for several minutes, opening doors and looking in rooms for some sign of occupancy. Eventually he opened the door to a large library with bookcases lining the four walls. A large one armed, one-eyed man sat at a desk in the rear corner, gazing out a window at the soothing green of the tea fields. He turned and flicked a shadow-smile as Lu entered.

"You have found me, Lu; a miracle of achievement for a man of your minimal capacities."

Lu seated himself opposite the old man.

"You make a game of demeaning me, hoping for advantage. I will not give you satisfaction. Do you know why I am here?"

Pemberton Yu leaned back in his leather chair and put two fingers to his lips.

"You would be wise to speak with respect to your superiors; you are in my hands now little brother. I am informed that you and the yellow Gaijin in San Francisco have bungled your way to a misunderstanding of my relationship with the American. Something about bringing certain objects out of Sinkiang Province for me ten years ago. It is unfortunate that I should be harassed over this matter. I am attempting to enjoy my few remaining months. Do you know that I have throat cancer? The doctors tell me I can live if they remove my vocal cords and most of my jaw, but I do not choose to pay that price. I say this to indicate that your small power to cause me difficulty is in no way intimidating. Now I ask your own question in reverse, what do you want?"

Lu studied his hands as they rested on the arms of his chair. His face turned hard in cold anger as he stifled outrage at the old man's disrespect. He represented the Ko Lau Hui, the senior council of the Green Gang. They could end the old man's life in a heartbeat if they chose to, tea estate or not, guards or not. But he was here for business and it was his duty to resolve the matter peaceably.

"Our investigation is concluded. The American risked his life for you and your father, General Yu. He risked dishonor and prison to carry out your task. He carried out his part of the bargain. At the moment it appears you may not have carried out your part. If this is true, it is intolerable. I have come to hear your side of the matter, to determine the facts. You must provide an explanation that can be weighed by the Hui: weighed to determine if you live or die. I do not speak of an abstract death at some future time measured in months, I speak of the here and now."

Yu giggled and leaned forward across the desk with an insolent look. These encounters were most enjoyable.

"In the good old days, the days before the Westerners became dominant with their ideas of human dignity, I skinned those who displeased me. It is almost a science, you know. You must regard the person as a dressmaker's dummy: arms, legs and torso, the head too. Front and back. You take a piece each day, and you skin slowly. It is most painful. I made a practice of keeping them alive as long as possible. I would force them to eat and exercise, even in their agony. They all died of course. The strongest one lived for almost a week with no skin at all: I would go each day and talk to him. Interesting. Would you like to be skinned, Lu?"

Lu felt a stab of fear, but he knew any sign of weakness could be fatal.

"No I would not, General. Nor do I think you are so addled as to believe you could get away with an outrage of that magnitude. Now, in the place of trading insults and childish threats, why do we not address these questions and resolve the matter? As we understand the affair, you promised to pay the American some dollars and give him two of the more valuable icons once his task was complete. Is that correct?"

Yu was tiring now: this was going nowhere. He wanted only to rid himself of this unctuous little man.

"Surely the American knows whether he was paid or not, why do you pester me with this fleabite? What I did or did not do with the American is of little consequence to either of us. You come here defending musty, arcane principles. You muck about in matters from dynasties over one thousand years old. This is the new millennium, Lu; bring yourself up to date. Find your way out; you will not be hindered. I advise you to chase larger game my friend. Your merchandise will never bring you a profit."

Lu leaned forward over the desk and spread his hands.

"We defend principles that are necessary to do business in this world, vital principles that will never change. You have me at a disadvantage, General. I can do nothing about your lack of cooperation just now. I think you know this recalcitrance will not be tolerated. No one defies the council. Why do you cause this trouble over so small a matter, why don't you simply explain yourself?"

Yu's face wrinkled in a benevolent smile. His eyes disappeared in folds of skin.

"You know the fable of the turtle and the scorpion, of course? In my old age, I have become the scorpion, anxious to cause difficulty where I can. You may leave now before my patience with your peasant stupidity runs out."

Lu returned to the country road outside the estate and asked the guards to call a cab from the telephone clearly visible in a niche by the open gate. There was no reply: the three men stared at him insolently. He flagged down a vegetable truck heading toward the markets of Vangaindrano, the nearest sizeable town. He called Tun and waited for almost two hours before the call was returned.

"Yu refuses to discuss the matter. He will not explain himself."

"Refuses? Why?"

"He is a rich old man. He claims to be dying. I think he is having fun with us."

"Very well. He can have his fun for the moment. We will go at this in another way. I want his itinerary for the next two months."

Lu's temper flared.

"For Christ's sake, that will take me weeks. Yu says we waste his time. We are all wasting our time."

"Your input is greatly appreciated. Do it."

# Chapter 59

Al knew he wasn't gaining the precious ground he needed, probably losing some. His chest felt paralyzed as he dialed, his lungs seemed unable to gather the air he needed.

"Al Deforest calling for Robard Tun."

A young girl's voice chattered in Chinese, directed away from the phone. Tun came on a moment later.

"You try my patience, Mr. Deforest. I told you I would be in touch when I was ready."

"I...I must ask for another favor. We're trying to get a two-month delay here, the delay you asked for. It's hard; the owner Mr. Barlow is an experienced businessman. We intend to make an offer for the business equal to the Dutch offer. We need a convincing down payment. Mandy; my wife M...Mandy, wants to invent a mythical Certificate of Deposit for $200,000 at an overseas bank, one that cannot be cashed until the term of deposit is up. We'll use it as collateral. But Barlow or his bank will check, we're sure of that. We need to survive that credit check."

Tun ached with desire to be rid of this pest, this grubby sweating businessman scrabbling for money. He was silent a moment, and then he chuckled.

"I guess a bold thief is better than a timid one. Even if I agree to provide a cover it will be flimsy; it will eventually dissolve, no matter what. I believe the Federal sentencing guidelines for your class of felony provide for a minimum of ten years. Do you wish to risk it?"

"Yes I do. No question about it."

"Use the Bank of Luxembourg in Luxembourg City. I'll need two days to arrange a telephone cutout. Someone will call you and provide an account number. This arrangement will be valid for one telephone verification, and then it disappears. It will never survive an audit. Do you understand?"

"I do. We can work with this. We're very grateful, and surprised too."

"As it happens, our investigation is nearing completion. Your story appears to be supported by what we have learned. If it remains so, we will provide an…uh, opportunity for collection. There are no time guarantees, Mr. Deforest; you are still taking an enormous risk. Also, it is time to make a home for your new funds, assuming you are not imprisoned, and assuming you can collect from General Yu. Write a letter to the Bank of Bimini branch in Hamilton, Bermuda. Send them $500 cash, no traceable checks. Provide a code word."

\* \* \*

Mandy finished her presentation and sat down fully alert, watching Barlow for a reaction. Barlow had listened patiently, never interrupting but clearly groping for a better understanding. He trusted the Deforests completely. It did not occur to him the strange tale might have been fabricated. Now he shrugged helplessly, pulling nervously on one of the fleshy wattles at the sides of his mouth.

"I don't know Mandy, this just seems…irregular. You say Al has a large account in Luxembourg, but the bank won't honor a withdrawal request for two months? Why is that?"

"Well, it's similar to a Certificate of Deposit here in our country. The funds can't be transferred until the term has expired. But it can be used for collateral."

"Why haven't you mentioned this collateral before? It certainly would have made a difference in my discussion with the Dutch: they think the deal is agreed to now, even though no documents have been signed. I don't know what to tell them. And these telegrams from your bank, do they amount to a negotiable instrument when the maturity time on this CD arrives? They appear to amount to a letter of credit, valid in 60 days, but I can't tell from the wording."

He had heard the story twice. He understood the words but was having difficulty forming a picture of the proposition. She smiled reassuringly and covered the high points once more.

"Al's Aunt accumulated a small fortune investing in utilities and communications companies. The Depression made her mistrust U.S. banks. She did some research and decided that Luxembourg offered the safety and privacy she was seeking, so she purchased an estate in Luxembourg City, held it for one year and sold it. She transferred the proceeds to Bank Generale de Luxembourg, avoiding U.S. taxes on the gain She left the account to Al, but it's costly to move the money back here, the transfers are heavily taxed, so we never considered the money for purchasing your business. Then Al had an idea: if you would accept an assignment of these funds as a down payment, we can afford to purchase the business. You can get the money out over ten years with no tax penalty Mr. Barlow, and it will always be an asset of your estate whether you bring it here or leave it in Europe."

Mandy felt light as air, afloat in the room. This was the moment she had sought all these years. She couldn't tell if she had pulled it off. She continued, trying to be cheerfully nonchalant.

"With the down payment, there should be no problem with a bank loan for the balance. We'll meet the purchase price the Dutch have offered. The banks won't care; with our down payment they'll have plenty of collateral. Give us this chance, Mr. Barlow; you know Al and I can develop the business better than any group of foreigners. You know we love the business and you know our reputation is tops throughout Northwest Oregon. You would be investing in us, instead of a remote group of foreigners. I told Al this morning today is bound to be our day. You only need to say yes."

There, that was it. Everything. Was it enough?

Barlow thought of Mandy as his own daughter. He knew that few men could have done as well with the financial aspects of Barlow Enterprises as she had. He saw her strength now: the clenched jaw and the burning dark eyes and he wanted to chuckle.

"All right, girl, here's what I can do. First, I'll need to verify this account of Al's, either through my bank or personally. When you complete the bank loan we'll do an assignment of assets and that will be it. I don't mind accepting assets in a Luxembourg bank: there are advantages owning overseas assets. If all this works, we'll close the transaction and you two will own the business."

But Barlow was unwilling to throw away the Dutch at this point.

"I won't turn the Dutchmen down until your financing is complete. I'm going to call them and temporize: tell them another buyer is in the picture and they'll have to wait until I can determine the best offer. They've threatened me with a deadline, but I know they want the business badly: they'll go along. But understand this Mandy, if they threaten to pull out, I'll sell to them. They're qualified and I can't let them slip away on a promise from you and Al. That's the best I can do."

Joy bubbled in the laugh she could not stifle. She put her hand to her mouth.

"Thank you. You'll never regret giving us this chance. Ten years from now Barlow Enterprises will be the biggest funeral business in the Oregon, and the best."

Barlow raised his eyebrows, still troubled by her proposal, unable to say why.

"I hope so, Mandy."

She called Al from her office, whispering into the telephone.

"He believed me. He's going to call the Dutch and put a 60-day hold on the closing. If we come up with the money, we have the business. I think we've pulled it off, darling."

Al was thrilled and frightened at the same time. In a quick and disturbing thought he pictured the two of them in the executive offices. Then he pictured them in a courtroom. The consequences of failure here frightened him at an elemental level. He had never felt this unease in combat flying. His voice was fragile and apprehensive.

"W…W…We still need for him to verify the bank deposit personally, we'll never make it if he goes bank to bank. It's all over for us."

Mandy knew how Mr. Barlow would approach the matter.

"Oh, I know him so well, Al. We don't need to worry. He'll place the call himself. He has to."

She replaced the receiver and leaned back in the chair, feeling as inauthentic as a woman could feel. Heat flushed her face as she thought of her behavior. She had tricked a man who provided shelter for them in desperate need, a man who had always been generous. Suddenly she felt fear too, stark and vivid; it glittered before her eyes. If Howard Barlow did the unexpected and asked his bank to verify the deposit, their fraud would be exposed by tomorrow evening.

She felt sure he would not press charges, but they would be disgraced and fired. They would have to start all over, with a fearful handicap. Again. She had placed them in harm's way. Now luck must come into play.

# Chapter 60

Al and Mandy were in the deep relaxed sleep that follows a great fuck. The phone rang at 3:10 in the morning. Robard Tun's voice penetrated Al's sleep-fogged brain.

"You need to be at the airport in Seattle tomorrow afternoon, Pan American flight 5317 to Sydney and a connection to Cape York Regional Airport in Queensland, Northwest Territories. A man will meet you at Cape York. Pick up your ticket at the counter under the name Fairfield."

"Wait a minute, where? Who am I meeting?"

"Get yourself to Seattle-Tacoma International before 3:00 PM tomorrow afternoon. Pick up a ticket at the Pan Am counter in the name of Max Fairfield. You're on Flight 5317. Your destination is the town of Barnagal. Yu will be there two days from now. He isn't cooperating, so we are arranging for you to be in Barnagal to meet him. The rest is up to you. Don't fail. By the way, you will reimburse us for all expenses."

"OK. Pan Am 5317, Max Fairfield, I've got that part. I'll be there. What do you want me to do?"

"Whatever is necessary, it's up to you. We have found your quarry and localized him, now you must get his cooperation. I warn you, Yu is tough and dangerous. He travels with two bodyguards, perhaps more. We will supply you with a single man and weapons if you wish. I have no taste for this affair; I hope Yu is not injured and I am indifferent to your fate. The outcome should be interesting. I suggest you take along a plentiful supply of cash. Now, can you hear me Mr. Deforest?"

"Of course. I've been hearing you fine all along."

"I meant are you listening, for this is important. The people I represent, the Elders, want you to know they are finished with this affair. They have gone far enough. Your Mr. Tuck is repaid in full. What happens between you and General Yu, or what does not happen, no longer interests them. We will make no further intervention."

Al opened his mouth to ask another question, but Yu was gone. He turned on the nightstand light and carefully noted 'Flight 5317 tomorrow 3:00 PM. Fairfield.' Mandy had come instantly wide-awake. Her heavy lashes flew up in anticipation as he turned to her.

"That was Tun. Yu will be somewhere in Australia day after tomorrow. I have to go there and convince him to give us our money."

"What? How the hell are you supposed to do that? They should help, he's their man after all."

"He didn't say. It's up to me. I don't know what I should do. Tun said this is the end; there's no more help if I can't convince him."

"It sounds dangerous Al, didn't you say Yu was some kind of a warlord in China before the Communists took over?"

"He's supposed to be violent, even with only one arm and one eye. On the other hand, I seem to recall he liked me. We sat in the dirt at the side of that airstrip drinking tea while his men loaded the plane. I remember that much. He was witty, charming. Maybe that will help."

She went to the dresser and withdrew a passbook.

"You'll need money. Go to the bank in the morning, the savings account has $3600 in it. Just leave $50 to keep the account open."

"I'm a Funeral Director, what do I know about this business?"

"Should you take your gun?"

"I'd never get it through Customs in Australia. I'll worry about that once I'm inside the country."

"I've almost lost you twice. For God's sake, be careful Al."

He sat looking down at his bare feet; the toes were curling anxiously, as if someone else controlled them.

"I don't think I'll have that luxury, Mandy."

She saw Al looking at his feet and looked at her own. They were cute feet. It was a comfort. She hugged her knees to her and turned to him, her hot dark eyes alive with love.

"You think you'll lose everything again. You think it will be like the time overseas. Just remember this, my love: I've been your wife. I've borne you children. I've been your family. I know…I know you lost so much over there, Al. I will never die on you. I will never go away like the others did."

She crossed her arms under her breasts and looked down, fighting hard against the tears. She would not cry. Not now.

"Do what you have to do. You may need to kill him."

Al nodded. He thought about Yu, about the long trail that would join them now. He felt no need for vengeance against this hazy shadow from his other life, wasn't even sure there was cause. What he felt was a beginning tingle; the hunt would start now. He had forgotten about the hunt.

Al was packing a small valise the next morning when the doorbell rang. He paid no attention. He was in a rush; he needed to be at the Portland

Airport in ninety minutes to catch the commuter to Sea-Tac. He looked up when Mandy came in and saw a flicker of apprehension on her face. Her voice was small and frightened.

"Two men at the door. Policemen. They want to talk to you."

A knot of unreasoning fear shriveled him.

"Jesus Christ, I've got to get on the road, I'll miss the commuter. What do they want?"

"They're FBI, they didn't say."

He snapped the catches on his valise savagely and placed it by the bedroom door out of sight of the living room before he went to the front door. Mandy hadn't let them in. They stood on the doorstep in snap-brim hats and overcoats, looking like pleasantly bland functionaries.

"I'm Al Deforest, what can I do for you?"

"May we come in?"

"Yeah, sure, but we need to move this along, I'm late."

They removed their hats in the foyer. The shorter one spoke.

"I'm Agent Turner, this is Agent de'Allesio. We're interested in your connection with Robard Tun, an importer in San Francisco. Is there anything you'd care to say about your relationship with the man?"

Al didn't get it. They had been to Tun's once and called him twice. Where had these guys come from? He shrugged.

"There isn't any relationship. I'm an artist: he's trying to get me a special type of gesso found only in Ceylon. And what business is that of yours?"

"Mr. Tun is under investigation. There are a number of allegations, serious ones. That makes us interested in all his friends, all his associates."

"There isn't any relationship. How did you find me?"

"Surveillance. We'd really like to sit down and talk about this. Do you mind?"

Mandy had been standing in the bedroom doorway. She moved to his side.

"My husband just said he doesn't know anything. He requested some imported art material from Mr. Tun, nothing more. Please leave, you're not welcome here."

Agent Turner stared at her and the silence grew tight with tension.

"It's in your interest to cooperate with us. We only want to have a discussion here."

"Are we under arrest?"

"Oh, heavens no, ma'am. We just need to clarify a few things."

"Then get out. Get out right now."

They watched the two men get in a white four-door Chevrolet and drive off. Fear brought an irritated vitality to Al's voice.

"Son of a bitch. We're in the tightest spot of our lives and the goddamned cops show up poking their nose up our ass. Talk about timing, this one wins the prize. I'm going anyway, they can take a leap."

Mandy hid her foreboding.

"Even if they bugged Tun's office, all we asked for was debt collection—sort of. No, I don't think they know anything. That was a fishing expedition."

Al shrugged, trying to push through the massive uncertainty.

"OK. We will d...defeat the enemy o...on the field of mortal combat. I'm on my way, wish me luck."

"I wish you love; all my love. Be safe."

*　　　　　*　　　　　*

Al was asleep when the din of the engines changed, diminishing to a whisper. He was instantly awake, looking for an emergency landing field before he realized he was not the pilot. He looked out the window to an expanse of green tidal flatland that stretched almost to the horizon, broken occasionally by sluggish rivers and streams that parted marsh grass and reeds. Stands of Cypress and Mangrove followed the rivers, stunted and deformed by life-struggle in water that changed from fresh to salt twice a day. Far to the east he could see a large body of water stretching away to the horizon. He consulted the stylized airline map: it was the Coral Sea.

The DeHaviland Twin Otter pitched up on a wingtip and Al craned his neck to see forward, looking for the landing site. Just before they rolled back to level he glimpsed two runways arranged in an X three miles ahead. They descended in mildly turbulent air as the pilot prepared to land. Al grinned in pleasure at the smooth float above the runway followed by the gentlest of landing shocks. He liked it: this guy knew what he was doing."

A crowd of twenty or so awaited the airplane. Most were men; ranching people of European descent dressed in faded jeans, hats, and cowboy boots. The few hatless individuals displayed suntanned faces and startlingly white foreheads. The co-pilot came out, opened the cargo door, and began placing bags on the tarmac in humid tropical heat. Al's was among the last; most of the greeters were gone when he turned to look for his contact. A mixed-race, middle-aged man stood to the side dressed in the only suit to be seen. Al was vaguely disturbed by his slight build and apologetic smile. Then, when the man came close Al could see the hooded eyes: hawk's eyes.

"I'm Al Deforest, are you here to meet me?"

The man removed his sweat-stained hat and squinted up at Al.

"Yes. I am Martin Livingston; I practice law in Mount Bartle Frere, that's south of here. I also represent the business interests of your advisors in this matter. We'd better go to my car directly; it's quite a drive to Barnagal. We have rooms at an inn ten miles south of town. It's best if we are not seen in town until we are prepared."

"Prepared for what?"

Livingston turned as they walked toward a battered Fiat, the only car in the small dirt parking lot beyond the concrete block open-air terminal.

"Do not pretend ignorance with me Mr. Deforest. I am here to render what assistance I can. I think you face a dangerous situation. You need to be open with me."

Al summarized his mission as Livingston hurtled down the poorly maintained two-lane road toward Barnagal, and then got to the point.

"Tun said I was on my own once the meeting was arranged. It's entirely up to me to persuade Yu to pay what he owes me."

Livingston kept his eyes on the road and the throttle to the floorboard.

"I know the General well, I was a Captain in his command back in the Thirties. We called ourselves the Guiyang Provincial Irregulars, though in fact we were little more than bandits. My name was Yomei Quing then, the name I was born with. We fought the Japanese and the Communists at the same time."

He chuckled, and the words gained strength.

"Then in 1937 he turned around: he made a deal with the Japanese and spent all of the war on their side, fighting Mao and Chiang both. He is amazing. I can tell you this: if the man has decided not to honor your bargain, words will have no effect on him. He is very strong in his thinking, a very successful man in this part of the world. You will need to influence him in other ways."

Al felt exposed and vulnerable. What could he do against this powerful man? He had only words and the moral persuasion of a bargain made but not kept.

"I had hoped to appeal to his honor, Mr. Livingston, the word he gave to a man who risked a great deal for him. Is this enough?"

Livingston was silent as the miles slipped by, lost in thought. Finally he nodded and spoke, shouting over the whipping din of wind from four opened windows.

"I think moral persuasion is useless, he will take it as weakness. You will be ignored. Talk if you like, but be prepared to inflict sudden lethal violence if Yu chooses to ignore you. There will be no middle ground with this man."

He took his eyes off the road to look at Al directly.

"Can you do it?"

Al felt cowed, far from home and among strangers, fearful of making a mistake.

"I...I had hoped to settle this peaceably. I am reluctant to consider violence, especially here in a foreign land without friends or support."

"It is good that you share your feelings openly. If you mean what you have said, we should turn around now, there is a flight for Brisbane in the morning. You do not belong here."

Al closed his eyes, wondered where his courage had gone. Had his injuries so cowed him that he would fold up here in the face of danger? Apprehension tore at his insides as he took a deep breath. He could not permit a failure.

"No. I can't go home empty-handed Mr. Livingston. I…we're in a bad spot, I must be successful: there's no choice for me. How many guards will be with him?"

"I have never seen more than two here in Australia, but I have not always witnessed his travels."

"Then I want two more men, tough men. And weapons."

Livingston had doubts. This white man lacked conviction; he seemed a green willow in the storm.

General Pemberton Yu exited the lobby of the New Frontier Hotel, headed for his limousine and the airport. He was used to the delightful Madagascar climate at 26 degrees south latitude now, and this wretched tropical heat was bothersome. But he was happy. He had just concluded the sale of 270,000 pounds of unprocessed opium milk at 16 American dollars to the pound. Tomorrow, when the funds had been deposited, the raw product would be delivered dockside at Cape Negras, Burma.

The profitable deal took his mind from the increasing discomfort of his cancer. Until a few weeks ago there had been no pain. Now, in the night, he could actually feel the small, metastasized colonies taking root throughout his body, tiny flickering stabs in his chest and abdomen and legs. He wondered when they would reach his brain, his heart. The deadly colonies were diminishing him.

Two bodyguards flanked him, one slightly ahead and one behind as they made their way down the small main street. Ahead of him two Oriental businessmen got out of a car parked at the curb chattering in noisy dialect as they argued some point. Yu casually noted that one of the men carried a briefcase, but he gave them no further thought. He was deep in self-congratulation about the deal. The going rate was 11 dollars and his product had brought a fine 5-dollar premium.

As they came abreast the hotel alleyway the two businessmen approaching them split, apparently making way, one going to the hotel wall and one walking near the curb. The man near the hotel wall threw his briefcase lightly, apparently playfully, at the bodyguard to Yu's rear. As the bodyguard reflexively concentrated on his catch, the businessman rocketed a kick into his crotch that landed with a thud of total impact. The bodyguard went down instantly, senseless. The second businessman was now behind Yu's other guard. He stepped into the man, threw an arm around his neck from behind, and snapped it with a violent jerk.

Before Yu could register danger, a white man came from the alley pointing a small pistol.

"Into the alley now."

Yu complied automatically, his mind coming alive to danger too late. Green eyes regarded him as the stranger spoke

"Do you know me?"

Yu's eyes searched the alley, looking for an escape route.

"The better question is do you know me? Do you realize what you have done here, you fool?"

"You promised me money, General. You never paid. I'm here to collect."

Recognition came to Yu in that instant: the green eyes. He smiled in amusement.

"Well, well: the Lieutenant. I do not recall your name, but I know the eyes. We once drank green tea together as I recall."

He snorted in disdain and continued to survey the alley, looking for a chance, an escape route.

"There was no need to pay a dead man. And now you will do what, Lieutenant? You will kill me? Cancer kills me as we speak. Perhaps you offer me a merciful end. But tell me, how will you collect your debt if I lie dead in this alley? You are shit, Mr. Lieutenant, you have made a grave mistake."

The gun lowered and Yu thought it was over, the fool was backing down.

Al's mouth tasted foul, his legs had vanished and he was afloat. The insane idea of an apology occurred to him. But he had gone too far down this dark path: there was no return. The truth was, he could never leave it like this. Yu's one-eyed face glared at him, taunting him. He spoke to Yu quietly, with no apparent menace.

"My shit is your shit, General."

Yu heard a pop and he was down in the alley. There was no pain, but he saw blood beginning to well out of his trousers at the knee. He knew he had been shot. Anger took away his control.

"You fucking idiot, you've shot me. Your life is over: you'd better finish it now or I will finish you. No one does this to me. No one. Never."

Al's face turned to stone.

"Get up and walk to the car back there. If you don't I'll shoot you in the other knee and still make you walk back there. Eventually, if I have to, I'll shoot your arm off. Then I'll shoot your eye out. You'll get no merciful death from me."

He flexed his cramping fingers and re-gripped the pistol.

Yu saw the gun move to his other knee and he capitulated in shock and dismay.

"Stop. Christ, I need medical attention. We can settle this."

Al removed his finger from the trigger; it was tightening involuntarily under the stress of the moment. He carefully de-cocked the pistol and turned to Livingston.

"Have those two put him in the car. Search him for anything he could use to commit suicide. Send the men to a store for bandages and aspirin. We need to move out of here right now."

Livingston nodded.

"I know a place on the Bugong River; we'll go there. I'll come back to town for the supplies. It's best if the men don't know where we are."

Yu groaned, he could feel a peculiar buzzing in the injured knee and the pain was starting.

Al followed as the men carried Yu to the car.

"You knew the Elders were looking for you, trying to determine if you had paid. You knew they would not be denied. Why did you let it get this far, go this badly?"

Yu cursed in pain and frustration.

"No one orders me. No one tells me what to do. Not in this life, not in the next life. If you had come to me in person, it might have been different. The money means nothing to me, my pride means everything."

Al shook his head silently, not understanding this complex man.

"How the hell was I supposed to come to you when no one knew where you were?"

Martin Livingston watched from the car. He laughed softly; delighted with the violence he had just seen. He had badly misjudged the American. He had taken him for a sentimentalist, too soft for decisive action.

They drove several miles north of the town and turned into a rutted two-lane road that passed through a field of reeds eight feet high. After twenty minutes of jouncing, they emerged into a clearing containing several ramshackle buildings. Livingston spoke.

"A fishing camp for the local ranchers. They come and fish for Bream and Tulapai in the summer time. No one will be here for months."

They left Yu in the car and searched the shacks. The largest contained several chairs, two iron cots without mattresses, and a long table covered with fish scales. It looked good to Al.

"This is the one, let's bring him in here."

They returned to the car and opened both rear doors. Yu pointed a finger at Livingston as they reached in for him.

"I know you. You served under me in China before the war. You had better help me, you rice-plucking peasant, or you're a dead man. Help and I will make you rich. Take a stand against this crazy man."

Al jerked Yu roughly from the car and he fell on the soggy ground, moaning. They carried him to the shack and placed him on the fish-skinning table. Al turned to Livingston.

"OK; so far, so good. Go back to town now and get the medical supplies. Stop at a market and get some food, we may be here a few days. Go to the tavern and check us out, then come back here. Oh, get a case of fruit juice. I'm sure the General is losing fluids here. We don't want him going into shock."

After Livingston left, Al drew a chair up to the table. Yu lay looking upward, his eyes following flies as they passed through slivers of sunlight from the carelessly shingled roof.

"Here's your situation, General: you're seriously wounded and losing fluids. You could easily go into shock. We can treat that. But the wound will become septic in a day or two and we can't treat that. Soon, you'll have gangrene in that leg. Eventually, you'll die. You whine to me about your cancer. It's nothing compared to what you face right here, right now. Think about it."

"What do you want?"

Al pulled a scrap of paper from his pocket. He had no idea how much Yu had promised him, but Mandy had a brilliantly simple idea: collect from Yu what they needed plus $150,000. She had computed an amount at compound interest from November 1949 up to last Thursday.

"You promised to pay me $300,000 back in 1949. If you had done that, the amount would be $487,430 today. That's at four percent interest, compounded. And you promised me icons, valuable icons. I want my money. I want the money wired to the Bimini Bank, to the branch in Hamilton, Bermuda. I have the wiring instructions with me. I want my icons air-expressed to a post box in Gold Beach, Oregon. You will give written instructions to Mr. Livingston to accomplish this by telephone: detailed instructions that will overcome the reluctance of your employees. He will make the necessary calls. When I verify that the funds are in my account we will take you to a hospital."

Yu wanted to live. He wanted to kill this mother-fucking American.

"That will take days. You need to show mercy."

"I don't think so. This is Wednesday afternoon; if you cooperate the transfer can be completed by tomorrow noon. In the meantime we'll see that you have aspirin and fruit juice. If you don't give the instructions to Mr. Livingston, I will shoot out your remaining eye. Then we'll all sit here with the flies and see what happens."

Al called Mandy from a telephone booth in the fishing village of Dufkin Bay at mid-morning Friday. Her voice was rich with satisfaction.

"It's all there, Al; over $487,000. And the package came: two icons. One is Terra Cotta with jade inlays and the other is a gold and jade oriental woman holding some sort of scepter. It's very heavy. I nicked the metal and its soft—I guess it's gold. How in heaven's name did you do it?"

"Well, I surely didn't invoke heaven. You need to move the money to the secondary account right away; that should prevent any monkey business from Yu's boys. Rent another safe deposit box for the icons and move them, too. I'll tell you all about it when I get home. I can wrap up here today and catch an airplane tomorrow, should be home by Wednesday. It…it's been very bad. I love you."

He returned to the fish camp clearing and got out of the car. The sun was bright off the tin and tarpaper shack roofs and he glanced at his watch: five minutes to compose himself and he would go in. He knew what to do, but Yu's face kept appearing before him. Inside, Livingston looked up from the paperback he was reading.

"Everything all right?"

Al nodded but didn't answer. He walked to the fish-skinning table and leaned over Yu.

"You did your part, the money transferred. It's hard for me to believe, but you did. We're even now, I guess."

Yu's eyes opened and looked at Al, but he said nothing. Al fished the small pistol from his pocket and shot Yu between the eyes. The small red hole was still for a moment, and then bright red blood began to pump from it.

Amazingly, Yu struggled up to his elbow and then to a sitting position. He began to scold noisily in Chinese as blood coursed down his face. Al turned to Livingston in disbelief.

"How can he be alive? What's he saying?"

Livingston was shocked. He shrugged in dull confusion.

"I don't know how he can sit up. He's in some sort of daze; says he's angry with you because the blood will spoil his shirt. He's not making sense."

Al turned back to the noisy General and fired a second shot into the top of his head. Now Yu fell back on the table. This time he was still.

The mid-day ebb tide was beginning to flow strongly to the sea now. Al and Livingston carried the pitifully light body to the Bugong River shallows and dropped it in. The body returned to shore. Livingston warned him.

"Don't go in far. Watch your feet carefully; fresh water crocodiles are in this river.

Al found a long stick and waded into the creek. He pushed Yu's body into faster moving water toward the center of the river.

Martin Livingston drove him to the airfield afterward, silent until they pulled into the small dirt lot.

"There's a last flight to Brisbane at five this afternoon: they'll honor your ticket even though you're a day late. I've done my job here. Good luck to you…I guess."

His dark remote eyes turned to Al.

"You are a savage man, Mr. Deforest; I misread you rather completely."

Al nodded and got out without a word. He closed the passenger door and reached to the rear seat for his bag. Livingston had a final question.

"He kept his part of the bargain. I thought you might let him go. Did you think of sparing him?"

Al bent down to look directly at the man.

"He kept the bargain eleven years late under threat of death. And never in life would I have spared him. I put him down and I won't lose a second's sleep over it. He would have killed my wife and children along with me. I had no choice and I have no regrets."

"I think maybe you have died inside, Mr. Deforest."

He thought about it, but it wasn't true. He had never felt more alive.

Livingston waved a hand, a goodbye gesture.

"The gate agent will be here in two hours, you should sit out of the sun. Goodbye, Mr. Deforest."

Al started for the terminal, and then turned back to the battered car.

"I want you to tell Tun what has happened here. I don't want trouble with Yu's organization."

"I will give a full report. Don't worry about reprisals. You fired the shots, but Yu's people will understand who has killed him."

Al walked to the open-air concrete structure and sat on a mildew-stained concrete bench in the humid afternoon heat that somehow made him cold inside. He sat and felt vague and wispy, as if something had escaped and left a sac of emptiness inside him.

The following week Al traveled to Hamilton, Bermuda. Officials at the Bank of Bimini arranged an ordinary savings account for him at the Bank of Luxembourg and transferred $200,000.

Four days later the Deforest application for a business loan of $900,000 was approved at the Farmers Bank and Savings in Gold Beach, Oregon; the banker was friendly and smiled at them possessively. There was ample collateral; the loan was no problem.

While Al was in Bermuda Mandy carried the gold icon to Los Angeles in an ordinary canvas flight bag, wrapped in burlap. She took a cab from the airport to 57 North Rodeo Drive. The jewelry store had a black granite fascia and gilt Art Nouveau lettering: Gerard de'Aquille.

"I have an appointment with Preston Flax."

The clerk looked at her long-sleeved sport shirt, chinos, and loafers disapprovingly.

"And you are?"

"Angela Lansbury."

A gray wooly head appeared at a rear door. A gold ringed hand gestured her forward.

"Ah, Mrs. Lansbury. A pleasure. What have you brought me?"

Mandy plunked the shabby flight bag on a long wooden table.

"Just this, Mr. Flax."

Flax opened the bag and unrolled the burlap. His eyebrows went up and there was a faintly audible hiss as he inhaled. He placed a jeweler's loupe in his right eye and reached unconsciously for an adjustable examination light. He studied in silence for twenty minutes before looking up. The smile was enigmatic.

"If you can document the origins of this figure, it is virtually priceless."

"And if I can't?"

"Then I should say upwards of two million. May I arrange private viewing for a few of our best customers?"

"No."

# Chapter 61

They were near the end now. The two men had been together, off and on, for almost six days, much longer than either had anticipated. Goldkette would disappear to his office occasionally as management crises surfaced, but mainly it had been time together, a time to understand the tangled story.

They sat in the dark on cloth beach chairs on the back porch of Gus Goldkette's modest home in Burke, Virginia, digesting Edith Goldkette's veal in white wine sauce, fresh vegetables and home baked rolls. Edith and Mandy were off seeing a movie.

Al was nodding off when Goldkette spoke.

"More brandy, Al? Mine seems to have disappeared."

He wasn't much of a drinker these days.

"I don't think so Gus. I'll pass. An old guy like me needs his rest. We're going to the National Art Museum tomorrow, to see the Ed Mell exhibit. Then home in the afternoon. I hope I've helped you out of your pickle here. I still can't understand how my record could have been released. It's hard to believe it was an accident."

"It wasn't. We knew what happened before I called you."

Al sat up, startled.

"You did? Then why did you need me for all this? What happened?"

"Tuck always thought you could have been a General, Al. If you had been, you would have discovered Generals in this town spend their time at the budget front, not the war front. There are only so many dollars each fiscal year. The Armed Services all compete for the same pie. Sometimes it gets a little devious."

"I don't see what any of that has to do with my service record being released."

"Highly sensitive personnel records are kept at the National Holding Vault over in Spring Hill, Maryland. That's the material on long-term hold, 25 years or more. *Heat Lightning* was on a 75-year diplomatic hold, enough time for national passions to cool, for those involved to have died. As it happens, a Marine Major signed out your record jacket. He does classified research for the War College. The guy is an Annapolis graduate, very bright, but somehow he filed your record with a stack of others awaiting routine declassification. Some of the material was blacked out in the process, but plenty was left to allow any good investigative reporter to uncover the story. Still, your file might have sat there another hundred years, but someone tipped off that media guy Lavendar. We'll never know who."

Al winced.

"Man, that poor son of a bitch must be hurting. Too bad, it sounds like he was a good one."

"Don't be sorry, the Major will be fine. Right now he has a letter of censure in his 201 File. Ordinarily that would be the end of his career, but in his case someone will come along in a couple of years and pull the letter. He'll go on without a blemish to whatever level he would otherwise have achieved. We'll protest, of course, but that's what will happen. The Major was a very temporary sacrificial lamb."

"Wait a minute, I must be missing something here. He's caused a major embarrassment for the DOD and the Administration, stirred up a diplomatic hornet's nest, and he gets a free pass? I don't get it. In my time, he would have been boiled in oil."

Goldkette grinned at his consternation.

"No. Not even in your time, Al. If you were on a suicide mission for the Chief of Staff, you would have received the same treatment. These things are rare, of course, but they happen."

"I still don't get it."

"Two years ago we started the new Air Superiority Fighter, the F-136; a blend of stealth and mind-boggling maneuverability. Just a few studies and tests at first: seed money, small potatoes. Well, it looked like a good airplane; it came out looking very good. So now we need money for advanced development and prototype production, big money. And we'll get it. Support in the White House and on both sides of the aisle on the Hill is overwhelming. It's going to be a great airplane. We've structured the program to put heavy funding into some of the most influential Congressional districts in the country: that's a tough combination to trump."

Gus Goldkette got out of his beach chair to get more brandy. Al still didn't see where this was going. It all seemed dumb: far-fetched and ungentlemanly. Gus returned with two brandy snifters. Al took his without protest.

"Well, the F-136 has to come from someone else's piece of the pie, in this case the Navy Shipbuilding program. So someone over there looked around for a program that would provide some temporary embarrassment for us, something that would put us off-balance and at a disadvantage in the budget wars. They came up with *Project Heat Lightning,* an example of young men behaving admirably on a muddled military mission, and run by yours truly. So I'll go on over to the Hill next week and provide classified testimony. I'll do my best to emphasize the quality of the military personnel and the dubious charge they received from their civilian masters. I'll talk about the discoveries and the intelligence validations. I'll talk about heroism. I won't speak of the appalling losses or our failure to act on the information. I'll dress it up as best I can, but no one will look very good. We'll lose some money over this, no question about it. That's OK; it won't be the first time. And later on, we'll have plenty of opportunity for payback."

Al understood now. He decided not to become angry. He wasn't an insider here, and he didn't know what was right and wrong in this odd, make-believe Beltway world. And a half-century had passed. He was older now, and more tired too, he guessed. He held his snifter up.

"Maybe I ought to have another one of these."

They sat growing drowsy; listening to the night insects, watching a growing thunderstorm to the east. Lightning illuminated the towering mass like an elaborate Japanese lantern. Gus's voice came to him from the darkness.

"We know what you did over there, Al."

Al was drowsing near sleep and now he jolted awake, wondering if he'd gone to sleep and dreamed something. The old warning flags came up: the ones that had kept his secret all these years, the ones that had kept him out of prison and maybe off the hangman's platform. He was suddenly very tired, bone tired. When did it end?

"What?"

Gus smiled to himself.

"We know you landed somewhere in the south of China on the way home from a mission: your 19th, I believe. We know you picked something up from a warlord named Yu, a fighting Provincial Governor. Tuck was devastated when he found out, he thought maybe you were part of the tip-off that made the Chinese ready for you on that last mission: the one that killed all those kids."

Al nodded and closed his eyes. Maybe he could just go to sleep again. When he woke, none of this would have happened. What should he say, what was there to say?

"I was one of those kids Gus, what happened out there changed my life forever. They're all gone. I would have been gone that day too, but for the slimmest chance. My flying ended there, I was never the same."

Gus waited, hoping Al would say more. There was uncomfortable silence.

"Oh, no one's going to do anything about it Al. That was all fifty years ago. It was Tuck you know; he turned you in after you went to him for help. He struggled, but in the end he served his masters. He was in agony because you were a favorite, but he wanted to know the truth. So the Defense Investigative Service launched a probe. You know them: they're the 'you catch 'em, we fry 'em boys'. They looked here in the U.S., they looked in Nationalist China and they even went to Madagascar. They were chasing their tails. There was nothing in any of the official records. Finally, they dredged up a Taiwanese who claimed to have been there that night, said he lit the torches around the airstrip and watched the American get out of the airplane. Then our Indonesian friends produced a rice-farmer who said he unloaded heavy objects from one of the airplanes parked at Isla Mattoon after a mission. He put them in a sampan and paddled to Chittagong where some one else took them. There were no corroborating witnesses. So the intelligence cheeses sat down and decided to drop the thing. You were a Medal of Honor winner. By that time, the entire operation was seen as something that wouldn't stand up to daylight: a lot more downside than up. So it was buried. And it will stay buried. I have instructions to skip the entire episode over on the Hill next week. Gladly."

More silence. Gus wondered if Al was angry. He decided to pick at the thing.

"Why, Al? Jesus. You'd done everything right up to that point. Tuck didn't care about the airplane you wrecked, no one could have salvaged an engine failure at that point in a takeoff. Your mission performance was exemplary. Tuck was making plans for you. So why? Let's talk, Al. Think about it, how can it hurt you?"

"Probably in a way I'm overlooking right now."

All the years, and Al really didn't know why. He had never dug hard at reasons. The closest he had come was a discovery, a phrase he had found, during his studies of occult and metaphysical processes. Saint Augustine had said, ' I am at the same time thoroughly tired of living and extremely frightened of dying'. Later, Oscar Hammerstein II used the same thought in the lyrics of Old Man River. The phrase pretty much summarized things for Al.

And now his reasons scarcely mattered. But here was Gus, a guy he could talk to. After all, the man didn't get the Air Force Cross for munching Cheese Doodles on the O-Club veranda.

"Well, let's just talk about theoretical possibilities. The truth is, I can't really remember what I was thinking about back then. I just don't have that part of my memory now. The head injury, there are things I just can't get to now. And I've never wanted to."

He watched lightning in the thunderhead, counting seconds between flashes: average time about 32 seconds. He smiled at the calculation: here he was 75 years old and his old squash still worked pretty well; brain injury or not.

"First of all, there was old man Yu, he got it going. He looked me up in Singapore while I was recuperating, told me what he wanted. A lot of money involved. But the big thing, the thing that busted my ass, was finding out they weren't going to train replacement pilots back in the States. And we just kept flying those missions. I don't think we brought back anything new in the last three months: twelve kids dead during that time. We couldn't see that we were doing any good at all."

He paused, pulling at the wattle of loose skin that had somehow grown below his jaw.

"We found out about the replacement decision from a Maintenance Officer they flew out from Ogden in a C-124 loaded with new engines for us. We found out from this ground weenie. The sleazy bastards at the Pentagon didn't even have the courtesy to tell us to our faces. We were chatting with that guy in the hangar. When he told us, there was dead silence; we all just looked at each other. He saw he'd made a mistake and tried to cover it up backing and filling. But we knew brother; we got it. And Tuck didn't know about it either, our Commanding Officer. How do you like them apples?"

Al stood and went indoors to the Goldkette refrigerator, well stocked with Sierra Nevada; his favorite beer. When he returned to the darkened back porch Gus appeared to be asleep in the hammock. He leaned over to inspect the younger man, wanting him to be awake so he could get this off his chest. Gus's eyes opened and an impish grin spread across his face.

"Just kidding. This is the Tale of the Century. Keep going."

"Well, a couple of missions later I lost that engine on takeoff and crashed. Then Singapore and Yu. After that, I decided to go ahead and do Yu's job. Not any one single thing involved, I was just god almighty tired and wanted to lash out at somebody over the stupidity of the whole thing. When the word came, when the arrangements were made, I just did it."

Goldkette sat up in the hammock, eyes wide,

"They were violent criminals. They could have killed you easily, or captured you and tried to get a ransom. It would have been a disaster for everyone. Where did you find the guts? I could never have done a thing like that."

"That's where you and I are different, Gus. Bottom line, I really didn't care at that point. But listen, I had my pistol cocked and ready to go when I climbed down that ladder. Not that it would have done much good. Did I tell you the younger Yu and I got along quite well? We had a nice chat sitting there and drinking tea in the darkness beside that dirt runway. I guess I believed old man Yu, figured they needed their merchandise out of China a whole lot more than they needed a political prisoner."

Al was tired of this yakking. He wanted to change the subject.

"Where is Tuck now? I guess the last time I saw him was more than forty years ago."

"Gone. He passed away a few years back. Retired in 1969 with 36 years of service, a Major General. He was a Deputy Assistant Ambassador in Germany for almost ten years after that. Then he taught Astronomy at the University of Montana for quite a while. Did you know he had a genius IQ? Not many people knew that. He completed all the course work for a PhD in Mathematics at the University of Michigan before the Army called him to active duty in 1933. Unusual man; well thought of."

"He was. Not much to look at, and it took a while to know him, to understand his methods. I finally realized he was just a very direct, unassuming man. There was nothing showy about him, but he was brave as a lion. I learned from him. Maybe we'll meet up a few more years down the road. I guess that's something I can look forward to."

He paused and an unwanted comment slipped out.

"I guess I'll never be well thought of in these circles."

Then he silently cursed himself: he was still needy, still fishing for complements in a field where he had disgraced himself. He was being whiny and coy. Gus picked up on the tone immediately.

"What do you want, Al? You made a life in spite of everything. You hold the Medal of Honor—deservedly so. You're wealthy, you have a beautiful wife: she's a perfect companion for your later years. What do you care what a few old soldiers think?"

Al didn't know what he thought. He wanted to get Mandy and go back to the hotel for some sleep.

"Did I tell you Mandy and I are going down to North Carolina on the way home? We'll stop and see Doug Trapnell. I just hope we can communicate with him. He's my oldest friend, you know."

Gus could hear the loneliness and isolation.

"But you must have other good friends?"

Al thought about it. He did have friends, plenty of friends around him: family, too. But he was remembering the tough, chestnut-eyed kid, the great pilot. He was remembering the crowded hot barracks at Moody Field where they first met back in 1947. It was all so clear to him, like it was just the other day.

"I do. But none like Doug. I'm glad I knew him."

# Chapter 62

Mandy closed the paperback novel she was reading and craned to look forward from her window seat in the small Air Force jet. She sighed: the trip had tired her, made her uneasy.

"I can see the McDowell Mountains up there. About twenty more minutes I guess. I'll be glad to see Mrs. Ten-Babies."

Mrs. Ten-Babies was a Gambel quail that visited their back yard each morning with her brood. At first there had been fourteen chicks, but now there were ten. Mandy was certain the quail had adopted an orphaned brood as well as caring for her own; it seemed impossible that one bird could have so many eggs. Now the babies were half-grown teen-agers who watched their mother searching for the seeds Al hid in different spots around the rear yard. The mother would cock her head, searching for signs in the sand before scratching with one foot while her comical bowling-pin body remained perfectly balanced above. The babies would repeat the motion exactly, each a small copy of the adult bird.

Al tried to look forward, but his view from the aisle seat was blocked. He could only see the brown patch of smog that spread southward from Phoenix toward Tucson. He remembered flying across the country in the Forties when smog was strictly a local phenomenon, sitting as a contained cap over notorious places like Los Angeles and Cleveland. Then, some time in the sixties, more cities sprouted the brown patch. In the eighties the patches had joined, forming a brown pall over much of the country on days of stagnant air. This was progress, he guessed.

He smiled at his woman.

"We'll be home in an hour. You can sleep a week if you want to."

"No, not a week. The kids are sending Jamie and Dakota on Wednesday. We'll have them for ten days, until just before Memorial Day."

Al nodded, pleased at the thought of time with his grandchildren. They were beautiful, curious, noisy, open kids, a joy to be with. He would start Dakota's golf lessons this time; she was going to be good, he could tell from the way she moved. Maybe he would take them to FiddleSticks so they could race the noisy little gasoline-powered go-carts and ride the bumper boats. They loved that. Mandy turned to him, rubbing tired eyes.

"How will Gus handle what you gave him?"

"Oh, I guess he'll go over to the Hill and tell them the good stuff about *Project Heat Lightning*, bullshit them about the rest. They like him; he doesn't expect any trouble. It seems the Navy stirred all this up to prevail in some budget dispute. The Hundred Years War was nothing compared to these Beltway battles."

Gus had given him a long complex explanation for the budget battles, but Al wasn't sure he could ever learn the odd Beltway calculus, wasn't sure there was anything to learn. He decided to skip any elaboration—a small mercy for Mandy's sake. She turned to him, concerned.

"You didn't tell him everything did you?"

"No, just a little bit off the record. I think he's a pretty good friend now, but there are limits. He knew some of it; they investigated us after I went to Tuck for help. Nothing came of it. They had suspicions about me but there was nothing on paper. I think they were glad to drop the thing. *Project Heat Lightning* wasn't exactly an example of Government courage and wisdom. And there was the medal. The investigators just took the first off-ramp they could. So I told Gus about the military stuff and stayed light on the rest; that should be enough."

He paused, thinking of Richard Tuck.

"Tuck turned me in. I never thought he'd do that. Not very helpful, was he?"

"We've really never had anyone to help us, Al. In the tough times we've always fended for ourselves, haven't we?"

"Got that right. I suppose we'll have to bury ourselves too."

"Oh God, Al, how would we do that? For that matter, who cares? To me, dead is dead: the never-ending sleep."

She shivered in her seat; this entire thing had been a scare, something unexpected after all these years. The arc of the juggernaut had barely missed them. She hoped it would end now. The coming media blitz was another concern.

"What about the press, TV? That repulsive man Lavendar?"

This was something Al didn't care to cope with.

"Oh, I don't know. It was all a long time ago, folks wouldn't be very interested. The tabloid press, maybe. You know, the ones who have never overestimated the taste of the American public. Short attention span: they'll all be gone in a day or so."

"I don't think so. People are interested in old stories. We're going to have a problem: they'll hang on.

"Maybe. I guess they'll drum up as much hysteria as they can; sell a lot of jock itch powder, that sort of thing. That reminds me, I saw one the other day that cured feminine odor and stopped callus growth at the same time. A modern marvel."

Mandy wrinkled her nose at the thought. He continued.

"I guess we'll just stay inside the gates and wait for it to die down. Not much attention span there, you know."

"We have to go out, Al. We have to get food, shop, see our friends."

"I'll get you a fake beard and dark glasses, maybe a raincoat. No one will know."

She giggled.

"Maybe you should write a book. Has that occurred to you?"

Al had considered writing the story these past days, but he rejected the idea. That awful time was a private memory for him. The flying and danger and comradeship were precious, he could not to share that with a gawping public.

"I don't think I could do that. No."

And now the sad end of Douglas Trapnell: over the years Mandy had come to understand and respect the odd, conflicted Southerner.

"I…I'm so sorry about Doug. He didn't have a very good life, did he?"

Al cringed inside; there were so many things he didn't want to think about now.

"No. Being away from flying was just too hard on him. It was what he had. He was OK later on, when he decided to stop feeling sorry for himself. He improved those tobacco lands and made even more money than his Daddy did. But it was just something to do; he never loved it like flying. He was gifted, I guess, and they took that away from him. Someone took it away from him."

He searched for something good in all the wreckage.

"Well he made it to 82 even with all the problems. That's something."

Al thought about his own aging, about what a sneak-thief time had become for him. Was time measured in months and seasons, or was it measured in books read, electric bills paid, bottles of Merlot consumed? It was going fast no matter how you measured it.

He was in pretty good shape except for little things: an arthritic toe that limited his morning hikes and a hip that locked up sometimes when he squatted. Both problems on the left side, and he wondered why. He had asked his doctor and received a helpless shrug—maybe in thirty years they would have some answers, maybe not.

And now there was his vision playing tricks on him even in the good eye. He had prided himself on uncanny peripheral vision in his flying days. He knew instinctively where everyone was in a complex air combat situation: one glance from the corner of his eye and he knew all the players, knew when to roll out and be on the enemy's tail. It had saved his life more than once, he was certain of that. Now sometimes he thought he saw something moving in the corner of his eye but when he turned nothing was there. Odd. And that stuff floating around inside his left eye like spots on a dirty window, the Doc smiled about it as he explained.

"Oh that's nothing. Just some fragments of the interior lining of your eye sloughing off. Happens to most everyone as they age. We call them floaters. The cure is worse than the problem."

Still and all, Al guessed he was lucky to be going as well as he was.

His mind turned to the car projects, always a source of pleasure. The Jag was close to done now: rebuilt engine sitting bolted to an engine stand in the garage, the polished aluminum cam-covers gleaming. The new floorboard and trunk were welded in, the bodywork complete and the car was in primer, ready for a dove gray finish, the original color. Then there would be the red spoke-wheels and graceful gray spats at the rear wheel wells. Wow, it would be a beauty.

He had done all of it himself. Well, almost all, he couldn't do upholstery. He had a bunch of Mexican guys over in Goodyear who did that for him. He had been there last month to check and was pleased with their work. The seats were pleated in soft gray Wilton leather, the door panels done, overhead liner and trunk-kit ready. All of it wrapped in plastic, nice and neat. When the old 51 coupe was running he would screw an orange crate to the floorboards for a seat and drive it over there for the upholstery installation.

And the 33 Ford awaited him, what a miracle that had been. He had been with Mandy up in Prescott Valley completing one of his landscapes. He still painted; there was quite a demand for his work. He did commission work now on a strictly limited basis, not wanting the hassle of art shows and gallery owners pressing their inevitable deadlines.

He had treated Mandy to lunch at the Gurley Street Grille in Prescott. They were headed home by a shortcut through an old neighborhood when he glimpsed a woman closing the doors on a one-car garage at the rear of a turn-of-the-century Craftsman bungalow. He thought he saw a flash from an old grille just before the doors closed. The garage was more of a woodshed, actually, set at the rear of an old fashioned driveway, the kind with two narrow strips of concrete and a grass median. Without thinking he wheeled a quick U and parked in front of the house. Mandy had not seen the car.

"What are you doing, Al?"

"Old car. I'm going to talk to the woman. Come up in about ten minutes."

It was a good story: her father's car, a new coupe purchased in late 1932 and driven for almost 60 years before the old man had been forced to park it. She had the original invoice and all the service records in the house. The car had been sitting for nine years, but she couldn't part with it.

Al offered her three thousand dollars sight unseen. The woman shook her head grimly. He talked it up, showing her wallet pictures of his restorations. His enthusiasm alarmed her but he didn't see it; she folded her arms across her chest and watched his manic capers disapprovingly.

Then Mandy came up the drive, cute and pert with her compact figure. She 'deared' and 'honeyed' and 'sweet-hearted' the old woman while resting her hand on a wrinkled arm. They left with the title: fifty two hundred bucks it cost him, a bargain. Now the old car sat at the rear of his garage restoration bay. The fading original tan paint was worn through to metal on the hood and trunk, years of hand-grime caked the steering wheel, the mohair upholstery was worn and ruptured and covered by a cheap rayon seat cover of WW2 vintage. But it was all there and all original, it would be a stunning restoration. Maybe he could talk his friend, Ron 'Sparthantuous' Cord, into coming over and giving a hand. They would have some good times.

He had found jack stands with strong caster wheels to support the car and to help him maneuver it crossways at the end of his restoration bay. Sometimes he went out and just pushed the old Ford around the garage, delighted by its easy glide across the floor. Now he needed time to finish all these important things, they both needed time.

He turned to Mandy, absorbed again in her paperback.

"How much time, I wonder?"

She knew what he meant. She put the book in her lap and thought a moment, distressed and frowning, her lips compressed.

"I don't know. A few more years I hope. Things are so good for us now. A few more years, maybe a little more."

She was so strong, but he could see that she was down. He wanted to cheer her.

"We'll get them, don't worry about that. We're too mean to die. Besides, the bobcat needs me."

She snorted, understanding the element of truth in his statement. And the bobcat was another miracle: it had appeared one morning, peering in the bathroom window from a perch on the roof, round eyes staring upside down at Al, giving him a start. Now the cat came almost every morning, making a stop on the way to its den from a night of hunting.

Al was sure the cat was a good omen sent to them by the Anasazi: the ancients who once ruled their rugged beautiful land.

**The End**

# Epilogue

In 1970, an Australian survey party searching for manganese deposits came across the wreckage of *StarBuster* in the Burmese jungle ten miles from the Indian border. Lt. Padraig Dwyer flew *Starbuster* on her last flight December 2, 1949. No remains were found in or near the wreckage.

In 1992, Mr. Winston Pardee, a military aviation expert from the Wright-Patterson Institute, was invited to speak at the opening of the Defenders of the Soviet Union Aviation Museum in St. Petersburg, Russia. While touring a warehouse holding aircraft under restoration he came across the battered engine and tail-boom from a P-61. He asked his host where the wreckage had been found and was told Soviet policy did not allow comment on items awaiting restoration. Then the host whispered that a shepard had stumbled across the pieces in Siberia many years before. Pardee committed the last six digits of the engine serial number to memory. After several months, the Air Force determined that the engine had been installed in *My Gal* three days before Lt. Arthur Trumbauer disappeared in it on a mission to Aksi, China, November 11, 1949.

Both discoveries received local media coverage before the State Department clamped on heavy security.

The Administration never proposed a DEW-line extension down the west coast of the United States.

Printed in the United States
2488

Manufactured by Amazon.ca
Acheson, AB

16365023R00057

# About the Author

**Paul Collin** began his entrepreneurial journey at the age of 16, just two weeks after earning his driver's license. He started by delivering pizzas, a job he continued until he eventually owned a Boston Pizza franchise, one of the most successful casual-dining brands in Canada. Fascinated by business, capitalism, and free enterprise from an early age, Paul pursued expertise in bookkeeping, generally accepted accounting principles, corporate law, and contract law.

This passion drove him to excel in his career, culminating in a role as a cost planner for a $425 million budget at Royal Dutch Shell Group, then the world's largest publicly traded company. During his time there, Paul's research uncovered evidence of what he described as corporate capture, or—at the very least—an economic super-entity that runs the world.

The time for passive observation has long passed. We are standing on the precipice of an economic shift that could either reinforce the stranglehold of the few or create an opportunity for genuine, transformative change for the many. This is not a fight that belongs to a select few nor is it a battle to be waged from the sidelines. It is a collective responsibility — one that calls on each of us to act with intention and purpose.

Every dollar spent, every investment choice, every voice raised in dissent has the power to shape the future. The systems we see today, with their monopolies and imbalances, will not reform themselves. They are entrenched, but they are not invincible. It is up to us to demand a new world — one where competition is restored, where economic power is distributed more equitably, and where long-term prosperity benefits all, not just the few.

The wealth of nations, and the well-being of their citizens, rests in our hands. If we act now, we can rewrite the story of the future — one that is more just, more inclusive, and more resilient. Let us rise to the challenge. **Let's invest in a future worth living for.**

---

*"I sincerely believe, with you, that banking establishments are more dangerous than standing armies; and that the principle of spending money to be paid by posterity, under the name of funding, is but swindling futurity on a large scale."*

**—THOMAS JEFFERSON**

---

The fast-tracked trade deals of the Trans-Pacific Partnership (TPP) and Transatlantic Trade and Investment Partnership had big benefits for corporations. As economist Joseph Stiglitz points out, multinationals have the right to sue: It's the "worst part of the agreement," he says, because it allows large multinationals to sue governments. "It used to be the basic principle was the polluter pays," Stiglitz said. "If you damaged the environment, then you have to pay. Now if you pass a regulation that restricts the ability to pollute or does something about climate change, you could be sued and pay billions of dollars."

There were similar provisions in the North American Free Trade Agreement that led to the Canadian government being sued, but the TPP goes even further. Stiglitz said the provision could be used to prevent raising minimum wages or overturn rules that prevent usury or predatory lending practices. Stiglitz argues the deal — a 6,000-page mammoth whose anatomy would frighten even the most experienced biologist — should have been negotiated openly. "This deal was done in secret with corporate interests at the table."

## Taking Responsibility for Your Own Life

It's time to take radical responsibility for everything in your life and become the executor of your every decision. Every dollar you spend participates in this current scene, whether you like it or not. The choice is simple: Recoil and be covertly belittled for every day you have left, or step forward into resilience and integrity, and cut yourself off from this corporate capture. The math alone illustrates that this beheading is going to happen at some point, but the longer this situation is drawn out, the more defenses it generates. Every dollar counts.

In these pages, I've shown a few directions you can take.

indoctrination; and distract the masses with iGadgets, reality TV, hero worship, professional sports, social media, irrelevant cultural issues, and literally thousands of other modern-day bread and circuses; you become arrogant and careless."

The system has consolidated itself into a monopolized world. Awareness of this will set the stage for the transfer of wealth necessary in the next crash. All systemically financially attached corporations should be allowed to go bankrupt during the next downturn with ownership redistributed to the people, such as 20% to employees and 20% to the communities they operate in.

In 1983, 50 corporations dominated almost every mass medium. In 1987, the 50 companies had shrunk to 29. In 1997, it became 10, a shrinkage marked by the $19 billion Disney-ABC merger, at the time the biggest media merger ever, which was then dwarfed shortly thereafter by the $350 billion AOL-Time Warner merger in 2000. Today, six corporations collectively control U.S. media: Time Warner, Walt Disney, Viacom, Rupert Murdoch's News Corp., CBS, and NBC Universal. Together, these "Big Six" dominate news and entertainment in the U.S. And there's more to come: AT&T is in talks to merge with Time Warner for $100 billion, and Monsanto, probably the most hated name on the planet, dissolved its ugly name into Bayer in a $67 billion merger.

Free trade and the free market have previously proved profoundly beneficial to the world and taken hundreds of millions of people out of poverty — but we no longer have a free market. The corporate monopolies have turned free trade into *trade deals* that benefit themselves. They also have put the world at systemic risk since, and including, the crash of 2008-2009, which shoved hundreds of millions back into poverty.

acronyms, dancing across the board. Instead of two players, there are several dozens of teams looking at the same game board, and each team has a head spokesperson — a spokesperson who never truly speaks their own mind. It's those minds that are contemplating the board, and they are the only ones allowed to touch the pieces and engage in action.

Institutions like the Brookings Institution, Fraser Institute, Rand Corporation, antitrust agencies, and the FDIC need to get their heads out of the sand. Credibility may well come back into vogue if Elon Musk's Department of Government Efficiency enters the mess, while simultaneously funding studies like the one I've highlighted. Spread the information; demand a directional change for a more decentralized corporate world; and in the meantime, *vote with every dollar.*

With recent record mergers and acquisitions because of near-zero interest rates, the control has become more condensed, and you need to demand change. The FDIC says one of their core missions is "Expanding Economic Inclusion for the Underserved." The best, fastest, and easiest way to do all that is to increase competition and decentralize global corporate control — period.

It's time for a redistribution of wealth; a one-time emergency transfer from the 1% to the people. Their stealing, pillaging, and ransacking apparatus over the last 20 years was designed to enrich and empower an extremely small group of shadowy, powerful, wealthy men. As ZeroHedge recently put it:

"When you control the currency and interest rates; rig the financial markets; buy the politicians; write the laws and regulations; own the corporate propaganda machines known as the mainstream media; operate a high tech surveillance state; create a dumbed down populace through government school

- **JPMorgan Chase, Jamie Dimon, Chair:** JPMorgan Chase is the world's sixth largest bank by total assets, with total assets of $2.35 trillion.

## What It Boils Down To

The current economic climate is particularly ripe for a significant financial shift, and I think with Trump 2.0, we'll get it.

However, any rapid and dramatic shift is likely to come at a cost. Retirees/pensioners and other long-term people who have invested heavily in traditional or conservative assets might find themselves at a disadvantage; they are perpetually easy prey, easily forfeited in this chess game. Pawns may outnumber the collection of other pieces on the board, but they rarely can overpower; they are just used by the powers that surround them. As such, they could see their investments diminish or fail to grow as expected, leaving them wondering what went wrong, which is usually the case. Any substantial gains in Asia, or elsewhere for that matter, could contrast sharply with potential losses or stagnation in their portfolios, highlighting a stark divide in the financial outcomes for different groups of investors.

I've never been much of a chess player, but I am familiar that *The Art of War* as a good manual for how to look at the game. The best war to fight is the one you never get into. You want your enemy to strike first, and that's what's taking place in the world today. Financial warfare is an entirely different kind of attack. It's a game of ghosts and covert maneuvers, and the pieces on the board have to be defined with an economic lens. Instead of pawns and rooks, we have precious metals, credit-default swaps, HFTs, EFTs — endless

It is imperative that we address these issues not only for the sake of financial stability but to foster a healthier, more equitable economic system that encourages social harmony. Here are just a few examples.

- **Barclays Plc, John McFarlane, Chair:** He spent 18 years with Citibank, as head of Citibank in Ireland and the United Kingdom, then became group executive director of Standard Chartered Plc. based in London and Hong Kong. He was chief executive of the Australia and New Zealand Banking Group Ltd. (ANZ), then joined the board of the Royal Bank of Scotland, then the board of Aviva Plc, where he became chair. He was president of the International Monetary Conference (the annual meeting of the heads of the world's major and central banks) and was chair of the Australian Banking Association.

- **Capital Group Companies Inc., Timothy D. Armour, Chair:** Connected to three board members in three organizations in seven industries.

- **State Street Corp., Joseph Hooley, Chair:** State Street is organized into two main divisions. The Global Services business is a custodian bank with $28 trillion in assets under custody and administration. The Global Advisors business provides investment management services and has $2.45 trillion in assets under management.

- **AXA, Thomas Buberl, Chair:** AXA was the second most powerful transnational corporation in terms of ownership and has corporate control over global financial stability and market competition, with Barclays and State Street Corporation taking the first and third positions, respectively.

CHAPTER 6:

# The Guillotine

**THE INDIVIDUALS LISTED BELOW HAVE** some of the most influential positions in global holding companies. While it may be challenging to secure direct meetings with them, it is essential that we initiate a constructive dialogue about the potential conflicts of interest that arise from their interconnected roles. We should strongly encourage them to reconsider overlapping board memberships, which concentrate power in a way that could exacerbate systemic risks. These risks are not theoretical — they can directly affect the stability of the broader economy and, by extension, our entire conception of a civil society.

They are likely to counterargue that *they are civil society,* or that *civil society arises because of them,* but such concentration of influence in the hands of a few large entities has far-reaching consequences. It opens the door to financial practices that prioritize speculative assets and derivatives over the interests of ordinary depositors — you — and ultimately make taxpayers vulnerable to potential bailouts, or worse, even bail-ins. More critically, the lack of meaningful competition creates a situation where prices are manipulated and innovation is stifled, enabling firms to extract disproportionate returns with little regard for the real value they provide. This imbalance, felt most acutely by everyday people, has ripple effects throughout the global economy and warps our social norms.

lineups to ATMs, *acting above bankruptcy law*. This fundamental theft now conflates with *attempted murder!*

Later, as expected, the pensioners were begging for austerity and pension check reductions just to feed themselves. It's been widely reported by online economists that this contagion has occurred throughout Italy, Spain, and Portugal — one by one, all the debts and obligations sewn together by the super-entities will topple the whole charade. The top companies are simply above the rule of law — too big to fail — and the top-level politicians just follow their wishes.

As far as claims against anyone in business, there are courts for that, and a lot of judges are very reasonable. I fought and won a legal battle over a tax issue after three appeals. These kinds of things — court cases and bankruptcies — make you a much better businessperson. All multifaceted business owners have had court cases over disputed opinions, and some business owners simply have very sophisticated opinions.

I suggest that the public demand that any industry-leading company that has more than 5% of market share be dissolved — and not broken up as in 1911: Standard Oil made Rockefeller twice as rich 12 months after his monopoly "crumbled."

This time around, a rule requiring the smaller units to have 20% of shares held by the community and 20% of shares held by employees is a must. A major one-time redistribution of wealth is justified in an economic emergency brought on by those putting the public at a systemic risk.

Since you are being robbed anyway, you may as well join the fight and arm yourself with information of your own choosing. In this kind of covert warfare, you need to win as many battles as you can.

Elected officials can consult with whomever they want, of course, but when they hand over control to presidential campaign donors and run near-monopolies, there must be oversight and transparency — and not one dime from taxpayers in the form of bailouts or subsidies. Why is a business leader whose company should have gone bankrupt — and technically did — selecting who should run the U.S. government? It's not just nepotism; it's near feudal, or feudal clientelism.

I believe that understanding economics is crucial for lifting people out of poverty globally, yet it remains a largely ignored approach. Everyone is simply too busy with their own scramble to participate in making the world better. Given that we are all on this downward spiral, war seems inevitable. While no one wants that — no one wants the world to go crazy — without an economic backbone to support one's psyche, the various options of not going to war just do not materialize.

## Finding Something Better

My aim is solely to help people understand that there are better approaches. With the world's debt now at $152 trillion and the average standard of living in decline since 2000 (a decline not seen in decades), it's clear that urgent individual action is needed.

By going through bankruptcies, you learn a great deal about that law, or the rule of law, and would be more likely to understand when a country's people vote 60% (Greece) to shove the debt back at the bankers, as they should be allowed to.

If creditors had poor judgment, and if their policies could not have encouraged otherwise, it's the creditors who should be brought to justice, and not their customer base. Instead, in Greece, they closed the banks and let pensioners pass out in has four major groups: Big Agriculture, Big Meat, Packaged Food, Supermarket Retailers and Fast-food Franchises. In the food industry, the top four companies hold market shares of beef (82%), chicken (53%), soy and corn (85%), pesticides (62%) and seeds (58%). Doesn't this equate to not having equal and open access to food?

- Healthcare is another industry where abusers are violating the Sherman Antitrust Act. Title 15 of the United States Code, Chapter 1, deals with prohibitions against restraint of trade or commerce. Through mergers and acquisitions, a smaller number of hospital chains now operate a large percentage of hospitals, outpatient facilities, and other healthcare services across the country. Their size and market share give them considerable leverage over pricing and healthcare delivery. Same with pharmaceuticals and benefit plans: They have taken healthcare as a percentage of the U.S. economy from about 3% to 20% — in 30 years. If we do not stop this steady march toward monopoly now, the federal government, state governments, pensions, and the American way of life will collapse. We will be held hostage merely by the premise of wanting to live a healthy life.

These two examples in combination should make anyone with an ounce of empathy sick to the stomach; however ...

- Banking is simply the worst abuser of power, with a near-monopoly on this aspect of human life; and most large banks are listed as *too big to fail,* so they generally just behave recklessly. Bernie Sanders said it quite perfectly: "If they are too big to fail, they are too big to exist."

so much pent-up cultural and economic energy. An ensuing crisis seems even more probable than the one that set up the crisis in the early 1980s. Given the choice between the status quo and a disruptive figure like Trump, I choose the disruptor, because simple math shows that the status quo is already dead. We need innovation, now, before the pain is forced upon us.

Fundamental reform at the Federal Reserve is more likely under Trump than the alternative. Democrats simply do not encourage financial literacy. Just pick one and listen to them as proof! They speak of change while completely and successfully dodging the core need of ending the massive manipulation of financial markets — and this is felt so clearly underneath all the woke noise.

The FOMC should be abolished, and the Fed's interventions should cease. Interest rates and true price discovery would be much better determined by the market, something that is essential to capitalism, and free and open movement of capital is essential to a free society. When we have that, people's natural inclinations to participate come forward. What we have today is mounting paranoia and personal entitlement — the sound of which is easily heard — and the ensuing tensions between people feel unnatural.

Essentially, the Federal Reserve, as we know it today, should be dismantled. If only the Democrats were literate about this, they'd agree. Giving some numbers to the problems helps to express exactly what this sense of entitlement is actually advocating for:

- Michael Pollan, a *New York Times* writer and food critic, reported in an article dated October 9, 2016, called "Big Food Strikes Back," that the $1.5 trillion food industry as negative interest rates or extensive quantitative easing, in an attempt to stabilize the economy. We may be approaching a significant phase shift in economic conditions, where existing strategies and policies are insufficient to address new challenges, marking a transition to a potentially more unstable economic paradigm.

The information about how the system was manipulated is becoming ever more exposed and is leading to a surge in extreme shifts in voting patterns around the world. It's ratcheting up to a big, sloppy turf war. If you are not deadly serious about this topic, perhaps next week you'd like to start.

## Some Good News

The positive news is that established powers are making significant efforts to regain control through taking measures, such as mergers and acquisitions, implementing laws like the Patriot Act, and transferring internet oversight to international bodies like the United Nations. Despite these efforts, though, the situation is so vast and complex that I believe they are increasingly losing control, and this trend escalates daily.

But if you are wise above it, you will recognize that you can only defy fundamental accounting for so long. Delay does not fix a system that is broke.

## The Trump Effect?

Will the new president solve all our problems? No. Will he bring new ideas or clean up the system? Maybe.

Unlike career politicians who are often entrenched in the belief that current practices are sustainable or workable, Trump has not been part of that mindset. Transitioning away from current debts will be painful but is essential to release

## What to Know Now

Everyone ought to be aware of how this process works and place their investment strategies accordingly, especially if notions like freedom are part of one's identity and sense of how to get through the world. I expect the greatest transfer of wealth in history to take place very shortly. The global debt is unsustainable, and the largest pensions will be looted to pay for it via hyperinflation.

That is why I call it perverse. Countless lives are working away, squirrelling their pizza-guy wages into little nest eggs, placing their trust most deeply where their wages are stored, and having so little idea of how vulnerable they actually are. Quite the contrary: There is tremendous confidence generally expressed about one's choices, merely on the grounds of belief.

We all have to do the best with what we are given, yet the financial landscape is becoming increasingly volatile, with a growing likelihood of errors or misjudgments by policymakers. Central banks might make decisions that have a negative impact on the economy, such as raising interest rates too quickly or withdrawing liquidity too aggressively, potentially leading to unintended consequences and increasing economic instability. Within the Eurozone, the risk of internal disruptions is rising, which could threaten the stability of the euro and lead to a possible restructuring of their currency.

Concurrently, there is momentum in global currency and trade wars as, driven by national interests, countries might engage in competitive devaluations and retaliatory trade measures. This fragmentation aims us all toward inconsistent economic policies and increasing tension among nations. The signs of economic failure are becoming more apparent, pushing central banks toward more extreme measures, such

This is all unfolding now. The U.S. printed over $5 trillion to $10 trillion in the last decade, ECB leader Mario Draghi said they will do "whatever it takes," and Japan has printed full blast alongside it all — the third contender in the race to the bottom.

The real theft here is in bailing out banks. If true free markets were around, those companies would have been closed or sold off to more trustworthy competitors, or nationalized.

The anxieties balled up in this mechanism will certainly blow up at some point — by design, if you ask me, and I'm far from alone in thinking so — so it's best to pick a spot on the roulette wheel and plan ahead.

I don't want this to happen. I am not longing for disaster; it's just baked into the cake. The core of the establishment that caused this never gets talked about enough, and most are either too incompetent or washed over by it all to see it. Meanwhile, the decision-makers behind the curtains have big smirks on their faces as they front-run the swings in the markets.

You have to ask yourself: Don't they get bored? When a person has nothing to strive for, and all capital just flows toward them, how do they derive any passion? A moderate amount of struggle is good for one's health; without that, life is either boring or perverse.

When it comes to the establishment and the elites, I pick the latter.

Over the last four years, the Plunge Protection Team and Exchange Stabilization Fund, or Federal Open Market Committee (FOMC), has represented 40% of the upside move in the S&P index. This is either clear state planning or a banana republic that has abandoned free markets. Can they hold the markets up? And *should* they?

Certainly, over the last 100 years, the fractional reserve banking system has taken hundreds of millions out of poverty and has brought about productivity gains and innovative technology that have been incredible, but over time, greed has crept in and eroded the already-shaky rigged system to its core. This "soft landing" that you may have been hearing about is a slow and steady creeping in of poverty, seen in a loss of intellectual capacity or productive discussion, and intellectual resilience.

The biggest revenue source for the IMC is the U.S. government, to the tune of $700 billion — *each year*. That is a single budget item on the government's balance sheet, which infiltrates the entire world through proxies, mapped out in the list above, which are all financial-holding companies. GE and Westinghouse, just as an example, are two large defense contractors that, along with Pfizer, own much of the mainstream media.

If that circuitous setup wasn't bad enough, newly made bail-in rules have made the money you think is yours not yours anymore at all. You have loaned that money to this circus, and you may think it is insured (they tell you that it's insured), but the system is so intertwined that when one bank fails, all are pulled down with it. Such a catastrophe ties up your wealth much longer than you could imagine.

This type of system erodes trust or confidence, and the natural response is a currency and trade war between countries. All this continues to undermine the desire to participate in a system that we can all rely on. If this doesn't add up to "divide and conquer" in your mind, remember:

*Corporate capture is alive and well in the G20 countries.*

CHAPTER 5:

# War Pages

**IT'S TIME TO REVIEW.**

- Your money is being inflated away to keep the industrial-military complex (IMC) funded.

- The IMC dictates the controlling shares of the major companies in the world, notably the major media networks.

- The IMC has taken over control of these companies through the Corporation Act.

- The top 147 companies own 40% of the shares of 43,060 transnational companies.

- The chairpersons of the boards of those 147 advise the Federal Reserve, and the Fed is a private entity.

- These chairs have controlling interests in shares of these companies through organizations, such as the Council on Foreign Relations, which is how their top few shareholders want things.

- With the controlling share of the media (that is, all mainstream messaging), it is difficult for individuals to have autonomous opinions or maintain independent action.

*This keeps the rich, rich, and the poor, poorer.*

dollar price continues to the upside — of course — because the dollar's value can fundamentally only move to the downside.

This is a watershed moment for freedom. That ease of having a gravity-fed pipeline for prosperity takes away all the heavy lifting. Bitcoin removes the heavy lifting in this life, always made heavier by the inflation of the currency supply. While your dollar travels shorter and shorter distances, Bitcoin steps in tandem, maintaining your purchasing power. Without Bitcoin in your possession now, it's as if that water was walking away from you, farther uphill and just a little further out, each and every day.

(unchangeable). Knowing these tokens are limited and can hold important data and have their ownership controlled by an individual — you — why would you not want to be that owner? Why would you not want to know that your assets — your life's value — is not always near at hand?

Once you truly see this utility and value, you cannot but question why a government or army has been demeaning our currencies in addition to wanting to control *everything attached or connected by the currency*. Hence its constant proliferation, a scheme of total and complete dominance — now and into the future of unborn souls.

Talk about artificial insemination.

If you look at money and consider it labor (in other words, you did some work and traded it for paper money), then that dollar bill has pent-up work, energy, or productivity stored in it. Bitcoin is the same: It has stored value in it. As long as two people are connected via computer, they can transact between each other without government approval, which would otherwise extract some of that value while it traveled between the two negotiating parties.

Let's say you lived in a village and had to travel uphill for a full kilometer to get water. One of your neighbors decides to dig a ditch over that whole distance and use gravity to make the water run down to the village. Would you build another ditch beside it to get water? Would you continue the trek to fetch the water you need by the bucket? No. You'd make a deal with the neighbor and put forward the terms of an exchange.

Bitcoin has not gone away, and it's not going to. That would be like saying we'd rather live without plumbing. Bitcoin has been around for 16 years and keeps gaining traction, and it's

Since you can only keep this current economic fantasy going for so long (you can only defy fundamental accounting for so long), kicking the can down the road or sweeping it under the carpet will eventually force these big kids to recognize the sun is setting and they have to go back inside to Mom and Dad and face the music. They spent all their allowance and stole from the other kids to keep the party going. And Mom, Dad, physics, and mathematics won't be denied; it's simply childish to uphold the fantasy of no harm done.

If you apply "as above, so below," look at how crazy this unravelling is. Look at the Paris Olympics. Look at the generalized salaciousness and desperation. Look at the gender war. Look at how deeply boys suffer in schools. Look at the suicide rate among veterans and farmers. Look at the righteous worry of your average woman. Look at the Middle East. It does not matter where you look, unless you only look *within* to find your own peace and truth amid this impending catastrophe.

Protect yourself. Now. Today. Acquire some bitcoin, and don't look back. Ride it out. And trust physics. Trust math. There are only so many bitcoins, and countless dollars will be put into creation and circulation. That means the price of finite things has an infinite value, while the value of something that is ever larger is of lesser value.

It comes back to the inequality thing, and what pairs with it is novelty. As the dollars lose their purchasing power and the bitcoin stays steady and becomes harder to purchase, people will seek the unfortunate *novelty* of safety.

Of course, I'm not a financial advisor, but do yourself a favor and HODL (hold on for dear life). Bitcoin can be used in the transfer of ownership rights, the registration of identification or property, and with transparency and immutability voluntarily give the bank your future time, as well. You may think your "money" is insured in said bank, but the system is so intertwined that when one bank fails, all are compromised.

It's like millions of spiders are competing for the same real estate to spin their webs, and a thick web of frauds, not "loans," is continually capturing every moment of human thought and feeling around the globe. That means it's worth investigating and taking action. You either position yourself in relation to these systemic frauds or the actuarial science pressurizing its payout mechanisms will eat you alive. You are the morsel, and the banks are without remorse.

We have arrived at a point in history where we are all looking into the thin air for where all our trust went. At the level of nations (China, USA, Russia, and Iran, to name today's key players), where trust is always a game, the fragility of the system becomes all the more apparent.

The U.S. has printed more than $5 trillion to $10 trillion or so in the last decade, and the European Central Bank (ECB) said years ago that "we will do whatever it takes" to keep the system ticking. It's like keeping a terminally ill person alive well after their own life forces gave up. The ECB, the Fed, and the Bank of Japan have been printing money at full blast for *years,* falsifying the story for everybody.

## Where Is the Fraud?

The real fraud here is in bailing out banks; if true free markets were around, those companies would have been closed or sold off to more trustworthy competitors or nationalized. The fact that they haven't illustrates just how powerful they have been allowed to become — by governments, yes, but equally by all of us, because we are forced to use them.

have exacerbated social inequalities, now effectively pushing millions back into poverty.

Isn't that strange and counterintuitive? This situation reflects a paradox highlighted by George Bush during the 2008 financial crisis, when he acknowledged the abandonment of free-market principles in a bid to preserve the free market itself. This contradiction underscores the impact that systemic corruption and overreach can have on economic stability and social equity.

Truly, both the Plunge Protection Team and Exchange Stabilization Fund should not exist in a free market. They keep this list of problems firmly in place. It simply counters the entire notion of progress and civilization. The current financial model is nothing short of an insult to the *human spirit* that brought us to this place of peaceable enjoyment, compared to more primitive and shorter-lived times.

Human beings have an innate sense of justice and fairness, and this enforced "stabilization" does not allow that natural mechanism to take its course. It makes things very unstable socially, financially, politically, and interpersonally. Family itself has basically fallen apart. This core perversion prevents our own inner moral compasses from finding true north, and that reverberates in every facet of human life — right now. We have nothing to be proud of and yet everything to be proud of — if we can just get this nasty *hungry uncle* who eats 40% of everything away from the table.

Since we do not have a free market, start protecting yourself from the unsustainable economic system you are in. New bail-in rules have made the money you think is yours (in your bank) *factually not yours* anymore. You have loaned that money to the bank. And by the interest you pay on a loan, you

CHAPTER 4: THE BITCOIN BUBBLE

The economic game has turned into "who can steal more and get away with it," but Bitcoin, and more notably, blockchain, changes everything. Traditional trust is being challenged, and I see a move to computational trust where actions are transparent while the actors maintain their privacy — unless a law is broken. Meanwhile, the laws of finance are broken and toyed with every day, and the general public chooses to stick its head in the sand, letting the bullies run the show.

Is it because it's complicated or boring or because people have been dumbed down by media, medication, sugar, caffeine, and/or alcohol? Probably some of that, although maybe they have given up because they think their point of view does not matter or won't make a difference — that maybe the system is too big to change and will do what it pleases.

The choice is on, and it's yours: Let your money be inflated away to keep the military-industrial complex funded, or become a part of the shifting sands below its feet. Pointless wars keep the rich, rich, and poor, poorer. As distasteful as it is to say, war is very profitable.

The fractional reserve banking system has been instrumental in reducing poverty, boosting productivity, and driving technological advancements over the past century. However, as time has passed, the system has become increasingly compromised by greed, undermining any formative integrity it may have been catalyzed with. This erosion is particularly evident in the context of the military-industrial complex, which, bolstered by measures such as the Patriot Act and surveillance by the NSA, has justified extralegal actions under the guise of national security. These developments system where you don't have to trust: computational trust. Be free and be trustless!

My story here of freeing myself from the financial system is actually one of the oldest stories there is; simply put, it's a long, long story of *fleecing the people.* The Group of 49 is masterfully disguised so thoroughly behind the scenes, poking the bear of human goodness and treating the majesty of our existence like a mere circus animal. They want the crash because they can short-sell it faster than anyone, and they will profit by the misery of the masses. They want the problem to grow so the transfer of wealth into their pockets gets even fatter. That is why you must act *now*, because it is all too exciting to be a fat cat in this day and age — there are so many mice to pick on.

Things have never been riper for this cleansing, because any and all sideline cash will be deployed — fleeing to safety and security and growth, making for what I call *super-booms.* This transfer of wealth will leave pensioners confused and disappointed as their investments dissolve or fail to keep up with the changes.

If my definition of the Bitcoin blockchain is allowed to flourish, I believe it will help reduce waste and bring many of the unbanked or underserved in banking into the 21st century. With micro-payments and no middle intermediaries, like foreign exchange fees, the poor on the planet will finally get a break and be able to leapfrog into a society worth inheriting.

I am an idealist in my hope that we can make the world better. Most people believe the super-rich are too big to take down. That could very well be true because it has been that way for the last few hundred years, if not a few millennia, but I am still hopeful that awareness can achieve something.

*dual authentication.* It's all very new. It's just like when the internet came around: *www, email, http://, browser, ad blocker,* etc. They were new terms then, but now we use them without even thinking twice.

This "trustless trust," when applied to elections, would eliminate the massive bulk of human energy that is utterly wasted in the depraved carnival that follows every four-year election cycle. All the shouting, the accusations, the hatred, the commentators big and small, and the utter *distrust* it forces into our psyches ... it is such a profound waste. It creates *generational* waste.

But we don't have to put up with it or settle for it anymore. Kid Bitcoin is on the scene, and his buddy blockchain is going to clean it all up!

## Cleaning It Up

Encryption is used with the blockchain to ensure trust in transferring ownership, even if it's just ownership of a message. In the future, the National Security Agency (NSA), the Central Intelligence Agency, and all governments will demand extremely powerful encryption and systems to prevent spying. The blockchain could be used in sending private information securely, with processing power to lock out potential hacks and secure banking, communications, and privacy.

Governments are trying to control encryption, and that is an extremely dangerous threat to liberty and privacy. They say it's in the name of preventing money laundering, a war on drugs or terrorism, and so on, but it is really about controlling money, people, and companies. It is the only real *war* going on, and the only fight worth fighting. Simply do not *trust* any government or corporation, and move over to a

To put that into perspective: If you stacked $100 bills in a pile, $1 million would stand as high as your average dining room chair, $1 billion as high as the Empire State Building, and $1 trillion as high as from your kitchen floor to the moon.

How do you "mistakenly" make 6.5 trips to the moon! That alone should convince you of how phony-baloney the current dollar system has become.

Once we are using the blockchain for all types of things, the processing power becomes so big and decentralized that the tokens (bitcoin) become an even more excellent store of wealth. I don't expect the Bitcoin blockchain to be used as a currency by any large country anytime soon, but the first domino has already tipped in El Salvador. National economies will not be able to inflate it away to pay for their military or deficits, or as they will say, to *add currency* to grow with their economies (indebting the unborn).

The largest financial-holding companies will create a centralized version to use as currency, such as the United Kingdom's RSCoin or even a side-chain coin from the semi-decentralized Ethereum blockchain that is centralized by a foundation.

Truly, though, people should decide to use bitcoin as their money. It would eliminate so many fees and middlemen and bring the power of the individual back to the community level. That is what the whole Woke movement has been asking for anyway (too bad they've mistakenly left out finance from their arguments). It will eliminate foreign exchange charges and keep your finances private.

I understand this is complicated. It's like a new language: *Bitcoin, blockchain, encryption, processing power, hash rate, satoshi, millibit, hacking, validating a ledger, computational trust,*

CHAPTER 4: THE BITCOIN BUBBLE

Be cautious with blockchains like Ethereum, Steemit, and Hyperledger. These are more centralized and function like private networks rather than fully decentralized systems. In my view, a true blockchain should be completely decentralized and require more than 51% of the network's processing power to make any changes to its algorithm. While these centralized blockchains can be useful for specific business purposes, they don't offer the same level of decentralization and democratic control. I prefer Bitcoin because it has the highest processing power and the most decentralized network, which ensures that it remains the most democratic and equitable blockchain available.

My definition of a secure and trusted blockchain is that it must:

- Have 51% processing power to change code.
- Grow in decentralization as it evolves.
- Be permissionless.
- Not have any central authority.

Around the world, blockchain technology is being explored for everyday uses, such as car registration, land registration, and even elections and identification. Nonprofit agencies should be required to have 100% of their transactions transparent on the blockchain for auditing purposes. The blockchain could also be used to track military spending. It is actually quite limitless, wherever honesty and transparency are of use.

Do you recall, for example, that after the Iraq War, a defense contractor lost $2 trillion in bookkeeping receipts, and a recent report revealed that the Army then mistakenly made $6.5 trillion in accounting adjustments? Do you trust that?

Blockbuster. Change happens fast, and I see that same speed of transformation coming to Bitcoin and digital assets.

In short, learning about Bitcoin isn't just fun — it's crucial. The future of money is unfolding right before our eyes, and it's an exciting journey to be part of.

Ready to dive in further?

Bitcoin is not an investment. It is simply a token used to validate a ledger and is part of the most secure blockchain there is. Since it is validating the ledger with more processing power than has ever been put together for one purpose, it has become the strongest store of wealth available by default. Yes, bad and good news will move the daily price, but it continues to get more powerful every minute.

Bitcoin has had no downtime, no errors, and no hacks since conception. Bitcoin is not a belief; it pays for the validating of the most powerful blockchain created. It is a new science and a new technology. It has more users and more acceptance every day, as well. I compare Bitcoin's relation to the blockchain as being like a triangle is part of geometry. As it grows, so does price stability and available Bitcoin markets, and the weight on each corner of that triangle continues to distribute the load.

Yes, Bitcoin is attractive to criminals who would also steal your cash, gold, or any asset that you leave vulnerable. You will need to learn about dual authentication and cold storage to be secure. Being anonymous with your money is a constitutional right, and allowing any other entity to control your money means you are setting yourself up for being cut off should that entity deem it necessary. And *trust me,* that's the very design.

For me, the allure of Bitcoin was clear early on. I realized the financial system was a *fraudulent monopoly*, and I didn't trust it, so I pulled my money out and went all-in on Bitcoin, believing it was the future of money. Fast-forward to today, and Bitcoin is starting to be adopted by the traditional financial world. We're in the early days of this revolution, and that's why I believe Bitcoin is a great buy right now. In my opinion, all retirement savings should be in this non-inflationary asset: Bitcoin.

If you aren't comfortable with handling passwords or securing digital assets, I suggest looking into physical assets like gold and silver, but for those who are ready to dive into the world of digital money, Bitcoin represents a tremendous opportunity.

## Another Look at the Future

Finally, let's talk about the future. Many people ask, "Are all cryptocurrencies the same?" The truth is that they share some key features: They're all fast, low-cost, and some permissionless, just like juice, beer, pop, and other beverages are mostly all water — in the high 95% water content — even though they taste completely different from each other. But Bitcoin, with its credibility, global adoption, and decentralization, stands apart.

As governments and corporations start holding bitcoin and it becomes used for things like pensions and cross-border payments, the pace of change will accelerate. Bank runs, for instance, could happen in minutes rather than days. The financial system is shifting rapidly, and while the U.S. dollar is entrenched, remember how quickly Netflix wiped out can be transferred to anyone else, simply by using a password (or private key). This makes it incredibly easy to send and receive bitcoin, and that's one of the things that makes it so powerful. Just imagine owning a little piece of this enormous digital ledger — that's really cool!

Why is this important? Well, owning bitcoin means you own a piece of this decentralized, transparent database. It's like owning a chunk of the internet itself. Because the Bitcoin system operates on a decentralized, open-source algorithm, it's immune to inflation and not controlled by any single entity — making it a *sound money* system. In other words, bitcoin can't be printed or manipulated by governments or banks. You have control, and that's huge.

The best part? Bitcoin's core use case is as *money*. You can store, send, and receive value almost instantly, without needing permission from anyone. This means bitcoin can be used in everyday transactions, from buying a cup of coffee to sending money across the globe. It's *permissionless*, *instant*, and *almost free* to transact with. Once the world fully understands this, bitcoin will become one of the most trusted forms of money in history.

Bitcoin also has many other potential applications beyond being used as money. For example, smart contracts can act as digital certificates of ownership, such as when you can prove ownership of a car or piece of real estate. This is already happening — Donald Trump, for example, started talking about releasing digital share certificates for his real estate, allowing people to buy fractions of properties like Trump Tower. This is groundbreaking! These use cases have been on the horizon for years, and I've seen them coming since 2012.

utility of energy management around the world. Without going into too much detail, just know that leading experts in energy management and audit management are extremely happy about this new technology breakthrough and are buying bitcoin like crazy.

Validating a ledger on the transfer of ownership, the way a notary would do, is an extremely powerful date stamp. Its permanence comes from the fact that everyone can view the transaction (while you are the only one who knows you participated in your own transactions). This is the silver bullet into the vampire's heart of intermediaries taking a fee to confirm something. This will eliminate a great deal of what I call waste in our economies. When the next big crash comes, there will be a lot of pressure on people to demonstrate their trustworthiness, especially entities and institutions.

Let's break this down step by step and take a deeper dive into why Bitcoin is so exciting and revolutionary.

First, there's the core of Bitcoin: its *ledger*. Imagine it like a giant digital spreadsheet — except this one is *secure* and *decentralized* and can never be altered. The Bitcoin ledger contains 21 million "cells" — these are the total number of bitcoin that will ever exist. Each of these cells is essentially a unique unit of bitcoin, with its own password. These cells can be divided into smaller pieces — called *satoshis*, or *sats* — with each bitcoin consisting of 100 million sats. In total, there are about 2.1 trillion sats available in the system, which means you can own a fraction of a bitcoin, down to the smallest unit.

## Making Magic Happen

Here's where the magic happens: Every bitcoin has a *unique address* (kind of like an email address or phone number) that cheat and easier to audit. The Bitcoin ledger gives the transaction an "atomic timestamp." As one Supreme Court judge with a background in corporate law said, "It was the strongest contract law [he] ever witnessed."

It's trust so firm that you don't even have to think about trust. It's absolute and true. It is literally stamped into time. Whereas a dollar's ability to purchase anything is always up for question.

Bitcoin's fundamental use case is a utility of notarizing, or witnessing, a ledger: That alone makes it extremely useful and very much needed in a corrupt world.

The real core of Bitcoin is where processors that are doing the validating are rewarded with digital tokens for their work. These tokens come in various denominations: Fractions are called satoshis or millibits, and full tokens are known as bitcoins. Essentially, the blockchain functions as a transparent auditing system, which is a revolutionary advancement in accounting principles.

Understanding it is crucial, because it represents the greatest advancement in business and human interaction since the computer.

Since Bitcoin takes a ton of energy to do the most witnessing in history (mining), you can use waste energy in a most productive way. Most hydroelectric sources — or for that matter, most energy sources in general — have waste energy that is not used because they are designed for peak-hour use time and the rest of the day is unused. The Bitcoin-witnessing process can use that energy for free and, at the same time, eliminate a whole industry of humans doing these auditing chores.

This brings us to the other fundamental use. Besides the powerful audit service, Bitcoin performs and creates another the temptation of deception that arises all too frequently due to human greed and fear.

Because Bitcoin is *sound*.

You set it, forget it, and walk away.

This is why more and more people are drawn to Bitcoin's *computational trust* — that decentralization aspect. It has the same feeling as something that is open-source: You can access it independently, and you have the confidence that it is there for you because so many sources of input are interested in keeping it secure and available. With Bitcoin, you don't need permission to see your own assets, and all its code can be studied and duplicated. This prevents deceptive practices from arising, like what usually happens within centralized systems. Microsoft operating systems can hide code and do malicious things, like tracking what you are doing and profiting from your data without you even knowing. The Bitcoin ledger can be witnessed, so its transactions are immutable, or extremely hard, if not impossible, to falsify — because that perversion of the data would have to infiltrate the whole network, not simply one accounting firm's independent, closed-door actions.

This means that it is definitely not profitable to try to change the ledger or audit trail that is Bitcoin.

The fundamental utility of its audit trail, or as Max Keiser, author of the *Book of Max*, calls it, "triple-entry accounting" for you bean-counters, is that the transaction is merely between a buyer and a seller. When a business sells something, it has to record that sale in a sales ledger (journal) and record the deposit of money (bank ledger or journal) or payment into another ledger, all while being validated every 10 minutes, which prevents perversions. Hence, its accounting makes it harder to born: smoke signals. That is the bit part: a collection of inter-actions that make up a language of sorts.

The coin in Bitcoin represents *value,* as with dollars. When we put these two things together, we have *binary value,* which is Bitcoin. Binary is *digital,* and value is an *asset.* Therefore, Bitcoin is a *digital asset,* no different from the Microsoft operating system from an intellectual property (IP) standpoint. The Bitcoin operating system has a kind of *IP value.* A placement stamped into existence.

Why people fall in love with this IP value or digital asset is that the binary language has evolved into doing amazing proof of work: that is, witnessing, or notarizing, a ledger, or set of accounting books, and the subsequent audit trail. The Bitcoin ledger is the most witnessed, or notarized, ledger ever created in history — the most powerful audit trail ever created!

In a world poisoned by corporate fraud, the importance of trust has escalated into *computational trust,* outsmarting the legacy bad actors.

It is like putting your audit firms — KPMG, Arthur Andersen (out of business because of the Enron fraud), or Deloitte Touche — into a super-computer calculator to audit all transactions ever made and all the transactions currently being made. Imagine the size of that! Instead of these audits taking place behind closed doors, and inherently being pressured to ensure the books always look good, this calculator is a peer-to-peer decentralized computer program that is being validated independently every 10 minutes. Every transaction ever made in this super-computer calculator is checked and double-checked, *and its validity and its value* remain uncontaminated by any form of leverage, or policy quirk, or even system is designed to be transparent and self-checking, and, in fact, it cannot operate in any other way.

It's a system that has so much power baked into the cake that you don't even have to trust it — trust is worked right out of the equation — unlike all the human-based systems that came before it, where trust is essential. Because the trust is essential, it is continually compromised. It is continually up for question. And it is continually put to the test.

Simply put, humans really do not like having things concealed from them. We are born into a trust-dependent system, and our mammalian brain somehow knows it to be a hoax, so when you place the trustless blockchain beside the constantly inflating bubble of the dollar system, it's easy to envisage a large bubble being burst by the clear transparency of Bitcoin's pin.

## Creating Traction

Let's get some real traction here with what is taking place inside all those computers, cranking out Bitcoin.

If we break down the word Bitcoin into "bit" and "coin," you start to understand why the technology experts named it Bitcoin. The bit stands for binary code as in computer bits and bytes: A bit is a zero or a 1 as is the base code in all computers. A bit is one digit, either a zero or a 1, also an "off" or an "on" of electricity moving through the wire or circuit — the language. When you can show the turning on and off of something, you can design a language, which in this case is a computational language, with bits.

An example would be smoke signals. Indigenous people learned if they disrupted the smoke over the fire, they could send a message between far distances, hence a language was documents from the Panamanian law firm Mossack Fonseca, revealed in 2016. Those documents exposed how wealthy individuals and public officials used offshore tax havens to evade taxes and launder money. The leak implicated numerous high-profile figures and led to widespread political and financial repercussions globally.

The real trick here, on trust, is that the wider the gap becomes between rich and poor, the busier the poor become, and the less time and energy they have to care about where their time is going. It's a vicious circle, and the divide can be seen, heard, and felt *everywhere* at this point. Simply *listen more than you speak*, and you will hear it very clearly: "The government isn't doing enough **for me**."

Again, it's become a very big turf war, and knowing who (*or what*) to trust is essential.

Trust is, essentially, power.

It's power from within. Within yourself or within a system, it is an interior process. When you look at the "system" that runs Bitcoin, it requires a tremendous amount of power. It's poetic, really: Bitcoin has 360,000 times more processing power than all the Google server farms put together, and that is how much *trust* is catalyzed, inherent to the technology.

I'm intrigued by a system that uses advanced math and encryption to keep things secure, and I've put my trust into it. The Bitcoin ledger rewards people with its digital currency, an inherently scarce asset (and therefore valuable) for helping maintain a public ledger of transactions across a decentralized network (that is, Bitcoin's *ledger* is not concealed as it is with a bank). In effect, you are rewarded for participating. The best part is that you don't have to trust anyone — the

CHAPTER 4: THE BITCOIN BUBBLE

available, so it can be no surprise that she tried to criminalize Bitcoin during her tenure.

According to Yellen, a high-pressure economic environment could be necessary to address the damages from previous downturns and avoid long-term stagnation. This approach, while intended to rejuvenate the economy, also raised concerns about potentially severe economic repercussions.

Like a bad tattoo, every chair of the Fed has had no choice but to follow the course (their only policy, really) and keep coloring over the previous version of the underlying problem. But putting a tattoo on top of skin cancer doesn't stop or disguise the growth of the cancer — the color and shapes only get bent out of shape in due course, and the *perversions* of our economy take over. The names used to describe the same phenomena of debt-lending in the name of debt-creation are absurd, too. Just sink your mind into any of them: *credit-default swap, quantitative easing, liquidity trap, quantitative tightening, open-market operations,* and *inflation targets...* Can you smell the baloney?

There are simply too many warnings from all directions about an impending economic downturn. Recent alerts from major financial institutions highlight severe risks and suggest that we might be on the brink of a significant economic collapse. These warnings underscore the urgency of exploring alternative financial systems, like Bitcoin, that promise enhanced security and transparency in an era when traditional systems (financial and political, including the media) are failing to inspire trust.

Today's decisions in the financial world are not the first rendition of this high-level stress. Once upon a time, there were the Panama Papers — a massive leak of 11.5 million

## Why This Matters

In an era where trust is increasingly compromised (if not outright dead), the significance of Bitcoin's robust validation system becomes just that much more pronounced. It's like the first poppy that blooms after a deadly combat.

We have witnessed a troubling erosion of trust in various areas of society, including our long-standing financial institutions. Major banks, once seen as the pillars of financial stability, and even civilization itself, have faced scandals and paid billions in fines for fraudulent activities — *all while selling you on their transparencies and trust*. It's fundamental nonsense, though, when you look at how the underlying capital is created. How can you possibly trust fluff? This has significantly undermined the public's confidence in the banks' ability to manage our finances responsibly, because it's a big lie.

It's a *campaign,* designed by a very select few — and a self-selected few at that.

Recently, in what added to the uncertainty, Janet Yellen, past chair of the Federal Reserve, indicated that the central bank would have to employ aggressive economic measures to counteract the lingering effects of past financial crises (i.e., 2008). This was a diplomatic/covert way of saying, "We're going to solve the problem with more of the same problem, and there's nothing you can do." That statement, although insanely paraphrased, is accurate. Most people believe there is actual money in great big gobs, sitting in every bank. What's more truthful in Yellen's announcement is that any innovation outside of the primary monetary instrument — the dollar — is simply not available to her. There's nothing you can do about her decision, and there's no other decision

## A Powerful Tool

Unlike anything before, in the entirety of human history, we now have computational powers to actually create transparency. It's not just *talk* anymore. Transparency is not something that some people value and practice while others do not. Transparency, because of this new technology, is cast, like iron, and with atomic precision, into *time*. Transparency has just been made visible, and permanent.

All previous forms of transparency have left way too much room for human error, or human emotions (like greed and fear), so they always go awry.

But not anymore. There is a new kid on the block. He's about 16 years old now, at the time of writing this, and he's an official badass. The thing that makes this kid such a badass is his *honesty* and his transparency.

He'll look right through you, and he looks right through dishonesty, and he looks right through fraud, and he looks right through our whole financial system, takes a big *snort*, and spits in the dead center of its eye.

This "kid" is BITCOIN.

Bitcoin has more processing power validating its ledger than has ever been put together for any single purpose in the history of civilization. It represents an unprecedented coordination of processing power — actual computers — dedicated to validating its *ledger*. This collective computational strength surpasses anything humanity has ever assembled for a single purpose in history.

*debt*. And because that future debt is created from a debt-based instrument (yes, debt can create debt in today's version of the economy), society goes into debt at increasingly faster rates with every spending initiative — *regardless of which side of the aisle it comes from.*

Either way you lose, because the monetary instrument is made out of fluff. Out of promises: Conservative, you lose; Liberal, you lose. It's very simple. And, unfortunately, it's also at this point in the human story, very perverse.

I remain in favor of the conservative side only because *it feels better to be productive, generating something of value and meaning, which you have expressed with your vitality and creativity,* rather than becoming dependent on a crashing system whose decreasing purchasing power always leaves you wanting — and quite literally needing — more. Note how those on the left continually express disappointment and disapproval that "government" isn't doing enough, for example.

With that basic lesson on accounting out of the way, my hearty encouragement for you to prosper, and all that macro-criminality in mind from the previous chapters, what do we do?

Let's get right down to it.

David Stockman, former director of the Office of Management and Budget under President Reagan, said in his book *Trumped*: "There is a $45 trillion bubble," pumped up by all that debt-based chicanery, and "nothing less than blockchain technology can help prevent these kinds of impending disasters, through transparency."

CHAPTER 4: THE BITCOIN BUBBLE

system, because humanity's dependency on it is essentially complete. Our economy drives around without any actual *value* inside it — and the top dogs know it. They also know that you and I have very few defenses against this ever-unfolding, inflationary process.

Aside from preparing and self-education.

And that's what this chapter is about.

Bitcoin and other assets that retain their value — that is, assets that have not been drained of their value into pure debt and speculations on top of that debt, offer portability, mutability, transferability, divisibility, and actually store value.[17]

Conservatives will argue that real wealth creation comes through possessing assets or running businesses. I tend to agree with them. However, because the money issued (the currency) that we use is not a store of value, the theory gets corrupted; only the tenacious among us succeed. No matter how invisible that corruption may be, when you take a deep breath and think about this, you are probably concerned about the house or property you are currently trying to own or getting that business into the black and out of the red. Even though the payment terms you agreed to eventually slip to the back of your mind, the constancy by which these payments arrived nag and tug at your time never entirely vanishes.

Similarly, the claims made on the liberal side of the argument often affirm that we have to protect everyone in society, especially the most vulnerable, by creating social programs. This is noble, and we can all be grateful for the various experiments over the years; however, they are funded through taxes, which (and this cannot be emphasized enough) ***means a future***

---

17    For a comprehensive explanation of these fundamental factors, watch Mike Maloney's series of "*The Hidden Secrets of Money*" — it's very valuable information.

because our financial instrument (the dollar) is continually catalyzed on the backs of debt agreements (and therefore inflation). It invariably is a system that can rob you blind in a heartbeat. Take a moment to think about that: It is a system that is *continually catalyzed.* It is constantly setting out from the bang of a starting gun. It is the treadmill. And everything — *everything* — rides on it. New debt comes into existence because it is born into existence on the backs of an earlier debt, and so on, and so on. The *value* of any given thing is sucked right out (like an innocent, furry little Gelfling at the hands of an evil Skeksi).

It's theft. Baked right into the cake. And it robs you every day. All day. The dollars always growing, catalyzing other debts, making prices rise because the *value* of the dollar is perpetually falling.

When you apply this equation to the social and political realm, it looks like this:

## Conservative = Liberal + No Difference at All

If you want your wealth extracted from you on the asset side of the equation, you vote conservative (i.e., housing prices rise, infrastructure bills, etc.). If you want your wealth extracted from you from the liability side of the equation, you vote liberal (i.e., expensive social programs that may or may not work).

Either way, the political system has been completely corrupted by using promises instead of sound money. It's like putting a bit of water in your gas tank every week instead of actual gas: Eventually, the car stops running. Even though the car still looks like a car, it stops acting like a car. At this point, there's very little you can do about today's financial records is not the point. You have bank statements, credit card statements, yearly mortgage statements, and perhaps some investment and retirement savings plan statements. These *statements of accounts* are a communication between you and your financial institutions that govern and record your transactions in an observable way. However, because of what you know now and what you understand from the last chapter, it's very clear what is happening on your side of the equation, but what is taking place on the side of the financial institution is not clear, *or transparent*. For now, remember this concept of a ledger.

You can also move forward confidently by knowing that this equation not only has implications for how you are faring across your life, but it also has social and political implications. When things are in balance, they also *feel* in balance. And when things are out of balance, the answer is clear: Things go sideways!

## Considering Value

When we take into consideration that the *currency* that flows through this equation is today 100% based on *debt*, the equation becomes *perverted*. The actual *value* becomes lost. The debt being serviced has no counterbalance, because a debt is only a *promise*. It is not an actual, tangible asset. When we express this equation in terms of the left-right/left-right/left-right-left paradigm we are ensnared in, we gain an insight into why the political system has outright stopped working for the people. The *value* is gone, and we *feel* this, because this equation is a *social ledger*, as well.

I wrote about theft — it's the main theme of this book, whether it's in finance, healthcare, education, or the arts, mortgage is gone, you essentially *rent* your house from the bank. You are merely maintaining and extending their permission for you to live in the house for another 30 days with each monthly payment.

Even though this next illustration is completely ridiculous at the time of this writing, when this equation is expressed in numbers, it looks like this:

$$100,000 = 75,000 + 25,000$$

Once upon a time, right?

## Back to the Pizza Perspective

Taking this out of the personal example and moving it back out into the world, that same equation shapes absolutely everything on Planet Earth. Truly. Right down to the pineapple on a pizza.

In terms of human relations, it's actually quite perfect. There's a reason it governs the world. There's a reason it took over: because it brought out a system to keep one another honest, to keep things "above board." It shows any given moment of an entity within its lifespan: the entity of your mortgage, your own financial well-being, the financial well-being of any business, the financial well-being of an entire country, and the balances owing between nations. This equation is nothing less than *the invisible hand.*[16]

With this equation (*and this is important for what is ahead*), every transaction made by this equation is recorded in a *ledger.* A record book. Whether or not you personally keep

---

16   The Invisible Hand, coined by Adam Smith, is nothing short of an "unseen" force that shapes the free market (aka, the free movement of "money").

CHAPTER 4:

# The Bitcoin Bubble

**BEFORE WE GET INTO THIS,** let's do a quick review of the most basic accounting equation. This equation, without exaggeration, has shaped pretty well anything humanity has achieved across the last few millennia:

**Assets = Liabilities + Owner's Equity**

Since that is a pretty big claim, and the natural counter-claim is that I'm being too simplistic, let's make this very relatable, using the idea of buying a house. Then, the equation looks like this:

**House = Your Mortgage + Your Downpayment**

In theory, you own your downpayment — but you put that up for risk if you cannot pay off the mortgage, so in reality, you don't actually own your downpayment the moment you put it up as collateral. As you pay off the mortgage, your equity *increases;* that is, the percentage of actual ownership increases, while the liability *decreases.* However, that house does not belong to you. It is legally the property of the bank, and it will not belong to you until it's completely paid off. And even after that, because of the taxation system, if you fail to pay your taxes or any of the other bills associated with that property, you can still lose your house rather easily. Until the rigging elections as he has strong ties to several of the companies that produce electronic voting machines. Many of these Soros-funded voting machines malfunction and even switch votes. Soros also pushes for a one-world government and has worked to erode American sovereignty, as well as the sovereignty of other nations, in pursuit of that goal.

This is the world *team* that set the tone and direction of the Group of 49. Instead of occupying Wall Street during the next big economic failure, we should take that movement and focus a great big light on these people. Do it through online platforms if you have to, calling them out on their monopolistic enterprises and overpaid executives. Protest at their homes and offices, and target their direct business holdings. There will never be a better time to let the industries fail that are systemically connected and transfer that ownership back to the people from the 1%.

This is a profound opportunity to ensure those who failed us suffer the consequences for their incompetence. And their theft.

CHAPTER 3: IT'S ALL ABOUT THE MONEY

**Larry Summers:** may not be very well-known, but his influence has been substantial nonetheless. Summers was a key player in economic policy in Bill Clinton's administration, serving various important positions within the U.S. Treasury until becoming the secretary of the Treasury in 1999. Summers, with his mentor Robert Rubin, were responsible for deregulating the U.S. banking system via the removal of the Glass-Steagall Act, making him more responsible than any other person for the economic crisis of 2008, as well as the economic crisis we are soon to face.

Summers and his cronies forced nearly every government in the world to sign the Financial Services Agreement, an addendum to the international trade agreements managed by the World Trade Organization. The only country that refused was Brazil, one of the few countries that avoided the worst of the 2008 crisis. Summers pushed all this deregulation to make the bankers richer — the 2008 crisis was essentially a massive wealth transfer from the people to the bankers. Literally: from *you* to *them*.

**George Soros:** one of the most notorious billionaires in the world. Soros became wealthy as a currency manipulator, famously making a billion dollars in one day by initiating a British financial crisis and betting on the outcome. During the 1997 Asian financial crisis, Soros was accused by the Malaysian government of bringing down the nation's currency through his insider-trading activities. He did something similar in England, prompting Thailand to call him an "economic war criminal." Soros is more well-known for funding political causes, as well as his machinations that helped lead to Europe's refugee crisis. Soros has also been accused of

This has been the maxim of the Rothschild family ever since. With so much money and power, the Rothschilds have incredible amounts of influence in U.S. and international politics, so much so that even Hillary Clinton has begged their forgiveness in leaked emails. This one family has the power to economically destroy any nation that doesn't do what they want.

These are the *lieutenants*, as I call them, who deliver the direction of the Rothschilds and Rockefellers to the leaders of the Group of 49.

**Henry Kissinger:** not surprisingly, one of David Rockefeller's closest friends since 1954. Kissinger, while serving as Nixon's secretary of state, oversaw a bloody coup in Chile, an illegal bombing campaign in Cambodia, and millions of deaths in Vietnam. However, because of his insider connections to the military-industrial complex, Kissinger ended up being awarded the Nobel Peace Prize, a decision so outrageous that several members of the Nobel committee resigned in protest. Although no longer alive, Kissinger wielded enormous influence as a consultant for some of the biggest names in U.S. and international politics. He was a mentor to Hillary Clinton and Barack Obama and was largely influential in the development of the U.S. system of perpetual war. His legacy is evident in the never-ending "War on Terror."

This War on Terror is a smokescreen orchestrated by the money men (Rockefeller/Rothschild and associates) for them to keep power and control the movements of money. The lower-level lieutenants and directors, executives, and government employees all buy into this deception and do as they are told. They are often rewarded with outrageous wages and share options, perks, and privileges.

Institute for Human Relations, which used Freudian techniques to influence the opinion of the masses. Graduates of this institute went on to assume leadership roles in mainstream media, the government, and corporations. David Rockefeller is the only surviving grandson of J.D., and, as such, continues his family's legacy by using his incredible personal wealth. He has openly admitted that his family's long-standing plan has been to create a one-world government, saying:

> "Some even believe [the Rockefellers] are working against the best interests of the United States, characterizing my family and me as 'internationalists,' conspiring with others around the world to build a more integrated global political and economic structure – one world, if you will. If that's the charge, I stand guilty, and I'm proud of it."

David Rockefeller has been instrumental in planning the advent of this "new world order" via his influence in the Bilderberg Group, Trilateral Commission, and Council on Foreign Relations.

**Sir Jacob Rothschild:** current patriarch of the British Rothschild lineage. The Rothschilds are arguably the richest family in the world and essentially own a majority of the world's central banks — which are private institutions in most countries — as well as the International Monetary Fund and the World Bank. The Rothschilds' best-known patriarch, Mayer Amschel Rothschild, once said:

> "Give me control of a nation's money, and I care not who makes the laws."

Who are the shareholders? The study shows that these people control 40% or the shares and have 60% of the voting control *by proxy,* or by sitting on each other's boards as directors.

When you follow the money, and do your own research as well, it points to these few families that a small number of business directors answer to. These individuals and families are the real people behind our political events, our planet's destruction, and our economic enslavement. It's time the world learns their names.

For more than 100 years, and arguably long before, the global economy has been controlled by a small minority of wealthy families and individuals with their own agendas. Through political and economic connections, these groups and their minions have funded both sides of wars and profited from them. They own the corporations that pollute our planet and our food systems, and exploit us all. They own the banks that make us slaves to debt. They own the politicians and police forces that are meant to serve us but protect them and their power with money. Regardless of where you live, these people are seeking only to procure even more power and influence, and control over every aspect of our lives.

I estimate the following two people with their families' wealth and connections own and control a sickening amount of the world's wealth: 30% to 60%. When we do that redistribution of wealth from the 1% to the 99%, these families will be hit hardest for their failures to lead us to a stable, equitable world.

**J.D. Rockefeller:** The first U.S. billionaire, responsible for monopolizing the American medical establishment more than 75 years ago. He and his descendants later funded the Tavistock

CHAPTER 3: IT'S ALL ABOUT THE MONEY

- A Financial Times Stock Exchange (FTSE)-100 CEO earns as much in a year as 10,000 people in working in garment factories in Bangladesh.[13]

- In the U.S., new research by economist Thomas Piketty shows that over the last 30 years, the growth in the incomes of the bottom 50% has been zero, while incomes of the top 1% have grown 300%.[14]

- In Vietnam, the country's richest man earns more in a day than the poorest person earns in 10 years.[15]

A very small number of families control and direct the *tone* of these people, and we have exposed who they are by following the money. I used the intense in-depth study done by Dr. Stefania Vitali, Dr. James B. Glattfelder, and Dr. Stefano Battiston, with the Swiss Federal Institute of Technology, to create a dataset and highlight the most important points. The dataset used 30 million company registration files and drilled in to find a smaller subset group of 43,060 transnational corporations and their connectivity, which represented 94.2% of the total operating revenue. Their study pointed to the top 80% in total control. That means 737 companies, or holding companies, accumulate that 80%. Top-ranked companies hold 10 times more control than expected based on wealth. It proved a group of 147 companies has almost full control, which they refer to as an "economic super-entity."

---

13   Calculations by Ergon Associates using CEO pay data from the High Pay Centre and the minimum wage of a Bangladeshi worker, plus typical benefits packages offered to workers.

14   P. Cohen. (December 6, 2016). "A Bigger Economic Pie, but a Smaller Slice for Half of the U.S." https://www.nytimes.com/2016/12/06/business/economy/a-bigger-economic-pie-but-a-smaller-slice-for-half-of-the-us.html#:~:text =Yet%20for%20half%20of%20all,the%20team%20of%20economists%20found.

15   Nguyen Tran Lam. (2017). "Even It Up: How to tackle inequality in Vietnam." Oxford: Oxfam. http://oxf.am/ZLuU

scrutiny of various organizations now considered exempt from such attention.

Moreover, restoring trust in global financial systems requires revisiting regulations like Glass-Steagall and rethinking accounting practices, such as mark-to-market, which have been exploited to the detriment of global trade. These measures will foster a fairer economic environment and bolster international trust and stability.

If in the pit of your stomach, you feel the need to move, to get out and shake something up —*good!* Here are a few more points to further inspire that gut feeling:

- Since 2015, the richest 1% has owned more wealth than the rest of the planet.[9]

- *Eight* men now own the same amount of wealth as the poorest half of the world.[10]

- Over the next 20 years, 500 people will hand over $2.1 trillion to their heirs — a sum larger than the GDP of India, a country of 1.3 billion people.[11]

- The incomes of the poorest 10% of people increased by less than $3 a year between 1988 and 2011, while the incomes of the richest 1% increased 182 times as much.[12]

---

9    "Credit Suisse Global Wealth Databook 2016." https://www.lse.ac.uk/International-Inequalities/Videos-Podcasts/Credit-Suisse-Global-Wealth-Report-2016

10    Oxfam calculations using wealth of the richest individuals from Forbes Billionaires listing and wealth of the bottom 50% from Credit Suisse Global Wealth Databook 2016

11    UBS/PWC (2016) "Billionaires Insights: Are billionaires feeling the pressure?" https://www.pwc.com/ee/et/publications/pub/billionaires-report-2016.pdf

12    D. Hardoon, S. Ayele, and R. Fuentes-Nieva. (2016). "An Economy for the 1%: How privilege and power in the economy drive extreme inequality and how this can be stopped." Oxford: Oxfam. http://policy-practice.oxfam.org.uk/publications/an-economy-for-the-1-how-privilege-and-power-in-the-economy-drive-extreme-inequ-592643

It's evident that a small group of powerful entities, the "Group of 49," operates with unchecked dominance that is no different than a predatory mob. It's imperative to recognize these realities and to seek solutions that prioritize fairness, competition, and human welfare over profit margins dictated by a select few.

To address this, we must first take personal steps toward decentralization:

- Support local businesses and avoid national corporations to reduce the stranglehold these giants have on our economy.

- Withdraw funds from banks — known for excessive fees and systemic risks — to mitigate their leverage over our "money" and purchasing power. Each dollar withdrawn has a multiplying effect, challenging banks' ability to manipulate markets.

- Establish crucial legal oversight. Antitrust agencies must rigorously enforce existing laws like the Sherman Antitrust Act, ensuring board members are held accountable for conflicts of interest.

- Mandate transparency through annual disclosures, under threat of legal repercussions.

- Reform corporate governance. Introducing legislation mandating community and employee ownership in the largest corporations — *20% each!* — would democratize decision-making and prevent future taxpayer-funded bonuses and bailouts.

- Mandate transparency in financial dealings. Implementing blockchain technology for auditing will ensure accountability, preventing fraud and enabling thorough

Japan's government in recent years was buying 60% of its own stock market ETFs (Exchange Traded Funds), actions indicative of desperation rather than sound economic policy. Again, if something needs constant, official stabilization, then it is fundamentally unstable. And chickens do come home to roost! It simply binds us all to a very big lie: Every dollar is faked, and therefore, everything done by the dollars has no real footing and there can be no real personal confidence when there is no trust.

The motivation behind all this is easily named: profit. Because we are all tied to it by degree, it is not so easily solved. Whether it's controlling pipelines in Ukraine and Syria or influencing policy decisions that lead to war, the directive remains the same: to maximize financial returns, often at the expense of stability, and with some degree of human cost. It's a system that no longer works for the people who contribute to it. It is a system that only works for itself.

Consider the alternative scenario: Had geopolitical decisions regarding Syria, Ukraine, Iraq, and Libya been different, the resultant stability could have mitigated migration crises and reduced fatalities. Instead, fear and political manipulation perpetuate conflicts that serve to maintain an establishment power.

Again, it's passive-aggressive population control.

The consolidation of economic control in the hands of a few, as highlighted by studies from institutions like Oxfam and the Swiss Federal Institute of Technology, should evoke outrage and a demand for change. The "economic super-entity" wields disproportionate influence, exploiting lack of competition across industries to the detriment of society. It's simply tectonic how this super-entity makes nations collide.

Schiff argues that the capitalist system, despite its flaws, is superior to alternative economic models because it encourages innovation, efficiency, and individual freedom. He emphasizes the importance of free markets and minimal government intervention, believing that economic growth and prosperity are best achieved through the principles of laissez-faire capitalism. Schiff contends that excessive regulation and government spending distort market signals, lead to inefficiencies, and ultimately harm economic stability and growth. His main argument advocates for a return to free-market principles as a solution to economic challenges and a path to greater prosperity.

Such a debate would be fantastic! Especially if a public forum hosted it regularly (like the media!).

Ultimately, the key to navigating these turbulent times is education. Equip yourself with knowledge, examine the evidence, and spread the word. This is not merely a matter of economic theory; it is about safeguarding our future together and the health of our planet.

## Troubling Indications

In a Steemit post from October 15, 2016, I highlighted troubling global economic indicators: a drastic drop in global growth not seen since 1955, plummeting home ownership rates in the U.S. to 50-year lows, and a job participation rate at its lowest in 38 years. Despite headlines touting low unemployment, these are largely due to an influx of new part-time jobs. The Baltic Dry Index and a recent World Trade Organization report have slashed growth forecasts to their lowest since 2009.

Central banks worldwide, from the European Central Bank to Japan, have resorted to unprecedented monetary easing, printing trillions of dollars and euros monthly.

separated by *intent:* one, to do harm via greed, and the other to do well by proliferation of jobs and prosperity.

It's as if the crimes are just so passé now, because the levels of inequality have the majority far too busy to do anything about it — except those who pick up books like this one. As the reader of this book, you can actually put yourself into a special category of human: of having concern, *and for taking action with your concerns.*

Equally promising would be having Ellen Brown and Bill Still lead reforms at the Treasury Department. Brown's advocacy for public banking, inspired by North Dakota's successful model, could revolutionize our financial system. Imagine a network of public banks in every state, making banking more accessible and equitable for all.

Further, fostering debates and collaborations between economic thinkers like Dr. Richard Wolff and Peter Schiff could help navigate the future. Wolff's focus on democratic markets and cooperatives contrasts with Schiff's free-market principles. Finding a middle ground between these approaches could lead to a more balanced and sustainable economic future.

Wolff argues that the current capitalist system, with its concentration of wealth and power in the hands of a few, perpetuates inequality and economic instability. He advocates for a shift toward democratic socialism, where workplaces and economic institutions are governed by the principles of democratic decision-making and collective ownership. According to Wolff, this approach would create a more equitable distribution of wealth and power, reducing the systemic imbalances and crises inherent in capitalist economies, and fostering a more just and sustainable economic system.

CHAPTER 3: IT'S ALL ABOUT THE MONEY

that immediate action is required to avert this disaster. While protesting may be a future step, right now, consider investing in tangible assets like silver coins or hedging against financial instability with Bitcoin. It's no different from having fire insurance for your house: You don't *want* it to happen, but if you live in a fire-prone area, it's probably an expense you'll work into your budget.

Deep reforms are essential, especially cutting back the influence of the banking and military-industrial complexes, which are currently masquerading as having your best interests in mind while their own policies are actually tightening their grip on the economy. These entrenched banking families are adept at manipulating the system to enslave future generations in debt, like a big leech, large enough to put a stranglehold on its victim.

Which, in this case, is the *unborn,* who have always carried the burden of a societal debt. Put simply, the *unborn* are already in debt.

How do you feel about that?

A transformative change would involve appointing figures to key positions who have a track record of financial reform. For example, Bill Black, with his expertise in criminology and banking regulation, would be an ideal candidate for leading the Securities Exchange Commission. His book (the title says it all), *The Best Way to Rob a Bank Is to Own One*, underscores the need for rigorous enforcement against financial crimes. Experts like Black could spearhead a cleanup of the financial sector and ensure that white-collar *criminals* face appropriate consequences, which is to distinguish these scam-stars from well-to-do entrepreneurs who earned their prosperity through their expertise. Truly, two different classes of people, percentage, certainly, but on a very, very large number. This disguises what the actual risks are in business.

One either holds back or plunges straight ahead. Either way, without knowing the real risks in the day-to-day operations of a business, the net result is stifled productivity, and a perpetuating *and growing* inequality. Imagine the profound change in people if we were to redistribute that 5% to 10% more equitably. Instead, as trust erodes, we are vulnerable to numerous triggers: be it a shortage of gold and silver, massive sell-offs of U.S. treasuries, hot-war conflicts, or bankruptcy of major global firms. Any of these could precipitate a systemic collapse. Truly, the protestors of today have little idea of what they are pursuing.

It is best called "passive-aggressive population control," because with such a collapse, it's the bulk of the population that is caught holding the bag, while the scammers just walk away with that annual 5% to 10% they've been collecting, propping up the system for their descendants in whatever form is availed to them at the time.

It's just the facts when you follow the money.

The pattern of wealthy families capitalizing on such crises is well-established. History shows how figures like the Rothschilds advised their underlings to sell off crucial stocks during the Napoleonic Wars, just before the market crashed. They then bought assets at rock-bottom prices, leaving ordinary investors holding worthless shares. The scenario is no different today: Your pension, savings, and investments could evaporate as they did in 2008. It's going to happen again, and you need to call it what it is: THEFT.

If you've followed the money in this chapter so far and the ideas laid out in the prior two chapters, you'll conclude the people, because at the heart of this shift is the concept of trust. We can easily see and hear from a variety of sources today that trust in just about anything is gone.

Reflecting on the 2008 financial crisis, we recall the shocking collapse of Bear Stearns and Lehman Brothers. The catalyst for their downfall was a loss of *trust* among banks, which led to a full stop in overnight lending for an entire month. This crisis nearly closed our ATMs and plunged the global economy into turmoil. Today, we face something even worse, with colossal institutions — institutions deemed too big to fail — when in reality, they are about as steady as an elephant balancing on a tiny ball.

It's little wonder that the media is so far out in front of all this fragility — a strange Praetorian Guard — and that so much glamour and sheer effort is expended to keep us from looking behind the curtain! If the masses leave before the "bread-and-circus" is done, the producers have to face the facts that what they planned and executed led to a disaster.[8]

## Looking to the Future

The balance point of our future lies in adopting what I term "computational trust." Currently, a small group of 147 companies wields control over 40% of transnational shares in 43,060 corporations (this bears repetition because it is so staggering to think about alongside of what we *think* is democracy). This concentration of power siphons off 5% to 10% of *global* gross domestic product into their hands. A small

---

8    In Roman times, the "bread and circus" was a diet of entertainment or political policies fed to the masses to keep them happy and docile.

out foreign companies that should have faced consequences for risky and poor regulatory behavior.

Essentially, the banks swiped at least $4 trillion to $5 trillion from American taxpayers through "quantitative easing." Most of this cash ended up lining the pockets of the world's richest families — the Rockefellers and Rothschilds — because for every debit, there is a credit, and if you make debits out of thin air, someone gets to take the *credit!*

More recently, Ukraine and Syria are key because of pipelines and crops coveted by the "Group of 49." One of my favorite internet memes shows the map of Russia, which says: *"Look at how close they put their NATO bases to our borders."* Major North American shareholders just *order* more profits, and Western societies obediently comply — even if it means toppling governments and costing lives elsewhere.

There is a moral imperative to participate, and I know that by the end of this book, you'll be feeling it quite completely. Otherwise, we allow one another to become a culture of ostriches, hiding our heads in the sand, hoping the lions will stay on their own island and eat each other. The reality, though, is that cats *enjoy* hunting, and this is all going to come home to roost in a nasty, nasty way.

As we edge closer to the next recession (and it's much like the Coyote who ran over the cliff's edge and into thin air while chasing the Roadrunner who skipped easily across the clouds just moments before and safely to the other side of the canyon), the conventional wisdom of saving the "too big to fail" corporations must be re-evaluated. Something that has no floor beneath it should not be stood upon. The idea is not just about financial stability but about a fundamental shift in ownership and management, transitioning control to

CHAPTER 3: IT'S ALL ABOUT THE MONEY

pension funds, and insider executives plunder corporate profits, furthering the economic problems.

**Imperial Overstretch:** Empires often overextend themselves with too many commitments, enemies, and cases of blow-back. Attempting to manage 700 to 1,000 military bases, for example, leads to fiscal insolvency when reforms are not implemented to address these overextensions.

To address this, we must take two key actions:

1) End the Federal Reserve and stop borrowing for *deficits*.
2) Disband NATO, or close 50% of military bases. With a U.S. defense budget exceeding $700 billion annually and $230 billion in interest on debt, these changes would swiftly bring the U.S. budget closer to balance.

There is supporting evidence for these considerations.

**Defense Spending Waste:** After the Iraq War, a defense contractor lost $2 *trillion* worth of bookkeeping receipts (invoices). Recently, a report from the U.S. Inspector General revealed that the Army made erroneous adjustments totaling *$6.5 trillion.*

**Lack of Federal Reserve Audits:** The Federal Reserve has *never* been fully audited because the Government Accountability Office is restricted from inspecting several critical areas (who decided *that*?!). These include transactions with foreign entities, deliberations on monetary policy, and actions directed by the Federal Open Market Committee (FOMC). A full audit would likely expose practices that would outrage the U.S. public and shock the world, such as the Troubled Asset Relief Program (TARP — a great cover-up name!) — funds being used to bail

(ESF) have been responsible for about 40% of the upward movement in the S&P index. This clearly shows a level of government intervention that undermines true free markets.

Just the names alone have high contrast to where our countries began as a *free-market society* — what healthy market needs a "plunge protection *team*"? If a fund needs a permanent authority to keep it stabilized, doesn't that mean it is fundamentally unstable?

The reality is that what we think of as capitalism or free markets doesn't exist anymore. It is an unfair system, and the protestors have things at least partially right. Where they go awry is with proposing socialism as the solution. With the interference of both the PPT and the ESF, we can't call our economy a free market. It's crucial to name the problem correctly and to start protecting yourself from this now-fundamentally unsustainable economic system.

One innovative alternative is blockchain technology and Bitcoin, which cut out the banking middlemen and their associated costs. Embracing this community-driven currency, alongside efforts to end the Federal Reserve, could very well be the solution we need to eliminate the burdens imposed by these banking giants.

Before I dive into the cosmic waters of crypto and Bitcoin, though, let's sprint across what the global system looks like today, because right now, from a high-level view, history teaches us that time is of the essence.

All past empires have failed due to these factors:

**Extreme Economic Rigidity:** This rigidity is driven by ideology and an inability to reform economic institutions as necessary. Corrupt stock exchanges, which no longer function as true markets, turn into clubs of crooks. They exploit workers' trouble begins — interest payments on this fluff effectively transfer wealth from the average citizen to the wealthy elites *who control the printers*. There's a great explanation of this in Bill Still's documentary, "The Money Masters," which points out that Canada alone pays (at the time of this writing) more than $18 billion a year in interest to bank shareholders, and the U.S. pays a staggering $223 billion (by the time you are reading this, those numbers will only have climbed higher)!

How that happens is a curious thing to understand. For example, it's important to understand that the Federal Reserve (the U.S. central bank) isn't government-owned; it's privately held by the Rothschild group, among others. They get a 5% dividend, while the other banks that borrow from the Fed, also part of the same group, create money out of thin air — not backed by anything — and then charge *interest* when they "lend" it out (that is, *print* it into existence). They don't actually *lend* anything at all.

There's a name for that, which the average citizen is forbidden to do: *getting something for nothing*.

This whole cycle of interest and dividends has become a real burden on our economy — even if you are on the winning side, because both the winners and losers of a trade are propped up by this core fraud. Those who receive dividends are generally nervous about the next payout, no different from living paycheck to paycheck. Those who do not benefit by this leverage are often depressed.

As our *leaders* steer the economy into evermore precarious territory, they should face consequences for the outcomes of their own poor management (i.e., for having succumbed to greed). In fact, over the past four years, entities like the Plunge Protection Team (PPT) and the Exchange Stabilization Fund food: Healthcare and the media are similarly dominated by a small number of corporations. It's wild to think about how, historically, we went from a diverse and healthy 50 companies controlling the media to only six today! And when you look at things like AT&T's merger talks with Time Warner or Monsanto merging into Bayer, it really highlights this trend toward concentration of power, opportunity, and dignity.

On top of that, if you envision that all money is representative of *labor*, it illustrates a big issue. What we have now is a situation where those top budgets — those 147 companies that have a dominant say in 43,060 corporations — are sucking the productivity right out of everyone through fees, taxes, and various expenses, almost like a parasite on the body of society. It used to be that people could provide for their families with their labor and still have time for themselves, but now it feels like the system makes that nearly impossible.

It's something we need to address *together* because it's startling to realize that *69% of Americans today have less than $1,000 in savings*. That means more than two-thirds of the country is just getting by, living paycheck to paycheck, and one emergency away from destitution, which is a dangerous position to be in, especially when the next economic downturn hits. As a good friend of mine said in his book *I-Ching Ecology*: "... *it's passive-aggressive population control.*"[7]

Look at the banking system: One of the biggest misconceptions is that governments have to borrow money. In reality, they can print money to cover any deficits, avoiding those pesky interest payments. That is, "money" doesn't exist until they made it come out of a printer, and that's where the covert

---

7  Sarsons, Phil. *I-Ching Ecology,* 2013

CHAPTER 3:

# It's All About the Money

IT SHOULD SEEM REMARKABLE THAT a small group of families and financial-holding companies controls so much of our economy, particularly in sectors like banking and the military. If you've been sitting with that remarkable stat I gave to you from the start, it ought to be twisting its way into your brain by now and finding its way into your heart and into a sense of action. That so much policy-level control is concentrated in such a significant swath of human life, that an economic super-entity has monopolized major industries — it calls out for us to focus our efforts on holding these entities accountable. Otherwise, this — this one precious life of yours and mine — is all just *their story*.

Instead of just protesting general economic inequality, like the Occupy Wall Street movement did, we should shine a light on these companies and the people behind them, protesting outside their homes and offices, to call them out on their covert, monopolistic practices. One policy at a time, our freedoms have be siphoned into just that: their plan and their story.

Let's name some names, shall we? Let's get specific.

## Naming Names

Take the food industry, for instance: Just four companies control a staggering share of the market. And it's not *just*

as old as the hills — *older* than any silver coins tucked inside them. It's natural to contribute, and to care, and to take care of one another, so when we receive this tidy package of information on a daily basis, it extends the trust we originally gave to it.

That means the betrayal is daily. Perpetuated in fear, and yet masking a much deeper fear: that the utter greed of a small collection of controllers will one day be revealed, and we will see the manipulators behind the curtain.

Have you noticed just how much energy it takes to cast the news? The spectacle? The *precise* training newscasters have to step through to "properly" deliver the news? And have you noticed that it takes more and more force to hold the narratives of the day true to course? Have you noticed how much more glamorous the newscasters appear? The increase in pomp and technology to deliver *the same story?* The increasing arrogance of character it takes to press the viewpoints out into our consciousness? The show? The pageant and pageantry? The makeup bill alone has got to be an industry unto itself now!

It is all just makeup, washed off at the end of the day. Like any stage show, when the actors go home and the ghost light is put out on center stage to ward off the evil spirits, a cold, still truth is left behind, hovering in the air.

## The Cold Truth

Let's go behind the scenes, sit in that empty theater, and look into who is really running the show.

humankind has seen to date. Pundits of the blockchain (like me!) have come to know that the effect the blockchain *is having* on humanity has the combined impact of both the aqueduct *and* the printing press. You may as well throw in the automobile *and* the internet as well. It is truly a profound paradigm shift playing itself out, today.

However, the media is telling you how to think about it, and, surprise, not to trust it.

Who's doing the talking and the thinking there?

I estimate that at least 20% to 30% of all wealth generated by hard-working labor has gone to the establishment to buy $125 million paintings and pay for aircraft carriers to keep them in power — under the guise of keeping you safe. That's the story being told by these storytellers. It's overwhelming to listen to those kinds of stats on the news — *and it's designed to be so.* We have to vote them out to help swing the pendulum back toward true free enterprise.

I am not a socialist, but I would rather use that perspective to take these criminals down and bring the rule of law back in force against criminal banks, politicians, and corporations. One of Bernie Sanders' financial advisors is Bill Black, who wrote the book *The Best Way to Rob a Bank Is to Own One.*[6] When you listen to Sanders, his anger over this outright *robbery* of our own good thoughts is also very clear. We simply are not living inside the system as it was described to us — and *sold* to us.

The real crime here is essentially a mass betrayal of innocence. Of human goodness. The Gelflings. We are inherently a cooperative bunch, and we all want to do *good*. That fact is

---

6    Black, William. *The Best Way to Rob a Bank Is to Own One: How Corporate Executives and Politicians Looted the S&L Industry,* University of Texas, 2013

weight gain, low motivation, a lack of interest in people and what's happening around you... It's like waiting for a tragedy to come into your life, waiting for a sign, or waiting for a disaster to empower you to have something to talk about.

But meanwhile, the world turns, and it is inviting you deeply in, to participate in every decision. This is why you need to throw your brain into the pool of true knowledge out there and to begin testing yourself — *today!*

I believe we have been under corporate capture all our lives; it is actually getting better, not worse, because of awareness via the internet; and soon, this will speed up even more so through decentralized networks, like Steemit, using the blockchain. You can see the difficulty the established channels of information are having with every passing election: Fewer and fewer people are believing traditional media.

Think what you will about blockchain technology, but it is here to stay. No doubt people resisted the aqueduct: *"What's that? Water in pipes? I trust my bucket and my own two arms!"* Or *"A what press? A printing press? I trust my own carrier pigeons, thank you very much. They get the message through every time!"*

## A Vital Resource

Blockchain technology is the ultimate test of character. It is pure transparency and pure privacy, all in one. It is the biggest flip-off to the banks ever conceived. It's the biggest truth bomb available. It's an Occupy movement gone incognito.

It makes leaving a bank, as a mammal of habit, no less scary today than trusting a technology to carry your water or to put your message out to the masses instead of carrying it on a bird. It is a leap of faith into *the* most giant improvement force. (If you do not know Hedges, his "Empire of Illusion"[5] is a great starting place, although he has all kinds of presence across the web.)

## Being Prepared

Hedges is one of these voices that truly help you *prepare*. You know right into your bones that a lot of things are no longer right in the world. The preponderance of mental illness — *and physical illness* — is a pretty simple indicator, and when *everyone* is feeling this, it's like the air becomes rather thick, and slicing through it with the truth takes some intellectual heavyweights. I have a knack for finding these voices, and the list of authors mentioned here are enough to get you going.

Getting hooked on the truth is worth it. Getting hooked on reason is also worth it. Reason is the "blood and guts" of real compassion. It's tough love, first applied to yourself, setting you free.

Getting hooked on the truth is like taking your brain for a swim, like throwing your brain into the pool. Every day your brain takes this exercise, your willpower grows from every article you read, and your brain builds up its power of discernment, so get hooked — *today*! Otherwise, it just feels depressing as you fall behind, bloated with information swirling around you rather than within you. You can take on more than you think, and you have so many actions right at your fingertips that will make a difference in your willpower and your curiosity about life. It becomes its own kind of zeal.

The choice to not get hooked on truth is simple. And the outcomes are simple as well, all expressing a kind of giving up:

---

5    Hedges, Chris. *Empire of Illusion: The End of Literacy and the Triumph of Spectacle,* Nation Books, 2010

power traveling through a narrow channel and into a single gullet. With that in the front of your mind, can you honestly say we truly have a free market? If so, why are so many protesting "capitalism," when, in fact, we do not have a capitalist *free-market* system? It has simply been socialism for the rich, and for everyone else to wish they were never born.

All that protesting is so interesting (the Occupy movement, and so on, which has moved away from the bank bailouts of 2009 and moved on to Identity Politics instead). It's like an enforced envy, and the masses start craving the very thing that is destroying them: socialism. They want a piece of the pie.

I follow independent reporters who have gained my trust through many hours of reviewing their work. I avoid (or at least take with a grain of salt) most news organizations owned by the mainstream because they have a conflict of interest and bias toward their shareholders. A few I appreciate are Greg Hunter, Greg Mannarino, John Williams, Paul Craig Roberts, Catherine Austin Fitts, Peter Schiff, Rob Kirby, Harry Dent, David Morgan, Chris Martenson, Andy Hoffman, Bill Still, Chris Hedges, and Mike Maloney.

I am doing all I can to expose this new weird hybrid of fascist-Stalinist control over people who otherwise believe they are free. The control of humanity's fundamentals can easily be confirmed, and I know I'll leave enough breadcrumbs throughout this book for you to find this out for yourself. If we are lucky, we'll avoid, *however narrowly,* a complete socialist takeover.

I believe what Chris Hedges is saying, unfortunately: that this current system will have to be brought down with is biased completely toward the corporate and political interests that I touched on in the opening chapter.

It's just plain untruthful.

## A Question of Trust

The question becomes who do you trust?

---

*"There are no longer any independent networks: ABC, CBS, CNN, NBC ... they are all now cogs in huge conglomerate media companies, are not run by journalists. They are run by former government officials and corporate advertising executives and have no interest whatsoever in telling the truth."*

**—DR. PAUL CRAIG ROBERTS**

---

It comes right back to that fact of 147 companies owning 40% of the shares of 43,060 transnational companies. The authority moves upward, while the *narratives* move downward. Let that sink in. This stat answers so many questions, or the things you talk about with your friends, the frustrations you express or carry, or the things you hear people say, like: *Who's moving the markets, are they front-running the markets, do they like monopolies, do they regulate the little guy out of business, do they buy elections, do they own media, banks, the military-industrial complex ... Who is running this show?*

You need to know that 62 *people* own more than half of what the global population does. Picture it: a constant siphoning of your purchasing power to some fat cats who are buying everything. It's a legalized siphoning — a river of purchasing

CHAPTER 2:

# The Media

**LET'S BEGIN THE STORY WITH** the storytellers.

It's perplexing just how much energy the media spins on what can only amount to *proliferating biases*. It's *funny* just how much energy the media spins on describing biases, but as the prejudices of the media become clear, there is nothing funny about it.

It's a *campaign,* and a constant one at that. In masquerading as an information source, when it is, in fact, an unending campaign, it is insulting. Every entity struggles to hold our shrinking attention spans, and each has to pick and choose how to shape a story, but when you listen to the timbre of what is being reported on, the campaign of fear and control rings out very loudly in every word.

The media, whose fundamental and lawful task is to be *unbiased*, focuses selectively on certain issues while ignoring others. Within that, the media spins the oldest theater tricks available, directing you toward what they think you *ought* to think and feel. They shape public opinion —your opinion — by prior design.

Realizing this gives a feeling of a constant moral shock. Tragically, their job is to help us question, not to shape our thoughts and emotions. As you look into who owns the media, who foots the bill, the *narrative* that the media supports

this writing, I expect a 40% to 70% loss in value of the riskier parts of pension holdings, just as one example.

*When it happens,* people ideally will scream for transparency. After decades of saving and dreaming of a peaceful, relaxed retirement, this next crash ought to have the masses asking, *What the hell?* Accounting firms, rating agencies, clearing houses, and government will be forced, no differently than in other crashes, to pony up and be honest with the people: *Since we don't have a sound money system, everything you've been hoping to achieve in your life was actually an asset whose creation benefited the lender.*

It's enough to tick people off. And once that becomes concretely experienced by the masses, that's when the upheaval will begin.

But why wait for that? Why not get out *now*, while you still can?

You don't have to work your way up to do it, either. You can be a pizza driver and not participate in this.

These corporate behemoths not only have the power to set prices to maximize their profits, with little threat of competition, but they also influence the politics of these markets, which have much farther-reaching impact on societies. Small retailers also pay a price for corporate dominance. In the U.S., the Justice Department recently ran a probe into allegations that AB InBev (the Anheuser Busch beer company) is curbing competition by buying up distributors, making it harder for micro-breweries to get their products onto store shelves.

Do you wonder why the Oxfam study did not mention banks (finance) or petroleum companies, as among the few that really control the big decisions? These 49 leaders of the boards of directors of the largest-holding companies set the tone and direction for all the largest institutions on the planet. A move of their fingers has no less of an impact than Caesar. This is extremely hazardous; they have made themselves too big to fail deliberately to protect their wealth. It hides the real motions of money, *while the rest of us scramble about in odd jobs to pay the bills.*

Awareness is our first defense: You are, in fact, a powerful individual. Since the same rule of law for rich and poor is our second defense, insisting on the equality gap to begin trending toward a morally balanced direction would be paramount.

## Protecting Against the Future

I believe the next 2008-style financial crash is long overdue but always could be delayed by extending what I call fraudulent-zero or negative-interest rate policies, or even just printing more money. This crash will hurt so much and acutely increase in its pain the longer it is delayed. At the time of

Go back to following the money, and it all makes sense. It's the best divide-and-conquer ever.

The frustrations you have, and probably are longing to express, also make sense by realizing all this. You have the right to express those frustrations, to whatever degree you also feel and understand them.

Just as I did.

## A Practical Education

Rather than let you stay lost in all that traffic, I want to help you. Once this chapter concludes, I want you to make a pot of tea or freshen up your coffee, make a tray of snacks, and block off the rest of the day to settle into the rest of this book.

As I climbed my way up from pizza driver to working in the finance department of one of the world's largest firms, it was one heck of an education.

The fundamental lack of competition presents opportunities for these top companies to set prices that enable them to extract returns over and above their real value and productivity. Examples include household names such as Google, which has 90% of the global internet search engine market and in 2024, reported profits of $100 billion. Google not only defines how the internet is used but also has a major influence on data protection laws around the world (which begs the question: Who, exactly, are their laws protecting?).

Other monopolistic companies are less in the public eye but nevertheless have a significant impact on people's lives. For instance, some 80% of the corn harvested in the U.S. is genetically engineered (GM) by Monsanto, a company that also dominates the global research agenda for GM crops and their safety standards.

brought about productivity gains and technology that has been incredible, but over time, greed has crept in deep and has eroded things to the very core.

Do you remember *The Dark Crystal* — the momentous 1982 Jim Henson film about good and evil, played out between the evil Skeksis and the noble, slow-moving Mystics, with the innocent Gelflings caught in the middle? Do you remember early in the film where the Skeksis capture a Gelfling, trap it in a kind of electric chair, and drain the poor, soft little creature of its *essence?* It's like that. We are the Gelflings, and this core group is draining our essence. And things are not looking good.

The existence of an economic super-entity, as the study's authors call it, has never been documented before. The fact that these large datasets have only recently become available is incredible. It's an achievement and probably an important step along the way to an actual transparency for our financial system. Do you *really* know where your money is, or where it came from? Really and truly, do you?

It seems to me to be common sense that this disproportionate playing field is easy to spot if we just look around. We don't see too many price wars at our local gas stations, utilities, banks, etc. Might it be because they have the same shareholders? The world's 49 largest-holding companies are financial companies, and their few leaders essentially control markets. You might see different logos, such as Shell, Esso, or BP, or Coke versus Pepsi, but these leaders set the companies' tone and direction. To me, this is a near total monopoly in each industry and the economy as a whole, with different logos simply floating about. And isn't that the smart way to make more money?

every $1,000 you withdraw from your accounts, you hit that bank by $10,000 of leverage they have otherwise been using, courtesy of your efforts. Things are most likely more leveraged, and in the name of national security, we are not allowed to know how bad it really is.

When you take back your money, you literally *take back your power*. You take back your purchasing power, which is something you ought to be guarding *with your life*.

What really saddens me is that mainstream media simply cannot even begin to report on this essential fraud, or military spending, or the fact that only a few in the extremely powerful super-entity control our behaviors.

Let's turn back to that guy I mentioned earlier: Greg Hunter, the independent reporter formerly with CNN and ABC who moved to a platform on YouTube and now has more views than most CNN anchors could ever wish for. What do you think are the ingredients of his magic recipe?

I'd call them ...

**Truth.**

**Curiosity.**

**Talent.**

**Reason.**

## Talking Truth

Other than guys like Hunter, it's super-entities that control the media—the story.[4] The world is a pretty good place and the system has taken hundreds of millions out of poverty and

---

4    http://www.bibliotecapleyades.net/sociopolitica/sociopol_mediacontrol92.htm

or pensions to the least-risky assets. I suggest you seek out a financial advisor who would readily enjoy this book, for all your needs, but in my opinion, most of them are paid for by corporations and live off your fees, so they totally present a conflict of interest.

There are several out there who really get this stuff. Some of these key players may even know about this paper I'm referencing. There is power in the individual — still — and the first thing you could do is shop local and/or avoid all national companies. Next, you could take your money out of the bank and put it in a lockbox or buy physical silver.

## Taking Back Your Power

Seriously! The strategy is as old as the hills, and there's probably some silver in those hills.

Think back to all that traffic, just that big, numb buzzing that is our day-to-day ... That is the sound of powerlessness. It is the sound of a machine that you did not build, a machine that needs you inside it, keeping busy — *playing your part.*

Yet, despite the demands you acquiesce to, and how you wrap them into your sense of purpose and personal mission, if you can step out of that machine, the more space and time you will have to feel ... like yourself.

Simply stated: The banks are stealing your money with fees and fraud.[3] Put more accurately: They are stealing your purchasing power. Continually. Every minute of every day, your ability to purchase the things you need, or want, is evaporating. Banks are allowed to leverage your money and put everyone at systemic risk by at least 10 times — that is, for

---

3    http://www.cnbc.com/2015/10/30/misbehaving-banks-have-now-paid-204b-in-fines.html

## The Big-Money Picture

If companies like the Brookings Institution, Fraser Institute, Rand Corporation, antitrust agencies, and the Federal Deposit Insurance Corporation (FDIC) truly worked for *the people* — *for me! for you!* — they would fund studies like these *annually* and build back their credibility, rather than just building up more power. Right?

With decades of record-level mergers and acquisitions because of near-zero interest rates, the control has become more condensed. The FDIC says one of their core missions is "Expanding Economic Inclusion for the Underserved." Doesn't that *sound* nice? Isn't that a nice piece of news, something to play in the back of your head as you go through your day? But what do they mean by that? What is the "service" they intend to deliver?

What actually happens is that those who are put in positions of power no longer need to listen. The entire Corporations Act creates a kind of immunity, and with every passing year, that separation between you (who must participate) and the decision-makers (who set the terms of *how, when, and where* you can participate) get stronger, with ever-increasing distance between the two "participants."

This has made the world entrenched with too-big-to-fail actors, which quite oddly *reduces* global economic stability. The growth goes into the hands of a few while the majority suffer from their decisions (e.g., Covid, much?). In other words, they are very densely connected and prone to systemic risk, and even systemic rebellion!

It's hard for me to resist, and I am not a financial advisor (I'm just the pizza guy, remember?), but I suggest your money is at risk right now and you should move your investments this knowledge was made more commonplace. Ask yourself how many Great Depressions you'd choose to live through, or how many houses you'd like to give back to the bank. When you truly apply your imagination to these tasks, you'll feel this tremendous sense of *how much time you owe to someone else.* Once your imagination truly takes hold of this, it goes a long way to preventing those connected few, those 100 people, from front-running how your day-to-day looks, transferring wealth and time away from you, and leveraging that into their investment companies.

It's all traffic. Deliveries made *from* you *to* them.

The study starts from a list of the world's largest companies, from a sample of 30 million. Yes — huge: 30,000,000 companies in one dataset, called *Orbis 2007.* As they looked at the balance sheets of all these companies, they zeroed in on a small subset group representing 94.2% *of the total operating revenues.*

Make sure that sinks in: 94%.

That means about 737 companies, or holding companies, have a significant "say" in how things operate — *how things behave.*

It should make you wonder. In fact, I *hope* it makes you wonder. I hope it makes you wonder about *democracy.* I hope it makes you wonder about credibility. I hope it makes you wonder how we even got to this place. Weren't we peaceful farmers somewhere along the way? How did so much power get into the hands of so few people?

Doesn't my vote *count?*

*how things are. I'm okay with being who I am, and how I am.* Or something like that. If that is the case, then I invite you to play that script back to yourself the next time you are inclined to complain about the world, or people, or your neighbor, or anything really, because we are all part of a much larger pattern of *behavior* — behavior that is being shaped on our behalf and not of our own freedoms.

## Following the Money

You have to follow the money to understand your own complaints in this life. You have to follow the money to discover whether your strongly held opinions have an actual independence, or autonomy, or influence, and even validity. It's the mask of society and civility; when it gets pulled back, we all find the Joker smiling behind it. It's damn scary if you haven't done it yet. But I assure you, it's there, and I'm here to guide you.

I boil it down to fewer than 100 people making all-important big-money decisions for the globe. If you've ever yearned for a bit more "equity," just a bit more pie, just another mouthful of ease, then in my opinion, it is profoundly important to follow the money, to know if we are even going to be able to change things. *And you know you want to.* It's natural. You want to make a difference. And you've been frustrated — possibly for years — because your efforts have felt simply like driving in circles.

When more people get hooked on going deeper into this type of analysis, they generally cannot stop, because it is so *empowering.* And we would be much more empowered, forming better decisions and rules, making global economics more stable and, therefore, less likely to cause volatile swings, if

I'll get back to the accounting terms in more detail, but for now, just think about *behavior,* and keep that sensation of percentages fresh in your mind.

*One* mainstream media article commented on this study: "The Capitalist Network That Runs the World."[1] It sounds pretty gentle — just how the world should be: *"Capitalism runs the world."* It's an easy thing *not* to think about as we walk down the street, or drive around in our cars, or go about our business, day in, day out. It's just a statement. Nothing negative is mentioned in this. Rather than be something to question, it just lands in most people's ears as a fact, and it probably should remain that way.

But when you allow your imagination to dig a little deeper into those numbers again, it is no longer a big leap to accept other stats, like: *62 people hold more wealth than the bottom 50%.*[2] When you think about all those company meetings, and who holds the decision-making power ... about the few who really make the decisions, especially via *proxies,* then these claims start to make sense: We're tied to the dollars, the dollars make all of us move, and this one handful of people who have a stake in how the whole picture comes together also have a stake in how we behave.

Not bad for a pizza driver, eh? You might want to take a moment and read that paragraph once more. I encourage you to let it sink in. When you sit in a traffic pattern for long enough, you start to question the traffic.

Now, you might think: *So what? What can I do about this, and why should I bother? I'm comfortable,* you may say. *I like*

---

1    https://www.newscientist.com/article/mg21228354-500-reveale etwork -that-runs-the-world/

2    https://www.theguardian.com/business/2016/jan/18/richest-62-billionaires-wealthy-half-world-population-combined

you will dive into the idea of what living in a "free market" ought to look like.

> Relationships between 43,000-plus transnational corporations have identified a relatively small group of companies, mainly banks, with disproportionate power over the global economy.

Think back again to those 43,000 companies and all the different facets of human life their activity must cover; the media is just *one* of those facets. Even though we are all consuming greater and greater amounts of media with each passing year, the *entirety* of the media is just one slice of this very finely sliced pie.

Of the influence it wields, a small group holds a 40% interest of it, and by extension, a 40% interest in the rest of human activity around that slice of the pie too. It's as if this central group ate out the center of the pie and left the crust for the rest of us. (Not a bad deal if you like pie crust, but let's face it — we all like a bit of the filling to come along with it!)

So, shouldn't this be, um, *discussed* somewhere? Openly?

Imagine if an uncle whom you've invited over for dinner ate 40% of everything on the table, drank 40% of all the liquids that were on offer to everyone, and then ate 40% of the dessert. He had damn well be a good uncle for everyone to give in to that behavior, or else there is something pretty wicked in that family dynamic.

Again, it's back to the *behavior.* The traffic ... That 40% figure is a percentage of influence in how things get done, how things get shaped, how stories get told, and how we experience the stories themselves. It's both behavior and consumption, united. It's both debit and credit, held by one buyer.

Now, imagine the 43,060 largest companies. Imagine how many people are working for these companies. Imagine all that competitive energy, all that creativity. Imagine it zipping about. Imagine all these people stepping through their lives — like traffic — and going through whatever motions they need to get through, to manage their 9-to-5, Monday through Friday routine ... all the corners they turn, the traffic they have to navigate in getting to their work and back home to the family, or back home to their cat, and all the little purchases they each had to make along the way.

Now, go back to that paragraph: 147 companies own 40% of the shares — of all that activity; 147 companies have a say in how all that activity gets done.

As you imagine this, you're probably starting to feel some questions coming on, like ...

## What to Ask

Why is it so profoundly important that the media (or any industry, but I'm choosing the media because its bulk messages tend to be parroted by most of us), which holds so much sway, are owned and controlled by such a small handful of people? For better or worse, the answer becomes obvious pretty quickly: They may have a conflict of interest with the founding purpose of having a reporting mechanism in the first place. Don't get me wrong — we have excellent reporting in the world — the best that money can buy — about emergencies, entertainment, weather, and so on; just not on this most important item. Simply: The process of obtaining information is skewed.

This study I mentioned, and its subsequent impact — on you — is the point of the book you are holding, and I hope

CHAPTER 1: A CAREER AS A PIZZA DELIVERY DRIVER

follow-up versions. This is probably the first time you have read about it, but to understand how bringing people out of poverty works, this study is probably one of the most important things on the planet.

Mainstream media, rating and regulatory agencies, and accounting auditing firms have not dwelled on this because their agencies and shareholders are part of those that benefit from keeping it out of sight. Luckily, thanks to the internet and new ways of sharing information, I have discovered and can share it with you.

For example, Greg Hunter (USAWatchdog), an independent reporter formerly with CNN and ABC, has moved to a platform on YouTube and now has more views than most CNN anchors. All this without getting paid by shareholders, but by reader donations and advertising streams alone. It's a heck of an achievement, especially if you let your imagination wander into what he is competing against and what he is revealing.

This 36-page, intensely detailed study shows clearly that 147 companies own 40% of the shares of 43,060 transnational companies. At the time of this writing, combined with today's speed of information, those numbers have no doubt changed — and not in our favor.

If you're not a numbers person, no problem, but do take your time with this information. It describes something so huge that it would be impossible to deny its effect on your own life.

Imagine just one transnational company. Just one. Pick the biggest chain store you can think of. One that does business across the globe and is probably known in every household. You can probably name one that is in the top 10.

and each entry foretells something about something else that has yet to come.

It all comes back to the patterns within it all: how we spend our time and what we spend upon our health. As within, so without. As above, so below ...

I went on to owning many other small companies and continued to do my own bookkeeping. And I continued watching the patterns. At my last 10-year gig, I was in the finance and IT department of the world's biggest company.

Remember this the next time you tip the pizza guy: You don't know what's going on inside the guy's head. If he's using his time well, you'll never see him twice.

## Understanding What Lies Beneath

While I was learning bookkeeping, I developed a very good understanding of those GAAPs and just how deeply the flow of numbers travels through our day-to-day. In my 35 years of accounting, only a few times did I almost fall out of my chair when I heard of various new rules coming into play. Specifically, these three: short-selling, mark-to-market accounting, and HFT. It was like someone said there would no longer be gravity; that by a stroke of pen — some policy, a fundamental rule of physics was simply not going to be obeyed anymore *by choice.*

But a quick look in the rearview mirror spells that choice out much differently: H-U-B-R-I-S. And I guarantee you, we are in for a helluva ride.

This was shown in an in-depth study by three PhDs: Stefania Vitali, James B. Glattfelder, and Stefano Battiston, at the Swiss Federal Institute of Technology in Zurich. No doubt you haven't heard of it because this study was barely reported on by the mainstream media and has had no

CHAPTER 1:

# A Career As a
# Pizza Delivery Driver

**EVEN CHEAP PIZZA HAS A PATTERN TO IT** — in fact, *especially* cheap pizza. The pepperoni, pineapple, green pepper, mushrooms, onions, anchovies ... Whatever way you slice it, when you peel back the cheese and start looking at what it's made with, and then who made it, that pattern underneath it all becomes very much apparent.

My career might have started as a pizza delivery driver, but I quickly moved my way up. *Way* up. Outwardly, that's a mundane start, but when you drive all day on deliveries, you get to see a lot about how people behave, and you *think* a lot about how people behave. You are not only part of the patterns dictated by the traffic flow — you see yourself and those around you as part of that pattern, too; a colossal timing, a clock, and each action ticking along inside that big clock.

Beyond the four-cheese pizzas (tomato, bacon, and shrimp for extra pleasure), I was applying my mind while zipping about, watching stuff, putting things together, seeing the patterns. I stuck that out until I owned the company. That included taking up my own bookkeeping, which was its own kind of traffic: debits, credits, purchases and revenues, liabilities ... they each deliver a good, or a promise, or a problem,

electricity) early, making millions. The same goes for curing cancer. I discovered that the medical system is rigged and fraudulent by doing my own research. I learned that cancer is metabolic, not genetic, and by making lifestyle changes and hitting the tumor with an antiparasitic (Ivermectin and others), you can cure cancer! Mark my words: This information is trending on the internet, and it is not going away. Those who get their news from the corporate world will be late to this awareness, and this book can't help them — it is for the open-minded.

---

*"Even if you slam the brakes on this freight train,*
*and throw it in full reverse, it still likely won't stop in time—*

*prepare accordingly."*

**—E.J. ANTONI, PhD**

---

general say, "Some are too big to jail." This confirmed that the system was rigged against the average person.

A few other troubling areas were learning about Jeff Skilling's involvement with Enron and introducing mark-to-market accounting, watching a 2% inflation target get standardized, and seeing generally accepted accounting principles be challenged or actually changed with moving goalposts, like negative interest rates. Establishing an Exchange Stabilization Fund and a Plunge Protection Fund/Team all seemed to go against the free-market equilibrium we learned about in Accounting 101.

The real discoveries of what I call "corporate capture" made me realize that "damn, things are not fair."

I know most readers just want to know how on earth I hacked the financial system to make millions and then followed that up with hacking the medical system by curing my own cancer.

The answer is by understanding that the system is rigged in both fields and by seeking independent information via the internet and libraries. You can do the same due diligence with your own best interests in mind.

The next chapters prove my corporate capture concept via peer-reviewed research. Then I discuss the blockchain technology I foresaw early as a utility — and how I made millions by learning the binary value in digital assets commonly referred to as Bitcoin or the derivatives in binary value (digital assets), such as Ethereum (ETH), Tether (XRP), and 7,000-plus others (cryptocurrencies).

When people finally understand (in a few more years) that Bitcoin is just a term for an advanced technology, they will see how, as a pizza driver (businessman), I saw a rigged, fraudulent system and moved to sound money (Bitcoin backed by

# Preface

**AS I REFLECT ON WHERE** my entrepreneurial spirit came from, I think of when I was young and wanted to make a lot of money — billions, I would dream of. I began my first career with pizza delivery at 16 years old and stuck to it until I was the owner of the Boston Pizza franchise. On my way to that achievement, the steps of handling the bookkeeping and organizing the office, file folders, and calculators felt like fun. I embarked on learning about business and found that courses in double-entry accounting, audit trails, and financial statements were interesting.

One of my first memories is learning about short-selling stocks. In 1985, I learned that you could bet against a company. I thought that couldn't be good karma for the company. Insider information being used to gain financially, and I called it out as a bad idea, even though the defense was that it created faster, more accurate price-stock discovery. Later, I questioned high-frequency trading (HFT) and the ability of trading companies to set their data connection lines closest to the stock exchange and be a nano-second faster than competitors, only to front-run the trades. This also was not criminalized in the name of fast stock-price discovery for everyone else.

I soon realized the system was rigged. As years went by, I heard President George Bush Jr. quoted as saying, "I have abandoned free-market principles to save the free market" (Lehman Brothers and Bear Stearns), then the U.S. attorney

CHAPTER 4: **The Bitcoin Bubble** .................................... 49

Back to the Pizza Perspective *50*

Considering Value *51*

A Powerful Tool *55*

Why This Matters *56*

Creating Traction *59*

Making Magic Happen *63*

Another Look at the Future *65*

Cleaning It Up *69*

Where Is the Fraud? *73*

CHAPTER 5: **War Pages**.............................................. 77

What to Know Now *80*

Some Good News *81*

The Trump Effect? *81*

Finding Something Better *84*

CHAPTER 6: **The Guillotine** ......................................... 87

What It Boils Down To *89*

Taking Responsibility for Your Own Life *92*

ABOUT THE AUTHOR .................................................. 95

# Contents

PREFACE ........................................................................... 1

CHAPTER 1: **A Career As a Pizza Delivery Driver** ..................... 5
Understanding What Lies Beneath  6
What to Ask  8
Following the Money  11
The Big-Money Picture  13
Taking Back Your Power  14
Talking Truth  15
A Practical Education  17
Protecting Against the Future  18

CHAPTER 2: **The Media** ............................................... 21
A Question of Trust  22
Being Prepared  24
A Vital Resource  25
The Cold Truth  27

CHAPTER 3: **It's All About the Money** ............................... 29
Naming Names  29
Looking to the Future  35
Troubling Indications  39

Copyright © 2025 by Paul Collin.

All rights reserved. Except as permitted under the U.S. Copyright Act of 1976, no part of this publication may be reproduced, distributed, or transmitted in any form or by any means or stored in a database or retrieval system without the prior written permission of the publisher.

This publication is designed to provide competent and reliable information regarding the subject matter covered. However, it is sold with the understanding that the author and publisher are not engaged in rendering legal, financial, or other professional advice. Laws and practices vary from state to state and country to country and if legal or other expert assistance is required, the services of a professional should be sought. The author and publisher specifically disclaim any liability that is incurred from the use or application of the contents of this book.

*Publisher's Cataloging-in-Publication Data*

Names: Collin, Paul, author.

Title: Corporate capture : how I made millions in BTC and cured my cancer / Paul Collin.

Description: Grand Forks, BC: Paul Collin, 2025.

Identifiers: ISBN 978-1-0693482-0-3 (print) | 978-1-0693482-1-0 (ebook)
Subjects: LCSH Collin, Paul. | Cryptocurrencies. | Bitcoin. | Electronic funds transfers. | Investments. | Personal finance. | Success. | Conduct of life. | BISAC BUSINESS & ECONOMICS / Bitcoin & Cryptocurrencies | BUSINESS & ECONOMICS / Corporate Finance / General | POLITICAL SCIENCE / Political Ideologies / Conservatism & Liberalism | BUSINESS & ECONOMICS / Government & Business
Classification: LCC HG1710.3 .C65 2025 | DDC 332.4--dc23

978-1-0693482-0-3 (Print)
978-1-0693482-1-0 (eBook)

Printed in the United States of America

# Corporate capture

## How I Made Millions on BTC and Cured My Cancer

Paul Collin